Water Capitalism

Capitalist Thought: Studies in Philosophy, Politics, and Economics
Series Editor: Edward W. Younkins, Wheeling Jesuit University

Mission Statement

This book series is devoted to studying the foundations of capitalism from a number of academic disciplines including, but not limited to, philosophy, political science, economics, law, literature, and history. Recognizing the expansion of the boundaries of economics, this series particularly welcomes proposals for monographs and edited collections that focus on topics from transdisciplinary, interdisciplinary, and multidisciplinary perspectives. Lexington Books will consider a wide range of conceptual, empirical, and methodological submissions, Works in this series will tend to synthesize and integrate knowledge and to build bridges within and between disciplines. They will be of vital concern to academicians, business people, and others in the debate about the proper role of capitalism, business, and business people in economic society.

Advisory Board

Doug Bandow, Tibor R. Machan, Walter Block, Michael Novak, Douglas J. Den Uyl, James Otteson, Richard M. Ebeling, Douglas B. Rasmussen, Mimi Gladstein, Chris Matthew Sciabarra, Samuel Gregg, Aeon J. Skoble, Stephen Hicks, C. Bradley Thompson, Steven Horwitz, Thomas E. Woods, Stephan Kinsella

Titles in the Series

Economic Morality: Ancient to Modern Readings, by Henry C. Clark and Eric Allison
The Ontology and Function of Money: The Philosophical Fundamentals of Monetary Institutions, by Leonidas Zelmanovitz
Andrew Carnegie: An Economic Biography, by Samuel Bostaph
Water Capitalism: The Case of Privatizing Oceans, Rivers, Lakes, and Aquifers, by Walter E. Block and Peter Lothian Nelson

Water Capitalism

The Case of Privatizing Oceans, Rivers, Lakes, and Aquifers

Walter E. Block and Peter Lothian Nelson

LEXINGTON BOOKS
Lanham • Boulder • New York • London

Published by Lexington Books
An imprint of The Rowman & Littlefield Publishing Group, Inc.
4501 Forbes Boulevard, Suite 200, Lanham, Maryland 20706
www.rowman.com

Unit A, Whitacre Mews, 26-34 Stannary Street, London SE11 4AB

British Library Cataloguing in Publication Information Available

Library of Congress Cataloging-in-Publication Data

Block, Walter, 1941- author.
Water capitalism : the case for privatizing oceans, rivers, lakes, and aquifers / Walter E. Block and
Peter L. Nelson.
pages cm. -- (Capitalist thought: studies in philosophy, politics, and economics)
Includes bibliographical references and index.
ISBN 978-1-4985-1880-2 (cloth : alk. paper) -- ISBN 978-1-4985-1881-9 (electronic)
1. Water-supply. 2. Water rights. 3. Privatization. I. Nelson, Peter L. (Peter Lothian), 1946- author. II.
Title. III. Series: Capitalist thought: studies in philosophy, politics, and economics.
HD1691.B575 2015
333.91--dc23
2015032605

∞™ The paper used in this publication meets the minimum requirements of American
National Standard for Information Sciences Permanence of Paper for Printed Library
Materials, ANSI/NISO Z39.48-1992.

Printed in the United States of America

Prior to the writing of histories, from before the dawn of civilization, the Homers of earth braved the elements to reach new vistas. This book is dedicated to those maniacal mariners who have revolutionized society in ways that the petrified toe-dippers of the world never believed possible. May ensuing adventurers continue that quest for excellence!

Contents

Maps   vii

Acknowledgements   xiii

1   Privatize the Oceans and All Other Bodies of Water   1

2   Why Privatize Anything?   15

3   Why Privatize Bodies of Water?   21

4   Aquatic Ownership Concepts   31

5   The Process of Privatization Homesteading, Abandonment   37

6   Existing Law Governing the Seas   49

7   Oceans—Concepts of Oceanological Ownership   55

8   Rivers—Concepts of Potamological Ownership   75

9   Lakes—Concepts of Limnological Ownership   97

10   Aquifers—Concepts of Hydrogeological Ownership   105

11   Mainstream Views on Ocean Management   115

12   Piracy   123

13   Case Studies   131

14   Debate—Technological Viewpoints that Inform Homesteading, Technological Units   171

Appendix: Literature Critique   201

Bibliography   233

Index   269

About the Authors 285

Maps

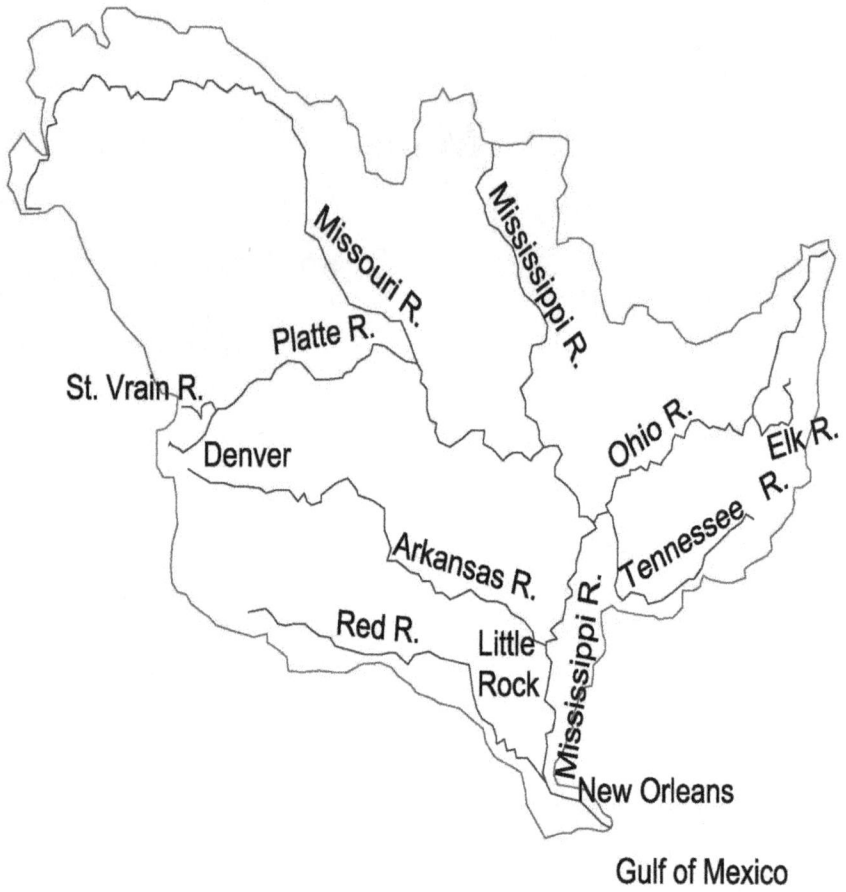

Figure 0.1. Mississippi River Watershed

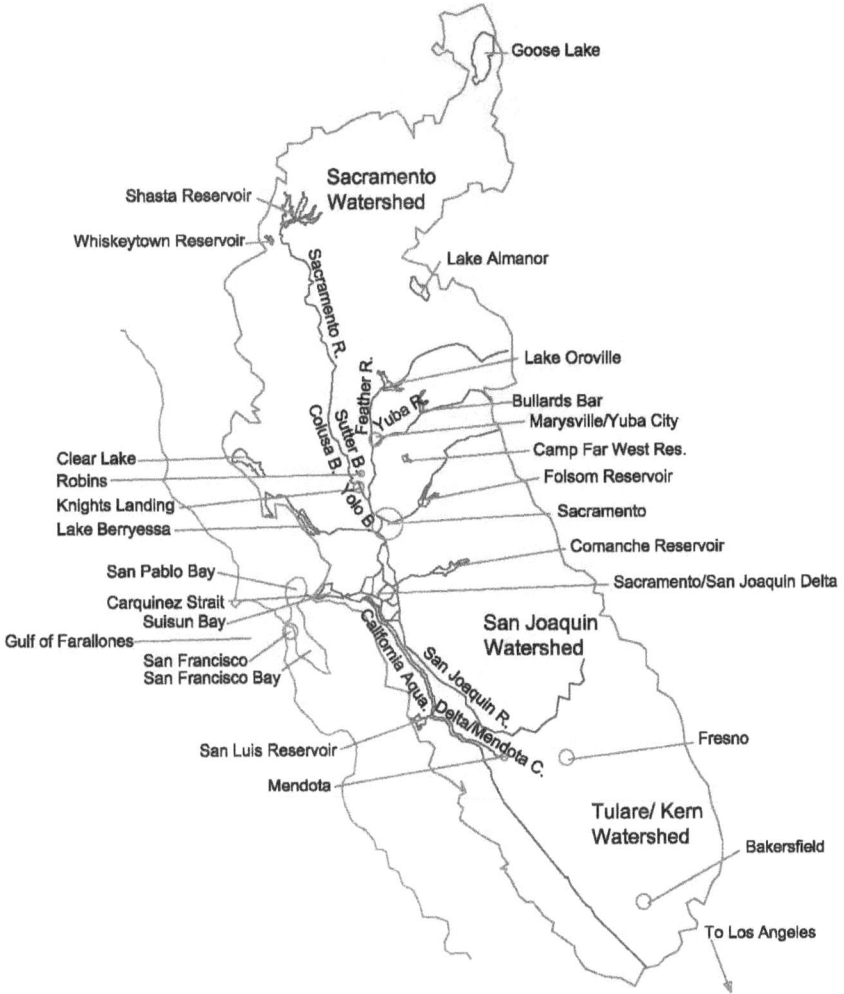

Figure 0.2. Central California Watersheds. Note: The Tule/Kern Watershed (including Fresno and Bakersfield) does not drain to the ocean.

Figure 0.3.   Gulf of Aden and Environs

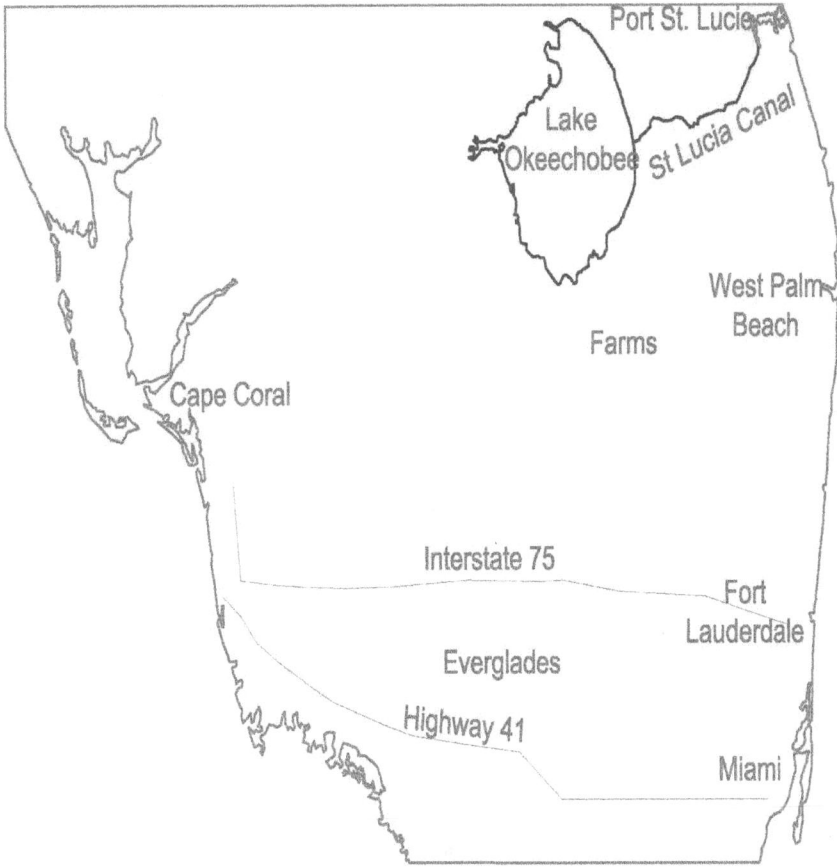

Figure 0.4.   South Florida

Acknowledgements

We authors wish to thank our intellectual predecessors. Together we are particularly beholden to those who established the Austrian School of Economics: Carl Menger, Eugen Böhm von Bawerk, Ludwig von Mises, and especially Murray Rothbard. It was the latter who through his adherence to the non-aggression principle, to private property rights, to libertarian principle, shines as a beacon for all those who wish to bring about the just society. Without these pillars of wisdom, this book would not have been possible.

We wish to thank Llewellyn Rockwell. It was his web site that provided the connection wherein the two of us, strangers no more, were able to embark together on this journey. We wish to thank the following students at Loyola University in New Orleans who provided great help with editing: Megan McAndrews, Christian Light, Ricardo Fast, Gage Counts, and Anton Chamberlin.

BLOCK'S ACKNOWLEDGMENTS

I thank Nathaniel Branden and Ayn Rand who first introduced me to libertarianism, and Murray N. Rothbard who completed my political philosophical education to full anarcho-capitalism and also to Austrian economics. I also thank my wife Marybeth for being there.

NELSON'S ACKNOWLEDGMENTS

Important, though not of the sort that is usually recognized in an acknowledgment section of a book, is my 6th grade teacher (name withheld) who through his interminable lies, taught me to avoid paying homage to authority. For it is through him that my journey to the freedom principle started.

I especially wish to acknowledge J. Craig Green, P.E. as the water rights engineer and most importantly as the philosopher of freedom who mentored me in libertarian thought. Prior to meeting him, I had never met or read another Libertarian, though I had evolved into one. He aided me to overcome a few hurdles in my intellectual odyssey.

In addition to those scholars listed above, I owe a deep debt of gratitude to such writers as Lysander Spooner, Herbert Spencer, and more recently, Adam Fergusson, as well as many others.

Finally and not least, my wife Jeanne has provided me the support and the space to pursue this endeavor.

Chapter One

Privatize the Oceans and All Other Bodies of Water

"My life is like a stroll upon the beach, As near the ocean's edge as I can go."
—Henry David Thoreau, "The Fisher's Boy," (1900)

This book is dedicated to the study of water privatization. No. That is not quite right. We, the authors of this book, will indeed analyze the arguments in favor of allowing private individuals to own bodies of water; but more: we shall also *advocate* this public policy, and attempt to refute objections to such a state of affairs.

Whoa. We have not, so far, said much of anything. Indeed, only one paragraph of this book, the previous one, has so far appeared for the reader's edification/consideration. And yet, we fear, we are already in grave danger of shocking our entire audience. When people wrap their minds about this concept (private property for oceans, lakes, rivers, and aquifers) and realize we think they should function in much the same way as ownership of pizza, shoes, and cows, we realize many will likely call for the committal to a mental institution of the authors, that is, us.

Noble reader, if you have not yet thrown away this book, a wild ride awaits. For herein, you will find free flowing ideas that may challenge assumptions you have held since your first grade teacher taught you of the "gallant" deeds of the men of yore.

To begin, we must establish the basis of proprietorship. What does it mean to own anything? Ontologically, humans know that from a very early age, babies begin to claim ownership of the things around them. Before the age of two, it is "My hand" or "My Mommy" or "My ball." Metaphysically, we each understand that this visceral, unobservable relationship with the environment exists. But as we grow in our comprehension, we come to

1

understand that most objects of our surroundings are in fact not ours. The question arises, "Is it my hand after all?" Do I own myself . . . or anything else for that matter? How much hurt do I feel that what I want is not mine? Perhaps the entire enterprise of ownership is evil. Many adopt that position. Proudhon (1840), for example, infamously wrote, "Property is theft."[1]

Some 2400 years ago, Aristotle (350 B.C.) asked that very question. While he observed that many denounce the evils of property, he answered "These evils, however, are due to a very different cause—the wickedness of human nature." St. Augustine suggests that this observation is the beginning of good works.[2] He furthermore stated that "as for the good things of this life, and its ills, God has willed that these should be common to both [the righteous and the unrighteous]" (Augustine, 426, Bk. 1, Ch. 8). In other words, while we are to enjoy those goods we have; we are not to covet those things which belong to other people even if we regard them as wrongdoers. This enjoyment of goods is a right which ought not to be abrogated by others.[3] The term for this philosophy is "Natural Law."

The rights to property precede manmade laws. Just as Augustine used Natural Law to judge the righteousness of states and empires, so St. Thomas Aquinas said that the natural law is above the laws of man.[4] John Locke (1764, Bk. 2, Ch. 2, Sec. 4) further developed the concept of the absolute right of ownership. For in his natural state even prior to civilization, men exist in:

> . . . a state of perfect freedom [i.e. anarchy] to order their actions, and dispose of their possessions and persons as they think fit . . . without asking leave, or depending on the will of any other man.

Men value property because it generates rents. To the economist to reverse the preceding sentence, rents are the value generated by the asset. However, beyond the frontier, income is negative. That is to say that the effort to generate revenue is of more value than the proceeds. At the current time, much of the sea and other bodies of water are beyond the pale.

The frontier is a sort of a boundary. In one sense, it is the line between one country and another; but here it refers to the edge of possible rents.[5] The costs of necessary infrastructure, travel, etc. to access these out of the way places, exceed the rents available. These outlays include finding ways to bypass ill-conceived man-made laws and restrictions promulgated by power-seekers who relish controlling others. The authors maintain this price is unnecessary and destructive. Artificial constraints and the wars required to enforce them dissipate[6] the rents.

As for Proudhon, he had it exactly backwards. Not only is property, per se, not theft,[7] there cannot even *be* such a thing as theft unless there is first (private) property. For, suppose A "takes" something now in B's possession, but B does not own it as his property. Can A's action constitute theft? Not at all. Theft, or robbery, can only occur if the A in our scenario dispossesses B of something he *owns*. If B does not actually have a property right in that which A takes from him, A's action cannot logically be considered theft. Of course, the object A relieves from B could have been borrowed by B from C. In that case, there is still theft on A's part, only the owner is someone else, C. But if *no one* owns what A takes from B, then there cannot be any theft that has occurred. On the contrary, property stems from the very expenditure of effort to bring it from outside to inside the frontier, from negative value to positive.[8]

Having, in our own brief way, established the basis of private ownership,[9] consider that this goodly frame the earth (Hamlet: Act 2, Scene 2) now supports some 7 billion people.[10] During the end of humanity's experience with farming alone (circa 1800 AD), right before the next stage, manufacturing, there were fewer than 1 billion souls on the planet.[11] Thus, manufacturing receives the credit for giving life to over 6 billion members of our species.

The era before farming was hunting and gathering. The best population estimates during this prior epoch is about 4 million. Extrapolating from the earlier calculation, the contribution of farming to life support comes to around 800 million.

But that occurred, almost exclusively, on the land. How are we doing on the seas? To ask this question is to answer it. We are not doing too well at all. Indeed, subject to some qualification, it is no exaggeration to say that mankind is still stuck in the hunting and gathering stages insofar as the oceans are concerned. Apart from fish farms, most of our efforts in this regard involve chasing down the denizens of the sea and catching them. Yes, our modern day implements, nets, radar, and diesel powered trawlers, are far more sophisticated than the spears and arrows of yore,[12] but for all of that, our *modus operandi* in the aquatic sphere is all too reminiscent of our pattern on the land circa 10,000 B.C. In other words, we are pretty pathetic.

To extrapolate from these numbers that occurred on dry land, if human society were to move from the hunting and gathering to the farming state on the oceans, the projected increase in population on the seas, then about 18 billion more people could live on our planet without accounting for any possible increase of landed inhabitants, and comfortably so.[13] That is to say the overwhelming majority of the ocean surface would be as empty as the Nevada deserts or Antarctica. But efficient farming on the earth's surface required private ownership. The fact that there was starvation in the former U.S.S.R. and in twenty-first century North Korea serves as dramatic, and tragic, evidence in favor of this claim. The absence of private property in the oceans, then, does not mean any individuals have been murdered, as in those totalitarian embarrassments to humanity; but it does imply that not as many have been allowed to come into existence as might otherwise have been the case. Each human is unique and precious. Amongst the people not brought to life because of the non-ownership of bodies of water are hundreds of potential Mozarts, Einsteins, Miseses, Ron Pauls and Mother Teresas.

To make this point in another way, chapter 3 shows the economic disparity between the sea and the land. The solid surface of the third planet from the sun makes a wildly disproportionate contribution to economic welfare. That is not to claim that were water privatized, it would yield three times as much wealth as the land. The five continents might have certain advantages over the rest of the earth's oceans in terms of economic productivity.[14] However, if this disparity were radically reduced, we would all be so much better off. chapter 3 further dramatizes the disproportion that existed in the old corrupt Soviet Union.

Okay: More human beings alive means greater economic welfare through private ocean enterprise.[15] No one has yet convinced anyone. (Folks: this is just the introductory chapter; the real excitement comes later!) Objections abound. This introduction is not written to *convince* anyone of anything substantive. Rather, it is a plea to keep reading. The anti-war people say, "Give peace a chance."[16] This book claims, "Give private property rights in water a chance." Indeed, private property is the way to peace in ways many do not begin to contemplate despite how outrageous this policy prescription may now seem.

We, the authors, immediately anticipate a series of possible complaints. Were this subject not so controversial, these objections would belong in the back of this tome, located after the positive case for water privatization. And, indeed, the following criticisms and refutations will be investigated and digested throughout the remainder of the book. For now, the authors can hear the following challenges and dare the reader to forestall them.

OBJECTION ONE

Imbeciles! You can't privatize bodies of water. There is such a thing as the water cycle. Water appears in the ocean. Some of it evaporates. The condensation forms clouds. Some of the liquid water falls back into the sea. So, the ocean owner has property in the clouds, too? Some of the clouds migrate to the land where they let go of their precipitation into lakes, which feed into rivers, which end up, guess where? Yes, back into the ocean. So the owner of the sea has to have property rights not only in clouds, but in lakes, rivers and streams too? Or is it that the proprietor of the river (ha, ha, ha) owns the ocean too, since "his" river replenishes the latter?

RESPONSE ONE

Give me a break. Land, too, moves. Think mud-slides, volcanoes, ice floes,[17] and so on. Water is akin to fast-moving land, and land to slow-moving water.[18] There is a soil and rock cycle too. Mud washes into the Mississippi River. It silts up downstream. Meanwhile tectonic activity both destroys land and brings new mountains and continents into existence.[19] Were deep earth movement to stop pushing up new mounts, the continent would eventually end up as a flat surface a few feet below the waves. If there were not this "land cycle," the entire country would eventually move downstream and become submerged. For example, French Frigate Sholes (Northwestern Hawaii, Undated) was once an island more or less the size of Hawaii, but it eroded away after the volcanos stopped making mountains at that location. But if a cycle in water precludes private property therein, then, too, it should have that same effect on the land. After all, a cycle is a cycle is a cycle. Should society really want to go back to communal land ownership, to collectivized farms Soviet style, and give up on the magnificent benefits that private property in land bring in their wake? Hardly.

OBJECTION TWO

Dunces! There are other, better, ways to deal with over-fishing, oil spills, species extinction of marine animals, presumably the reason you are making these outrageous claims. You undoubtedly have not ever heard of Individual Transferrable Quotas (ITQs), Territorial User Rights in Fisheries (TURFs), Total Allowable Catch (TACs). Yet you have the audacity to write a book about aquatic economics? All society need do is set up a quasi-market to buy and sell rights to catch fish, and viola, the problem is solved. Proposing private ocean ownership as a means of dealing with this admitted problem is like hitting someone over the head with a baseball bat to kill a fly rather than using a fly swatter. And it is just as dangerous, if not more so, to the body economic as would be the bat to the physical body.

RESPONSE TWO

Quasi, semi, demi, market-based schemes such as ITQs, TURFs, and TACs are highly problematic.[20] In some ways they are an improvement over no market at all, but in other ways they are inferior. So, let us call it, at least at the outset, a dead-heat between quasi markets[21] and their entire absence. However, as shown in this book, what cannot be denied is that full bodied markets, with complete private property rights, are superior, and vastly so, compared to either of these options.

These imitation arrangements amount to those "ill-conceived man-made laws and restrictions promulgated by power-seekers." They increase the transaction costs to develop fisheries by muddying property rights. Those control freaks who setup such institutions interject their beliefs regarding the proper volume of taking even though they have no personal interest and pay no cost for being wrong. True property owners know intimately how to manage their assets because their livelihood depends on it. (Or else they learn quickly or go bankrupt thereby making them unable to do more damage.)

Why, then, settle for ITQs, TURFs, TACs and all the rest of the alphabet soup bastardizations of true free enterprise? We would not apply any such system to cows or corn or canoes. Why to fish? The vast productivity of fish farms *vis a vis* these compromises is a case in point.[22]

OBJECTION THREE

You lunatics! Fish are a fugitive resource. They do not at all stay put like cows. They are forever roaming all through the seven seas, sometimes ranging over thousands of miles. Unless you are advocating that one big firm (Rothbard, 2004) own all the oceans, rivers, lakes, aquifers, and clouds too (they are all *connected*) these species will swim from the property of one owner to another, and then to yet another.

RESPONSE THREE

Cows, too, move around. Yes, not as much nor as quickly as denizens of the sea, but that is just the point. If land is akin to slow moving water, and water to fast moving land, then this applies, at least sometimes, to the species that inhabit both. Yes bovines have less range than whales.[23] And how did ranchers deal with that issue? Initially by branding. What would be the aquatic equivalent? Whales could be made to wear electronic devices or sport biological markers.[24] Would there be theft of these sea going mammals? Probably yes, the human condition being what it is. But there is also cattle rustling, and that does not stop private property in cows. Next came barbed wire fences. Is there any oceanographic equivalent? Of course there is; one such is electronic fences.[25] The main reason we do not yet have them has nothing to do with technical challenges. It is because—wait for it—there are no recognized private property rights in bodies of water. If the same obtained on land, we never would have had barbed wire fences either. Subject to the needs of these sea creatures, with water privatization they will travel where *we* want them to go, not where they wish. Private property in oceans will end the epoch of "non-restrained fish migration." They will have no more liberty to travel than do barnyard animals. This will amount to the "barnyardization" of fish, a process long overdue. This may sound like cruel and unusual punishment, but why should water animals be treated any differently than those which occupy the land?

A BETTER APPROACH

As mankind's resources become increasingly scarce with the passage of time as the population rises, it is important to look at privatization of the world's seas, rivers, oceans, lakes, and, yes, mud puddles too. Such a claim sounds like the ravings of a mad man, even to us, who have just written it. And, yet, there is method in our "madness."

Private property rights have benefited every arena of human experience they have touched. The economy of the USSR collapsed mainly because of the absence of this system. The US economy is one of the foremost in the world largely due to its relatively greater reliance on this institution. Even in the US, where private property rights are relatively clear and stable, this is not at all the case with rivers, lakes, aquifers. As a result, confusion reigns while attempts to improve the environment with anti-pollution laws and the like only aggravate the problems and lead to increased incarceration rates.

There is simply no reason on earth for us not to apply to the oceans these precious lessons we have learned on the land. It is our contention that these two arenas, land and water, are not as dissimilar as might first be imagined. Property rights, profit and loss, and free market capitalism, that have worked so well in the one context, can do so, equally well, in the other.

The world's oceans, apart from the territorial seas and exclusive economic zones of nations, are classified as the high seas. Neither individuals nor nations have property rights in these aquatic areas. Partly as a result of this communal ownership, the "tragedy of the commons"[26] has come into play and fisheries have been depleted while other marine animal and plant life suffer as well. If an entrepreneurial system were instituted in the world's oceans, it is arguable that pollution would decrease and plant and animal species would be far better conserved.

And yet, vast areas of human activity occur where private property rights play no role at all: oceans, seas, rivers, aquifers, and other bodies of water. But why should we expect that there would be any better results from "aqua-socialism"[27] than we have experienced from socialism on land? Indeed, the evidence is all around us attesting to this fact: whales are an endangered species (McClendon, 2010; Sandle, 2013; Nimoy, 1986; World Wildlife Fund, 2013); fish stocks are precipitously declining (Cook, et. al, 1997; Gaia, 2012; Myers, et. al. 1997; Roland, 2012); oil spills are a recurring problem (Casselman, undated; ITOPF, 2013; Rockwell, 2000B; Rothbard, 1989A: Sharp, 2010) rivers are polluted, some so seriously that they actually catch fire (Rotman, 2014); lakes are becoming overcrowded with boaters, swimmers, fishermen, etc. (Tahoe, 2011; Photobucket, Undated). There is no market mechanism to allocate this scarce water resource amongst the competing users; deep sea mining is in a state of suspended animation due to unclear titles; the legal status of offshore oil drilling rigs is uncertain.

We, the authors, cannot answer all objections to ocean, lake, river, and aquifer privatization, nor explain how they would function under full free enterprise. Not, at least, in this introductory chapter. But, we hope we have at least whetted your intellectual appetite, and have encouraged you to read the remainder of the book. We have no warrant to believe that socialism, the absence of private property rights, is any more workable on water than on land; it is long past time to explore ways in which this institution can be applied to aqueous resources. Topics to be covered in this book include:

GENERAL CONCEPTS OF AQUEOUS OWNERSHIP

The disparity of gross domestic product on land and water will be addressed; and while the tragedy of the commons is bad enough on land, it is worse on water.

Most importantly, the book discusses: Who will rightly own the rivers, lakes and oceans? On what basis will property rights in these bodies of water be distributed? It starts with the Lockean principles of homesteading. While Locke discussed his theory in terms of land, herein the application to water will be studied. The investigation will proceed with the mechanics of privatizing bodies of water. Also of interest is the concept of abandonment of an aqueous asset. Are abandoned water bodies subject to homesteading by another person? If so, what are the limits and duties to the abandoning agent, if any?

Concepts for privatization of water will account for how it differs from land as well as how it is similar. Water flows from one place to another. Unlike land, usually regarded as a solid, water is a fluid. Would ownership apply to the water itself as the physical molecules, to a geometric volume in which it temporarily rests as a particular location, or to a flow rate as a specific volume or mass over a period of time at a particular location? Four types of water bodies are studied herein:

CONCEPTS OF OCEANOLOGICAL OWNERSHIP

Oceanological[28] ownership must account for the salt water itself either as the physical solution, particular volumes by location, or by flows (currents). Property rights in the oceans, it will be argued, will have strong and positive implications for fishing privileges; transportation; mineral extraction from oceanic fluid; potable water extraction from salt water; mineral extraction from the floor of the seas, etc. Ideas regarding possession of these various assets have sharply negative implications for the UN Law of the Sea Treaty. Since property rights imply boundaries between one person's holdings and those of another, we will explore how "fences" in the water can be established. Related discussions will include methods for apprehending trespassers and thieves and rectifying damages they inflict upon the rightful owners. Unless the owner of an asset does the dumping, those who leave garbage in any part of the ocean belonging to someone else would be considered criminal trespassers.

Certain natural processes cause transfers of water to and from the fluid available for the uses listed herein. For example, when the polar ice caps and/ or icebergs melt or freeze, does this imply theft of water from the owner of the ice on the part of the proprietor of the ocean, the reverse, or neither? What about gains and losses stemming from the natural water cycle? Unusual events such as the following are discussed in subsequent chapters:

- Suppose a volcano creates a new island; who is the rightful owner of it?
- Would the owner of an ocean or a miner beneath the waves be responsible for a tidal wave emanating from his property which inflicts severe damages inland?
- What happens when a surge emanating from X's part of the ocean destroys Y's boat?
- What about lighthouses? Who would be in charge of them, during the epochs they were needed?
- Who will get to own the oceans? On what basis will property rights in these bodies of water be distributed?

CONCEPTS OF POTAMOLOGICAL OWNERSHIP

Potamological[29] ownership must account for the water itself, fluid flow, floods, draughts, fishing, transportation, mineral extraction from the liquid, and the riparian[30] zone, pollution, erosion, sedimentation, recreational swimming, and boating, etc. In Toto, Riparian, and Priority schemes for water use will be compared and contrasted for strengths and weaknesses.

Subsequent chapters will investigate the locus of liability when erosion occurs, whether natural or anthropogenic. Based on the concept that "Everything that is, is somewhere,"[31] eroded material will be deposited downstream of the erosion. Assignment of liability will also be discussed. When a river overflows its banks, can the contiguous landowners sue for trespass? Or can the river owner charge for a water delivery? When a river such as the Mississippi or Sacramento changes course, what are the implications for ownership titles?

- Who will get to own the rivers? On what basis will streams and river flow be distributed?
- Suppose a watercourse overflows its banks and damages holdings alongside. Who pays? Does anyone?
- Who will determine whether a dam can be built on a river? Would it be possible, with private property rights, for a gigantic project, such as the Tennessee Valley Authority or Shasta Dam, to be built under free enterprise? What should happen to these amenities if and when there is a libertarian government?
- Suppose there is a mud slide from a farm into a river. May the owner of the former bill the holder of the latter for undermining his land, or does the latter sue the former for trespass?
- What happens if a river changes course and eliminates a previously occupied building site?
- How does a landowner re-establish access if his only previous access was via a navigable river that has become non-navigable?

CONCEPTS OF LIMNOLOGICAL OWNERSHIP

Private Limnological[32] property rights in lakes and ponds must address the water itself, floods, fishing, transportation, mineral extraction from the liquid, mineral extraction from the lake bottom and/or the riparian zone, pollution, sedimentation, etc.

As in the case of oceans, how can fences best be established? What is the mechanism for access to the lake bottom if it is under separate ownership for mineral extraction? Suppose an individual or corporation owns a lake. Is access to the shore necessarily included? Suppose there are four owners of contiguous land surrounding a lake including the riparian zone. Do they each come to own a slice of the lake; do they all four, together, own the entire lake; or neither? In addition to those challenges, this book will discuss rights and limits regarding the extraction of water from and discharge of material to the lake.

- Who will get to own the lakes? On what basis will inland waters be distributed?
- Who is at fault if a power boater cuts the line of a fisherman?
- Should those who have rights to sail on a peaceful, quiet lake be able to enjoin motor speed boats?

- Can a miner legally extract salt from under Lake Erie? What if the mine collapses and the Lake drains into the mine? Imagine that the salt dissolves and converts it from fresh to brackish, then what?
- How will free enterprise deal with mosquitos and standing water?

CONCEPTS OF HYDROGEOLOGICAL OWNERSHIP

If ownership of Hydrogeological[33] resources (aquifers and ground water) is to become a reality, this concept must take into account water extraction, fluid flow, underground rivers, soil structure, permeability rate, pollution, unconfined aquifers, confined aquifers, and artesian[34] water, the interaction between surface and subsurface water, ground subsidence, etc.

Excessive pumping of groundwater from an aquifer has serious consequences for surface features. Pumping creates a drawdown cone.[35] As a result, the gradient of the phreatic water surface[36] steepens, and the flow rate increases. The loss of water from surface rivers and lakes intensifies and leaves less water for the owners of those facilities. Where the soil structure of the aquifer is weak, extraction can cause collapse and result in ground subsidence. The slow percolation rate affects a delay in observable consequences of pumping on surface water. The chapters regarding groundwater and aquifers discuss the resulting liabilities, and demonstrate that a system of private property rights is vastly to be preferred to present institutional arrangements.

- Who will get to own the aquifers? On what basis will ground water be distributed?
- Should Person A lower the pressure of an aquifer and thereby cause an artesian spring being utilized by Brewery B to go dry, is A responsible for damages?
- Posit that a Town A aggressively pumps water from an aquifer and, since the water seeks a level surface, none is available to a user B, 10 miles away? How would B prove it?
- Suppose a farmer extracts water from a collapsible soil and the ground surface subsides leaving his neighbors in a newly created flood zone?
- What if a bunch of Johnny-come-latelies draw from groundwater hydraulically connected to a river, and, thereby, deny irrigation farmers the rights that were homesteaded 100 years ago? How would the victims prove it?

NOTES

1. Here is the entire quote from (Edwards, 1969, 124). "If I had to answer the question 'What is slavery?' and if I were to answer in one word, 'Murder,' I would immediately be understood. I would not need to use a lengthy argument to demonstrate that the power to deprive a man of his thoughts, his will and his personality is a power of life and death, and that

to enslave a man is to murder him. Why, then, to the question 'What is property?' may I not likewise reply 'theft,' without knowing that I am certain to be misunderstood, even though the second proposition is simply a transformation of the first?" Unlike Proudhon, your authors see a real difference in that the slave has the very attributes that he lists while property isolated from humans as simple goods has none of those properties.

2. "The confession of evil works is the first beginning of good works" (Southgate, 1862, p. 671).

3. Assuming an evil state acquired some property by war, Augustine (426, Bk. 4, Ch. 4) said "Justice being taken away, then, what are kingdoms but great robberies? For what are robberies themselves, but little kingdoms? The band itself is made up of men; it is ruled by the authority of a prince, it is knit together by the pact of the confederacy; the booty is divided by the law agreed on. If, by the admittance of abandoned men, this evil increases to such a degree that it holds places, fixes abodes, takes possession of cities, and subdues peoples, it assumes the more plainly the name of a kingdom, because the reality is now manifestly conferred on it, not by the removal of covetousness, but by the addition of impunity. Indeed, that was an apt and true reply which was given to Alexander the Great by a pirate who had been seized. For when that king had asked the man what he meant by keeping hostile possession of the sea, he answered with bold pride, 'What thou meanest by seizing the whole earth; but because I do it with a petty ship, I am called a robber, whilst thou who dost it with a great fleet art styled emperor.'" Interestingly, Augustine based the story of Alexander and the Pirate on Cicero.

4. "Man can make laws in those matters of which he is competent to judge. But man is not competent to judge of interior movements, that are hidden, but only of exterior acts which appear: and yet for the perfection of virtue it is necessary for man to conduct himself aright in both kinds of acts. Consequently human law could not sufficiently curb and direct interior acts; and it was necessary for this purpose that a Divine law should supervene." Aquinas (*Summa*)

5. The concept "rent" is used in three different ways in economics. First, there is ordinary rent, of the sort we discuss in the text: if you own a house or some land or a car, you can rent it out to a tenant and earn a fee on your property. If you use such properties yourself, you are enjoying an implicit rent: you are benefiting from their use, presumably to a greater extent than the amount you could collect from a renter. Second, is "economic rent." This is defined as an amount of money over and above that which is necessary to keep a factor of production in its present position. For example, suppose a professional athlete earns $10 million per year, and that his next best option, from which he earns an equal amount of psychic income, is $2 million annually. Then, he is earning a salary of $2 million, and an economic rent of $8 million. Were his salary as an athlete reduced from $10 million to, say, $3 million, he would still remain as a ballplayer. In contrast, were his income as an athlete decreased to $1 million, he would quit and take up alternative employment at $2 million. The third use of this word is "rent seeking." This concept, created by the Public Choice school of thought, refers to the attainment of an illicit payment, say, from restricting entry of a potential competitor, or gaining a government subsidy. For a critique of this third nomenclature which claims that "booty seeking" or "theft seeking" is more accurate, see Block (2000A, 200B). The point we are making in the text is that certain lands, say in the wilds of Alaska, or, some bodies of water, for example in unused parts of the ocean, are not (yet) economic goods, and hence do not (yet) create any rents for their owners.

6. If governments set up barriers to accessing (far away located) raw materials, or land, or under water resources, then the rents that would otherwise arise from owning them will be lost, or dissipated, by such laws. For example, if a government placed a tax on developing land in the Antarctic, it might preclude such entrepreneurial activity.

7. Of course, *some* property is indeed stolen, or is the result of theft. That occurs when someone steals the rightfully owned property of someone else. But this is an entirely different matter.

8. This statement does not endorse the labor theory of value. Value is subjective and stems from the appreciation of the beholder not the laborer (unless the beholder and laborer are one and the same).

9. For more on this see Bylund, 2005, 2012; Grotius, 1625; Hoppe, 1993B, 2011A; Kinsella, 2003, 2006; Locke, 1948; Paul, 1987; Pufendorf, 1673; Rothbard, 1973, 32; Rozeff, 2005; Watner, 1982

10. United Nations, Department of Economic and Social Affairs, Population Division, 2013. World Population Prospects: The 2012 Revision.

11. Schoenbach (2000). All population estimates herein are based on this web page as it existed on Jan.1, 2014.

12. Which lead to the very opposite problem, species extinction due to the tragedy of the commons, about which more, much more, in later chapters.

13. We, the authors, are not Malthusians. For modern day followers of this fallacious and pernicious school of thought, see Brown, 1963, 1972, 1981, 2009, 2011, 2012; Commoner, 1990; Ehrlich, 1968; Ehrlich and Ehrlich, 1981; Gore, 1992; Suzuki and McConnell, 2007; Suzuki and McKibben, 2004; Suzuki and Hanington, 2012. For critiques, see Bauer, 1981; Boudreaux, 2008; Friedman, 1972, 1977; Robbins, 1928, 1966; Rothbard, 2011B; Simon, 1981, 1990, 1996; Sowell, 1983; Williams, 1999; Wittman, 2000. Sowell (1983) states: "Every human being on the face of the Earth could be housed in the state of Texas in one-story, single-family homes, each with a front and a back yard. A family of four would thus have 6,800 square feet—about the size of the typical middle-class American home with front and back-yards." Also, the bet between Ehrlich and Simon, discussed below (endnote 22), is of particular interest in this regard: For the story of the two bets from the point of view of Ehrlich refer to: Center for Conservation Biology (2005).

14. We are not at all sure of this claim. It is entirely plausible that when privatized, the seas will have important advantages not yet apparent to us.

15. This sounds like that old advertising jingle, "Better living through chemistry" but if the cliché works, our motto is to use it.

16. As it happens, we entirely agree with them, but that is entirely another matter. We would only add that we oppose both Republican *and* Democratic wars of initiatory aggression, not just the former, as is the case with all too many in the anti-war movement.

17. Is this terra firma or fluid? That is the entire point. There is no unambiguous way of answering this question. The connection between land and water is greater than most people appreciate.

18. In fact, land moves through several mechanisms, to wit: erosion, settlement, expansion, tectonic movement, earthquakes, and landslides, to name a few. Land-like properties of water include incompressibility, platform for transportation, milieu for life support, valuable natural resource, etc., but most importantly: the surfaces and volumes are remarkably stable.

19. The Juan de Fuca Plate is an example. The ocean bed subducts (literally to take away, but in the case of tectonics, to dive under or disappear from sight) and then melts under the North American plate. Meanwhile the forces push up the Cascade Mountains and create volcanoes such as Mt. Hood and Mt. Rainier (Colorado U., Undated).

20. The same applies to analogous tradable emissions rights (TERs) for dealing with air pollution and school vouchers which misaddress education. For critiques of the former see McGee and Block, 1994. Of the latter, North, 1976, 2011; North and Friedman, 1993; Rockwell, 1998, 2000A, 2002; Rome and Block. 2006; Rothbard, 1971, 1973, 1994, 1995; Salisbury, 2003; Vance, 1996; Yates, 2002A, 2002B; Young and Block. 1999..

21. This is precisely the system of "market socialism" advocated and implemented by the Hungarian Communist Party. See on this Arnold, 1994; Bradley, 1981; Bardham and Roemer, 1992; Gordon, 1996,1999; Machaj, 2007B; McGee and Block, 1994; Murrell, 1983; Ollman, 1999; Roemer and Bardhan, 1992. Yunker, James A. 1995. If there is any one person responsible for these violations of full-bodied capitalism it is that semi-socialist, Milton Friedman. See on this Block, 1999B, 2003B, 2003C, 2010B, 2011A, 2013A; Block and Barnett, 2012–2013; McChesney, 1991; Rothbard, 2002; Friedman and Block, 2006; Kinsella, 2009B; Lind, 2012; Machan, 2010; McChesney, 1991; North, 2012; Rothbard, 2002; Vance, 2005; Wapshott, 2012; Wenzel, 2012; Wilcke, 1999

22. MacArthur "genius award" winner Paul Ehrlich had a famous bet with free market economist Julian Simon over whether we were running out of resources such as nickel, copper, chromium, tin and tungsten, etc. The former lost. After Ehrlich lost his Malthusian bet to Simon, Ehrlich offered another: the fish would soon disappear. Simon's response? Sure, if we can include farmed fish as well. Ehrlich lost his enthusiasm for that bet. See the second Simon-

Ehrlich bet, the one that did not occur. See on this Bailey, 1995, p. 132; Colander, 1998, p. 382; Center, 2005; Murphy, 2007, p. 54; Regis, 2004; Worstall, 2013. Source Sailor, 2013

23. Deer and buffalo range more widely, and more quickly, but, again, not as fast as many sea species.

24. A proprietor could also possibly breed his stock to show unique characteristics, such as color or patterns on the skin, to establish ownership.

25. More on electronic fences in water can be found at (Maceina, et al, 1999).

26. On the tragedy of the commons, a theory introduced by Hardin, 1968, see also Smith, 1981; Rothbard, 1982; Leal, 1997; Block, 1999A; Cordato, 2004. For a fallacious critique of this crucially important insight, see Ostrom, 1990. For a rejoinder to Ostrom, 1990, see Block, 2011B and Jankovic and Block, forthcoming.

27. Aquasocialism, as used herein, refers to "water socialism": the communal or govern-mental ownership of water and/or bodies of water.

28. Of or related to the study of oceans; derived from the Greek ωκεανό.

29. Of or related to the study of rivers; derived from the Latin *pōtāre*.

30. The riparian zone is the wetted perimeter of the river plus the banks of the river up to the normal high water and/or the top of emergent plant species. In subsequent chapters, the term "riparian" will be used to describe water rights based on ownership of land adjacent to a river which includes title to the riparian zone.

31. Also translated from the Greek as "All existence . . . must of necessity be in some place." (Plato, 360).

32. Of or related to the study of inland waters; derived from the Greek λ I μνη.

33. Of or related to the study of groundwater; derived from the Greek ὕδωρ+ γῆ

34. Artesian water refers to an aquifer where the hydraulic grade line is higher than the ground elevation. Pumping from the aquifer could lower the hydraulic grade line and cause un-pumped artesian sources to stop flowing.

35. A drawdown cone derives from the fact that a pump removes water from the aquifer faster that it can flow towards the well. The deeper the "funnel," the faster it can be discharged.

36. Phreatic water surface: (technically) is the surface (or line when viewed in cross section) where the pressure is zero under atmospheric conditions. It is the top of the seepage zone (US, BOR 1987). In simpler terms it is the surface of free water within a soil matrix. If one drills a hole in the ground, free flowing water will rise to the phreatic level. A steep gradient supports rapid movement.

Chapter Two

Why Privatize Anything?

Private property is more ethical and efficacious than either government ownership or non-ownership, i.e. the commons. These two desiderata are considered in turn. First up is morality.

MORALITY

State Ownership vs. Private

When one person deals with another, each in a private capacity, this commercial interaction can be fully voluntary. A sells a car to B for $10,000. Each of these consenting adults in this capitalist act goes into the deal willingly. Neither is forced, at the point of a gun, to engage in the transaction. [1]

Matters are different, very much so, when the government is involved on one side of the deal. For the state, necessarily, involves the initiation of violence against innocent parties. Some might argue that this is a necessary evil, but it cannot be denied that it is wicked. For whenever the government acts, it brings an undue advantage to the one at the expense of the other. In the case of the car sale, if A is willing to sell for $9,000, but a sale for less than $10,000 is forbidden by law, then B is oppressed—violently.

In addition, it finances this tyranny with money forcibly taken from the taxpayer. It cannot be cogently argued that the citizens of a country have agreed to pay for services provided for them by the state through taxation, as in the case of the golf or tennis club, for there is no evidence of any such contract. Schumpeter (1942, 198) states: "The theory which construes taxes on the analogy of club dues or of the purchase of the services of, say, a doctor only proves how far removed this part of the social science is from scientific habits of mind."[2] In the view of Rothbard (1973):

> For centuries, the State (or more strictly, individuals acting in their roles as 'members of the government') has cloaked its criminal activity in high-sounding rhetoric. For centuries the State has committed mass murder and called it 'war'; then ennobled the mass slaughter that 'war' involves. For centuries the State has enslaved people into its armed battalions and called it 'conscription' in the 'national service.' For centuries the State has robbed people at bayonet point and called it 'taxation.' In fact, if you wish to know how libertarians regard the State and any of its acts, simply think of the State as a criminal band, and all of the libertarian attitudes will logically fall into place.

Whatever the necessity of violence against innocent taxpayers, in terms of ethics, it is difficult not to give the nod to the private sector. After all, taxpayers are necessarily exploited; they are compelled at the point of a gun,[3] to pay the amount of money required of them, whether they wish to do so or not. In sharp contrast, while the private sector surely experiences fraud, it is not at all a necessary condition; the overwhelming majority of commercial interactions in the market are voluntary. What about coercion as a means to right a wrong such as fraud? The very repugnance of unprovoked force necessitates the need to forcibly restore order. So, in terms of sheer morality, privatization is justified as it transfers economic activity from the government towards relatively moral private actors.

The Commons vs. Private Property

What about the moral implications of common vs. private property? Here, too, it is clear that the latter is vastly superior to the former. For under common property, it is unclear as to who owns what. Suppose, for example, that shirts, to pick a rather mundane example, were all owned in common. It would then be exceedingly difficult for ordinary, well-intentioned, ethical people to know what they may wear, and what not. Most likely, they would fight with each other as to who could wear what. The government would then step in to create order out of the ensuing chaos, but we have already dealt with that particular institution. And the same applies to water resources, when they become scarce. Who has precedence in the commonly owned lake? The boater, the swimmer, the surf boarder, the fisherman? It is impossible to make any such determination. Since chaos and government control are hardly ethical ways for civilized persons to deal with one another, we must again conclude that the free market with private property rights is the only moral system of the three of them.

EFFICIENCY

State Ownership vs. Private

Second, what about efficaciousness? Here, too, the private sector comes out ahead of either governmental ownership or unowned resources. On a pragmatic basis, government ownership is far less efficient than private enterprise. Whenever there are at least semi-controlled "experiments" in this regard, the latter performs the same tasks at a far lower price than the former. That is, it costs bureaucrats two, three and even four or more times the amount of money for a given task to be done than for entrepreneurs. When it comes to moving a ton of garbage, or a ton of mail, tasks undertaken by both, private enterprise accomplishes this at a small fraction of the expense of the statist system. [4]

Is this a mere accident? Is this an empirical finding limited to a small number of years? Is it the case that private enterprise is more efficient than government bureaus only in a small geographical area? No, no, no and a thousand times no! Markets outperform state services in all times and places because they have an important advantage over those other institutional arrangements. When an entrepreneur cannot cut costs and improve services, he loses customers. If this process continues for a long enough duration, bankruptcy is the inevitable result. When the weakest performers leave the stage, the average of all the remaining others increases. But this weeding out of the inefficient (Hazlitt, 1946) cannot occur in the so-called public sector. There is no automatic penalty for an underperforming government bureau. This statist need not disappear when it does a poor job. For example, suppose the Food and Drug Administration approves of a bad drug, or prohibits a good one. Will the FDA automatically lose profits and go bankrupt? Of course not. Far more likely, perversely oftentimes, it is more heavily subsidized. The squeaky wheel gets the grease. This is not to say that the poorly run government airline or steel mill can never be laid to rest. This can occur, at least theoretically. But for this result to occur, the political process must give its imprimatur: a far more complex and convoluted process. It is no accident that the FDA, the Fed, Fannie and Freddie, and hundreds of other government bureaus that have failed, are still in operation.

Nor is the stick the only competitive advantage the market holds over the statist sector of the economy. There is also the carrot. When a private entrepreneur successfully satisfies customers by lowering prices, innovating, increasing quality, cutting costs, he earns more profits than otherwise. He can thus expand his base of operation. He can purchase the plant and equipment of his previous competitors, the ones who are going out of business due to inefficiency. He can attract new investment better than others who were not as effective. This cannot occur in the public sector, at least not legally. Any innovative bureaucrat who brings about efficiencies[5] to better serve his clients is prohibited by law to pocket the fruits of his labor. If he tries to do so, he can and will be imprisoned for theft.[6]

At present, if McDonalds falters, Burger King, Wendys, and a whole host of other fast food emporia will take up the slack immediately. But, imagine, if the government were in charge of the fast food industry, and provided burgers, pizza, chicken wings, fish, salads, and all the rest. Now, stipulate that it did a poor job. Would there be any automatic response rectifying the situation? Of course not. Rather, this statist fast food supplier would limp along for years as does the US Post Office, the motor vehicle bureau, and other state suppliers of goods and services.

The Commons vs. Private Property

In the case of commonly versus privately held property the latter is likewise preferable, for the former suffers from the problem of the tragedy of the commons. When no one owns a meadow, and all ranchers can feed their stock at will, over-grazing and the devastation of the paddock are assured. The group as a whole loses out, but only individuals can act. And yet each herdsman has an incentive to allow his bovines to enter the meadow as long as any grass at all remains. In the western US, deadly range wars have ensued from just such conflicts of interest.

Similarly, if food is served as individual portions, there is less of a temptation to overeat than when all diners may dig in. With personal servings, and no one allowed to grab food from anyone else's plate, people may eat at a leisurely pace. But if the meal is in effect owned in common, the rate of ingestion will increase, as each person fears that others will grab his share if he is dilatory. This is precisely why communes, kibbutzim, entire socialist nations, and other organizations where goods are owned in common do not prosper: the tragedy of the commons.[7]

NOTES

1. This is not to deny that sometimes private individuals defraud others through swindles. It is only to say that it need not necessarily be so. That is, there are millions, nay billions of trades, purchases, sales, of this sort that occur every day, with not an iota of compulsion or deception involved.

2. For literature attesting to the necessarily violent nature of all government, see Anderson and Hill, 1979; Benson, 1989, 1990; Block, 2007B, 2010A, 2011C; Casey, 2010; DiLorenzo, 2010; Gregory, 2011; Guillory & Tinsley, 2009; Hasnas, 1995; Heinrich, 2010; Higgs, 2009, 2012; Hoppe, 2008, 2011B; Huebert, 2010; King, 2010; Kinsella, 2009C; Long, 2004; McCon-

key, 2013; Molyneux, 2008; Murphy, 2005A; Rothbard, 1973, 1975, 1977, 1998; Shaffer, 2012; ; Spooner, 1870; Stringham, 2007; Tannehill, 1984; Tinsley, 1998–1999; Wenzel, 2013.

3. Some might disagree with this claim, and maintain that by living in the country, the citizen has agreed to pay taxes. This argument from club dues is circular: it assumes as correct the very point at issue: that the state has the right to compel "dues" in the first place. Further, if taxes are truly voluntary, there ought to be a signed contract attesting to this claim. There is no such thing. For further criticism of this point see Anderson and Hill, 1979; Benson, 1989, 1990; Block, 2007B, 2010A, 2011C; Casey, 2010; DiLorenzo, 2010; Gregory, 2011; Guillory & Tinsley, 2009; Hasnas, 1995; Heinrich, 2010; Higgs, 2009, 2012; Hoppe, 2008, 2011B; Huebert, 2010; King, 2010; Kinsella, 2009C; Long, 2004; McConkey, 2013; Molyneux, 2008; Murphy, 2005A; Rothbard, 1973, 1975, 1977, 1998; Shaffer; Spooner, 1870; Stringham, 2007; Tannehill, 1984; Tinsley, 1998–1999; Wenzel, 2013.

4. For empirical evidence buttressing this claim, see Adie, 1999, 1990a, 1990b; Ahlbrandt, 1973; Alston, 2007; Anderson and Hill, 1996; Bennett, 1980; Bennett and DiLorenzo, 1982, 1989, 197; Bennett, and Johnson, 1980; Blair, Ginsberg, and Vogel, 1975; Boardman and Vining, 1989; Borcherding, 1977; Borcherding, Burnaby, Pommerehne, and Schneider, 1982; Butler, 1985, 1986; Chapman, 2008; Clarkson, 1972; Crain and Zardkoohi, 1978; Davies, 1971, 1977; De Alessi, 1982; D'Souza, Bortolotti, Fantini, and Megginson, 2000; Dewenter, and Malatesta, 2000; Fitzgerald, 1989; Frech, 1976; Hanke, 1987a, 1987b, 1987c; Lindsay, 1976; Megginson and Netter, 2000, 2001; Monsen and Walters, 1983; Moore, S., 1987; Moore, T., 1990; Moore, and Butler, 1987; Poole, 1976; Priest, 1975; Savas, 1987, 1979, 1982, 2000; Vining, and Boardman. 1992; White, 1978

5. This sounds like a logical contradiction in terms, but it is not. Civil servants are not homogeneous. Some will inevitably be more efficient than others.

6. Unless his cronies are sufficiently powerful.

7. For a critique of the notion that the tragedy of the commons leads to economic inefficiency, see Ostrom, 1990. For a defense of this theory, and (in effect) a rejoinder to her, see Block. 2011B; Jankovitch and Block, forthcoming; Smith, 1981.

Chapter Three

Why Privatize Bodies of Water?

"Prima sapientiae clavis definitur, assidua scilicet seu frequens interrogatio . . .
Dubitando enim ad inquisitionem venimus; inquirendo veritatem percipimus."
[Relentless and frequent questioning is crucial to understanding . . . For in
doubting we are led to inquire, and by inquiry we perceive the truth.][1] —Peter
Abelard, *Sic et Non* [*Yes and No*], (Anno Domini 1120, p. 320)

À la Yentl, when the yeshiva boys were swimming, too many landlubbers
with less reason would just as soon limit their pool exposure to dipping a toe
while firmly standing on the shore. Meanwhile, prior to the writing of histories, from before the dawn of civilization, the Homers of earth braved the
elements to reach new vistas. This book in general, and this chapter in particular, is dedicated to those maniacal mariners who have revolutionized society
in ways that those toe-dippers never believed possible. May ensuing adventurers continue that quest for excellence!

APPLICABILITY OF PRIVATE
OWNERSHIP TO BODIES OF WATER

Ethics

As demonstrated in chapter 2 regarding all goods and services, the case for
privatizing anything is both ethical and economic. This applies to bodies of
water as much as anything else. When rivers, lakes, oceans, etc., are privately
owned, there is neither the tragedy of the commons, nor the initiation of
violence against innocent people. Individuals can deal with each other on a
voluntary basis.

The moral aspects are vital when it comes to water. At the time of this
writing, China is claiming parts of the Pacific Ocean, several small islands

21

and more to our interest, the water itself. These resources are seen by some as under the control of neighboring countries such as Vietnam, Philippines, South Korea, Japan and others. Hopefully, these conflicts can be settled peacefully. Would matters improve if only individuals, not nations, were to be seen as owners of aquatic property? Although an answer to this question must necessarily be speculative, there is a strong case in this regard for a positive reply.

First of all, if China and Japan get into a war concerning these matters, many people will die. If on the other hand two individuals from each of these countries maintain conflicting claims as to water ownership, there will be far fewer deaths, and this cannot be considered ethically irrelevant. Posit that C from China and J from Japan each claim an identical portion of the South China Sea. How will such a clash be settled? Is it likely that C and J will start shooting at each other? No, because both are private, non-coercive establishments, and when they cannot agree, their first recourse is usually the courts, not the bullet or the bomb.[2] There is no national pride at stake between entrepreneurs C and J, as there would be between states China and Japan. This is yet another reason to expect private property to reduce tensions.

To which court might J and C turn, in order to settle their differences? Under a pure free enterprise system, to private courts themselves.[3] In the present day and age, they would have other options, including arbitration: the Better Business Bureau, the American Arbitration Association, the American Stock Exchange, etc.[4] While it is true that China and Japan might also agree to arbitrate, it is our contention that there would be greater pressures on "mere" businessmen to do so than for leaders of powerful nations.

Secondly, as we have seen in the previous chapter, whenever government takes one side of a commercial interaction, coercion is necessarily involved for at least one party. This does not at all apply when both participants are private.

Productivity

There is a gigantic disparity of GDP on land and water. It is exceedingly difficult to obtain exact statistics on the disproportion of productivity on the land mass and in the seas. But the best guesstimate we have is as follows[5]:

Land–25% of earth surface	Water–75% of earth surface
Land–95% of GDP	Water–5% of GDP

What could account for such a gigantic disparity? The tragedy of the commons is certainly one possible explanation. Apart from the USSR until 1991, and Cuba and North Korea as of 2014, vast portions of the earth's land mass were owned privately,[6] while hardly a drop of water apart from a few bottling plants and many small bottles of it, was in private hands. This means that the deleterious effects of communism strike our water resources, while land is relatively free of this scourge. Even apart from that cause, there is good and sufficient reason to believe that land would be more effective in producing wealth than water. The former is more stable than the latter. More people would likely occupy land than even privately owned water, and thus economies of scale would be stronger on the former than the latter. Then, too, water is probably more dangerous for mankind than land. While typhoons and hurricanes attack both, the destructive force upon people is heavier in the sea, where mass drownings can occur. So, even under private ownership, there would likely be a disparity. Land would still be more productive a resource than water.[7] However, that the disproportionality would be so severe is preposterous. Under private ownership the oceans, rivers, and lakes would become more productive, without in any way reducing the contribution made on the land per capita. In this way, gross world product would inevitably increase, and markedly so, under privatization.

Contemplate now the productivity of land in the former USSR where the disproportion is also very dramatic, albeit less so than on the seas[8]:

Land: Public–97%   Private–3%

Crops: Public–75%   Private–25%

Here, there is little mystery as to the source of the disparity. Again, the tragedy of the commons rears its ugly head. Farm workers would leave tractors out in the field to rust, while taking meticulous care of the teeny home garden plots which they were allowed to own.[9] People take great care of their own private property from which they can gain, and less so, far less so, of resources they do not control and from which benefits to them flow not at all. Sovietized agriculture, which led to mass starvation, is a good vantage point from which to view ocean non-ownership. The two are intimately connected.

Ethically, under individual ownership no one would necessarily violate the rights of anyone else. Were that was all there were to it, privatization on this ground alone would be justified. But there is more.

Practicality

Mankind is also likely to become far wealthier under private ownership of bodies of water and in this way, to put a positive spin on the matter, get just that much closer to curing poverty. Short of divinity men cannot walk on water. So how could people live and work on the oceans, lakes, and rivers beyond a few boats?[10] Without the ability to actually live complete, exciting, and fulfilling lives in vast numbers, is increasing the aqueous proportion of the gross world product by something on the order of 600 percent, or more, realistic?

In fact, people do live in and on the water, albeit in small numbers so far. It is this sort of pioneering a vast wilderness that will teach men how to live in this wild new environment. As with any evolution, no one can predict exactly how it will happen. But there already exist important clues to viable ocean living.

One form of oil drilling platform intended for deep water amounts to an unusual "boat." Imagination is the key. Fancy a large deep cylinder weighted at the bottom so that it floats upright or an array of deep pontoons fixed together so that they retain orientation. Such a device would be stable, as deep ocean oil platforms are, because of the great bulk below the level of the waves. With proper anchoring, come storms, hurricanes, and high-water it would remain steady and unaffected.

Once such a foundation is moored in place,[11] any platform and structure could be built upon it. Oils rigs already occupy such spaces. Envision locating a small platform off the coast of a country such as China or Iran with highly restrictive media services. It would be a perfect location for direct radio or television broadcasting with no regulations whatsoever.[12] Similarly, such an institution could be located anywhere on the waters of the world and, when combined with satellites, would be able to broadcast ubiquitous Internet access and phone service.

Picture a platform off the coast of New York City or of Edinburgh, Scotland. Such a platform could support a stable hospital—readily accessible to anyone at low transportation cost—able to provide the latest innovations in medical care regardless of self-serving old fogies lobbying for more restrictions and limits to competition.[13] This facility could be exceedingly lucrative. But what about utilities? The technology is already in place to generate power from waves, desalinize seawater, and treat sewage. The possibilities are boundless.

What we are talking about is the establishment of small colonies not terribly different from Plymouth Plantation. The challenges might be equally as daunting. On the positive side, we now have modern technology; on the negative, the environment appears far less stable, at least at first glance to us landlubbers. From such colonies for those with resourcefulness, new countries would evolve. Would it be too pricey? By no means. Challenging yes, but with the increasing limitations, oppression, and taxation throughout the countries of the planet, much expense for the escape to Sanctuary[14] becomes imminently affordable. Besides, one must ask which is more affordable: a floating platform 12 miles offshore or an equally sized square block in midtown Manhattan.

The best part of this is that the increase in the number of countries would create competition to existing governments. As freer jurisdictions attract immigrants and older countries lose denizens, those old world monstrosities would be motivated to relax their rules. As occurred throughout the world even as far away as Austria-Hungary during the centuries during which Massachusetts and Virginia were growing into freedom loving jurisdictions, a new era of liberty across the globe might develop. Thus, private ownership and development of the oceans would even improve conditions on land.

Not only is privatization of the waters morally and ethically timely, private development is also extraordinarily practical.

Sewage and Water Lines

Let us move from the highly abstract to the very practical. Consider the benefits of privatization in cases closer to home; indeed, those aspects of water privatization which flow in and out of all our houses.

Water and sewer service (and certain other utilities) require delivery and/ or collection of high bulk relatively non-differentiated masses to or from widely dispersed areas with many customers to or from a centralized location.[15] Providing these types of services may be impossible without some kind of rule from above. Or rather, so it would seem.

This appearance of impossibility under present institutional arrangements, leads either to the government supply of these amenities, or state authorization of "private enterprise" to do so only under strictly regulated circumstances as "utilities." The fear on the part of many people is that, under private enterprise, firms would adopt a monopoly position and take advantage of it. To wit, with outrageous pricing they would come to own pretty much the entire capital value of the homes and businesses they supposedly "serve."[16] Therefore, so the argument goes, they must be told what methodologies to use, how much capacity to supply, and at what prices, along with being ordered about pretty much every other decision they make. It is difficult for some people to see how provision of these services could be arranged in any other way. Were competition allowed, the presumption is that there would be needless duplication, consisting of dozens or more sewer and water lines, where one set would fully suffice, thank you very much.

How would sewage and water pipes be handled in the free society? Admittedly the market is challenged by long thin facilities transporting high bulk materials like sewer and water; the same difficulties apply to gas, power, telephone (before the advent of cell phones),[17] and roads and streets.[18] The issue even includes services such as postal delivery and garbage collection; although they are not "long and thin," they are indeed hulking masses.[19] A significant part of this challenge to the efficacy of free enterprise stems from the appearance that one firm performing these functions, rather than a plethora of competitors, would be far more efficient.

From the *ex post* view, e.g., given that the homes, stores, and other such facilities are already built, then, it must be readily admitted, the problem is just about unsolvable. To get hundreds, let alone thousands of people to agree to any one provider for each of these things: gas, electricity, water, sewage, telephone, roads, postal delivery, garbage collection, etc., would be well-nigh impossible. This is commonly referred to by economists as high transactions costs.[20]

On the other hand, a system that allows competition in these services, with say a half dozen providers of each, would appear to be wastefully duplicative. Imagination boggles the mind at the thought of six different gas delivery firms, each with its own pipes, a dozen garbage pickup services, each with one twelfth of all the clients, or ten separate lines on the telephone poles, let alone a telephone pole for each separate provider. This scenario convinces most people that the free enterprise system might be all well and good in many industries, but not for this sort of thing.

However, from the *ex-ante* point of view, before the buildings to be served are first constructed, the supposed challenge evaporates entirely. The qualms enunciated above derive from a lack of imagination. Two free market approaches are presented herein: (1) Using existing technologies from an *ex-ante* viewpoint and (2) speculating on alternative technologies. *Laissez faire* capitalism reveals itself to be efficacious in the face of this challenge as it always is.

Consider a real estate developer with a few hundred acres at his disposal. He can do one of two things. First, build all the homes, stores, recreation centers, office towers, and so on, that he intends to construct, worrying not at all about how any of these long thin things will serve his clients. He will allow the new owners to make contracts with all of those providers on their own accounts. Or second, he will first contract with providers of each of those services and have all such "utilities" arranged before he sells any of the buildings. Then, he will market the homes, factories, stores to their new owners, with a side order condition: they have to accept the providers of the long thin things with whom he has contracted. Is this "package deal" a permanent arrangement? No, of course not. The overall real estate developer may have had to enter into a contract of some duration, for example, three years, but, after that time if the new owners are not happy with the sewage service, or the mail delivery, they can, by a majority vote of all the condominium owners, change them and enter into new contracts with more satisfactory firms.

It should by now be clear that Adam Smith's "invisible hand" will lead construction firms to engage in precisely these sorts of condominium or collective arrangements. Who, after all, would want to purchase a house or store, knowing full well he would face the *ex post* challenge of very high transactions costs, or wasteful duplication? If the buildings were sold without this package deal, they would fetch a very low price on the market, if people would be willing to pay any positive price for them at all. On the other hand, if the homes and stores were sold as part of this package deal, where these necessities were put into place beforehand, then a much higher price would be garnered by the developer.

Secondly, government provision or supervision of utility services locks out innovation. Just because wastewater is currently collected by sewer pipes does not mean that is the only way. In times past, it was stored in cisterns and periodically pumped out and carted away in honey wagons. Gutters in the street were also used.[21] In those days, no one could imagine underground plastic pipes serving those functions. With regard to water in times past, who could imagine a cement-lined ductile iron pipe wrapped in plastic? No one; that is who. Is there another technology in our future for handling water and sewage? Who knows, but the point is we never will learn so long as these services are provided or regulated by municipalities and special districts.

Furthermore, take garbage disposal. In our day and age, it is collected just like the archaic cistern and smelly old honey wagon system for wastewater in the days of old. Is it so far-fetched that an underground pipeline might one day gather puréed refuse? Could it come to pass that persons seeking valuable minerals might pay to pick up trash? Once again, no one will know these things until the invisible hand has free reign.

There is also the issue that when government errs in the provision or regulation of these services, there is no automatic feedback mechanism to deal with the situation. Since profit and loss are limited to private enterprise, that institution is unavailable to bureaucratic managers. Yes, there is the political system, but it is very cumbersome; it may take years until another election, and very few of them turn on statist provision of water and sewer services. In sharp contrast, in the market, with the dollar vote, people are not similarly constrained. To see the quandary, imagine the situation in which a buyer of a violin also had to accept a year's worth of gasoline, a ticket to a concert and a month's worth of restaurant meals. But that is exactly the model everyone must face when he steps into the voting booth.[22]

So, while this problem looks insuperable from the *ex post* point of view, it is a challenge to the free enterprise system that can easily be overcome when looked at *ex ante*. Moreover, the free enterprise environment leaves open the possibility, and the motivation, for revolutionary technologies to entirely transform these tasks.

NOTES

1. All translations of Hebrew, Greek, Latin, or French, unless indicated otherwise, were performed by Nelson.

2. Admittedly in times past, dueling may have been the recourse. However, even then, deaths are usually limited to one. For a defense of dueling, see Block, 2013B.

3. This is not the appropriate venue to defend private vis a vis government courts. For readings on that see Anderson and Hill, 1979; Benson, 1989, 1990; Block, 2007B, 2010A, 2011C; Casey, D, 2010; Casey, G, 2012; DiLorenzo, 2010; Gregory, 2011; Guillory & Tinsley, 2009; Hasnas, 1995; Heinrich, 2010; Higgs, 2009, 2012, 2013; Hoppe, 2008, 2011B; Huebert, 2010; King, 2010; Kinsella, 2009E; Long, 2004; McConkey, 2013; Molyneux, 2008; Molyneux and Badnarik, 2009; Murphy, 2005A; 2010, 2013A, 2013B; Randy, undated; Rothbard, 1973, 1975, 1977, 1998; Shaffer, 2012, pp. 224-235; Spooner, 1870; Stringham, 2007; Tannehill, 1984; Tinsley, 1998-1999; Wenzel, 2013.

4. On private arbitration see Berman and Dasser, 1990; Marcus, 2009; Popeo, 1988; Tannehill, 2001; Young, 2002. Of course the formation of the *Global* Arbitration Association, the *Oceania* Stock Exchange would be both welcome and expected.

5. "Globally, the market value of marine and coastal resources and industries is estimated at $3 trillion per year or about 5 per cent of global GDP." (United Nations, undated)

6. In the United States, 27.7 percent of the land is claimed (unjustly, we would say) by the federal government (Gorte, et al, 2012). In contrast, governments at all levels own virtually all the water.

7. We realize that in making this claim we are, strictly speaking, violating the diamonds-water paradox that so bedeviled economists such as Adam Smith before the marginalist revolution in the 1870s, (Jevons, 1871; Menger, 1871; Walras, 1874). We plead innocence however. We are merely reporting and/or speculating as from whence Gross World Product will emanate.

8. Sources: Allen, 2009; Belov, 1955; Eberstadt, 1988; Feshbach and Friendly, 1992; Grossman, 1985; Nove, 1993; Nutter, 1957; Pejovich, 1979; Sakoff, 1962; Smith, 1976.

9. See Bradford (1630-1651) regarding the failures of communism at the Plymouth Plantation.

10. Those involved in sea-steading have studied this issue, and claim this is possible to an extent not dreamed possible by most. (The Seasteading Institute, undated; Google Images, undated; IndieGoGo, 2014)

11. Is an anchor necessary? Perhaps such a structure should move about, though there could develop a commons issue.

12. The film, *Pirate Radio* was a less technical predecessor to this.

13. For an excellent analysis of the problems of medical licensure and its restrictive entry attributes, see Friedman, 1962, chapter 9.

14. "Sanctuary" refers to Nolan and Johnson's, *Logan's Run*.

15. A water treatment plant or a sewage treatment plant, for example.

16. This fear is entirely ungrounded. It is obviated by contractual arrangements which would preclude any such occurrences. Assume that nevertheless prices head skyward, then this fear is still unwarranted because a new more consumer-oriented provider would move in and take over. An innovative new technology might eliminate the supposed need for such a monopoly. Those sky-high prices would motivate inventors.

17. We mention this even though the problem has now been overtaken by technology. We do so since we want to demonstrate that libertarian property rights theory can solve all such problems, at all time periods, and does not rely upon modern technology.

18. Roads and streets as well as all utilities are discussed in other sections of this book. The gist is either that an original developer would include these in a package when he markets a residential or commercial lot and provide a system for maintaining them, or a homesteader will have established an access route. In some cases for a late arriving developer, a right of way must be purchased. Then difficulties may arise. For a solution to this challenge, see Block, 2009C.

19. These are included in the sense that a single provider of these services, too, will likely be more efficient than several competing ones. This is sometimes called a "natural monopoly" in the economics literature, but this is misleading, since "monopoly" properly refers only to government grants of privilege, and these play no role in our present analysis. However, there are differences, too. Of relevance is that the garbage (or postal delivery) truck is already there,

right in front of the house that it is going to skip by; no such thing occurs with the hardware or grocery store. Suppose there are three garbage removal firms, A, B and C. A has clients 1, 4, 7, 10; B has 2, 5, 8, 11; C has 3, 6, 9, 12. All houses are located in this order: 1, 2, 3, 4, 5, 6, etc. That means A, B and C each has to pass by two-thirds of all houses. This appears very inefficient. If so, then profits and losses will dictate the outcome. That is, one company can come in and offer the service at, say, half the price, and thus put the others out of business. If that for some reason cannot happen, then, ipso facto, the three are more efficient despite appearances to the contrary.

20. It is hard enough to get five friends to agree to which restaurant and movie to patronize; this difficulty seems far, far worse.

21. To view a medieval street with a very large central channel refer to MESSYNESSYchic, 2013. On the contrary, the streets of the ancient Roman City of Ephesus in Iona had a stone lined trench with marble capstones on each side of the street which resembled a municipal combined sewer system (one that carries both sanitary and storm wastewater). A public latrine was connected to the tunnel (Ephesus, 2015).

22. As a real life example of this type of conundrum, in October, 2014, Coloradans faced an election. One of the ballot issues would have permitted casino-style gambling at a race track which would be taxed, and the proceeds earmarked to support public education. The measure went down to defeat. The question for a libertarian was this: How is it possible for your authors to vote yea or nay on such an initiative when they see it as an absolute right of entrepreneurs, without permit, to provide gaming, but oppose state funded schools as extremely egregious examples of state incompetence and corruption beyond redemption? How can anyone say *Sic et Non* (see Abelard reference above) if he opposes taxes and supports private schools which are free to teach whatever they desire and market their services as they wish?

Chapter Four

Aquatic Ownership Concepts

"Few things help an individual more than to place responsibility upon him, and to let him know that you trust him." —Booker T. Washington, *Up from Slavery,* 1901

GENERAL AQUATIC OWNERSHIP

The point of this chapter is to very briefly present the three ownership concepts without judgment or criticism. That follows in later chapters. The one exception is that since both authors are in agreement that riparian does not work, that is stated and defended in this chapter.

A primary reason for adopting private ownership as the mantra for dealing with the waters of the world is as Mr. Booker T. Washington said. Ownership is so closely related to responsibility that they are regarded as synonyms or at least nearly so. Ontological concepts of ownership cover a broad range. Traditionally, three have been applied to ownership or use of aquatic resources: (1.) In Toto, (2.) Prior Appropriation, and (3.) Riparian (Coleman, 2012).

Water is an essential resource necessary for life. It is so only when developed and made useful for only then can it generate rent.[1] Where it is in short supply, a functioning society needs a tool for stable and reliable distribution. As with other resources, aquacapitalism supplies the most dependable, constant, and fair supply mechanism (Friedman/Donahue, 1979). All that idealistic blather has no meaning unless what is to be owned is understood. Evidently, in the case of the precious fluid, it must be the H_2O; or is it so obvious? Water moves, flows, if you will. Try to grab some with your fist as you would a ball. It does not stay within your grasp. One could take a cup and dip it. At last you have some. But what good is that? Drink it, and it is

31

gone. One needs a supply so he can dunk his cup repeatedly. Folks want to know this for a fact: "My cup runneth over" (Psalms: 23, 5). They want it repeatedly day after day. Even that which is ingested into the body is eventually expunged. All concepts of aqueous ownership are necessarily usufructuary in nature.

Furthermore, people want "living" water. If this fluid sits around too long it gets stale, musty, and indeed fetid. For freshness, movement is vital. Having a container, even if constantly filled, is inadequate: it is not what we really want!

Does it take a pure mountain brook to satisfy our needs? Not really, especially when the deer and the antelope "do their thing." In addition, if one wants to travel on it, a babbling "brook" simply will not do. So, to be adequate in the long term water cannot be grasped, nor contained, nor dipped out of a stream in a vessel. Then what exactly is to be owned? In turn the above listed three concepts are now described.[2]

IN TOTO

The first definition of ownership for consideration is in terms of the space the water molecules occupy and their container. Here, control would be over the physical components that direct and contain the water molecules as well as the aqueous resource itself. This notion, we claim, is feasible. For a given portion of the river, the proprietor would control all of its aspects. He could alter its course (if it is a river, or current), change its grade, divert or remove water, float boats for transport, and swim in it. He could fence it off or post no trespassing signs.

This type of ownership is based on the Lockean theory of homesteading.[3] A pilgrim who mixes his labor with the resource thereby makes it an extension of his essential being. He comes to possess it as much as he owns his own person.

In Toto resource control would include the fish and other animals that live in the stream, lake, or ocean. The proprietor could harvest the wildlife. He could lease out his property for fishing.

Since water flows freely where it will, the definition must preclude the sort of illicit transfer that might occur at boundaries. In the case of a river, both halves would necessarily be controlled by a single entity; otherwise, the left bank owner would be tempted to remove all of the water before the holder of right bank could do so. In the case of possession by two or more individuals, shares would be proportionately allotted. Likewise, up and downstream owners would hold stocks in a united title based on the relevant technological unit.[4]

What is owned, in this conception, is whatever water occupies the given geometrical space at any particular time as well as the physical surface that provides the containment. Definitionally, the In Toto ownership concept implies proprietorship of the water based on possession, similar to that which occurs on land. For H_2O is nothing other than fast moving land from the libertarian perspective. This concept also is based on priority of homesteading. What is taken under control is both the land and the water at the same time. The proprietor of the ocean, river, or lake bed and/or the riparian zone[5] owns the water as well (In Toto). Unlike the traditional riparian concept, a single entity would own the entire technological unit. A river from source to mouth might serve as a good example. Whether tributaries were also included in the technological unit would depend on whether the boundary can be clearly defined in such a way as to reduce conflict between adjacent owners.

PRIOR APPROPRIATION

The definition of appropriation means taking possession of water in and of itself without reference to land according solely on the order of development. The basis of ownership is the Lockean concept of homesteading in that "First in use is first in right." This concept is also seen as feasible. For example, if an original immigrant starts to catch fish and makes that his livelihood, then he has instituted ownership over the creatures he catches plus the fishery upon which he relies plus enough H_2O in the body of water (ocean, river, or lake) to support his fishery, up to the intensity with which he draws his livestock and according to the extent he husbands his animals rather than simply hunts them on an opportunistic basis. That is, it might only be a portion of the fishery that he has claimed. Likewise, a farmer might establish a property in X acre-feet of a river per year to irrigate his crops; a boater might start a transportation enterprise, thereby giving him the right to enough depth to float his boats. These uses are based on priority of ownership. A Johnny-come-lately may create a new property right, but only after all previous proprietors have their needs filled, as established by the property rights they have garnered.

This type of ownership both involves the water and measures it. The first user constructed the device(s) necessary to utilize and/or divert what he needed.[6] In so doing, he mixed his labor with a natural resource. But what exactly does he own? It is not geometric in nature. The flow of water is what he possesses. For example homesteader A might own the first 1 cubic foot per second (cfs) of the water flowing along the river by priority or date of first use, B, the second 2 cfs, C, the third ½ cfs, and so on. If there are only 3 cfs in the river, the rights of A and B get fulfilled, C loses out.[7] Furthermore, some owners might homestead only the flow with no right to consume[8] whereas others might consume also. Ownership would also apply to in-stream use. A person can own the right to a non-consumptive flow of say 100 cfs so that he can float ships and barges. Indeed, that is often one of the very first uses to which a river is put. The owner may then charge a toll of boat owners wishing to use it as a highway.

This concept of ownership is robust. Say a Johnny-come-lately home-steads the 50th priority of a river for consumptive use. He does not get water until the first 49 users get theirs. In other words he only obtains water when there is a great flood. Now with this new owner, large storm events, up to a certain level, are no longer a problem because this 50th user needs a high discharge.[9] He is ready with his reservoir and needs that event to fill it. Previous river owners benefit from his activities, at least up to the capacity of his reservoir, because they no longer have to suffer inundation. Beyond that level, the 51st user might be quite interested in storing that excess water.

RIPARIAN

The third concept also involves property in water. "The riparian doctrine confers upon the owner of land the right to divert the water flowing by his river frontage for use upon his holdings, without regard to the extent of such use or priority in time" (Racanelli, P. J., 1986). Riparian water rights have a long tradition.[10] The concept is that ownership of the adjacent land includes the riparian zone and the geometric facilities listed above, typically to the centerline (unless he has holdings on both sides of the river), as well as the water in the river. Pure riparian ownership gives the proprietor the privilege of drawing water from the river as long as there is any in it.

This system tended to evolve where water was plentiful. In environments of abundance, it made sense because the small amounts taken had no obvious effect on the surface, volume, or discharge of the primary watercourse. But when the withdrawals become large with respect to the source, the riparian system breaks down. Historically, states have then stepped in with regulatory modifications. Such regulations limit the amount of water that an individual may take so that apportionment is more "fair" (whatever that means).

CRITIQUE OF THE RIPARIAN CONCEPT

The authors see two viable theories for ownership of water: In Toto and Prior Appropriation. Neither author subscribes to the riparian concept. To begin, fluid seeks a level surface; so, taking from one location amounts to effective-ly stealing from one's neighbors. The more stream side owner A removes from the body of water, the genuine resource flows into his portion of the stream. If he removes enough, even water located downstream would drift backwards to his territory.

For this reason each user would try to use as much as possible as fast as he could lest others get to it first. This is a standard "tragedy of the commons" situation. Why does this calamity occur? The precious resource, which is the water itself, is not owned under the riparian system. That is, it is a "commons," and suffers the same over use as all other communistically held assets. The real problem is that this system failed to come to grips with the amounts of water available to all users.

Consider a transportation company. It has no claim on the water which could easily dry up entirely. Meanwhile, the waterside proprietors could rightly charge tolls. With dozens or hundreds or thousands of owners each charging a toll, transportation would become impractical.

NOTES

1. Notice that in a primitive society, such effort may be as simple as submerging one's face and drinking.

2. The ensuing chapters of the book will delve much more deeply into economic and physical theories briefly touched upon in this chapter.

3. Homesteading briefly mentioned herein is discussed more fully in Chapter 5.

4. See our Chapter 14 for Rothbard's (1982) definitive definition of the "technological unit."

5. The riparian zone is that portion of a water bearing facility adjacent to the fluid that supports emergent vegetation.

6. Strictly speaking diversion is not necessary. A homesteader could use a stream for transportation, for example, and in this way establish a non-consumptive right to the amount of water necessary to float and move his boats.

7. "Water rights in Colorado are unique when compared to other parts of the United States. The use of water in this state is governed by what is known as the 'Prior Appropriation System.' This system of water allocation controls who uses how much water, the types of uses allowed, and when those waters can be used.

"A simplified way to explain this system is often referred to as 'first in time, first in right.' An appropriation is made when an individual physically takes water from a stream (or underground aquifer) and places that water to some type of beneficial use. The first person to appropriate water and apply that water to use has the first right to use that water within a particular stream system. This person (after receiving a court decree verifying their priority status) then becomes the senior water right holder on the stream, and that water right must be satisfied before any other water rights can be fulfilled.

"For example, assume three water-users exist on a stream system with adjudicated (court-approved) water rights totaling 5 cfs (cubic feet per second). The user with the earliest priority date has a decree for 2 cfs, the second priority has a decree for 2 cfs, and the third priority right has a decree for 1 cfs of water. When the stream is carrying 5 cfs of water or more, all of the rights on this stream can be fulfilled. However, if the stream is carrying only 3 cfs of water, its priority number 3 will not receive any water, with priority number 2 receiving only half of its 2 cfs right. Priority number 1 will receive its full amount of 2 cfs under this scenario. This process of allocating water to various water users is traditionally referred to as 'Water Rights Administration,' and is the responsibility of the Division of Water Resources" (Colorado Department of Natural Resources, undated). Prior Appropriation as described herein varies from Colorado water law in that it recognizes many uses, such as transportation or fishing, not traditionally counted."

8. Of course, with limited caveats, water is never consumed (Refer to Chapter 7, "Concepts of Oceanological Ownership," the "Water Cycle"). The term refers to the loss of water from the system. An example of a non-consumptive right would be power required to run a watermill that relies on the fluid in the watercourse but does not use it up. A consumptive right would include plant growth wherein H_2O is transpired in due course to the atmosphere. Many uses include both consumptive and non-consumptive aspects like a swimming pool that evaporates some but returns most to the source.

9. Discharge refers to the flow of water leaving a reference point.

10. In the earliest concept, riparian doctrine was based on streamside ownership. The proprietor of land adjacent to a body of water was entitled to continued flow. For more on this refer to Rice (1991).

Chapter Five

The Process of Privatization
Homesteading, Abandonment

"On ne résiste pas à l'invasion des idées." [One cannot stop an invasion of ideas.] —Victor Hugo, *Histoire D'un Crime* [Story of a Crime], 1877

WHY PRIVATE PROPERTY?

Why must we have private property rights? In order to be able to answer that primordial question, we must first be clear on exactly what this concept means. Simply, it is the right to use, and prevent others from so doing, the material that is owned. If Jones owns a pair of shoes, no one else may use them without his permission. He may exclude others from such utilization.[1] Also, he is permitted to lend them to others, or to sell them outright.[2]

Why is it imperative that we have private property rights? The utilitarian case for this institution is clear. It is very helpful to know who may, and may not, use all the goods owned by all the members of society. Who may use Jones' shoes? Why, Jones, of course, or anyone else to whom he gives permission. Who has the right to play with Smith's tennis racquet? Why, Smith, or anyone else to whom he gives permission. In that way, conflicts are kept to a minimum. In a society with clear titles to property, disputes as to who may, and who may not, use a pair of shoes or a given tennis racquet are kept to a minimum. Imagine the confusion were this not to be the case.

Another beneficial aspect of private property rights is wealth creation. When there is no option for individual ownership of property, the result is virtually always great poverty, often actual starvation, and typically on a massive scale.[3] Wrote William Bradford (1967) of Plymouth Plantation[4]:

37

At length, after much debate of things, the Governor (with the advice of the chiefest amongst them) gave way that they should set corn every man for his own particular, and in that regard trust to themselves; in all other things to go on in the general way as before. And so assigned to every family a parcel of land, according to the proportion of their number, for that end, only for present use (but made no division for inheritance) and ranged all boys and youth under some family. This had very good success, for it made all hands very industrious, so as much more corn was planted than otherwise would have been by any means the Governor or any other could use, and saved him a great deal of trouble, and gave far better content. The women now went willingly into the field, and took their little ones with them to set corn; which before would allege weakness and inability; whom to have compelled would have been thought great tyranny and oppression.

DEONTOLOGICAL JUSTIFICATION OF PROPERTY RIGHTS

Property rights also have a deontological justification, or normative rules based on ethics. When a person mixes his labor with land or other natural resources, he in effect imprints himself onto the latter. Locke (1948, pp. 17–18) explains this, brilliantly, as follows:

> ... [E]very man has a property in his own person. This nobody has any right to but himself. The labour of his body and the work of his hands, we may say, are properly his. Whatsoever then that he removes out of the state that nature hath provided, and left it in, he hath mixed his labour with, and joined to it something that is his own, and thereby makes it his property. It being by him removed from the common state nature placed it in, it hath by this labour something annexed to it that excludes the common right of other men. For this labour being the unquestionable property of the labourer, no man but he can have a right to what that is once joined to. . . . He that is nourished by the acorns he picked up under an oak, or the apples he gathered from the trees in the wood, has certainly appropriated them to himself. Nobody can deny but the nourishment is his. I ask then when did they begin to be his? . . . And 'tis plain, if the first gathering made them not his, nothing else could. That labour put a distinction between them and common. That added something to them more than nature, and the common mother of all, had done: and so they become his private right. And will anyone say he had no right to those acorns or apples he thus appropriated, because he had not the consent of all mankind to make them his? . . . If such consent as that was necessary, man had starved, notwithstanding the plenty God had given him. We see in commons, which remain so by compact, that 'tis the taking part of what is common, and removing it out of the state Nature leaves it in, which begins the property; without which the common is of no use.

Yes, mixing one's labor with the resource to be owned establishes an intimate connection between the person and the hitherto unowned natural resource in question. Moreover, if the first person to reach the virgin land and "mix his labor with it" is not the man with the best claim, and the second to arrive on the scene is, this undermines the entire procedure in determining land ownership. For if the second has a better claim than the first, then, for whatever reason, the claim of the third must be considered better than that of the second. But if any Johnny-come-lately may properly assert ownership over all prior "owners," then and to that extent there is really no such thing as private property rights at all. [5]

Locke, unhappily, is not the final word on this issue of homesteading, at least not for the libertarian, due to his dreaded "proviso": Locke (1690, pp. 287–88) says in this regard:

> Though the Earth, and all inferior Creatures be common to all Men: yet every Man has a Property in his own Person. This no Body has any Right to but himself. The Labour of his Body, and the Work of his Hands, we may say, are properly his. Whatsoever then he removes out of the State that Nature hath provided, and left it in, he hath mixed his Labour with, and joyned to it something that is his own, and thereby makes it his Property. It being by him removed from the common state Nature placed it in, it hath by this labour something annexed to it, that excludes the common right of other Men. For this Labour being the unquestionable Property of the Labourer, no Man but he can have a right to what that is once joyned to, at least where there is enough, and as good left in common for others.

Under this Lockean proviso, the appropriator of land must leave as good and sufficient for others before his own homesteading can be justified. This, however, has been subjected to withering criticism (Kinsella, 2009D; Machan, undated; Rothbard, 1998, 244–245). The problem is, under this limitation, it would be impossible to convert *all* of nature into private property, since, as more and more of it falls into individual ownership, less and less of it remains for others. Eventually, long before this process comes anywhere near completion, there will *not* be "enough, and as good left in common for others." According to Locke, then, the process must come to a halt, and a presumably significant part of the earth must be left to suffer under the tragedy of the commons, or non-ownership. Since the present book is devoted to the concept of privatizing *everything*, including the oceans, lakes, rivers, streams, tributaries, right down to each and every mud puddle, [6] we must reject this proviso as an unfortunate compromise with what in effect is Communism, or non-ownership of private property of the means of production.

It is relatively easy to think in terms of privatizing land. One clears the trees and rocks, plants some corn, and viola! in a few years, the process is done. The farmer is the owner of the cleared land in which he has built his farm. Yes, there are complications: for how many years does the procedure require? How many crop cycles? What about the intensivity or extensivity of the farming? That is, must there be one corn plant every square foot, every square yard, every acre, every square mile?[7] In a similar manner, how can a would-be homesteader know whether the property was previously possessed by one who may have gone on an extended vacation for such a long period that all signs of improvement have disappeared but who intends to return and resume his activities? To what depth into the earth does homesteading the surface entitle the homesteader?[8]

THE EXAMPLE OF CLIVEN BUNDY

On April 23, Shawn Regan (2014) attempted to settle the range war between Cliven Bundy and the Bureau of Land Management. The latter wants to charge grazing fees to the former for allowing his cows to graze on land it claims as its own. In the view of Regan (2014, emphasis added):

> Does this sound familiar? A rancher is grazing cattle on federal land, just as his family did for generations. Environmentalists come along and say the cattle must go; they would rather the land be used to protect tortoises than to feed cows. No, this is not the battle between rancher Cliven Bundy and the Bureau of Land Management that captured the nation's attention last week. And this story, instead of devolving into violence as the Bundy roundup did, ends with a handshake. It happened in 2003 in Arizona, across the border from the Bundy ranch in Nevada. Tony Heaton, the rancher, approached the Conservation Fund, a nonprofit environmental group, and negotiated a deal: The fund paid him several hundred thousand dollars in exchange for receiving his permit to graze on a 44,000-acre federal allotment near the Mount Trumbull Wilderness. No violence, no protesters, no armed federal agents—just a check and a contract. Heaton had been having difficulties with hikers and other land users on the allotment and realized it might be time to stop running cattle. Still, the permit had value. "I didn't want to just give it away," Heaton (now deceased) told *High Country News* at the time. Grazing buyouts such as Heaton's are quietly occurring in parts of the West and show how conflicts over federal land management can be resolved peacefully. *Call it free-market environmentalism.* And contrast it with a much more familiar story—one in which interest groups endlessly tussle over how federal lands should be managed and litigate at every turn. The range war brewing (as of summer 2014) outside Cliven Bundy's ranch in Bunkerville, Nev., is an example of the dysfunctional status quo on federal lands. Outside this small community 80 miles northeast of Las Vegas, dozens of protesters have clashed with federal agents, prompting officials to call off a controversial cattle roundup due to concerns over public safety. The Bureau of Land Management intended to confiscate Mr. Bundy's cattle for illegally grazing on federal lands that are considered habitat for the federally protected desert tortoise.

We beg to differ. This is not at all "free market environmentalism." In that view, land should be owned by the homesteaders of it. The proper owners are those that first used the terrain in question. And who would that be, pray tell? Well, the B.L.M. was created only in 1946.[9] In sharp contrast, the Bundy family had been utilizing the land under contention since the 1800s (*Inquisitr*, 2014). True, the U.S. government predates the Bundys, and Nevada joined the union in 1864, which may or may not predate that family's settlement. However, not a single solitary bureaucrat, federal or state official, ever homesteaded as much as one square inch of the spread. Therefore, under the free market philosophy, it is Cliven Bundy, not the BLM, nor the US government, nor the State of Nevada, that owns the land under contention. To claim the Heaton deal an aspect of "free market environmentalism" is to indicate a serious erroneous understanding of that philosophy. By libertarian law, no contract between a criminal gang and an innocent person can be binding on the latter.[10] Of course, not everyone would agree that the state comprises a cadre of felons. To defend this position would take us too far afield from the focus of this book. We content ourselves with our reference to the Rothbard quote in chapter 2 of this book.

APPLICATION TO WATER

But how would it work for water? At least on the land, that which is to be homesteaded is relatively clear: it is thus and such a patch of territory, extending from points A to B to C to D. But what, precisely, does a person own when he homesteads water?[11] It cannot be the molecules of water themselves, since they are far too fleeting. For example, water travels down the Mississippi River, under ordinary times, at the rate of approximately three miles per hour (Caleuche. Undated). Were a Mississippi River Corporation to own discrete particles, it would all too soon see its holding washed out into the Gulf of Mexico.

Let us suppose we start *de novo* regarding ownership of bodies of water. Who would get to own what? Simple. We take land ownership as our model and apply Lockean homesteading theory (minus this eminent philosopher's invalid proviso) to oceans, rivers, and lakes. The people who use these resources get to own them, in proportion to, or according to, the level of their use. So, putting present water rights to the side, who would come to be the owners of the Mississippi River? Why, the people who *use* it, who "mix their labor" with it. Those who drink it, irrigate with it, use it in manufacturing processes, swim in it, transport goods on it, and use it for recreation.

Homesteading, of course, is not the only possible way of awarding property titles, whether to land or water. Let us contrast this system with claim theory,[12] or the planting of a flag, and then maintaining ownership as far as the eye can see (perhaps from the vantage point of a high-flying plane).

There are many disadvantages with regard to claim as a basis for ownership of water resources (or anything else for that matter) vis a vis homesteading.

One point in favor of homesteading versus claim is that controversy, strife, war, fighting, is greatly reduced. As of this writing, Canada is claiming ownership (Guardian, 2013) of an area of the sea bed as big as its prairie provinces, without lifting so much as a finger to create any connection what-soever between it and this aquatic territory. The other northern countries[13] cannot be expected to look upon this initiative with any favor. Similarly, China is claiming seabed (Malakunas, 2015) thought by others[14] to be in-cluded in their own holdings. The U.S. flew B52 bombers[15] over this area in direct conflict with Chinese territorial ambitions. Tensions rose.

In a bygone era claims of this type of claim were based on how far a cannon (again we see the similarity to conquest), located on the coast, could shoot a projectile into the water. In the early days of rifles, this distance was some 2 miles. So, numerous nations claimed that amount of the ocean abutting their shores. When more powerful weapons could cover 6, 8, 10, 12 miles, these distances became the limits of their territorial ambitions to the sea. With greater distances, conflicts based on overlapping "limits" in-creased, that is, when the distance between national borders was less than these arbitrary figures. Applicable is the old adage, "two is company, but three is a crowd." But with overlapping jurisdictions established through this system, even two is a "crowd." Far worse for this justification, in an era of ICBMs, the premise breaks down completely due to massive overlapping claims.

Another difficulty with using range of cannon fire as a basis for owner-ship is that it is predicated on the dubious doctrine that "might makes right." Property titles are supposed to confer rights on their owners. When justified on the basis of cannon fire or missile "might," to escape the conclusion that rights are based on sheer naked physical force is difficult. Power may be precisely how the world actually works; but as a recipe for peace,[16] it is completely unsatisfactory. According to this doctrine, Hitler was "right" from about 1935 to perhaps 1943; then he became less and less "right" until in 1945 he became "wrong." But, he stood for precisely the same perspective all during this time period. Thus, "might" becomes a synonym for acting virtuously. If so, why do we need two words which are practically polar opposites to describe one and the same thing? The upshot here is that this doctrine is plainly incoherent.

What excuse for these land and water grabs is currently invoked? One is the continental shelf argument. The governments of Canada and China and other such states are in effect maintaining that the sea bed next to their lands, and also the water above this extension, are really part of the territory they already control (righteously, at least according to Ottawa and Beijing). If, in their view, they are sovereign over their respective land masses, this privilege should be extended outward into the oceans.

Problems abound. It would take us too far afield to make the case against any and all sovereign nations. We shall content ourselves with the contrary to fact assumption that this is indeed the case. But just because an entity owns land at the top of the mountain does not mean it can with impunity seize control of the abutting territory at the bottom. By analogy, land at the top of the mountain is akin to a given state. Territory at the bottom is analogous to the continental shelf extending into the water. Second, even if we concede, *arguendo*, that Beijing, Ottawa, etc., are the appropriate governors of the sea bed they claim, it by no means logically follows that they should be awarded, also, the water that lies above.[17]

ABANDONMENT OF HOMESTEADED PROPERTY

However, with this subject, we start to get pretty far afield because the issue of whether a property can be abandoned starts to come into play. May aquatic property be abandoned? If it may, and this applies to land also, how can someone determine whether any given piece of property is available for homesteading? If Columbus lands on a vacant shore line, how does he know that the owner has not simply stepped away for a few minutes? Simply, he cannot; and also shooting any competitors would not legitimately establish any rights either. Yet, there is no reason why a property holder cannot pull an Ellis Wyatt.[18] And if he did, there should be no legal requirement that he must leave a sign as Miss Ayn Rand (1957) said he did. So here we are again: how can a would-be homesteader looking at unused property possibly know whether or not it is available to be taken over?

In the libertarian view, once a person has succeeded in homesteading property, that is it; he is the owner, period. No one, relying on the heinous "use it or lose it" tradition, may take it away from him whether he "uses" it or not. He may bequeath it to his children, or give it to a charitable organization. Many people have in their chests of drawers unused clothes, or a car in the garage, sports equipment, a television, air conditioning, sitting unused. Under "use it or lose it" all these things are subject to loss. This horrid anti-libertarian system is not improved in the slightest when confined to water.

What about abandonment? In the free society, private courts would spring up. One of their tasks would be to take care of abandonment. Right now, under statism, abandonment is no (intellectual) challenge. There are land and property taxes, and as long as the owner pays them, no one can say he has abandoned his possessions. But under libertarianism, there would be no taxes. What then?

One of the roles of the courts would be to address abandonment. These adjudicators would set up their own rules. Say, if the owner of a property has not been heard from for 20 years, then his land or water may be deemed to have been abandoned. An auction would then be held, the proceeds going to the private court and the property in question to the highest bidder. The market would deal with the continuum problem of whether 15 or 20 or 25 years is the correct cut off point. Now, assume that only 90% of the people are associated with private courts. Well, that takes care of, presumably, 90 percent of the problem.

But what of the other 10%? Suppose a property owner, Smith, comes back after an absence of 50 years, and finds out that his property has been auctioned off to Jones, and that the private court kept the bid money. One possible assessment of this scenario is to say, "Tough cheese," Smith. He should have realized that while property rights are indeed sacrosanct, he lives in a society, and if he is gone for 5 decades without leaving word with anyone, he stands to lose title. And, it is not as if he had to do much at all; just register the fact that he was not abandoning his property.

Likewise, Jones is hiking on the prairie and discovers an apparently vacant, never-before settled parcel of land. At one time Smith did own it, but now the natural elements have dissolved all signs of any previous occupancy. Not knowing a thing about Smith, Jones registers an original homestead with the court. Then after his long absence, Smith finally returns to find his property occupied. The result is the same as above despite the lack of an auction. Smith should have registered his intent to return. Are these examples the same as "use it or lose it"? Not at all because Jones has mixed his labor with the land for these 50 years. Smith may not take it back without recompense to Jones for his care taking efforts and then only insofar as Jones agrees.

But what about the following case? Smith intends to be away for only a few days on a sailing trip. He sees no reason to demonstrate his refusal to abandon his property to any private court. Alas, he is kidnapped by pirates and held by them for 50 years. Upon his return he learns his property has been stripped from him. Not good. [19] Certainly, from a utilitarian point of view, it pays to give the back of our hands to the claim of Smith, pirates or no pirates. Extreme cases make bad law. Once the Smith's plight is publicized, it is easy to contemplate that 99.9 percent of people would take out abandonment "insurance," namely, registering with a private court that the owner has no intention of abandoning his property.

Let us argue by analogy. In the movie *Dr. Strangelove* there was a scene in which it was necessary to call Washington DC in order to stave off an end-of-the-world scenario. There were no cell phones in those days, and the private lines had been cut off. However, there was a pay phone, but no one had any change. Standing nearby was a coke machine with plenty of coins, but no one had a key to its lock. This scene took place on a military base, so there were rifles galore.[20] One character says to another something to the effect of "shoot that damn machine so that we can get coins with which to telephone the president and thus save the world." Another character recoils in horror: "You can't do that! That's *private property.*" The obvious libertarian response to this gratuitous and unwarranted attack on the institution which is the bedrock of civilization is, "Of course shoot the machine! But pay damages to the owners." In that way we can have our cake and eat it too: we can adhere to the niceties of private property rights, and, also, not act so as to encourage the blowing up of the entire planet. In like manner Jones can say to the Smith who is absent for 50 years, "Sorry, I didn't realize you had not abandoned your property; I now hereby return it to you. And, also, I shall be paying you whatever rent the court determines appropriate (or since it was an innocent mistake, charging a caretaker fee). The last thing I want to be considered is a trespasser."

The time period of supposed abandonment by no means need be limited to 50 years. For all we know it could have been 500 years. A strict, narrow, not to say barking mad interpretation of Smith's absence is that his heirs would one day, in five centuries, come back to claim their property rights which have not been abandoned, and that therefore no one was justified in taking hide nor hair of his holdings, ever. "Private property rights, yes, squatters, no," might be the motto of people who take such an extreme view. In the more moderate assessment of the present authors, after the passage of a mere two decades (if that is the number hit upon by most private courts) of nonappearance of the owner, the property in question may be assumed to be abandoned. If the rightful owner shows up after 5 decades, or 5 centuries, at worst the present owner will have to make compensation to the original owner Smith, and be compensated by the defense agency or private court which kept the auction bid money. However, the argument that the first best legal remedy is that Smith and or his heirs get not one penny of compensation is still a powerful one.

Yet one more very strong case leads in an entirely different direction. It may be argued that there is no unambiguous solution to this challenge at all: none coming from the left or right of the political spectrum and none that can be derived from libertarianism, which is not on the traditional spectrum at all. Rather, we are now faced with the continuum problem (Barnett and Block, 2008) for which only arbitrary solutions can be considered.[21] For example, it is undeniable that to go to bed with a five year old girl, no matter how "willing" she is, still constitutes statutory rape, since a child of that age is simply incapable of giving consent to any such act. On the other hand, this does not at all apply to a mentally competent 25 year old woman. If she agrees, there can be no rape involved in such interaction. But what is the age at which one conclusion stops and the other starts? Is it 15, half way between the other two ages? The problem is there are always females younger than that arbitrary cut-off point who are more mature than those older. For example, some 14 year olds may be in a better position to make such a determination for themselves than others aged 16 or more. So, should the age of statutory rape be 17? Or maybe 13? The point is there is no one single number out there such that everyone will agree to it. Some cultures and legal systems tend toward one end of this spectrum, others toward the opposite. The point here is that choosing a number of years for "legitimate" abandonment may well fall victim to this radical uncertainty in proper law. Various courts should make such a determination for themselves, and people should sort themselves out according to the decisions of these various institutions.

NOTES

1. Malcolm (1958, pp. 31–32) said of his teacher and mentor, Ludwig Wittgenstein: "On one walk he 'gave' to me each tree that we passed, with the reservation that I was not to cut it down or do anything to it, or prevent the previous owners from doing anything to it: with those reservations it was henceforth mine."

2. Often is heard from some official or self-proclaimed stakeholder words such as, "It is our park." To such an assertion, the authors ask, "May we then sell our share?"

3. The deaths of coerced agricultural collectivism in the USSR is a case in point. Chamberlin, 1937; Maltsev, 1996; Mises, 1922.

4. Regarding the case of the U.S. Pilgrims, see DiLorenzo, 2004, 2009; Ebeling, 2009; Galles, 2010; Maybury, 1999; Rothbard, 2006.

5. There are of course deontological arguments against private property rights. One of the most famous was articulated by Proudhon (840, 131) who averred "property is theft." But stealing cannot occur unless there is private property in the first place. Without property, there cannot logically *be* any theft. So Proudhon cannot be taken seriously, at least not on this point. There are other interpretations of "property is theft" other than the usual one that Proudhon opposed private property per se. Another interpretation is that he was only against stolen property, as emanates from "crony capitalism." See on this Amato, 2013; Osterfeld, 1986; Reichert, 1980.

6. Our motto might well be: "If it moves, privatize it; if it does not move, privatize it; since everything either moves or does not move, privatize everything."

7. For a defense and explication of homesteading which deals with these and other such issues, see Block, 1990A, 2002A, 2002B; Block and Edelstein, 2012; Block and Yeatts, 1999–2000; Block vs Epstein, 2005; Bylund, 2005, 2012; Grotius, 1625; Hoppe, 1993, 2011A; Kinsella, 2003, 2006; Locke, 1948; Paul, 1987; Pufendorf, 1673; Rothbard, 1973, 32; Rozeff, 2005, Watner, 1982.

8. For an analysis of this question see Block, 1998, 2008, 2009C; Block and Block, 1996; Epstein and Block, 2005; Nedzel and Block, 2007, 2008.

9. "The BLM was created in 1946 when the Department of the Interior merged two older agencies: the General Land Office, created in 1800 to sell off the public lands and encourage settlement; and the Grazing Service, created in 1934 to manage grazing on public lands" (The Thoreau Institute, 1998).

10. On this refer to: Anderson and Hill, 1979; Benson, 1989, 1990; Block, 2007B, 2010A, 2011C; Casey, D., 2010; Casey, G., 2012; DiLorenzo, 2010; England, 2013; Gregory, 2011; Guillory & Tinsley, 2009; Hasnas, 1995; Heinrich, 2010; Higgs, 2009, 2012, 2013; Hoppe, 2008, 2011A; Huebert, 2010; King, 2010; Kinsella, 2009C; Long, 2004; McConkey, 2013; Molyneux, 2008; Molyneux and Badnarik, 2009; Murphy, 2005A; 2010, 2013A, 2013B; Rock-

well, 2014A, 2014B; Rothbard, 1973, 1975, 1977, 1998; Shaffer, 2012, pp. 224–235; Spooner, 1870; Stringham, 2007; Tannehill, 1984; Tinsley, 1998–1999; Wenzel, 2013.

11. In this chapter we eschew all questions concerning the transition period. At present, there are owners of water rights: the legal ability to transmit certain amounts of liquid from a lake or river onto their landed property. We deal with such issues in Chapters 7, 8, 9, and 10.

12. In contrast to claim theory is conquest theory. That is the concept that by overpowering and defeating the present owner one becomes the new lord. That is nothing other than theft. In the libertarian philosophy defended in this book such a vanquisher is obligated to return his ill-gotten goods to their rightful owner. The same principle applies whether the offender is an individual, corporation, or state. Claim theory has some similarity with conquest because it is usually implemented by a small unopposed military force acting on behalf of a state while ignoring the rights of current occupants. If necessitated by the resistance of previous residents, it is eventually enforced by full scale military invasion.

13. Russia, United States Norway, Sweden, Finland, Denmark (via Greenland).

14. At least by Japan, South Korea, Thailand, The Phillipines, Viet Nam and other Pacific countries.

15. Of course, Washington, DC in effect claims control of the entire planet given that it has some 1000 military and other bases posted in some 160 other countries and seems to feel free to invade, sanction, or threaten each and every place or nation. See on this Department of Defense, 2007; Vance, 2010.

16. The present book is an attempt to make the case that private property rights should prevail for bodies of water. Or, which institutional arrangements would be employed if we lived in a free or libertarian society. Thus is it radically prescriptive, not descriptive. This is a far cry from how such matters are currently discussed.

17. Only the *ad coelum* doctrine would justify such an extension from seabed to the liquid that lies above. For a critique of this viewpoint, see Block and Block, 1996.

18. A character from Ayn Rand's *Atlas Shrugged* who was an oil magnet and abandoned his property. This applies, also, to Francisco D'Anconia, another hero of this book.

19. Suppose that farmer Green goes off on a trip and leaves no provision for his livestock to be fed, milked, etc. His neighbor, farmer Brown, makes good these oversights on Green's part. Green returns after 50 years. May he demand his property back from Brown, who has been homesteading for lo these many years? Not bloody likely. Farm animals need care. Some might say that land does not need care; but it does if it has been improved as is assumed in this illustration.

20. Unlike several real world cases where gunmen shot at US soldiers who were prevented by law from carrying fire arms.

21. We owe a debt of gratitude to Matthew A. Block for his contributions to our thoughts on this matter.

Chapter Six

Existing Law Governing the Seas

"The waters of the sea rush on past Gravesend, tumbling the big mooring buoys laid along the face of the town; but the sea-freedom stops short there, surrendering the salt tide to the needs, the artifices, the contrivances of toiling men." —Joseph Conrad, *The Mirror of the Sea*, (1906)

In this chapter we deal with the Law of the Sea, Admiralty law and the law of salvage. We conclude by rejecting the non-scarcity objection to water privatization.

LAW OF THE SEA

The UN Law of the Sea Treaty (1982, 25) reads in part as follows:

> . . . the area of the sea bed and ocean floor and the subsoil thereof, beyond the limits of national jurisdiction, as well as its resources, are the common heritage of mankind, the exploration and exploitation of which shall be carried out for the benefit of mankind as a whole, irrespective of the geographical location of States. . . .

This is highly problematic from several vantage points. First, it collides with the well-established principle of John Locke (1948, pp. 17–18) that ownership stems from homesteading. In order to stake a legitimate claim to any part of the earth, in this view, one must "mix one's labor with" the land, or by extension, the water. The UN document states in effect that this need not occur. People far-removed from the water, those in land-locked areas who have never so much as seen an ocean, let alone mixed their labor with it, can nevertheless claim a share of it. In the view of Rothbard (1974) in sharp contrast:

> . . . if a producer is not entitled to the fruits of his labor, who is? It is difficult to
> see why a newborn Pakistani baby should have a moral claim to a quotal share
> of ownership of a piece of Iowa land that someone has just transformed into a
> wheat field and vice versa, of course, for an Iowan baby and a Pakistani farm.
> Land in its original state is unused and unowned.

In this particular case, neither the Pakistani nor the Iowan could lay claim to any part of seas, since neither of them lives[1] within hundreds of miles of these bodies of water, nor did either "mix his labor" with that resource.

Second, if the oceans are the "common heritage of all mankind" this would imply that every person on the planet should have an equal share in their benefits. But why should the fisherman from Iceland work in behalf of the Iowan or the Pakistani, for example, give them a portion of his catch, when neither of the latter would share the fruits of the land with him? Why should the former share with the latter if the latter refuses to share with the former?

Third, why distinguish aquatic resources in this manner? Why not assert that the land, too, is the "common heritage of all mankind." Would it not be aesthetically pleasing if not only the oceans but the dry land, too, were owned by all inhabitants on the globe? Of course a scheme of this sort was actually employed in the USSR not only with Sovietized agriculture, but also included all basic factors of production. It does not seem reasonable to utilize a scheme in the seas that ended up with massive starvation on the land. Nor do the authors of this UN document see the need to counter this criticism, much less succeed in rebutting it.

ADMIRALTY LAW

Admiralty law, also known as maritime law, and the law merchant, is a distinct subset of overall law that deals with the proper relationship between shippers, dock-owners, marine commerce, transportation by sea, insurance, salvage and other matters affecting those who use bodies of water. It is international in scope, since, typically, lawsuits in this domain are between citizens of different countries (Lombardo and Mulligan, 2003; Mulligan and Lombardo, 2008; Sechrest, 2004A, 2004B).

Admiralty law is part of the common law tradition. Jurists in this practice did not so much make new law as attempt to discover what the law would be, were it based on the libertarian code of private property rights and non-aggression. States Rothbard (1998):

> . . . it is generally accepted, by limited-government and by other political
> philosophers, that the State is necessary for the creation and development of
> law. But this is historically incorrect. For most law, but especially the most

libertarian parts of the law, emerged not from the State, but out of non-State institutions: tribal custom, common-law judges and courts, the law merchant in mercantile courts, or admiralty law in tribunals set up by shippers themselves.

Sometimes called maritime law, or the law of the sea,[2] this legal system held sway for several centuries, mainly during the medieval period. However, vestiges of it are still in operation in the modern day, for example the topic to be discussed in the next section.

Law of Salvage

The maritime law of salvage relates to the entitlements of salvors[3] vs. owners of shipwrecks or general property lost at sea. In general the title to the ship or property remains vested with the owner immediately prior to the time of the loss, even if the loss occured centuries ago. The Salvor has a right to reimbursement proportional to the value of the salvaged property. While many issues remain unresolved, case law has established precedents which govern.[4] Salvage law was not typically passed by legislatures. Rather, as Kinsella (2010) tells us:

> Historically, in the common law of England, Roman law, and the Law Merchant, law was formed in large part in thousands of judicial decisions. In these so-called "decentralized law-finding systems," the law evolved as judges, arbitrators, or other jurists discovered legal principles applicable to specific factual situations, building upon legal principles previously discovered, and statutes, or centralized law, played a relatively minor role.

Nor were these "judicial decisions" of recent origin. Anderson (1993) explains:

> The legal concept that a marine salvor is entitled to a reward for the saving of imperiled marine property has been a recognized part of the admiralty law for more than 3,000 years. The origins of the concept may be traced from antiquity, as set forth in the Edicts of Rhodes, through the laws of the Romans, as set forth in the Justinian Digest, to the Medieval Laws of Oleron, the Code of the Hanseatic League down to the founding of the Republic.[5]

What proportion of the value of the saved boat went to the owner and how much to the salvor? Did the former give money to the latter as a reward, or in effect in the modern parlance as a tip as occurs in a restaurant? No. The latter earned part of the value of the ship as a right not as something emanating from the good will of the owner. Typically, one-third of the value went to the latter, and two thirds to the former. However, as Anderson (1993) explains, matters were a bit more complex than that. The awards were based on considerations such as the following:

1. The degree of danger from which the vessel was rescued;
2. The post-casualty value of the property saved;
3. The risk incurred in saving the property from impending peril;
4. The promptitude, skill and energy displayed in rendering the service and salving the property;
5. The value of the property employed by the salvors and the danger to which it was exposed;
6. The costs in terms of labor and materials expended by the salvors in rendering the salvage service."[6]

How would matters change when the seas come under the jurisdiction of libertarianism and private property? Certainly, rules in this context would take as a jumping off point the laws of the sea merchant based on the findings of private jurists over the centuries. However, matters would change somewhat under individual ownership. For example, each owner of a patch of ocean, or lake, etc., would be free to set up his own rules of salvage. Then the various owners would compete with each other in terms of which rules, all of them of course compatible with the non-aggression principle (NAP),[7] satisfied customers to the greatest degree, at the lowest cost. But the admiralty law has passed the test of time. The presumption, then, is that those owners who employed it would prosper to the greatest degree, and those who jettisoned it would experience the opposite result. But this is only a presumption. It is possible the entrepreneurs of water resources could do better than ancient jurists. If so, they would be free to employ their business acumen in the direction of maximizing profits.

OBJECTION: NON-SCARCITY

It may well be objected to the privatization of the oceans that they are not scarce, and that property rights apply, only, to resources that are not abundant. There is of course a great amount of truth to this claim. If a good can be used by all, then no one may properly be precluded from utilizing it. This insight is at the core of the libertarian critique of intellectual property, such as patents and copyrights (Kinsella, 2001). However, are the oceans, rivers and lakes scarce? Are there more people who want to use them than is available? Well, yes and no. Shipping channels in the seas are for the most part non-scarce. If this were the only consideration, our book would still be relevant to public policy, since as population grows this will become less and less true. Better to contemplate privatization before it is actually required than afterward. However, shipping channels are far from the only consideration. Whales and various varieties of fish are not only become scarce, but some species are even endangered and some already extinct. The oil and minerals that lie beneath the water are scarce, in the sense that there are more people who want them than are available.

Is the air a free or scarce good? There is still plenty around. It will be scarce on the moon or Mars when civilization finally settles there,[8] but not, yet, on earth. Rather, we refer to paths through which airplanes travel. This is if not already soon to become a scarce good which must be rationed, if mid-air crashes are to be avoided. Something of the same situation is fast occurring on the seas. At present, there is room for all the boats, with the exception of near harbors. But before too long, pathways in the ocean will have to be rationed, lest ships start to hit each other to an unprecedented degree. Before a few house boats, artificial islands, constructed peninsulas, permanent residential on yachts, and scattered deep sea platforms supporting dozens of people evolve into large floating megaplexes with thousands of denizens, an understanding of seasteading might be helpful.

NOTES

1. In this statement, we assume a boy in northern Pakistan, perhaps Baltistan.

2. Not the U.N. version, of course.

3. A salvor is one who salvages items lost at sea.

4. Examples of such cases may be found in the *Admiralty and Maritime Law Guide* (undated).

5. The present authors assume this refers to the Republic of the United States, but are not sure.

6. For more on the law of the sea as it pertains to salvage, see Anderson, 1993; Doane, 2013; Kinsella, 2010; Lipka, 1970; Wilder, 2000.

7. This principle, the foundation of the libertarian philosophy, states that it is illicit to threaten or initiate violence against a non-aggressor. For more on this see: Albright, 2013; Rothbard, 1973, 1982; Huebert, 2010; Rockwell, 2014A, 2014B; Block, 1976; Rand, 1957.

8. Thus, it will become an economic good, and a price will be charged for it, in a similar manner to oxygen tents and canisters on earth.

Chapter Seven

Oceans—Concepts of
Oceanological Ownership

"He who dreams not creates not. For vapor must arise in the air before the rain can fall. " —Louis Henri Sullivan, "Education," (1902)

Resolved: Private ownership of oceans would rid or mitigate the earth of many seething trepidations, to wit: oil spills, pollution, species extinction, piracy to name a few. The benefits would be so vast as to be only open to conjecture.

OBJECTIONS AND SHORT RESPONSES
TO PRIVATE OWNERSHIP OF OCEANS

The concept of private ownership of oceans must seem preposterous. Some of the more obvious and difficult objections will now be considered. Herein, these objections are shown for what they represent: a fretful pessimism regarding the ingenuity of our fellow humans and in the benefits of freedom and free enterprise. These short answers merely hint at the full benefits of private ownership described later within this chapter.

(1) *Who will get to own sea water, ocean floors, and rights of transit on or below the surface? Everyone and anyone can access the sea. How can some avaricious magnate presume to take over and cut off our access and enjoyment?*

As a matter of fact, the open ocean is not all that accessible at present. The seas are now in effect owned by governments who purport to act for the common good. Many of the benefits such as sport fishing and oil drilling are frequently denied. People should be free to initiate enterprises. In so doing, they take on the role of homesteaders, that is, they reveal and make valuable a resource that did not previously exist.[1] In the free society, such ingenious pioneers would own at least their portions of the waters and submerged land.

(2) *On what possible basis can property rights in the vast expanses of undifferentiated oceans be distributed?*

Each initiative involves a certain expanse, depth, or path to implement. As increasing activity of individuals impinge upon neighbors, boundary definitions would evolve to define the limits of respective enterprises. Such borders could include physical markers, invisible lines such as latitude and longitude, and methods not yet conceived.[2]

(3) *Since buoys, the closest equivalent to survey pins on land, revolve around their anchor, precise boundary demarcations are impossible.*

In a non-crowded environment such as the ocean, precise property limits exceed the requirements of titleholders. Should certain expanses become congested and precious, ocean surveyors would devise more exact demarcations, perhaps electronic fences. Perhaps triangular witnesses in the form of radio beacons such as LORAN[3] would be used for property location as well as for navigation.

(4) *What about navigation aids such as buoys, lighthouses, LORAN, and GPS?*[4] *Who would be in charge of them, how would they be financed, and what responsibilities would their owners incur?*

Use of navigation systems like LORAN and GPS can be by subscription wherein those in need purchase a reference frequency that changes monthly or an access code. Buoys and lighthouses can be installed and maintained by those (such as harbors wishing to attract traffic) with an interest in physical demarcations. Liability for malfunctioning of any of these systems would operate much the same as it does on land. We already have long experience with such difficulties. There is no need to reinvent the wheel. Extrapolation from legal precedents can be employed.

(5) *To whom would fish, which swim freely, belong?*

The current state of fishing throughout the oceans illustrates perfectly the tragedy of the commons. Avoidance of the threat of widespread extinction of valued species speaks to the value of private titles. Private proprietors would establish a much improved condition because they would be keenly interested in preserving their resources.[5]

(6) *Suppose some people wish to strictly control sharks and other predatory species while others wish to release them into the wild?*

Sharks have potentially beneficial influences on the ocean as well as valuable uses, but they are predators after all. The herdsmen who wish to breed and rear them would be of course free to do so. However, the owners of said sharks would be liable for the damage they create.

(7) *Would miners need permission to access or construct mineral extraction operations on or beneath the ocean floor?*

The ocean floor resembles land; indeed, is land. The homesteading process includes a path of entry. That is, in order to make a valid claim, one must arrive on the scene to first explore, then to "mix one's labor" with the virgin resource. For a would-be entrepreneur under a densely developed sea, access rights must be acquired from previous developers, unless ownership of the ocean floor was established before that of the H_2O in the ocean itself. For non-crowded zones, access would be implied in the homestead and subsequent developers would necessarily work around such entrance routes.[6]

(8) *Would the owner of an ocean or a miner beneath the waves be responsible for damage to property on land and/or to floating craft caused by a tidal wave or surge emanating from his property?*

Such damage would be resolved according to the following principles: A tsunami resulting from a natural event over which said owner had no control would impose no liability. That is a risk which those who wish to live and work on or near the sea have chosen to assume. If the surge stemmed from the actions of the proprietor, he would.

(9) *Suppose a volcano creates a new island; who is the rightful owner of it?*

New dry land (above-water) would be up for grabs for the first homesteader, but it may not have many takers. Such new land tends to be sterile, and its weak structure frequently means rapid erosion and eventual disappearance. Access across privately held waters could prove a challenge and further inhibit would-be entrepreneurs. Such an emergent island may not be new.

(10) *Certain natural processes through gains and losses stemming from the natural water cycle cause transfers of water to and from the ocean. When the polar ice caps and/or icebergs melt or freeze, does this imply theft of water from the owner of the ice on the part of the proprietor of the ocean, the reverse, or neither?*

"Possession is nine tenths of the law," and "innocent until proven guilty" are the bedrocks of rational law. If it can be proven (see point 7) that some untoward action on the part of the defendant caused this difficulty, then the plaintiff prevails. Otherwise, not.

GENERAL OCEANOLOGICAL CONSIDERATIONS

Ownership of oceans must account for the salt water itself either as the physical liquid, particular volumes by location, or by flows (currents, movements). Property rights in the seas have strong and positive implications for fishing privileges; transportation; mineral extraction from the fluid or the oceanic floor; potable water extraction from the saline solution; etc. Property rights imply boundaries between one person's holdings and those of another.

Related discussions include methods for apprehending trespassers and thieves and rectifying damages they inflict on the rightful owners. Unless the proprietor of an asset does the dumping, those who leave garbage in any part of the ocean belonging to someone would be considered tortious trespassers.[7]

Ideas regarding possession of these various assets have sharply negative implications for the UN Law of the Sea Treaty (1982). In the view of that pernicious document, the oceans are the common heritage of all mankind. According to "article 25, concerning the *Right of access to and from the sea and freedom of transit*: 1. Land-locked States shall have the right of access to and from the sea for the purpose of exercising the rights provided for in this Convention including those relating to the freedom of the high seas and the common heritage of mankind. To this end, land-locked States shall enjoy freedom of transit through the territory." States Rothbard (1994, p. 35) regarding land, but his view certainly applies in the present context:

> Georgists[8] and other land communalists may claim that the whole world population *really* 'owns' it, but if no one has yet used it, it is in the real sense owned and controlled by no one. The pioneer, the homesteader, the first user and transformer of this land, is the man who first brings this simple valueless thing into production and social use. It is difficult to see the morality of depriving him of ownership in favor of people who have never gotten [sic] within a thousand miles of the land, and who may not even know of the existence of the property over which they are supposed to have a claim.

On this basis, one might as well claim ownership to the sun, the moon, and the stars (we fully realize and decry that many greedy politicians claim just that). But, anyone may claim ownership to anything, if there is no homesteading requirement. At the very least, this will set up innumerable conflicting claims, with no principled way of resolving them. In other words, the UN Law of the Sea Treaty rests on the despicable mantra, "Think war, not peace."

The Water Cycle

Prior to looking at ownership considerations, drawing the limits of analysis is necessary for making the case for private ownership of bodies of water. A review of the water cycle helps achieve an understanding of where a body of water starts and stops. For this study, the authors have assumed, *arguendo*, as a first approximation, that the quantity of water throughout the entire planet Earth is stable and unchanging.[9] The oceans provide a good starting point because they are by far the largest reservoir of water on the earth.

The oceans contain about 1.5 billion cubic kilometers at an average depth exceeding 12,000 feet (Elert, 2003). Water enters the oceans from all land bodies and leaves primarily to the atmosphere through evaporation. Examples of other minor losses from the oceans include infiltration through the ocean floor and, at least temporarily, through freezing at the polar ice caps. Ocean currents circulate around the earth.

The water cycle (Fig. 7.1) begins with evaporation from the ocean surface. The water vapor[10] mixes with the other gasses of the atmosphere and circulates to all parts of the earth. About 12,900 cubic kilometers circulates in the atmosphere at any given time (Elert, 2003). Air currents circulate it to form weather patterns. The constant change in location of the gasses is the reason why owners of bodies of water cannot extend their ownership of the moisture into the atmosphere but can only possess the water actually flowing through their ocean, lake, stream, or reservoir.[11] In other words, water lost through direct evaporation specifically from, say, the Mississippi River could fall as rain in the watershed of the River Don in southwestern Russia and/or any other place, and vice versa.

Where the temperature falls (high elevations, the north and south poles, areas experiencing winter, and zones shaded from the sun) the water vapor condenses into liquid or deposes to ice. Droplets and crystals are small and remain suspended in the atmosphere where they form clouds. During the daytime the clouds cool the earth's surface as well as the lower atmosphere.

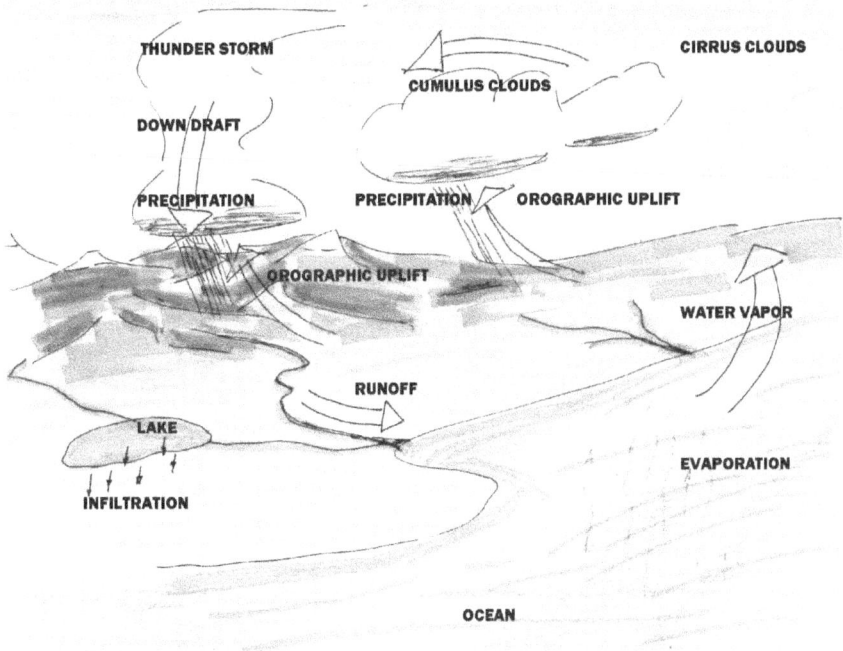

Figure 7.1.   The Water Cycle

Gas becomes denser as it cools. To provide the air for the increase in density, it moves towards the space under the clouds creating a current. The current spirals into the center of the system and ascends. The moisture in the incoming and ascending air becomes cooler so that it condenses. Through this process, the clouds and the water droplets within them become larger. The updraft formed as the air ascends helps to support the condensate at higher elevations.[12]

Additionally, the atomic weight of water molecules (H_2O = 18) is less than that of other major components of air (N_2 = 28, CO_2 = 44, O_2 = 32, Ar = 40).[13] Since the space occupied by each molecule is the same regardless of weight;[14] where the concentration of moisture is high, the atmospheric pressure must necessarily be low. A current of air will flow from relatively dry high pressure areas towards low pressure ones where it rises; the water condenses; and the concentration increases as described herein.

When the size of the droplets increases beyond the ability of the rising air to support them, they fall to the surface as precipitation. Precipitation landing on the ground runs-off in a down slope direction. If it is frozen, it eventually thaws and then runs-off.[15] As it runs off, much of it will infiltrate (soak into the ground) or will evaporate. That which evaporates is added to the atmospheric moisture described above. The water that infiltrates may continue to percolate through the ground until it joins a river, lake, or ocean; or it may enter a plant through the roots. That which enters a plant will be transpired where it is added to the atmosphere.

Runoff collects first in small rivulets and then into streams and rivers. The infiltration that is not transpired collects as groundwater in aquifers which in turn spill into rivers. The discharge collects in first lakes and eventually the oceans thus competing the cycle.[16] The following numbered subsections correspond to objections in the introductory portion of the chapter.

(1) Determining Oceanic Ownership

At the root, people love the oceans. They find the wide open spaces exhilarating and the potential for earning a livelihood inexhaustible. Who does not feel adrenalin at the speed of a dolphin racing a ship (Fig 7.2). In today's world, beaches are overcrowded, pollution has rendered vast expanses unusable or severely compromised;[17] and heavy traffic impacts transportation and recreation.[18]

One of the criteria for ownership is scarcity. If something is not scarce it cannot be owned. Why? This is because the purpose of ownership is to distinguish "mine" from "thine." But, if we can all have as much of the good as we want, and we can because it is not scarce, then no possible conflict can arise between us. If no possible conflict can arise between us, then the need for private property rights does not exist. Not only is there no need for them,

Figure 7.2. Dolphin churning up a rooster tail.

it is impossible for them to exist. Take air for example, including the clouds. It makes no sense for anyone to grab up any amount of this material since, at least at present, there is more of it around than any of us want.[19] However, on the moon and/or Mars, which hopefully mankind will one day occupy (if our governments don't blow us up before that becomes technically feasible.), air is indeed scarce. Private property rights would and should apply to it.

Back to earth, is the Atlantic Ocean scarce? Well, yes and no. "No" in the sense that there is still an abundance of space for people to occupy. Most of these bodies of water are empty most of the time. However, as indicated by commercial and recreational choke-points, it is being filled up with people, boats, oil rigs, etc., more and more; and soon conflicts over its usage will abound. A gradual process of homesteading will end with private property rights. To figure out the how and why of this at present, before that time comes, triumphs over hashing it out when there are actual people with conflicting demands upon this body of water. The key for sorting out ownership proceeds from the recognition that he who initially uses or mines a resource, is mixing his labor with that resource and, thereby, making it his own. This chapter analyzes ways of understanding the resulting ownership concepts and speculating how the process might unfold.

Consider those fish and sea creatures whose life cycles require migration (salmon, whales), the water holdings, in a geometric fenced sense, would have to be large, but not so large that we can't have dozens of different firms owning various parts of all the oceans. The oceans are composed of four aspects: the surface (for shipping, whales, and other air-breathing aquatic mammals), the water below the surface (fish, submarines, scuba divers), material on the ocean floor (manganese nodules,[20] methane clathrate crystals),[21] and the resources under the ocean floor such as oil. Should ownership be vertical or horizontal? Using an analogy from the land, vertical ownership implies that the *ad coelum* doctrine is correct: anyone who owns a patch of land on the surface of the earth owns territory in a decreasing cone shape right down to the core of the planet, and upwards, in an increasing cone shape, toward the heavens. This would imply that slant drilling is improper and that one could charge a fee to airlines for flying overhead. The doctrine has been roundly condemned in the libertarian literature (Benson, 2005; Block, 2008; Huebert, 2011; Marcus, 2004; Rothbard, 1982).

Rejecting *ad coelum* in the seas as well as the land, then, implies denunciation of integrated vertical ownership. The people using the ocean's surface for transportation do not own any water below for fishing, nor even less, manganese nodules on the floor of the ocean, nor even less resources below this level. At least four owners of the seas can exist one stacked right above the other. This, of course, leads to neighborhood effects problems. If the proprietor of the surface rights uses this so intensively as to forestall access to the ocean of the other three owners, he would be in violation of their property rights; ditto for any of the other three. Here, we can again benefit from analogies from the land. Vertically partitioned ownership rights occur on *terra firma* as well. Upon occasion, the owner of farm acreage will lease or sell the rights to the minerals below. These contracts stipulate that the owner of the terrestrial volume below may not build so close to the earth's surface such that he caves in the buildings of the proprietor above him nor interferes with his crops. Similarly, consider condominium owners of the first, second, third and fourth floors, assuming each owner holds sway over one complete floor. They, too, have to cooperate with each other in a manner that respects all rights. No one in a floor above is allowed to inundate his neighbor below with overflowing water from a bath tub. There are limits as to the decibels any of them may emanate at different times of the day, on different days of the week. Such restrictions are, or at least should be, stipulated by deed of title. So, the scenario of four owners of the ocean, stacked one above the other, is not far-fetched.

Some of the ideas expressed above appear to lead to a "tragedy of the commons" wherein a miner of manganese nodules, for example, could create havoc for fishermen or shippers. A mistake in mining methane clathrates could release natural gas into the water thereby reducing the density of the solution and, thereby, cause a ship to sink.[22] If so, then the miner would be inhibiting, or even prohibiting, the use by other users. As in other cases of property ownership, priority sets the limits. If shipper A has established a right though homesteading to run 100 ships per month and then suddenly increases it, miner B who needs access would be damaged. The key is to be able to define what was homesteaded and to define the quality of what is owned, as heavily polluted vs. lightly polluted. So, as the first on the scene, if A has established the right to run 100 ships per month, then B must schedule his access around that traffic. If sometime later, the shipper increases the traffic, the increase must not interfere with the mining operation. With these two properties of ownership, object and quality or priority, the owner can point to a trespasser and say, "Cut it out."

One may not perform a simple act and, thereby, claim the entire ocean. If a Robert Nozick (1974) throws a can of tomato soup into the Atlantic,[23] eventually, molecules from this foodstuff will percolate all throughout the earth's seas. With a sufficiently powerful microscope, they will be found everywhere. Does this mean that eminent Harvard philosopher can be said to be the proper owner of this entire resource, based on libertarian homesteading principles? No, of course, and for several reasons. First and most important, tossing soup into a body of water is an act of pollution. It is a negative in terms of the use for which most people would want to put this resource. But does not the Austrian school of economics maintain, and correctly so, that only subjectivism[24] can shed light on economic issues? Yes, it does. Suppose that an entire continent were heavily wooded, from one end of it to the other, so much so that if one tree were burned, all of them would share in this fate.[25]

Based on subjectivism, and the Lockean-Rothbardian theory of homesteading, the person responsible for this one act could end up as the owner of all the land on this continent. Surely, that would be highly problematic. Based on these considerations, only "positive" homesteading can suffice to establish ownership. Burning trees, and polluting (inter-connected) waterways simply will not suffice. However, if a more limited space, such as a landfill, is polluted to an extent that it is unusable for anything else; and if the landfill owner was the original homesteader or current owner, then this would be a legitimate use. Likewise if the homesteader of the Houston Ship Channel, for example, used it as a dump for pollution that also would be a legitimate use. Of course, trying to extend that to the entire Atlantic would be over-stretch of gargantuan proportions.

Other reasons why a single can of tomato soup, no matter how widespread are its molecules, and abstracting from the fact that this is an act of pollution, cannot count as a legitimate homesteading strategy are *de minimus* and *continua*. What does that mean? The former legal concept appropriately maintains that the law cannot take into account trifles. Strictly, speaking,

batting our eyelashes can send forth reverberations that may negatively impact someone else's property. But, just as in the case of a butterfly's wings,
this effect is far too small for the law to recognize. The latter concept maintains that there is no clear dividing line between what counts and what does
not count as sufficient homesteading. As in the case of pornography, "we
know it when we see it." The amount of labor necessary to establish property
rights varies from place to place, from epoch to epoch, from culture to
culture. There are clear cases on either side of this line, but when acts come
close to it, there is no objective way to distinguish success from failure
(Block and Barnett, 2008).

Free-acting entrepreneurs offer the best chance to realize the importance
of ocean resources. For what is speculating in the oceans if not discovering
new opportunities to bring value, prosperity, and enjoyment to people
throughout the world? In so doing, they take on the role of homesteaders.
That is, they reveal and make (more) desirable a resource that did not previously exist (or had less significance than before their efforts). As long as
manganese nodules and methane clathrates remain trapped on the ocean
floor, they remain valueless. Indeed, in the case of trapped or frozen natural
gas, they pose a danger of sudden and unexpected releases that have resulted
in damage (Associated Press, 2003). That is to say, they have zero or even
negative value as long as they remain untapped. Insofar as ownership of the
seas is unimaginable or verboten, enterprising individuals will not consider
the rich potential that is otherwise available. Those objects remain articles
only—not resources. Likewise, the lack of value engenders contempt. Pollution and overcrowding remain intractable problems.

To the contrary, ingenious pioneers should be proud no matter whether
they start new enterprises, finance others who do so, or simply produce
music and paintings to express the beauty to be found. More than anyone
else, those adventurers benefit the entire human species. Folks who mix their
labor with the waters of the planet should, and in a libertarian civilization
would, own at least their portion as an extension of their very being. They
bring the unimaginable and novel to treasured reality. The only question is
how to define exactly what is to be owned.

(2) Demarcation of Property in Oceans

Each inventive homesteader would discover some value heretofore not recognized, or at least unappreciated. His initiative would involve a certain
expanse, depth, and/or path to implement. In developing his enterprise, the
value, now a "resource," would become an extension of his personhood. It
would become "his." Starting with the current unoccupied seas, at first there
would be no concern about delineating the exact extent of his possession.

As increasing activity of such creators impinge upon neighbors, boundary definitions would necessarily become imperative. Methods for demarcation would evolve.[26] Noteworthy is the concept that spatial geometry may not always be the only, or even the best, definition of what is owned.

(3) Property Limits and Boundary Surveys

Early on for those enterprises that did involve geometrical extent, precise physical property limits would undoubtedly remain unnecessary. As development continued apace, certain expanses would become precious. Property owners would call for oceanic surveyors to devise more precise demarcations, perhaps electronic fences.

However, it is necessary to keep in mind that some enterprises might involve spatial extension in only the most superficial manner and not impinge upon other uses. For example, one can imagine that a fishing business could coexist with shipping. Those enterprises do not necessarily require a specific spot, volume, expanse, or path. However, should the usage become intense, priority in terms of initial time of homesteading would take effect. If the shipper was there first, the fishermen would have to yield. If multiple shippers found themselves in conflict, specific paths would necessarily be staked out with the better routes going to the earlier homesteaders. Without limiting the possibility of future improvements, routes can even today be accurately identified using global positioning. In earlier times, LORAN, lighthouses, and marker buoys ascertained locations. In the future, technologies only dreamed about at present will become reality.

For enterprises requiring a specific expanse of ocean, such as an anchored living platform or a subsurface factory, these same techniques would provide the necessary means to identify the specific place occupied by the residents and/or manufacturers.

(4) Navigation Aids

A major question with the preceding concepts centers on the provision and ownership of navigation aids. Surely GPS, LORAN, buoys, lighthouses, and maps do not appear as if by magic. Who would create them; who would own them? Who would be in charge of them, how would they be financed, and what responsibilities would ensue?

The key to financing revolves around the needs of the owners. A skipper must be able to identify when to turn his vessel to avoid colliding with an anchored residential platform.[27] To avoid the expense of damages resulting from an accident, the shipping company would be happy to purchase the exceedingly cheap by comparison subscription to a GPS provider. Expecting to take advantage of that need, an enterprising firm would want to provide that service.

Another method, which can be expected to operate in tandem with systems like GPS or LORAN, are devices like buoys and lighthouses.[28] The owner of a residential platform, wishing to avoid being struck by a wayward vessel would install and maintain lighthouses on the platform along with fog horns, navigation buoys, and/or aquatic fences. Likewise, private harbors, just as they do now, would construct similar aids and would employ pilots and tugboats to help ships wishing to enter. As the ocean usage becomes more and more intense, these systems would become more refined and accurate.

The process is similar to what happened on land. The first homesteader may have been a farmer. He simply started to till the land. There was no boundary per-se. Sometime later, a second one settled on another parcel of ground. For both, there might have been some vague concept of an edge to each property based on the practical limits of what each individual was capable of husbanding. Only when the land became so intensely used did precise property lines develop. For an example from the relatively recent past, the reader is referred to the historical map of the Arabian Peninsula and Vicinity (Undated). On it, he will see nations, but except very close to the coast, he will find dashed, indistinct or non-existent borders. We, the authors, envision a similar process, not of countries, but of homesteaders gradually filling in the oceanic territory with ever more detailed and exacting definitions of proprietorship.

(5) Possession of Aqueous Species

The vehement commitment these days to "the open ocean"[29] notion illustrates perfectly the folly of common or non-ownership. Without secure titles, a fisherman must harvest fish lest he find them already taken by others. The unmitigated need to obtain the catch as soon as possible compels all anglers to try to beat the others to the punch. In earlier times, when trawlers, sonar, and, most importantly, a smaller human population was not capable of applying serious pressure on desired species, non-ownership did not create conflicts. Now with declining aqueous populations, a hunter/gatherer culture is no longer viable.

To avoid of the threat of extinction, valued species must be privately owned. On land, ranchers prudently husband their herds to preserve their future livelihood. Aquaranchers[30] would care for their charges with the same due diligence. They would be motivated to devise "seabreaking"[31] methodologies for keeping their schools (herds, flocks) healthy, viable, numerous, and flourishing. New species have come into being through competitive breeding and bio-engineering on the land;[32] why not in the oceans, too? Essential to aquaranchers' endeavors are secure titles. Who would find the necessary commitment to preserve a school of fish if someone else can take it at any time? Who would devise a new and better salmon, if he could not legally protect it from competitors?

(6) Sharks

Sharks are dangerous animals. In the free society, when libertarianism rules the waves, these predators will not likely[33] be allowed to roam freely, spreading havoc wherever they go. No more so than applies to vicious animals on the land. Block (2010) writes as follows:

> Another otherwise libertarian who does not fully support private property rights is Baden (2001): "I'm a guy who, with my wife Ramona, ran 500 ewes for years. Yet we publicly support the return of the wolf to wild areas." This, despite the fact that "The reintroduction of wolves necessarily means that more livestock and pets will be prey" (ibid). And again (Baden 1995): "In Montana, and in Idaho as well, few issues are more complex and emotional than those concerning wolves. For three generations people vilified, mythologized, and killed wolves. More recently, many environmentalists, myself included, have sought to restore this ancient predator to Yellowstone Park and wilderness areas. Returning the wolf replaces an important part of the ecological tapestry that humanity has unwoven. . . . With careful management, humans and wolves can coexist. Even with 75 wolves in northwestern Montana, only two cow calves were killed last year."
> If Baden, a Montana rancher, were talking about releasing wolves onto his own property, while building strong fences to keep them penned in there, that would be one thing. His neighbors might feel threatened, but that is another matter. However, this otherwise free market environmentalist is proposing no such thing. Instead, he is advocating the introduction of this vicious predator into the wilds, where no fences will keep them from the private property of other landowners. It would be one thing if Baden were the typical watermelon: green on the outside but red on the inside. Then, he would be, merely, an ordinary leftist, or coercive socialist. Those are a dime a dozen. But this is clearly not the case, here. Rather, this author has impeccable[34] free enterprise credentials (Baden and Stroup 1981, 1983; Stroup and Baden 1982). This being the case, it is then proper to characterize him as a left libertarian. No matter how he is characterized, one thing is clear: it is a violation of private property rights to release wolves onto territory where they can have access to the persons and property of others. Let Baden keep those wolves to himself.

In other words, sharks are to the water as lions, wolves and tigers are to the land. If it is improper for there to be "predator freedom" on *terra firma*, this should apply, as well, to the Kingdom of Neptune. Sharks are merely lions, wolves and tigers that can swim very well. They must all be kept imprisoned, if human beings are to be safeguarded.

(7) Oceanic Mining

Quite simply the ocean floor is underwater land. As such, all of the same characteristics apply. It can be surveyed and delineated into parcels just as any other type of land. Pins can be set out to define property limits. In anticipation of the markers being covered over time by mud and debris, witness landmarks can be used to reestablish them. Then, there is also modern electronic technology. [35]

The issue of access might at first seem formidable. But just as on dry land, in order to inaugurate a homestead, one must enter. Access rights are part and parcel with the formation of new assets. For a would-be entrepreneur under a densely developed sea, access rights would be acquired by or purchased from previous developers just as well drillers and miners do on dry land.

(8) Liability for Natural Disasters

The assignment of liability for disasters would be the same or at least similar to all other liability cases. Damage stemming from an event beyond the owner's control would not subject him to the obligation to pay. For example, under current technology, earthquakes cannot be prevented. The Juan de Fuqua plate is subducting beneath the North American plate. The process stresses both plates. When the resulting strain becomes so great, the fault gives way; and an earthquake occurs. No liability would ensue. If, on the other hand, someone were to conduct an operation that caused an underwater land slide, he would be liable for all resulting damages.

(9) Newly Formed Land

Should a new island form in the middle of the ocean (Hasegawa, 2015), new dry land would be open to homesteaders. Though such islands tend to be sterile and structurally weak, [36] innovators might very well devise uses from which value can be derived.

Should such an island occur in a shipping lane, ocean going vessels would have to detour. In a crowded environment, the detour would incur an expense to reestablish a lane through someone's property. That loss could be costly. Shipping route owners should consider insurance, or they might also want to contract for emergency options to buy or rent alternative routes prior to emergencies. At rift zones, underwater land is being constantly formed, but at a sluggish pace on the order of an inch or so per year. Such microscopic expansion would become part of the holdings of the adjacent landholders.

But, suppose, that a large island suddenly arose out of the sea and that this spontaneous occurrence stemmed from geophysical forces beyond the scope of human ability to counteract. Would the first to use this newly developed land become its owner? Or would that benefit accrue to the owner(s) of that patch of the ocean in which this new island appears? The libertarian would generally agree that the island would not automatically belong to anyone. It would also not go to the person who discovered it or stepped on it. As discussed in this chapter, a land dweller who has no contact with the sea and has not mixed his labor with it has no oceanic rights. So it is with the ocean inhabitant: He has no rights to land he has not so much as touched. Such an original protuberance would go to whoever proceeded beyond mere discovery with a commitment manifested by the work necessary to make it so. How could a shipping magnate who steered around that irritating obstacle in his way claim possession? He could not! How could a resident come to own it who lived on a platform on the very patch of sea where the island appeared? He could do so only by settling on it with accompanying due effort to put it to beneficial use.

Problems with the forgoing analysis could crop up. What if a landlord historically leased out the surface all around the island before it appeared? Then no one could legitimately get to the landmass.[37] The libertarian perspective considers whether anyone can garner legal access. For example, the owner of the ocean surface could settle it at his leisure (barring approach by aircraft used by another homesteader). Alternatively, someone might own the land under water for the purpose of mining manganese nodules and it then somehow rises above the surface of the sea without human cause; he would still own it and continue to harvest them. He could properly continue his operation as before without interruption. The fact that it is now above sea-level whereas before it was not changes exactly nothing. He was and now still is mixing his labor with his asset making it his own. As a third illustration, posit a homeowner who lived at that very location on the water's surface, he would lose out because he unwisely built his house right above this undersea volcano.

Similarly, posit that a meteor lands on farmer Jones' lower forty. Would he own it? Or would this space visitor belong to an astronomer who swooped down in a helicopter and parked on this largish meteor? Our answer is: the farmer is the legitimate owner of the meteorite. This case is similar to the one where there is an apple tree planted in A's land, but is located on the border of B's holdings. Some of this fruit drops into B's territory, since several of the branches of A's tree hang over B's land. B gets to keep those apples that drop down onto his holdings. In like manner, the owner of that patch of ocean in which this new island appears gets the first shot at homesteading it, unless a predecessor already has homesteaded the ocean floor which is now above the surface. And, the farmer, not the astronomer, gets first crack at the meteor.

Figure 7.3.   Glacier Calving

(10) Gains and Losses from the Natural Water Cycle

What of the case of the polar ice caps either melting and raising the sea level, or enlarging, reducing the height of the oceans, and exposing more land (see Fig. 7.3). These are important challenges. Again, we resort to that bedrock of law, "innocent until and unless proven guilty." Posit, then, that no one is at fault. [38] Not the owners of the ocean, nor those who use too much or too little air conditioning, underarm deodorants, or those who have too large or small a carbon "footprint." Blame it on sunspots, for our purposes. In the former case, some low lying areas of land will be flooded. That would be tough cheese for its owners. They take their chances when they build in such vulnerable territory. Certainly, at least in the free society, no one else would be compelled, through the tax and subsidy system of the government, to make good their losses. In the latter case, it would be the owners of the newly uncovered land who would gain from this development. Despite his land becoming exposed because of the receding waters, the proprietor of the sea bed in this area would still retain his possessions.

NOTES

1. Does a falling tree make any noise in the forest if there is no one around to hear it? Who knows? We don't really care. However, if there is a forest with no people around, presumably, the trees exist. But, they are not yet a valuable resource until and unless a human being comes along and interacts with them. Thus, while the trees did "previously exist," they were not yet economic goods.

2. It is our claim that this system would be viable no matter what the level of technology. In a bygone era, the markings might have been "from this here rock to that there whatever." Nowadays, however, with sophisticated electronics, GPS systems, property boundaries could be much more precise.

3. LORAN is an acronym for LOng RAnge Navigation.

4. GPS is an acronym for Global Positioning System.

5. In chapter 1 and chapter 8 we present, and criticize, ITQ schemes directed at this challenge.

6. For more on this, see the literature surrounding forestalling: Block, 2001, 2003D, 2004, 2008, 2010A, 2010B, 2011D; Block and Whitehead, 2005; Epstein vs Block, 2005; and the "Blockian proviso" described in endnote 37. Also refer to Kinsella, 2007, 2009D.

7. Trespass and other criminal activity are discussed in more detail in chapter 1, the introduction and chapter 12, Piracy.

8. Georgists are followers of Henry George, an otherwise strong advocate of economic freedom, except for land. He urged a 100 percent tax on this factor of production, replacing all other taxes, since he thought land ownership, alone, was unproductive. For a sharp critique of Georgism, see Rothbard, 1997C.

9. While the quantity of water is unchanging for all practical purposes and certainly as a first approximation, this assumption is not entirely true. A few reasons for changes in the amount of water on earth include: (1) The solar wind consists of plasma containing mostly protons and electrons which upon entry deionizes into hydrogen and then oxidizes into water, a gain for H_2O. (2) Icy comets collide with the earth and melt, another aquatic increase. (3) Water is reduced to hydrogen and oxygen through electrolysis, a loss. (4) Water combines with carbon through the photosynthesis processes of plant growth, another decrease. (5) Burning changes hydrocarbons into carbon dioxide and water, a gain. These and other processes can be dismissed as small compared to the total amount of water on the planet; though, over geological time they can become significant.

10. An often overlooked fact is that water vapor is, by far, the most significant greenhouse gas. By comparison, carbon dioxide has virtually no effect. A frequently observed illustration of this fact is that the earth's surface remains relatively warm on cloudy, humid nights as compared to the more rapid cooling on clear nights. The hot and dry summer Utah desert tends to become quite cold at night.

11. Ownership of the atmosphere is beyond the scope of this book; though, the authors believe the application of similar concepts could form the basis of another study. This will become applicable when and if scarcity emerges in this context. We claim scarcity has developed and is now in the process of further development in bodies of water.

12. If the temperatures at the higher elevations are cold enough, snow or ice (hail) forms. The exact processes behind the various forms of precipitation are beyond the scope of this book.

13. Nitrogen, carbon dioxide, oxygen, argon, respectively.

14. "Avogadro's law states that all gases at the same temperature and pressure under the action of a given value of g [gravitational constant, for Earth it is 32.2 ft/s^2] have the same number of molecules per unit of volume . . . ." (Daugherty, 1977, p. 8).

15. Or it may flow as a glacier to a lower elevation where it then melts.

16. Rivers such as the Humboldt in Nevada or the Sevier in Utah which terminate in undrained salt lakes or sinks rather than an ocean are beyond the scope of this book. Suffice it to say that even water infiltrating into or evaporating from a sink eventually reaches an ocean.

17. Refer to Exxon Valdez Oil Spill Trustee Council, Undated; NOAA, Undated; and Goto, 1975.

18. Refer to Bosphorus Strait (Maritime Security, 2013) and Singapore roads (Raunek, 2012).

19. Clean air is another matter. The way we analyze this matter, there is no shortage of clean air. There is plenty of it all around us. The only problem is that some people place dirt in it, e.g., pollution, an entirely different matter. For an analysis of the causes and cures for air pollution, see the best essay ever written on this matter, Rothbard, 1982.

20. "Polymetallic nodules, also called manganese nodules, are rock concretions formed of concentric layers of iron and manganese hydroxides around a core" (International Seabed Authority, Undated).

21. A methane clathrate ($CH_4 \cdot 5.75H_2O$) is a flammable source of energy or "burning ice." The methane burns, and the ice drips away as water. Thomas, Undated and Zizka, 2015.

22. Could an enemy sink a ship by pumping air into the ocean? Theoretically, yes; but such an attack would require a massive, expensive, and difficult to move infrastructure. Target ships would notice and avoid the danger zone.

23. See also Friedman, 1983.

24. States Hayek (1979, 52): "And it is probably no exaggeration to say that every important advance in economic theory during the last hundred years was a further step in the consistent application of subjectivism." Also, see the following on this issue: Barnett, 1989; Block, 1988; Buchanan and Thirlby, 1981; Buchanan, 1969, 1979; Butos and Koppl, 1997; Cordato, 1989; DiLorenzo, 1990; Garrison, 1985; Gunning, 1990; Kirzner, 1986; Mises, 1998; Rizzo, 1979, 1980B; Rothbard, 1979, 1997B; Stringham, 2008.

25. While not the entire continent, consider Wisconsin in 1871 (Hipke, Undated).

26. This matches the pattern of land development. Initially, there was the "open range," when land was plentiful compared to the number of settlers. But as the latter increased, more and more efforts were undertaken to demarcate "mine" from "thine." For one analysis of this phenomenon, see Demsetz (1967).

27. In the view of Coase (1960), if a boat hits a dock, the person responsible for the collision is the least cost avoider, not necessarily the captain of the ship. We reject this Coasean "analysis." See on this Block, 1977.

28. For an analysis of this institution, see Barnett and Block, 2007; Bertrand, 2006, 2009; Coase, 1974; Van Zandt, 1993.

29. Freedom of the seas, or freedom of navigation is a well-established legal principle. The United Nations statement is but the tip of the iceberg in this regard. For other support of this doctrine see Parks, 2013; Thaler, 2013; Slow Fish, undated; GreenPeace, 2007; Grotius, 1633[1916]; Reppy, 1950. It would appear that "freedom of the land" or "freedom of riding on the land" is the rough analogy of this doctrine, applied to terra firma. What would be the logical implication of such a claim? Why, land socialism, of course. If all and sundry are "free" to roam around the land exactly as they wish, with no by-your-leave from anyone, this would constitute the death knell for private property. Ownership, and such "freedom" to aggress against others are simply incompatible with one another.

30. The term "aquarancher" is used herein to refer to the private owners of aquatic species and who care for, breed, and harvest in a manner similar to a rancher of beef on land and radically different from a hunter.

31. For example, groundbreaking innovation on the sea.

32. A few examples include the following: The fertile species beefalo was created at first accidentally and then intentionally by Charles Goodnight in the mid-18th century. The non-fertile cama was created in Dubai by cross-breeding a female llama with a male camel. The theoretically, but rarely, fertile mule is a cross between a female horse and a male donkey.

33. Of course, if the owner of a patch of ocean wants to harbor these creatures, whether because they are scavengers and keep the water clean, and/or for biological research or future pharmaceutical purposes (one day new discoveries may be made which will utilize their DNA), and can keep them to himself, for example with electronic fences, he may of course legally do so. But, if they escape his clutches and do harm elsewhere, he would be as responsible as if his dog bit someone.

34. Clearly, though his free market principles are deep, they are not "impeccable."

35. It is our view that private property rights are justified, but pragmatically and deontologically, at any epoch in history. Of course, modern GPS technology is a recent innovation. But in former years, there would have been no need to demarcate land at the bottom of the sea, so our contention can be preserved.

36. Newly formed islands tend to slump and erode quickly.

37. Refer to Block's proviso: Imagine three concentric parcels as in the illustration:

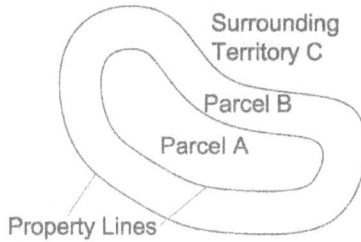

Figure 7.4. The Blockean Proviso

The question we face in this analysis is if B came first, who would come to own lot A? No one. The "Blockian proviso" argues that the owner of B controls A, an area with which he did not mix his labor, and that this is illicit: it would be, so to speak, a violation of the natural homesteading rule, and should be prohibited by law (of course, not by government; rather by private courts and police). This is contrary to the Lockean-Rothbardian homesteading theory of justification in land titles, since in that view, if you don't own a patch of land, you may not control it; you may not prevent others from homesteading it; and, apart from the Lockean proviso, *all* land, and in our view water too, must be privatized. But, unless B allows paths to be built on land he did indeed homestead, he in effect controls area A. In this example, *no one* homesteaded area A. It is entirely empty. B in effect controls it, in that he won't let anyone else into area A. But B didn't homestead area A either. No one did. But suppose someone wishes to homestead area A as an untouched wilderness. Is he not allowed to do that? Is not the very act of homesteading B and denying access to the backwoods A a sort of labor on A and thus a de facto homestead of A? No, it is not. It allows someone to own something with which he has not mixed his labor, contrary to the homesteading theory. May untouched wildernesses not be owned, then, according to libertarian theory? No, they may be owned. For a discussion as to how this can occur, compatible with homesteading, see Nelson, 2015A and B; Block and Edelstein, 2012. For a critique of the Blockean proviso, see Kinsella, 2007, 2009A, 2009D. For a defense of it: Long, 2007.

38. If it can be proven beyond a reasonable doubt that anyone is at fault, then of course the guilty parties would be considered tort-feasors and be made to pay damages.

Chapter Eight

Rivers—Concepts of Potamological Ownership

"[I]t is clear that the main tenet of socialism, community of goods, must be utterly rejected, since it only injures those whom it would seem meant to benefit, is directly contrary to the natural rights of mankind, and would introduce confusion and disorder into the commonwealth. The first and most fundamental principle, therefore, if one would undertake to alleviate the condition of the masses, must be the inviolability of private property." —Vincenzo Gioacchino Raffaele Luigi Pecci, aka Pope Leo XIII [1]

Resolved: Private ownership of rivers, streams, and other waterways is deontologially justified and would reduce the level of confusion and uncertainty regarding water rights. Many students of public policy will experience shock at the concept of private ownership of rivers. After all:

OBJECTIONS TO PRIVATE RIVER
OWNERSHIP AND RESPONSES FOR FURTHER DISCUSSION

(1) *Water is a natural resource which can be used for drinking, washing, irrigation, transportation, etc. If a greedy company or individual owns any, it or he would be able to hold the surrounding community hostage and demand excessive profits for his water since humans must have it to survive. This fluid in natural channels existed prior to man; so, no one individual may properly claim it. Rivers are the common heritage of all of mankind. No selfish corporation should be allowed to own any of them.*

Who among us is not greedy? If selfishness precludes riverine ownership, why not also cars, cats, and clothing? Are bureaucrats not jealous for power and privilege? Clearly they can and do impose nasty, debilitating conditions

75

on water use designed to inflict damaging political aims on the populace to keep it in place. Since a river is like any other natural resource, owning it is as appropriate as privatizing land, factories, capital goods, farms. Far from being evil, profits provide the message that one is providing a valuable service to society.

(2) *Rivers flood. Suppose a waterway overflows its banks and damages holdings alongside. Who pays? Water flows everywhere without regard to property lines. Protection from inundation is, therefore, a public good. If a single land owner builds a levee next to a stream, he is not protected because his neighbor may not also have one. To shield one landowner, all neighbors must be protected. Furthermore, to avoid the problem of free-riders, all must contribute. The taxing and regulatory power of the state exists precisely to address this type of issue.*

Yes, there may be free-riders, at least according to some. But fairness enhancing market mechanisms will evolve as private actors protect their interests. More to the point: since when are government programs immune to free-ridership? Who wants the incompetent and vicious creators of "Obamacare" to have charge of flood protection? Shall we accord this task to those who have long mismanaged the Post Office?

(3) *If natural channels, or any channels for that matter, are under private proprietary control, who owns the fish?*

Fishing rights are no different than any other resource. The possibility of fairness with regard to aquatic species requires private ownership. Indeed, private ownership protects the viability of species, even, or especially, when endangered. While nothing touched by human hands is or can be perfect, would this be better than any other alternative? Yes. Non-ownership creates the tragedy of the commons. Public management is notorious for creating shortages.[2]

(4) *Who owns the minerals underneath a river and how would he access them?*

As with water, humans value minerals as raw materials. A would-be miner will be well motivated to negotiate access rights with a river owner. The owner on-the-other-hand, in addition to profiting from the income from the miner, needs the products that will be made from the mined material. Again, there is a strong analogy with the land. It behooves farmers to find minerals beneath their land; they can negotiate with mining companies for access.

(5) *How would a property-owner reestablish access if his only previous access was via a navigable river that becomes non-navigable?*

Users in a free market needing access would create or purchase right of way should the river dry up. Alternatively, if he were the original homesteader and if the river was emptied by overuse from a competitor, he could sue for the return of his water. In sharp contrast, the government would steal water as necessary to maintain or keep a river accessible only if support from users was forthcoming (bribes in short).

(6) *What happens when erosion causes the river to change course? What happens if the change of course eliminates a previously occupied building site?*

Indeed, rivers do change course on occasion; it happens naturally. Again, it is a matter of comparison between central direction and free enterprise.[3] State control does not cause rivers to stay in "their place." People do lose property from such events, but under public ownership they are protected only with funds mulcted from innocent persons. Private proprietors are motivated to anticipate risks and provide recovery mechanisms that elude bureaucrats. The failure of the state apparatus before and after the post Katrina tragedy[4] ought to encourage people to at least keep an open mind on this issue.

(7) *Suppose there is a mudslide from a farm into a river. May the landowner of the former send a bill to the holder of the latter for undermining his land, or vice versa for trespass?*

In the same way, landslides and avalanches will occur, and only capitalist control will provide adequate methods for retrieval of losses. These natural disasters will happen despite supposed state mitigation efforts. Private control works for two straightforward reasons. First, everyone looks to protect his property or will have paid a sufficiently low price so that the loss from such an event will not be burdensome. Second, those afraid of such an event will take steps to alleviate the threat. Unless the slide stems from a misfeasor's actions, no payments are due.

(8) *How would damming rights operate? How can an owner gain license to inundate the property within the proposed reservoir? May he collect all of the water or dry up everything downstream? Would it even be possible, with private property rights, for a gigantic project, such as the Tennessee Valley Authority or Shasta Dam to be built under free enterprise?*

States that build dams take land to be inundated by force under eminent domain procedures. That is not ethical. The private builders would have to obtain the reservoir area through free negotiations[5]—returning value for value to those who are displaced. There is no limit to the size of a project except one: The developer must obtain the resources from willing sellers. The TVA would be verboten should the then current owners have been unwilling to sell or lease.

GENERAL POTAMOLOGICAL CONSIDERATIONS

Those tired objections, heard many times, fail to account for the dynamic capabilities of entrepreneurs performing valuable services in a free market.

So far this chapter has focused almost entirely on the legal ramifications of private ownership of rivers. If A does thus and such, which has this or that effect on B, and the two of them cannot agree to this activity, what remedies do either of them have to persist in, or block, that activity? Before addressing the preceding objections in greater detail we now focus on an entirely different question: how will private ownership of the river function on a day to day basis, and in ordinary times, when there are no legal conflicts between any of those involved in the use of this resource? For example, how much will the owner of the transit rights charge to those large boats which ply the Mississippi in both directions? Will the price be based on tonnage? On length or width of the ship? What about fishing? If Tom Sawyer sticks a fishing rod into the water, does he pay by the hour? By the number of fish caught? By their weight? And what of swimming? Who pays whom for that? By the hour? Day? Should there be a season pass?

These questions are important. It is crucial that they all be addressed both from the point of view of making the case for privatization, and, if that should ever come to pass, these speculations might be of some practical help to the entrepreneurs in question.

We confess, however, that it is extremely difficult to answer these questions with any degree of precision. It is as if shirts were always a government monopoly, and now some maniacs were proposing that this industry be privatized. The questions would come thick and fast: what color would they be? Would the same sizes be used? How many stores would sell them? Who would produce them? They were always "free" before (paid with tax money); what would they cost now? Would they be sold in mom and pop shops or large warehouses? Do such questions sound absurd?

Difficulties appear to abound, but not to one who has ever experienced a free market in shirts. The point is, it is challenging to anticipate the market, to determine what thousands, millions, billions of entrepreneurs and customers would do. For one who has lived with a free market or even one relatively so, the introductory interrogation is equally ridiculous. As indicated by the continuing debate, all we can do is speculate. So, let us begin.

Would the X River Corporation charge large boats for travel on its premises? Almost certainly, and the price would be based on tonnage, miles travelled, etc.[6] Swimming and fishing with a single pole might well be for free; as a loss leader, promoting good will, an advertising ploy. Pleasure boats might have to pay more on weekends, and little or nothing during the weekday, in an effort to install peak load pricing. Would people have to put coins in toll boxes? More likely, particularly for large boats, they would register their trip beforehand, and keep a running balance.

Ownership of rivers must account for the water itself, fluid flow, floods, draughts, fishing, transportation, mineral extraction from the liquid, mineral extraction from the riparian zone, pollution, erosion, sedimentation, recreational swimming, and boating, etc. Homesteading provides the preferred methodology for taking ownership. To address both the natural resources and the objections, geometric, riparian, and priority concepts for proprietorship will be brought to bear.

(1) The Water Itself

Fresh water is a valuable commodity. Where it is in short supply, a functioning society needs a tool for stable and reliable distribution. Aqua-capitalism supplies the most dependable, constant, and fair supply mechanism. As described in chapter 4, the three ways to implement ownership include In-Toto, Prior Appropriation, and Riparian.

IN-TOTO: A necessary feature of the ownership of a geometric portion of the river is that the water will always be flowing through it, at least in most cases. The constituents include the river bed, natural banks, the gradient,[7] soil, rocks, vegetation, natural levees and floodplains, and/or artificial levees. Since the maximum flood can only be estimated on a stochastic, or probabilistic, basis, the exterior limits of the facility in its natural state are difficult to define. Over time, individuals with no direct interest in the river may homestead areas subject to flooding. Boundaries will evolve, but the homesteaders must either accept the risks associated with natural phenomena dating from time immemorial or take mitigating actions. But geometric ownership does not include the water itself; that is, any particular molecules of it, because, as the river flows, these specific atoms will soon enough move downstream. What is owned, in this conception, is the previously described facilities constituting a technological unit that contains the liquid as well as whatever water occupies the given geometrical space at any particular time.

RIPARIAN: The second type of aquatic ownership involves the water. "The riparian doctrine confers upon the owner of land the right to divert the water flowing by his land for use upon his land, without regard to the extent of such use or priority in time" (Racanelli, 1986). Riparian water rights have a long tradition. This concept is that an owner of the adjacent land, including the riparian zone and the geometric facilities listed above, often to the center-line,[8] as well as the water in the river. Pure riparian ownership gives the proprietor the privilege of drawing water from the river as long as there is any in it. This system tended to evolve where water was plentiful. In environments of abundance, it made sense because the small amounts taken had no obvious effect on the surface, volume, or discharge of the primary watercourse. However, fluid seeks a level surface; so, taking from one location amounts to effectively stealing from one's neighbors. When the withdrawals become large with respect to the source, the riparian system breaks down.

Historically, states have then stepped in with regulatory modifications. As organizations that evolved out of, and remain nothing more than, marauding gangs (Spooner, 1870; Rothbard, 1961), states cannot resist taking a cut for themselves of whatever they control. The water under riparian systems has tended to become state property de-facto. An individual's riparian right then became subject to licensure. The real problem is that this system failed to measure the water quantity.

PRIOR APPROPRIATION: This type of ownership both involves the water and measures it. Prior appropriation is based on Lockean (1948) homesteading theories. The system described here bears similarities with the system developed in the western United States by the pioneers who immigrated into this vast land. As such it advanced from the bottom up. Say Anderson and Hill (2004, p. 8): "Property rights that evolve from the bottom up . . . are much more likely to conserve resources and promote investment."

The first user constructed the device(s) necessary to utilize and/or divert what he needed.[9] In so doing, he mixed his labor with a natural resource. But what exactly does he own? The flow rate of the water. For example homesteader A might own the first 1 cubic foot per second (cfs) of the water flowing along the river by priority or date of first use, B, the second 2 cfs, C, the third ½ cfs, etc. If there are only 3 cfs in the river, the rights of A and B get fulfilled; C loses out. Furthermore, some owners might homestead only the flow with no right to consume[10] whereas others might consume also. Ownership should also allow for in-stream use. A person can own the right to a non-consumptive flow of say 100 cfs so that he can float ships and barges. Indeed, that is often one of the very first uses to which a river is put. He can then charge a toll of boat owners wishing to use it as a highway.

This concept of ownership is robust. Say a Johnny-come-lately homesteads the 50th priority of a river for consumptive use. He does not get water until the first 49 users get theirs. In other words he only gets water when there is a great flood. Now with this new owner, large storm events, up to a certain level, are no longer a problem because this 50th user needs a high discharge. He is ready with his reservoir and needs that event to fill it. Previous river owners benefit from his activities, at least up to the capacity of his reservoir, because they no longer have to suffer inundation. Beyond that level, the 51st user might be quite interested in storing that excess water.

(2) Flood Protection

Flood protection should be viewed not as a public good but as a valued service. In a libertarian society, individualized protection could be used. One who wishes to live and work in a risky zone, could build his house and place of business on an existing or artificial mound above any expected floods. This approach has been used from prehistoric times.

Many buildings within floodplains are built on stilts, see Figure 8.1. Whether on a mound or on stilts, people protect their homes, businesses and belongings from damage. For physical protection of a larger area, levees and/ or dams can be built. For example, a Flood Protection Service Company could issue subscriptions for defense against inundation. If a sufficient number of the populace signed up, the company could purchase right-of-way and build a levee along all or part of the river. Yes, there might be those who did not want to participate, but they would pay a rather steep price for refusing.[11] Since no embankment is 100% secure and risk remains, the company might well issue insurance-like guarantees against flooding that would not be available to non-subscribers.

The residents of a high risk basin could form an association to build a dam which would both store storm runoff and make irrigation water available during dry periods. Neither of these solutions to this fact of life involves the use of initiatory force. Each player makes his own choices and lives with the consequences. This is as it should be and is what is meant by a libertarian culture.

Figure 8.1. Building on Stilts

FREE RIDERS: Much concern regarding water ownership appears at first glance to involve free riders, as in the case of flood protection. The concept "free rider" is a perfectly coherent one, at the level of ordinary discourse. We all know exactly what it means. For example, most men seem to be free riders when audacious women appear in public. They enjoy the sight yet do not have to pay for it. Some restaurants even take advantage of this situation, by hiring coquettish waitresses, in the hopes that they will bring male customers in through the doors (but, of course, then such men are not free riders).

However, as a matter of technical economics, "free rider" is incoherent. Why? This is because the only way a person can establish anything in this discipline is through "Human Action" (Mises, 1998): buying, selling, renting, borrowing, lending, bartering, etc. For example, if a man purchases a newspaper for $1.00, he thereby *demonstrates* in a manner impossible for the so called free rider (Rothbard, 1997A) that he values the periodical at $1.01 or more. Similarly, the vendor reveals in a way impossible to dispute that the value he places on the paper was $0.99, or less. In contrast, how do we *know* that the man really appreciates the sight of a beautiful woman dressed provocatively? He may smile, but that does not indicate, apodictically, any such thing. For all we know, he is smiling for unrelated reasons. No, unless he puts cash on the barrel head, which a free rider never does, we can never know. There is an idea in the "market failure" literature which usually follows hard on the heels of the "free rider": that we should make him pay for this enjoyment, and/or subsidize or compel the creator of this external benefit[12] to do so even the more; that is, either the government should tax men who look at women in mini-skirts, and/or subsidize women who wear such apparel. Rothbard's (1997A, 178) *reductio absurdum* of this idea is as follows: "A and B often benefit, it is held, if they can force C into doing something. . . . [A]ny argument proclaiming the right and goodness of, say, three neighbors, who yearn to form a string quartet, forcing a fourth neighbor at bayonet point to learn and play the viola, is hardly deserving of sober comment." The problem in either example is that the supposed beneficiary has no way of demonstrating in a manner that cannot be contradicted, that he really does enjoy what he is being given. And, even if we stipulate that the free rider does benefit, from whence comes the justification that it is licit to *compel* him to pay for this?

The concept "indifference" as in the case of "free rider" also makes perfect sense as a matter of ordinary language. We are all indifferent between this chocolate bar in the candy store, and the one placed right next to it. We are happy to have either one of them. However, in the event, we picked out *this* one, not *that* one. Perhaps this one was closer to hand, or for some other reason more desirous, or accessible. The point is, as a matter of technical economics, it is impossible to *demonstrate* indifference. Whenever we buy, sell, rent, borrow, lend, barter, etc., we express a *preference* for the thing we are receiving, *vis a vis* that which we give up. It is logically impossible for us to reveal indifference through commercial iteration. [13]

This matter of technical language is not limited to economics. It appears in physics, too. There, "work" is defined in moving a mass through a distance. But, if a man holds a pair of 50 pound barbells above his head for even a minute, sweat will come pouring down out of him. He will begin to tremble. He will be exhausted after a short period of time. For the layman, he will have "worked" and worked very hard. And, yet, by stipulation, since the weights did not move by even a scintilla, we may assume, no work at all was done in the technical sense. [14]

This present book is an attempt to apply technical economics (among other considerations such as law, history, common sense) to the exquisitely difficult task of making a case for privatization of bodies of water. It behooves us, then, to employ economics in its narrow professional sense, not to reduce its level of discourse to ordinary language. Accordingly, we must eschew the "free rider" concept as unscientific.

(3) Fishing Rights

What about the fish? Prevaricating libertarians and some conservatives are forever prattling on about "Individual Transferable Quotas" (ITQs)—permits to harvest fish. On the contrary, quotas do not adequately address problems surrounding fishing rights, let alone full privatization of aquatic resources. [15] They are inadequate because they are aspects not of full free enterprise, but rather of semi-demi-quasi-market like institutions. [16] ITQs are nothing more than state imposed manacles intended to pose as market oriented.

One problem with them is that they do not go far enough. Privatizing merely fish, while a good step in the right direction, leaves this industry suspended, as it were, in a sea of non-ownership. Private entrepreneurs should be allowed to own not only the right to catch fish, but the fish themselves, as in fish farms. Under ITQs, there is little or no incentive to do the equivalent of sowing, for example, what the farmer does when he plants the next crop. Provision is made under this system for limiting the reaping, so that fish stocks will not go extinct. This is a necessary condition for good governance, but not a sufficient one. With very tiny amounts of ocean privatized by fish farm firms, this oversight is corrected. What we advocate here is making of the entire fishery a farm if that is what the owners want, which is very far removed from ITQ schemes.

As long as all species of aquatic creatures are abundant, fishing rights could be somewhat similar to riparian rights. That is, fishermen with access could harvest to their heart's content. However, when pressure threatens the viability of a desirable type, free fishing is revealed to be inadequate when the ability of others to catch as much as they want is compromised. Private ownership of the fish precludes such overharvesting.

The viability of aquatic species and fairness require prior appropriation and private ownership. Private ownership protects the viability of species, even, or especially, when endangered.[17] In addition to the faunae, private ownership saves the flora because entrepreneurs are economically compelled to care not only for their animals but necessarily for a healthy habitat. Exactly the same dynamics apply to fish.[18]

(4) Raw Materials

In or below a river bed, valuable minerals may exist. The water, itself, may carry minable materials in, for example, the form of glacial flour which, if extracted, could be used for soil restoration of agricultural fields.[19] See Fig. 8.2.

Figure 8.2.   At the confluence of the Talkeetna River (on the right) and the Susitna River (straight ahead) near the town of Talkeetna, Alaska, the water in the foreground is approaching opaque due to the high concentration of glacial flour.

One resource frequently mined from river beds is sand and gravel. Open pit mining is the usual method. The Thalweg[20] can be moved to enable extraction of materials directly under the water. A miner who is the original homesteader should be free to move the river[21] wherever he wants and in so doing would possess the primary development around which other would be proprietors would have to work. For example, a late arriving Potable Transportation Company would be required by law to homestead or purchase adjacent land and pay to construct a suitable bypass channel for its operations. On-the-other-hand, if a PTC Corp were the first in use, then the mining enterprise would need to seek access to its mine. The miner could pay for general access rights and pay to provide the said bypass channel according to the requirements of PTC.

The same theories would apply to any other minerals to be extracted whether metallic such as copper or non-metallic like potash. Of course underground deep tunnel mining could be homesteaded separately after the establishments of earlier pioneers so long as it did not in any way interfere with the rights of the previous proprietors.

A miner could generate contaminants in the form of undesirable dissolved chemicals, fine suspended solids, or debris of any sort or nature. If he is the original homesteader, then all subsequent users must deal with the resource as they found it. A late arriving miner would assume complete liability for retaining his waste material or purchasing rights from previous homesteaders.[22]

(5) Erosion

When erosion occurs, whether natural or anthropogenic, damages are at least two fold. This process removes material from the river bed and/or the banks. The loss may cause assets nearby to collapse. A farm might lose agricultural land. A building might be deprived of its foundation. The other type of damage occurs where the eroded material is deposited.

Liability for the loss would depend on the cause. Natural erosion tends to deepen the waterway and steepen the banks. As a result, the adjoining acreage will eventually slide into the stream.[23] A land owner may attempt to stabilize the banks, but the power of water will eventually remove these protection devices.[24] Erosion is a natural phenomenon; so, one who cultivates adjacent property has no proper claim for the resultant damages. However, if the river owner has taken steps that increased the tractive force[25] of the flow, then he would be liable for erosion damages.

Based on the concept that "Everything that is, is somewhere," (Plato; Timaeus, 48e-52d) eroded material will be deposited downstream of the erosion. The eroded, and now deposited, material fills in the river bed, or during a flood, aggrades[26] the banks. In the former case, the capacity of the channel is reduced; in the latter, the land is covered by a layer of mud. If these assets have been previously homesteaded, and if the erosion was caused by malfeasance, then the misfeasor is liable for the damages.

Figure 8.3.   Erosion is in foreground and deposition is in the distance. Maximum size of displaced rock was about 18 inches. The photograph was 11 months after the event.

Aside from anthropogenic erosion and deposition, when a river overflows its banks, may the contiguous landowners sue for trespass? If a homesteader has settled in a flood plain, then he has come to the risk, and must therefore assume it. His land holdings include as an essential characteristic the risk of inundation. Likewise, prior water users retain their rights according to prior appropriation principles. That is, the flooded land homesteader gains no right to the water.[27] What if the erosion is so extensive that the river changes course?

(6) Change of Course

On occasion, it happens naturally. State control does not negate that fact.[28] People do lose physical property from such events,[29] but under public ownership they are deluded into thinking they are protected. Private proprietors are motivated to anticipate risks and provide recovery mechanisms that bureaucrats are not (Mises, 1944). If the natural river meandered, then a land developer would either have to live with that fact or take steps, read incur expenses, to stabilize the existing alignment. If a fishing enterprise constituted the original homesteader, then the meanders of the waterway might be an essential component of the fish habitat, and the land developer would neces-

Figure 8.4. Deposition from a major flood occurred 11 months prior to the photograph. Notice that more than 3 feet of 12 inch cobbles have been deposited in drifts.

sarily have to build his foundation at sufficient distance from the stream to allow the natural meandering required by the fishermen. On-the-other-hand, the latter must demonstrate that the continuing process of erosion and movement is in fact necessary for the health of the fishery as opposed to making permanent the existing curves. Without proof, an ambiguous claim to unlimited land to accommodate possible future migration would be material overreach.

However, due to the difficulty and expense of crossing, rivers often function as boundaries as shown in Fig. 8.5. When a waterway such as the Mississippi or Sacramento changes course, what are the implications for ownership titles? Generally, a watercourse remains the border despite a gradual process of erosion and aggradation. However, a sudden change has been seen as not changing the border. In 1876, a change of course of the Mississippi near Reverie, Tennessee, left part of Tennessee on the Arkansas side. Since this event was a sudden abandonment of an old channel rather than the effect of incremental erosion and deposition, the state line remains along the old channel and diverges from the current course.

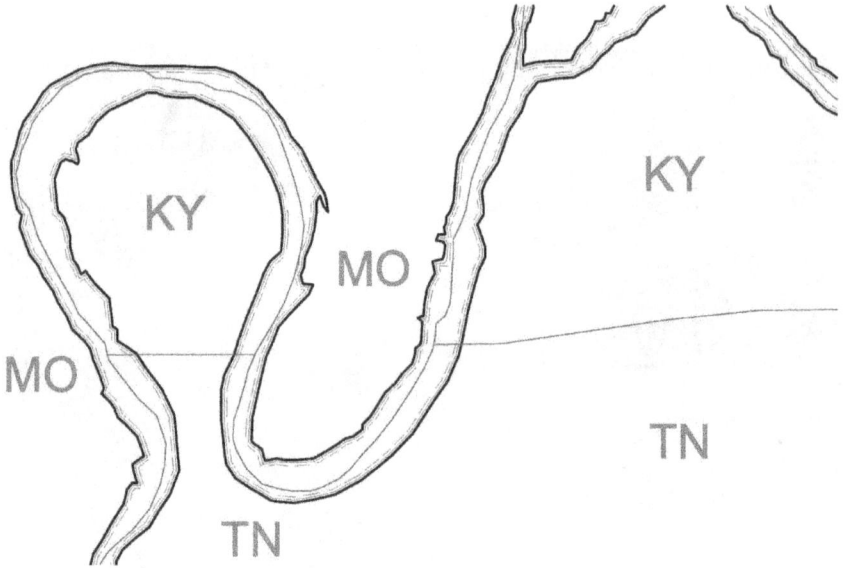

Figure 8.5.   The boundaries of Kentucky, Tennessee, and Missouri serve as a case in point. The border between KY and TN in this area is at 36 degrees, 30 minutes north latitude and between KY and MO is the Mississippi River. The result is the separation of part of Kentucky from the rest of the state.

(7) Landslides

A landslide has the potential to create much havoc. It can dam-up a river and/ or destroy nearby land holdings. Landslides can be either man-made or natural occurrences. In the latter case, no one bears liability for them. Private control alleviates such calamities for two straightforward reasons. First, everyone looks to protect his property and will eschew actions that increase risk, including the refusal to purchase ground that appears unstable or a river below such terrain, except at a low price that incorporates this possible danger. That is to say, the one who finally does take possession will have paid a sufficiently low price so that the loss from such an event will not be devastating. Second, those afraid of such an event will take steps such as slope stabilization methods or insurance to alleviate the threat. A proprietor of an asset subject to risk is responsible for taking steps to reduce it. Should he choose not to take such steps, or not obtain insurance, he would of course in the free society incur the entire burden of any resulting damages. No bailouts would be consistent with the libertarian point of view.

To the contrary, if an avalanche emanates from human decision-making, then of course the perpetrators would be responsible for subsequent damages. How, specifically, would this work? Although the courts would have to weigh in on this, here is the principle upon which they should operate, if they wish to abide by the libertarian philosophy. Suppose that from time imme-morial x tons of mud (dirt or other debris) flowed into the river per year. We would say that the farmer had homesteaded a right to continue at this rate. But, if x+y material began moving in this direction, the farmer would owe a debt to the river owner, assuming this was looked upon by the latter as a harmful trespass, only to the extent of y.

If it comes from a volcano, no one is responsible for it. If it is the by-product of the industrial process, then all bets are off (Rothbard, 1982) as far as lack of responsibility is concerned. Anthropogenic landslides are an en-tirely different matter. Should someone build a dam across a waterway and create a reservoir, new ground will become saturated. The foundation of a steep slope would be softened. Should this effect compromise the stability of a mountain, the perpetrator would be liable for all the resulting damages.

Under *laissez faire* capitalism, those who bear these responsibilities will tend to look out for their interests to avoid incurring such losses. Disasters from landslides would be expected to decrease. State run bailout programs will weaken the natural protections of the free market and the frequency of landslides would increase.

(8) Reservoirs

States that build dams take land to be inundated by force. The libertarian views eminent domain laws as neither practical nor ethical.[30] Some claim that existing landowners would jack up the price to take advantage of the state which is building an aerially extensive project like a dam. If the current owner does not want to sell at any terms of trade, then an eminent domain taking destroys infinite value with a finite payment.

Dams raise a lot of political debate. Advocates push discussions that center around its benefits: water storage, flood prevention, fishing, recrea-tion, increased land values, etc. Opponents emphasize the negatives: loss of wildlife habitat, damage to wild and scenic rivers, the ugly concrete struc-ture, dangers of failure with subsequent flooding, etc. Missing in discussions among statists is recognition of the proper owners of the resources involved and a sense of what "value" means. In the libertarian vision, only the title-holders should have the ability to determine which of the above considera-tions should dominate the actual outcome: to build or not to build. However, there is such a thing in law, and very properly so, as an injunction. If there is a clear and present danger, then even those private individuals who have amassed sufficient lands upon which to build a dam may nevertheless be prevented from so doing by the courts if a downstream plaintiff can prove his non-compensated risks are significant.

The would-be dam builder to be just in his pursuits must be a private entrepreneur. A coercive state must necessarily introduce partiality. Giving voice over the use of other people's property to so-called stakeholders, who have no standing in the matter whatsoever, is patently unjust. This point pervades the entire economy. It is by no means limited to watery issues.[31]

A private dam builder would want to run a clean, safe operation in order to provide a service, or multiple amenities, so as to maximize his returns. The income he expects to make provides the proof he needs that the advantages are indeed valuable to his customers. To realize profits, he would invest his own resources. He would have to obtain the reservoir area through free negotiations—returning value for value to those who are displaced. A property owner in the proposed reservoir could not have his property stolen through eminent domain. No, the developer would have to pay the asking price. He would have to compete with others who want the land for those or other purposes. For example, if there were essential wildlife habitat in the dam's target area, those desiring to save it would be free to bid for it.[32] The same goes for those wishing to develop this terrain for housing, or commerce. In this way, the true value of the existing environment versus the proposed dam and the newly created lake habitat would be exposed.

There is no limit to the size of a project save one: the developer must obtain the resources from willing sellers. A massive project such as the TVA could not displace owners unwilling to sell. Does that mean that large scale projects could not be implemented? Not at all. Entrepreneurs would devise methods for obtaining the necessary land. Prior to implementing the project they might test the feasibility by negotiating options to buy from existing occupants. They might offer money to buy at a sufficiently high price to cause everyone to sell. Methodologies would be as varied as human imagination.[33] Only violence would be disallowed.

HYPOTHETICAL DAMAGES
RELATED TO RIVERINE OWNERSHIP

The Question

Suppose X River has always flooded, from time immemorial. It caused damages of Y% before the libertarians took over society, and A became the owner of the river. Now, it floods again. The new owners should be responsible to pay damages to those who were harmed if both occur: 1. The damages were greater than Y%; and 2. The actions of A can be demonstrated to have caused the increased physical harm. Otherwise, A is innocent and is not responsible to pay damages.

Analysis

The short answer is "correct." A should not be responsible for damages.

That being said, the meaning of river ownership needs to be discussed. Property rights in a piece of land tend to be static. The land does not move, though dust can blow or be washed onto or off of the parcel.[34] The land can be surveyed, and the property right can thus be clearly defined. Likewise, a diamond can be owned. While it can be moved, it is a clearly defined object that does not change from one second to the next. In this sense the diamond is static.

A river is not static; prior to any development a river had the characteristics of a dynamic system.[35] Therefore, to have meaning the concept of owning a river must adapt to this dynamism. While the riverbed can be viewed as somewhat static, the specific water in the river changes from one second to the next. For a fast moving river and/or a short segment, it is possible for the water to be entirely displaced and replaced by different water in a mere moment. Over time, the flow rate in the river will vary. Despite the relatively static nature of the riverbed, the river itself will sometimes change course over time. Even an effort to stabilize a river to a particular course has damaging effects on other river and land owners.[36]

Because of this dynamic nature, a river, qua river, should be owned in ways that are different from static objects. For example, a new developer, B, might stake a claim to a river by diverting the water into a flume by which he drives a waterwheel to power a mill. In establishing such a use, B does in fact, aside from any manmade laws, establish a property right in the river. B does not establish ownership of "the river" *in toto*; but if he diverts, say, 1 cubic foot per second (cfs), he establishes a right to divert that amount of water from the river, as long as there is 1 cfs in the river, and so long as he subsequently returns the water to the river.[37] That is a non-consumptive use and is one of the earliest historical types of formal water rights and is the original source of the riparian theory. In contrast, a consumptive right enables the owner to remove water as for irrigation purposes and not return it.

The preceding paragraphs discuss ownership of the water flowing through a river. The physical and geometric components are also subject to ownership. Herein, the geometric components of the river include its lateral and longitudinal extents, the geologic surface of the river exclusive of the water, and the floodplain. Also included are natural and man-made features that contain, or purport to contain, the water within the river. Following are two cases of damage related to the water that can be caused by specific actions of market participants.

The first case is discharge to a river. If C owns a piece of land, historically, runoff resulting from rainfall entered it (or passed over other land to eventually be incorporated into the river). When C originally settled the land, it established, at the same time, a right to discharge rain runoff into that river. Furthermore, let us say that the soil contained harmful radium and that the land was and is erodible. At that same time, it established a right to discharge radioactive pollutants to the river. Merely discharging water and radioactive material in the historical amounts cannot be seen as (additionally) damaging to downstream users. They always suffered from those problems. If C plows its fields, the rate of water discharge will decrease[38] and the inflow of radium will increase. In so doing, C will have damaged anyone, D, located downstream who relied on that water. C stole D's water if his right predated the time of C's homestead. C has also damaged anyone who relied on the quantity of radium being limited. C trespassed by dumping *excess* harmful radioactive material into his facility, a swimming hole for example. But this is a case where the "guilty" party has no direct ownership of the river and only very limited rights to discharge water.

On the other hand, C might pave the land for use as a parking lot. That would increase the discharge rate of water and decrease the release of radium. The escalation of runoff would augment the flow rate in the river. C would have thereby boosted the flood risk of the downstream residents.

Actual physical damage is not necessary to establish a rights violation; a "mere" threat will suffice. Assuming D wants to control his risk to manageable levels and has constructed a building above say the 1% annual exceedance[39] level, he is now forced to raise his building higher to maintain the same level of risk. By imposing this increased risk and/or expense, it has already damaged him. The only ownership C has in the river is a right to discharge at the historic rate.[40]

The second example is the building of a dam. That can have the effect of damaging upstream residents. If A builds his weir but fails to obtain rights to inundate upstream properties, then he has damaged these neighbors. It may also have reduced discharge to existing downstream users thereby in effect stealing their water. This is a case where the guilty party has direct, though still limited, ownership in the river.

Thus, the long answer to the hypothetical is that it is necessary to determine exactly what property right and liability has been established, and then after detailed analysis the question becomes, "What damage, if any, did the activities cause?" If none, then A is innocent as stated in the hypothetical. The point in the long answer is that "ownership" rights and liability in a dynamic system are not nearly as easy to define as ownership rights and liability in a static system.

NOTES

1. *Rerum Novarum*, 1891.
2. "If you put the federal government in charge of the Sahara Desert, in 5 years there'd be a shortage of sand." Attributed to Friedman, Milton. For one example see Hawkins, 2011.
3. An economist was asked, "How is your wife?" His response: "Compared to what?"
4. See on this: Anderson, 2005; Anderson and Kjar, 2008; Block, 2004, 2005A, 2005B, 2005C, 2005D, 2006B; Block and Rockwell, 2007; Carden, 2008; Chamlee-Wright and Roths-

child, 2007; Chamlee-Wright, 2008; Cowen, 2006; Culpepper and Block, 2008; D'Amico, 2008; Dirmeyer, 2008; Lora, 2006; McGee, 2008; Murphy, 2005B; Raskin, Kjar and Rahm, 2008; Rockwell and Block, 2010; Stringham and Snow, 2008; Thornton, 1999; Vuk, 2006A, 2006B, 2008; Walker and Jackson, 2008; Westley, Murphy and Anderson, 2008; Wood, 2008; Young, 2008.

5. For an analysis of how private highways could be built in the absence of eminent domain laws, see Block, 2009C; Block vs. Epstein, 2005 for a critique and rebuttal.

6. In the early days of roads, streets and highways, when they were owned privately (Block, 2009C), travelers were charged for wagons based on weight carried, number of axels, and even width of wheel. Narrow ones paid more (think ice skates that would put ruts in the dirt road), and wide ones (think steam rollers that would flatten out the terrain) paid less. In scientific terms, pressure is weight divided by the area. For a given weight of truck, narrower wheels apply greater compression. Excessive concentrated force will destroy a road. For this reason, some agencies charge more for or prohibit critically focused pressure.

7. Gradient: the longitudinal slope.

8. The traditional ownership to the centerline derives by analogy from the common-law tradition of roads following the property lines.

9. Strictly speaking diversion is not necessary. A homesteader could use a stream for transportation, for example, and in this way establish a non-consumptive right to the amount of water necessary to float and move his boats.

10. Of course, with limited caveats, water is never consumed (Refer to Chapter 6, "Concepts of Oceanological Ownership," the "Water Cycle"). The term refers to the loss of water from the system. An example of a non-consumptive right would be power take-off to run a watermill that relies on the fluid in the watercourse but does not use it up. A consumptive right would include plant growth wherein H_2O is transpired to the atmosphere. Many uses include both consumptive and non-consumptive aspects like a swimming pool that evaporates some but returns most to the source.

11. This is the "free rider" problem of neoclassical economics. For our discussion of it, see section "Free Riders" in chapter 8.

12. Somehow, this pernicious doctrine is never applied to women's apparel. It is used, relentlessly, with education, another so called external economy. For example, Friedman (1962) applies his doctrine of "neighborhood effects," e.g., free ridership, to education. He maintains that we only consider our own benefits when we choose or refuse an additional year of schooling; we ignore the spillover effects onto free riders of such choices; that if we are more educated, we will become better voters, less likely to be criminals, etc.

13. For a discussion and further explication of this analysis, see Barnett, 2003; Block, 1980, 1999, 2003A, 2007A, 2009A, 2009B; Block and Barnett, 2010; Hoppe, 2005, 2009; Hudik, unpublished; Hulsmann, 1999; Machaj, 2007A; Nozick, 1977; O'Neill, 2010.

14. That is to say there is no *net* work done when that required to resist the potential work of gravity is perfectly negated.

15. McGee and Block (1994) discuss the inadequacy of tradable emissions rights to pollute.

16. Analogous to ITQs are school vouchers. For critiques see: North, 1976, 2011; North and Friedman, 1993; Rockwell, 1998, 2000A, 2002; Rome and Block, 2006; Rothbard, 1971, 1973, 1994, 1995; Salisbury, 2003; Vance, 1996; Yates, 2002a, 2002b; Young and Block. 1999.

17. Regarding conversion from public to private control of deer refer to McTigue, 2004.

18. Refer to chapter 7 regarding branding and/or fencing in oceans.

19. The Geography Site, 2006.

20. Thalweg refers to the lowest part of a valley whether dry or under water. Generally, the bottom or centerline of a stream will coincide with the thalweg.

21. If there are other owners (not the case here since the hypothesis is that he is the original homesteader of the river), he will have to make arrangements with them before moving this waterway.

22. One way for the would-be miner of material below the river to access it is by paying off the owner of this body of water. But, there is another possible technique: slant drilling. Here, the miner burrows down from a plot of land next to the river, into the territory lying beneath this body of water. Then, assuming that he was there first, he need not obtain the permission

from the owner of the river. The counter-argument to this possibility is the *ad coelum* doctrine discussed earlier (chapter 7).

23. For an extreme example, consider the Grand Canyon, or any canyon for that matter, where the eons long process of erosion continues.

24. After the 1976 flash flood in the Cache la Poudre River had washed-out Highway US 34 in places, a new highway was built with concrete retaining walls through the narrowest reaches. During the recent September, 2013 torrent, the base of the wall and the soil behind it was eroded until the road collapsed.

25. Tractive force is a function of friction (related to channel gradient) and weight (dependent on depth of flow). If a reach of river were paved with concrete, it would be smoother than natural. The velocity of flow would increase which would increase the friction. When the water hits an unchanged natural reach, it would be forced to slow due to the increase in friction. The forces, in the form of increased tractive force, would increase the rate of erosion for any given flow rate. This is one reason why erosion is frequently observed downstream of culverts.

26. Fills and raises the elevation by depositing sediment on it.

27. Should no one legally possess this water, then the land owner may stake a claim to it, store, and use it (homestead it) so long as all prior rights are filled any time he wishes to call for his newly owned water.

28. The Army Corp of Engineers will strive mightily, if ordered to do so by the political process, to try to ensure this does not occur. However, bankruptcy stemming from errors is not a threat to them; so, the presumption of correct decisions, either whether to "force" the river to continue in its present course or not, is untenable. Neither can their managers know how much money to throw at this problem (Mises, 1922).

29. And/or its value. The remedy for the first, in libertarian theory, is to sue the causal agent, if there is one. There is no legal cure for the second (Hoppe and Block, 2002).

30. Shockingly, Epstein (1985) and Tullock (1996), supposed libertarians, actually support such enactments. For a critique see Benson, 2005; Block, 1998; Block and Block, 1986; Block vs. Epstein, 2004, 2005; Gregory, 2006; Nedzel and Block, 2007, 2008; Paul, 1987; Speiser, 2005; Ward, 2012. Even China eschews eminent domain (Ward, 2012, his pictures are worth 1000 words each), and thus is more free enterprise oriented than the U.S. On the infamous Kelo case, see Block, 2006A; Epstein, 2005; *Kelo*, 2005; Kinsella, 2005.

31. For example, employees are frequently considered stakeholders. However, they can quit at will with no loss whereas an owner cannot walk away from the losses that he will suffer from a bad decision. Likewise, outsiders, or "stakeholders," are given rights to determine how other people's property may or may not be used. This phenomenon pervades the modern economy. If someone wants to tear down an old building, he must first be given permission to do so by the statists in charge of "heritage" buildings. If someone wants to build a high rise dwelling, the zoning authorities must give their imprimatur. They hold "hearings" in which strangers get to mouth-off about how the owners may use their own holdings. Often, the city planners make a deal with the property owner: he can build only if he grants concessions: a certain percentage of low income tenants, some land to be set aside for a park, etc. All of this violates the very core of the free enterprise system, private property rights. So called stakeholders have no stake.

32. Mind you, such a bidder would not have to purchase the entire area of the slated reservoir, only one parcel that he is unwilling to resell at any price.

33. For other techniques, see Block, 2009C.

34. Mudslides are merely large amounts of (wet) "dust" in motion. The land itself does not move. We abstract from the case of severe flooding, where a lake now appears where a farm previously existed.

35. It may be overstating matters somewhat to make an entirely sharp distinction between land and water. While we cannot fully subscribe to the notion that land is just like slow moving water, and water is like fast moving land, there is a grain of sense in this notion in that there is a continuum between the two, at least theoretically. But, as a practical matter, of course the sharp distinction we draw between the two is eminently justified.

36. An example of a major change of course is the Yellow River (The British Museum, Undated) in China. For over 2,000 years prior to the Boxer Rebellion, the River had been controlled with levees. The River originates in the mountains. It washes silt (loess) down from

the Loess Plateau. Where the River enters the eastern plains of China, the water slows and can no longer carry the bed load. (The bed load of a river refers to the solid material on the river bottom moving along with the water. Heavy material such as boulders and cobbles require a swift current; smaller particles such as silt require little speed. Velocity is related to slope. As the slope flattens at lower elevations, the speed slows. When it decelerates enough, even silt cannot be moved and the bed load settles in place thereby aggrading the river bed.) Eventually and repeatedly, the Chinese had to raise the levees in order to retain control of the river. Through this process, the profile was at times up to 200-feet higher than the surrounding land. The watercourse is renowned for its devastating floods. In 1897 during one such instance, the mouth of the River on the Pacific moved 400 miles northward to the Bohai Sea, from south to north of the Shandong Peninsula. A map of China shows that Henan, Hebei, Jiangsu, and parts of Shandong provinces constitute a vast alluvial fan. The Yellow River has over the eons traced paths covering the entire plain.

37. With due allowance made for possible evaporation during this process. In other words, once having established this pattern, he is entitled to continually engage in it.

38. Warning, technical scientific content to follow: Isolating from the effects of changes in vegetation, plowing disturbs and aerates the soil. Infiltration increases so that runoff declines. On the other hand, more soil including the radium would be mobilized. Paving the ground would contain the soil and attendant radium thereby preventing its mobilization while also obviating infiltration thereby increasing water runoff.

39. Exceedance: The amount by which something exceeds a standard measurement.

40. That rate is of course not static but rather dynamic and determined stochastically. That is to say the discharge varies according to weather and any "determination" of risk must be based on a probabilistic time series.

Chapter Nine

Lakes—Concepts of Limnological Ownership

"A lake is the landscape's most beautiful and expressive feature. It is earth's eye; looking into which the beholder measures the depth of his own nature."
—Henry David Thoreau, *Walden*, 1854

Much to the mortification of statists everywhere, this book advocates private ownership of lakes, ponds, and even puddles. Though the mortified will be shocked at the concept of turning "our" mirrors of the soul into the private preserves of robber barons; consider the following:

OBJECTIONS AND SHORT RESPONSES TO PRIVATE OWNERSHIP OF LAKES AND INLAND WATERS

(1) *Which robber barons get to own the lakes? On what basis will inland waters be distributed among such greedy tycoons? Is access to the shore necessarily included?*

Who says government bureaucrats are any less greedy? As with oceans and rivers, the original homesteaders will take possession of inland waters based upon whatever beneficial use the pioneer established. It is the "beneficial use" that enriches everyone in society.[1] The real greedy ones are those who expect to be fed for nothing. Access to an estate is an implied and necessary part of original exploration and settlement. No one, apart from Marxists and others at the furthest reaches of the political community, objects to private ownership of land. Why should lakes be any different?

(2) *How on this good earth would property limits be established, in water of all things?*

As the lake became popular and crowded, it would behoove proprietors to establish accurate property demarcations such as (electronic?) fences at least for large lakes. For small lakes with only one or two businesses, there may be no need for such delineations. But the optimal technological unit[2] may be such that only one owner may be needed for a body of water the size of Lake Superior. This is not something that can be established a priori.

(3) *What conceivable mechanism for access to the lake bottom would apply if it is under separate ownership for mineral extraction? Suppose an individual or corporation owns a lake. Is access to the shore necessarily included?*

To establish a homestead access is necessary, but not necessarily from shore. It could be from a river.[3] If the original homesteader was a miner of the lake bottom, then subsequent pioneers must work around his access route. Otherwise, he would of necessity attain access by negotiation with current owners. The identical issue obtains on the land. Does the farmer own mineral rights under his property? No, we do not buy into the ad coelum doctrine. It depends upon who gets there first, although, surely, the owner of the surface, whether of water or land, will have a competitive advantage.

(4) *Suppose there are multiple owners of contiguous land surrounding a lake including the riparian zone. Do they each come to own an unusable sliver of the lake; or do they, all together, own the entire body of water with all the infighting that would entail; or neither? As in the case of oceans, how can fences best be established (underwater, really)?*

In order to establish a homestead, personal labor must be mixed with the resource. If none of these owners had interest in the lake, then it would remain up for grabs. Ownership of adjacent land conveys no rights to the lake until homesteading extends into the water. On the other hand, it is more than likely that the owners of the land surrounding the lake would have been using it for swimming, boating, fishing, etc. They might have ensured that this resource was clean, well-preserved. If so, they would be considered the homesteaders and thus each own a share of it; though any prior downstream water appropriators could own the water and limit in-lake uses to non-consumptive purposes.

(5) *What are the limits regarding the extraction of water from and discharge of material to the lake?*

As one possible use of the lake, if the first resident should extract water, he could, if he wished, pump it dry (assuming the downstream river owner(s) did not already own the water). The rights of any predecessors must be fulfilled first. Likewise the dumping of liquid or solid matter must not damage prior owners. However, it is within the realm of possibility that a given lake could be used as a garbage dump, provided it did not violate any rights of downstream owners. Some land is used for such purposes, and we cannot rule out the possibility that some water may be, also.

(6) *Who is at fault if a rude power boater cuts the line of a fisherman?*
Must those who have rights to sail on a peaceful, quiet lake suffer the noise
of motor speed boats?

Let us say that the power boater is also the late arriver. If so, then his
boating operation necessarily must honor and protect all previous occupants.
He would be liable for cutting fishing lines. Should a predecessor indulge in
wind sailing, then the subsequent operator must not inhibit the experience of
the sailor. If, on-the-other-hand, he is the original homesteader, then later
immigrants must work around his activities. Private property rights determine which party must defer to the other, exactly as they do on land.

(7) *Mosquitos are bothersome. How will free enterprise deal with them*
and with standing water?

Mosquitos and standing water are natural phenomena. As such, the settler
of a lake or land adjacent to said body of water includes mosquitos as an
essential feature of the homestead. However, a land owner may enjoin a lake
oriented business if the proprietor has caused an undue proliferation of irrita-
tions that inhibit the enjoyment of his neighbor's estate. If he did not mitigate
this menace, and/or make private arrangements to pay those he had thereby
harmed for it, he would be liable for damages to the victim and/or an injunction.

GENERAL LIMNOLOGICAL CONSIDERATIONS

Private property rights in lakes and ponds must address the water itself,
floods, fishing, transportation, mineral extraction from the liquid, mineral
extraction from the lake bottom and/or the riparian zone, pollution, sedimentation, etc.

(1) Limnological Ownership

As with oceans and rivers, ownership goes to he who homesteaded first. The
subject of control would depend on what beneficial use the pioneer established. If all he did was husband fish, then a subsequent immigrant might
extract water or minerals etc. so long as he did not upset the fishing operation.

Suppose an individual or corporation owns a lake. Is access to the shore
necessarily included? If the labor invested to create the original homestead
involved this body of water only but no dry ground, then, with the following
caveat, access to neither the beach nor the fields beyond is established. This
is similar to how landed estates include the path that was necessary to initially occupy the plot; so, access to a water filled amenity is a necessary part of
the watery homestead. While such a trail is necessary for the establishment of
a plantation it need not be from shore. The pioneer's access could have been

either by river or by land. If the former, absolutely no access to the shore is included except as he chose also to mix his labor with previously non-settled ground. If the latter, it could imply possession of an extensive reach of beach if the industry included land-based operations along with the H_2O or, more likely, a mere right-of-way at one small spot sufficient for the aquatic use.

Regarding joint ownership of both the land and the lake, the homestead could have included farming along part of or around the entire lakeshore as well as fish husbandry within the pond. In fact, a full scope ranching operation involving both land-roving beasts as well as aquatic creatures would be an interesting business. Such an operator would require caretaking not only of the livestock but also of dry and wet forage, farming of feed, and habitat that encourages each species to thrive.

As with oceans and rivers, separate ownership is entirely possible. One homesteader could operate a mine on the lake floor, while another bottled water for sale, and a third ran a sport fishing concession. Potential uses are only limited by the imagination of entrepreneurs, subject only to honoring the property of previous homesteaders.

(2) Property Limits

For a small lake or early in the development process of a large one, exact property lines would likely be un-necessary (as was described in the Oceanological Chapter 7). For small lakes with only one or two owners, there may never be a need for fences.

For larger lakes increasing numbers of residents would boost the occasions of conflict. It would behoove proprietors to establish accurate property demarcations such as survey-able lines and fences. For spatially overlapping uses contractual agreements defining the limits of the original homesteads may become necessary. For example, a lakeside resort with a pleasure boating concession on the water and a fish canning factory could easily co-occupy a tarn.[4] Suppose that some of the vacationers wished to fish. Unless previous arrangements were made, since the cannery owns the fishery, any such act would be theft. However, the resort operator and fisherman could strike a deal where in exchange for value, 100 visitors per year could obtain permission to harvest two fish each, for example. If some guests were avid sportsmen, they could purchase more than one ticket. The resort could even auction off fishing vouchers. The only limit would be that all fish taken, combined, could not exceed 200 per year, unless a higher price were negotiated for a greater harvest.

It may be, however, that when we utilize the Rothbardian notion of "technological unit," that a lake of whatever size may most efficiently and properly be owned by only one party. This single corporation may be owned in turn by numerous stockholders. It is plausible that in the process of converting government owned, that is, unowned, waters into private property that the initial proprietors would be the historic users, in effect, homesteaders. After this new institution is set up, previous owners would be free to sell their interest in the loch to willing buyers.

(3) Access to the Lake Bottom

What is the mechanism for access to the lake bottom if it is under separate ownership for mineral extraction? If the original homesteader was a collier of the floor, then subsequent pioneers must work around his access route. Otherwise, a late arriving miner could attain access only by open negotiation with foregoing owners or underground as by slant drilling or as in the following case.

A consideration of Lake Erie sheds light on the extraction of salt from under water. Cargill (Correa, 2013), as of the time of this writing, has a mine operating beneath the lakebed. Access is from a land based portal in Cleveland, Ohio. This company functions without upsetting any other users. Most people on Erie probably have no idea of the mine's existence. But what if the excavation collapses and all the water drains into the resulting pit?

In that case, Cargill would be liable for all damages to other users.[5] Imagine that the salt dissolves and converts the lake as well as the St Laurence River from fresh to brackish, then what? The company would be liable for that also. It behooves Cargill to eliminate[6] the potential for such problems to develop. For example recent data indicated that convergence[7] could lead towards a potential collapse (Krouse, 2013). Immediately (prior to any government involvement) the mine shut down. Within a couple of weeks, corrective measures to strengthen the structural integrity were implemented; and it was back in operation with no ill effects to Lake Erie (Bull, 2013).

Mining of course is not the only use for a lake floor. No legitimate (i.e. non-state restrictions) reason exists to prevent homeowners from living underwater.[8] Presumably, at least for now before the concept becomes popular, the land would be cheap. In so doing, one would experience a close up connection to nature rarely seen in today's world. Visionaries could invent a new underwater sport such as racing along a lake floor with some sort of bubble vehicle.[9]

(4) Rights of Land Owners Adjacent to a Lake

In order to establish a homestead, personal labor must be mixed with the resource. Should an immigrant come up the river and establish a fish ranch, then the new entrepreneur would have at least fishing and boating rights. Conceivably, the entire lake could be developed with no reference or damage to adjacent settlers.

A more likely scenario is that the landed entrepreneurs would mix their labor with the lake. Then they would possess it according to the nature of their use. Possibly, the first of the many shore bound homesteaders could have taken possession to the entire body of water; or later pioneers might have also established rights. Refer to chapter 7, "Concepts of Oceanological Ownership" for additional information on the establishment of aquatic based homesteads.

Would the land owners adjacent to the lake have the right to leave that body of water totally untouched and therefore unowned, but based on their holdings, prevent all others from homesteading it? They could easily do so, at least in the era before helicopters and other technological breakthroughs that would enable would-be homesteaders to hop over their land holdings. But this would be an invalid act on their part. One difficulty would be that the lake would remain unowned. But this is anathema for the private property libertarian philosophy espoused herein. For just as nature abhors a vacuum, this political perspective eschews any valuable real estate in an unowned state. Ideally, every square inch of the earth should be owned by someone.[10] Secondly, such an act, called forestalling,[11] would logically contradict the homesteading ethos. For this states that man may only control land (or water) with which he has mixed his labor. But, here, in this case, the owners of the surrounding territory would control the lake in the sense of being able to prevent others from bringing it into the economy, without having homesteaded it at all.

(5) Extraction of Water from and Discharge of Material to a Lake

One possible use of an inland lake is extraction of its contents. If the first resident should extract water, he could if he wished pump it entirely dry (assuming the downstream river owner(s) did not already have rights in conflict with such an activity). A homesteader might wish to do so in order to use the H_2O for watering livestock, or he might want to develop additional land. However, the rights of any predecessors must be fulfilled first.

Another possible use is to release material (solid or liquid) into the lake. Once again the reason could be to fill the lake and thereby increase developable land. That could be an advantageous approach if downstream river owners had the rights to that water.[12]

The discharge of pollutants to aqueous assets has been addressed elsewhere in this book.[13] Assuming prior homesteaders are unharmed, one legitimate use of a pond, which can be seen as a large hole in the ground, is to use it as a dump. Admittedly, this sounds horrid. But the logic of private property rights in bodies of water must make room for such an eventuality. We do use some land for garbage disposal. Why should water be exempt from such a fate?[14]

(6) Boating Conflicts

As development continues apace, increasing boat traffic would be expected. Let us say that a power boater is a late arriver. If so, then his speedboat operation necessarily must honor and protect all previous occupants. Damage stemming from his boat to fishing lines, fisheries, shorelines, swimmers, slow sailboats, etc. would fall squarely on his shoulders.

Should a predecessor indulge in a wind sailing business and thereby establish a homestead, then the subsequent operator must not inhibit the experience of the sailor. The current user(s) of a pond might want to establish a joint covenant to enhance and preserve a quiet and peaceful condition.

(7) Insects and Standing Water

Mosquitos exist. They are a fact of life. Mosquitos are a paradigm case of so-called external diseconomies, in mainstream economics. But from the libertarian point of view the analysis of this phenomenon is similar to that of smoke or particle pollution, or noise, or unseemly odors. The perpetrator would be found guilty of a trespass (Rothbard, 1982). A settler in or near a lake has come to the mosquitos, as in "come to the nuisance." Barring trespass, he may implement defenses against these threats. That is to say, he may spray insecticides to reduce the population of irritants.[15] Such activities would be enjoined by prior occupants should they demonstrate damage beyond a shadow of doubt. For example, insects provide forage for fish. An original fishing homesteader would be damaged by the loss of food for his aquatic ranch and/or by any tainting of his product with pesticides that reduce its marketability.

Let us suppose that previous land owners reside in houses adjacent to the shore, or nearby. They are necessarily subjected to mosquito attack. With the caveats above they may take defensive measures. However, should a late-arriving developer cause an undue proliferation of insects that inhibits the enjoyment of the residents, the early residents may enjoin a lake oriented business from doing so.

Putrid standing water, with its noxious "fragrance," is an irritant in and of itself. However, if there was always a stinking swamp, it is up to the immigrants to either live with it or take steps to alleviate the problem. Should someone cause the stale water, then it is he who should be required by a court to clean it up.

NOTES

1. "It is not from the benevolence of the butcher, the brewer, or the baker that we expect our dinner, but from their regard to their own self-interest. We address ourselves not to their

humanity but to their self-love, and never talk to them of our own necessities, but of their advantages." —Adam Smith (1776, I.2.2)

2. In Rothbard's (1982) terminology.

3. Throughout this book, two dimensional terminologies are generally used because of reference to earlier times when people were surface bound. In the modern age of flight, aerial access might be sufficient in some cases. Then, right of entrance by shore and/or waterway would not be included.

4. For the uninitiated a "tarn" is a lake, often but not always an alpine or nordic lake occurring in a glacial cirque.

5. If there is a clear and present danger of this occurring, those affected could apply to a court for a cease and desist injunction. This option would apply especially if the firm would not have enough money to defray the costs of all those who would lose out did this mishap occur. For the argument that downtown nuclear enterprises would be legally verboten in the free society, see Block and Block, 2000.

6. No one can eliminate, in the sense of offering a 100 percent guarantee against, anything. However, this is or at least should be the goal even though the attempt may be unsuccessful.

7. Convergence refers to the ceiling and the floor of a mine approaching each other over time.

8. For a look at proposed and actually existing under water residences refer to: U.S. Submarine Structures, LLC, Undated; and Sorokanich, 2014.

9. Frankly, even to your authors, some ideas look preposterous: AutomotiveTv, 2008; but with the free market there is no telling where creative minds will go or what marvels they will develop.

10. At least at present there are some sub-marginal lands for which it would not pay to homestead: real estate in the wilds of Alaska, Siberia, or, for that matter, on the Moon or Mars. Eventually, hopefully, these areas will become owned, and thus enabled to provide welfare for human beings.

11. See on this Block, 2008. For more detail and an exception see the discussion on Block's Proviso, chapter 7, endnote 37.

12. That is so long as the developer maintained existing flow rates so as to not cause increased flooding.

13. Refer to chapter 7 "Concepts of Oceanological Ownership."

14. This can only be speculative, but perhaps our repugnance at this possibility stems from biology: we all begin life in an aqueous environment, after all.

15. The authors neither endorse nor condemn spraying insecticides. Stocking the lake with insect devouring species would have the similar effect of reducing obnoxious pests. Defensive measures depend strictly on the needs and resources of the lake owners.

Chapter Ten

Aquifers—Concepts of Hydrogeological Ownership

"There is something fascinating about science. One gets such wholesale returns of conjecture out of such a trifling investment of fact." —Mark Twain, *Life on the Mississippi*, 1883

Resolved: Non-ownership of aquifers, those concealed reservoirs of pure water, results in dry wells, polluted drinking water, sinking sand, and a plethora of intractable problems. Secure titles to ground water would equate to a secure, safe, and steady supply of said amenity without damage to others.[1]

Apology: This chapter about groundwater is an intensely scientific subject and is very difficult to make comprehensible on an intuitive basis because it all takes place underground and thus out of sight and out of mind. Very few people (perhaps no one) fully understand the subject. We want to make it understandable; so, please bear with us in our attempt to make the case that aquifers, too, should be privatized. Our hope for this chapter is to at least make a good faith effort in responding to this intellectual challenge.

OBJECTIONS AND SHORT RESPONSES TO PRIVATE OWNERSHIP OF AQUIFERS

The concept "exclusive title to unseen pools" may confound those statists for whom coercive control and a big stick are the only sources of good order. Those who rely on government operate out of fear and dread of shortages, of poisoning, of theft, of innumerable terrorizations. Among these false threats to their welfare are the following:

(1) *Exactly how can grasping tycoons be trusted to own our drinking water? On what basis would it be distributed?*

Who is it that has most succumbed to a grasping insolence? It is not businessmen, who must satisfy their customers. No: the employees of the state only answer to other people with the most arrogant countenance. Ownership goes to those who discover and put to positive use the subsurface water. It is this love of creativity that advances not only such entrepreneurs but all of culture.

(2) *Posit that a Town A aggressively pumps water from an aquifer and, since the water seeks a level surface, none is available to a user B, 10 miles away? How would B prove that his rights have been violated?*

This objection is the precise reason to favor ownership of subterranean resources, including groundwater. As with all commonly held amenities without clear titles, anyone with a drill and a pump is motivated to take water as fast as possible before it can be removed by others. The ubiquitous result is high and unsustainable use until mining the resource causes it to go dry. A clearly established proprietor will look to his own interest and only use it at the general rate of recharge.[2]

(3) *Should person A lower the pressure of an aquifer and thereby cause an artesian spring[3] being utilized by brewery B to go dry, is A responsible for damages?*

Assuming that the brewer was the original homesteader, then A is responsible and is liable to recharge the aquifer to its original artesian pressure. If A was prior to B in terms of homesteading this particular property right, then B has no just complaint. Again, this would be precisely the analysis used were there any conflict between two land owners, and there is no reason that would change matters merely because the issue now concerns water resources.

(4) *Suppose a farmer extracts water from a collapsible soil and the ground surface subsides leaving his neighbors in a newly created flood zone?*

In the first place, the farmer is a thief if he engages in such an act and does not own the aquifer or at least a share of it. Secondly, if the proprietor of the subsurface resource was the original homesteader, he has every right to cause subsidence.

(5) *What if a bunch of Johnny-come-latelies draw from groundwater hydraulically connected to a river; and, thereby, deny irrigation farmers the rights they homesteaded, some as long as 100 years ago via their predecessor owners? How would the victims prove it?*

The prior surface water claimants own their rights and the late arrivers are thieves. Proving it follows from the concept that water pumped from the ground does not appear as if by magic. Specific proof pointing to an exact offender would necessitate a hydrogeological study which would probably be rather complex. Appeal to the courts could be necessary.

GENERAL HYDROGEOLOGICAL CONSIDERATIONS

If ownership of aquifers (refer to Fig. 10–1 for definitions of the terms used herein[4]) and groundwater is to become a reality, this concept must take into account water extracted (or pumped from underground), fluid flow, underground rivers, soil structure, permeability rate[5] , pollution, unconfined aquifers, confined aquifers, artesian water, the interaction between surface and subsurface water, ground subsidence[6] , etc.

As shown in Fig. 10.2, excessive pumping of groundwater from an aquifer has serious consequences for surface features. Pumping creates a drawdown cone.[7] As a result, the gradient of the phreatic water surface[8] steepens, and the flow rate increases. Where the soil structure of the aquifer is weak, or if the fluid helped support the structure, extraction can cause collapse and result in ground subsidence.

The removal of water reduces the natural outflow to the surface (for example, at springs). Thus, rivers and lakes receive a smaller discharge, and the owners of these facilities suffer a loss. Slow hydraulic conductivity (say 1 foot per day for a given aquifer), as compared to surface flow (say 10 feet per second for a high plains river with a moderate slope), effects a delay in observable consequences of pumping on surface water. The reduction in this regard can occur years, decades, or even on occasion centuries after the onset of pumping: the less permeable the soil media, the longer the deferral. Never-the-less, if a homesteader has established a surface water right, the late arriving user who pumps would be stealing. The theft could remain undetected for years. This is all the more reason to support/allow the installation of a private environmental forensics industry.

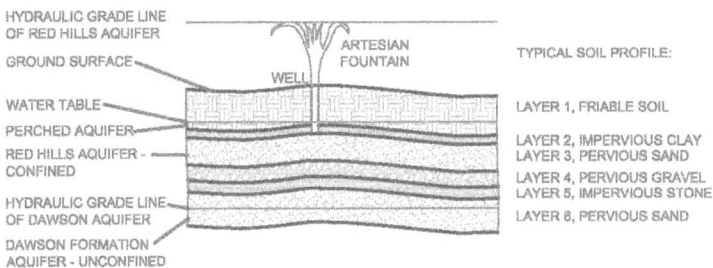

Figure 10.1.   Simplified Illustration of Aquifers

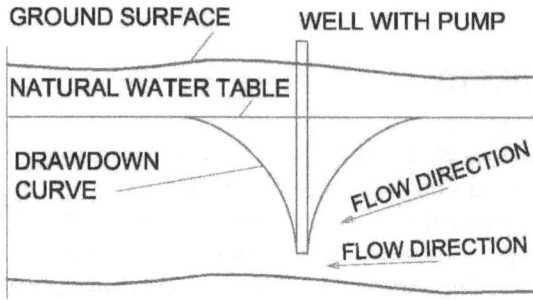

Figure 10.2. Phreatic Water Surface

The dynamics within the structure itself needs consideration. In an unconfined aquifer, the water seeks a level surface. When pumping occurs, fluid
flows from under all adjacent properties towards the well. Without responsible owners, everyone is motivated to mine this resource as fast as possible.
The same applies to a confined aquifer because the energy head[9] also seeks a
level surface. Pumping will lower that elevation thereby increasing the effort
needed to extract a given amount of fluid. Once again, flow towards the point
of withdrawal will occur.

(1) Determining Ownership of Subsurface Water

Ownership goes too those who discover and put to positive use the subsurface water. Through the act of drilling to find water, an entrepreneur mixes
his labor with a natural resource. In performing this act, he makes it an
extension of his being. Self-ownership thereby implies ownership of the well.

That is acceptable as a first approximation, but certain complicating facts
intrude into this simple idyllic state of affairs. If the digger is the first to
withdraw water from an aquifer, and if it is not a tributary to the property of a
downstream river owner, then this simple description may apply. If because
of this mining, a surface water body goes dry,[10] things become decidedly
more complex. It could turn out that the aquifer is in fact already owned by
previous homesteaders of surface resources.

Wells have been used for millennia. Even the first chapter of the Book of
Genesis implies that wells were in use.[11] Clearly a well dating back that far
can be assumed to include prior water rights.

So, who owns the water after all? An accounting of the relationship
between surface and groundwater is necessary.

(2) Pumping of Groundwater

The fact that water seeks a level surface is favorable to private ownership of subterranean fluids. Should the H_2O be extracted[12] from one location, it will flow from all other areas within the aquifer. Referring to the phreatic water surface as shown by Fig. 10–2, we see that a flow develops in the direction of the pump, from all directions. In short, the level of the groundwater is lowered throughout the aquifer.

Without clear titles, anyone with a drill and a pump is motivated to extract the water as fast as possible before others can take it. The omnipresent consequence is unsustainable withdrawal until excessive mining causes total depletion. Under this tragedy of the commons condition, those who own a well cannot depend on it. A secure proprietor will look to his own long-term interest and only use it at the general rate of recharge.

What if a cheater does take too much despite being revealed as a water thief? Other interested parties would enjoin him from further pumping; they would obtain a court injunction against such a practice, along with damages for water loss. As for that which was already consumed, he could be required to purchase sufficient liquid to restore the previous level. This operation would be very expensive to the point that the wise user will not want to face those consequences. And what are those expenses? First he must buy, presumably lots of, water from those who have had their own plans disrupted. Then he must pump it back into the aquifer. But it will not flow easily back into the ground. It will require much effort, i.e. much expensive energy. This is especially true if the aquifer is under pressure.

How would the victim prove it in court? The water surface can be measured. Should the water surface increase or decrease, then pumping is occurring at a rate that varies from the recharge rate. In the event of multiple owners, the pump records would expose the culprit.

(3) Artesian Aquifers

Artesian aquifers refer to the situation where the hydraulic grade line is higher than the ground level as shown in Fig. 10–1. A well dug into the water body results in a fountain the height of which is the energy potential minus the losses from the pipe friction and the exit (nozzle).[13] If the extraction exceeds the recharge, the pressure will dissipate until natural springs stop flowing.

Using the hypothetical brewery as an example, a Person C can indeed lower the pressure of an aquifer and thereby cause severe damage. Assuming that the brewery was the original homesteader, then C must keep his mitts off of the property of B. If C has already trespassed in this manner, then his punishment must at least include the requirement that he recharge the aquifer to the pressure upon which B relied. The expenses mentioned above would become astronomical. C might even have to buy out B, which would then give him a useless facility.

The situation becomes even more complex should there be an A who used downstream surface water from a river, which depended on the discharge from the aquifer, prior to either C or B. If so, then A's right takes precedence. That is to say that if the order of the development was A followed by B followed by C, then successive users must honor the preceding homesteaders.

(4) Collapsible Soil

Some soil may not be self-supporting or may undergo changes when it dries. Being incompressible, water may help provide structural support. Consider clay in a dry lake bed which cracks into polygonal shaped chunks when dry. The loss of water causes the material to shrink. When the depletion is underground, subsidence of the surface may result.

Another mechanism for loss of strength is underground erosion. If water moves rapidly, it may remove material and wash it downstream. The loss of material undermines the ground thereby causing the collapse of the surface. Some material such as limestone even dissolves and washes away as a liquid with the same result.

With due consideration of these processes, a farmer who extracts water from a collapsible soil and, thus, causes the ground surface to subside bears full responsibility for all damages that result. Should his actions leave his neighbors in a newly created flood zone, he must pay to make his victims whole. That could imply recharging the aquifer, if possible,[14] providing flood protection devices, or even buying the damaged property at the pre-damage price according to a court's evaluation.

This issue could become quite complex if a farmer has started to mine the aquifer. As long as surface development by other homesteaders has not occurred, then there is no harm and thus no foul. However, let us say that after surface development has proceeded apace, he decides to *increase* his pumping rate. Assume the new rate of extraction creates a negative pressure in the aquifer (read: suction). The process could cause the soil to collapse. Where conditions get this complex, the intermediation of the courts would be necessary on a case by case[15] basis. If the new developers can prove their case that it was only after they arrived that the pumping was increased and that caused the damage, then the farmer would be liable.[16]

(5) Late Arriving Groundwater Miners

It frequently happens that a bunch of Johnny-come-latelies draw from groundwater hydraulically connected to a river. They, thereby, deny water to surface water users with rights that were homesteaded many decades ago, and/or purchased from these owners. Such people steal this resource from these rightful proprietors.

Consideration needs to be made for the fact that the damage may not become apparent for an elongated time span. Proving it involves extensive engineering studies to trace the route of groundwater. Solid proof may remain elusive.[17] Surface water users may seek injunctive relief against water miners who they believe are stealing their assets. For such a complex situation, court adjudication may be the only reasonable path towards resolution.

An essential component of subsurface cases is whether the body of water is fully utilized.[18] Since the effects of pumping do not take effect on surface water until years later, one cannot simply call for the extracted water to be delivered, i.e., the shortage this year resulted from what was pumped and consumed years ago. That suggests severe limits on mining. On-the-other-hand, the drastic limitation of extracted subsurface resources could result in lots of wastage in most years if everyone is using only what can be counted upon. That suggests basing limitations on wet years. This conflict, which is built into the natural water cycle, further buttresses the need for active protection of one's resources and early adjudication before problems develop. Who is properly motivated to track down this information? Only property owners who have a personal interest in their assets care enough to exercise the necessary diligence. Government officials do not have the time, the budget, or, frankly, the interest to understand the dynamics of a particular aquifer. In addition, they would still lack the market's automatic feedback mechanism even if they did. When an entrepreneur errs, he loses his own money; do this too often, and bankruptcy is the inevitable result, assuming free enterprise and no "too big, or too connected, to fail" mechanism in operation. In contrast, when a government bureaucrat fails, and they are human too,[19] so this must occur, it is a rare occurrence when their function is eliminated: for example, the US Post Office, the IRS, Fannie and Freddie, the Fed, those who made the decision to subsidize Solyndra, etc.

NOTES

1. It would be amazing were this not true in the present case. The manifest benefits of private property rights applies to everything else under the sun: to species survival, to problems with Soviet collectivized farms, to roads. . . . If we own it, we take better care of it. The tragedy of the commons really is a tragedy. On species extinction see Anderson and Hill, 1995; French, 2012; Lora, 2007; Kreuter and Platts, 1996; Simmons and Kreuter, 1989; Anderson and Hill, 1995; Benjamin, 2012; DiLorenzo, 1998; Malek, 2007; Simon, 1981, 1996; on USSR farms,

Allen, 2009; Belov, 1955; Eberstadt, 1988; Feshbach and Friendly, 1992; Grossman, 1985; Nove, 1993; Nutter, 1957; Pejovich, 1979; Sakoff, 1962; Smith, 1976; on roads, Block, 2009C. On commons tragedies, critiques of Ostrom, Block, 2011B; Jankovic and Block, Forthcoming.

2. Recharge, in this application, refers to the addition of water to an aquifer whether natural or intentional. Pumping at a faster rate than recharge amounts to mining. As with all mining, depletion results. We do not assert no mining of water will ever take place. Mining of other natural resources does occur. We only aver that if it does, it will be because profit and loss considerations point in this direction. For example, aquifers would run dry if population is decreasing, the projected future uses are of insufficient present discounted value to justify conservation, or other cheaper sources of water are expected to come on stream.

3. "Artesian" refers to an aquifer where the hydraulic grade line is higher than the ground elevation. Pumping from the aquifer could lower the hydraulic grade line and cause un-pumped sources to stop flowing. Refer below to the hydraulic sketches.

4. The soil profile and aquifers represented in the illustration do not relate to any particular real life situation but rather illustrate typical geological formations that one might find in nature.

5. Warning! Scientific content follows: Permeability refers to the capacity of soil to pass water and is proportional to the hydraulic conductivity (K, a measurement of the speed of water though the soil). For relatively impermeable clay, K can be on the order of 0.0001 feet per day or slower (speed is distance divided by time similar to miles per hour). For sand and gravel with lots of open space interspersed in it, K can range from 100- to 1000- feet or more per day. Water in a layer of sand and gravel overlain by clay is a confined aquifer if filled to capacity, and pressure can develop. Should one drill into an aquifer under high enough pressure, an artesian fountain will occur. "Unconfined" means that the K value of the overlying soils is high enough that pressure cannot develop or that the aquifer is not full. What about puddles that won't evaporate? Such small bodies of water will always evaporate. If the puddle remains, it either has a water supply to replace evaporation; or the humidity is constantly at 100% (which never happens—except maybe in New Orleans, the home of one of your co-authors). Does this mean the aquifer is over-full? No, just that it is under pressure. Increasing the pressure has very little if any influence on capacity. If pressure increases too much, something will break, but the contained capacity will not increase. Balloons are an exception.

6. Subsidence refers to the gradual movement of ground to a lower elevation. It can occur because of dissolving of underlying rock such as limestone (a natural phenomenon), removal of water that provided part of the structural support (natural or manmade), underground mining (manmade) to name a few causes.

7. Refer to Fig. 10–2. A drawdown cone derives from the fact that a pump removes water from the aquifer faster than it can flow towards the well. The deeper the "funnel," the faster it can be discharged to the surface.

8. Refer to Chapter 1 for a detailed explanation. The vector of the slope of the phreatic surface indicates the direction of movement in an unconfined aquifer.

9. The energy head equals the phreatic water surface (straight horizontal line as shown in Fig. 10–2) or the potential energy plus the velocity head. The velocity head equals the velocity (speed of the fluid in a given direction) or the kinetic energy squared divided by two times the gravitational constant (32.2 ft^2/s for the planet earth).

10. There is an analogue on the land regarding the construction of a tunnel under someone else's property. How deep must the new construction be? (We now assume arguendo, that the *ad coelum* doctrine which states that the owner of acreage on the surface of the earth owns the decreasing cone-shaped territory down to the center of the earth doctrine, is false). The tunnel cannot be so close to the surface that it ruins the other man's crops, or caves in his buildings. The depth will depend upon the quality of the material involved. If it is under Manhattan, which is solid rock, the underground construction may come quite close to the island's street level. If it is built on a swamp, a thousand pardons, a wetland, such as New Orleans, the tunnel must be placed very far down, so as to not cause any damage to other's property. For more on this see Block, 2009C.

11. Refer to Genesis 1:6–8. What is being described is a flat conception of the earth's orb. The word רקיע (raqiya) refers to a covering as for example gold leaf covering a carving (compare

its verbal root רָקַע (riqqua) [hammer out], Num. 16:38). The usual translation of the Genesis application into other languages is a word, such as the Latin *firmamentum*, meaning "dome." (The word "expanse" from the cognitively similar expansion of metal into a "spacious" thin sheet has also been used.) This dome functioned to separate "the waters below from the waters above." Of relevance to this discussion is the term "the waters below." Whether one hiked downhill to the shore or dug deep enough, one found water. The ancients must have dug wells down to the water table to know this.

12. Herein wells are assumed to include pumps according to modern practice. In the strictest sense pumps are not necessary. In earlier times buckets attached to a rope were lowered into the water. Before that stairs were formed within wells, and people would hike down to the wet surface.

13. Energy losses refer to the conversion of kinetic energy to heat. Typical losses in flowing fluids include friction, bends, entrance (as to a pipe), exit, branch connections, impediments, expansions, and contractions. The amount of loss is dependent on such characteristics as roughness, velocity, and shape.

14. Because of the potential for extreme pressure and/or irreversible changes to soil charac- teristics, recharging an aquifer to restore a previous ground surface elevation may not be possible.

15. But the libertarian principles of homesteading, first user, private property rights, etc., would remain invariant. However, judges must always stand by to resolve close calls, disputes, grey areas, continuum problems. The reader is reminded that, in this book, "courts" refer to private for-profit mediation companies.

16. A similar pattern occurs with airport noise. If the planes were there first, they have the right to emit a given decibel level. Any homeowner who builds later on "comes to the nui- sance," and would have no case in a libertarian law court. However, if the airport *increases* its level of noise by a discernable amount, then and only then would the neighbors have a legiti- mate cause for damages and injunctive relief.

17. As an example of the potential for complexity in determining culpability, the reader is referred to Hood (2014).

18. Would that mean "fully utilized" in a dry year? We are talking about aquifers here; dry years will generally not have any effect within the space of single season.

19. This is something of a concession on our part.

Chapter Eleven

Mainstream Views
on Ocean Management

"I wish to have no connection with any ship that does not sail fast; for I intend
to go in harm's way." —John Paul Jones, Letter to Le Ray de Chaumont, 1778

This chapter addresses international agreements regarding environmental
amenities, which have implications for aqueous ownership: CITES and UN-
CLOS as well as another mainstream initiative: Greenpeace.

CONVENTION ON INTERNATIONAL TRADE OF ENDANGERED
SPECIES OF WILD FAUNA AND FLORA

What are the views of the powers that be in terms of oceans and the fauna
and flora that lie within these bodies of water? One of the leading groups that
may be considered in this regard is the Convention on International Trade in
Endangered Species of Wild Fauna and Flora (CITES). It is self-described as
". . . an international agreement between governments. Its aim is to ensure
that international trade in specimens of wild animals and plants does not
threaten their survival."[1]

Even at the very outset, their target can be seen as highly problematic.
For, if the goal is to preserve species, then how can *trade*[2] in these species
possibly "threaten their survival?" For trade enhances the value of anything,
and the more valuable something is, the more likely it is to be preserved. So
if preservation is the desiderata, one would think that every effort would be
made to *enhance* trade, not to reduce it, or, worse, ban it.

Before turning to saving sea creatures, let us consider the record of
CITES with regard to land animals, such as elephants. Unhappily, it illus-

trates a commitment to the deleterious prejudices of socialism.[3] According to this organization, the best, indeed the only way to preserve these creatures is to keep them unowned, and ban trade in their tusks and other valuable body parts. But this is the exact opposite direction to go in, if that is indeed the goal. For prohibition courts the tragedy of the commons. When everyone in effect "owns" the elephant, no one really does. Whereas, in sharp contrast, if there are specific ranchers who have these animals as their private property, they tend to take care of them, protect them. They might even allow hunters to shoot them, for a relatively steep fee, and use such funds to further safeguard their herds. Likely, they would charge much more for a pregnant member of this species than for an old male, or a female past the age of reproduction. An analogy arises with regard to the cow and the buffalo.[4] The former were traditionally owned on a private basis, and never came within a million miles of extinction. The latter were allowed to roam free, and were hunted until their very existence was endangered. If a cattleman slaughtered one of his charges, he paid a high fee: the alternative cost of a cow tomorrow; he would only do so if the benefits outweighed these significant costs. If he shot a buffalo when they were unowned, he paid no price at all,[5] since he would not have had that creature on the next day in any case. The benefits would thus far outweigh virtually any nonexistent costs. But the elephant, as far as the economist is concerned, is merely the economic equivalent of a massive buffalo exposed once too often to a crocodile beside the "great grey-green, greasy Limpopo River."[6] The two cases are functionally identical. Privatization, commerce, ability to export spells species preservation.

The CITES policy is a recipe for extinction. Why? The ever present problem of poachers will not go away despite the most draconian prohibitions of the most violent bureaucrats. No matter how clever environmentalists craft their legislation, creative people will adapt and find a way to get around it. Even worse is that the more perfidious the measures, the more profitable will be ignoring them. Rustlers find flouting these officials easy and morally acceptable because since the property is unowned, the idea that this activity is theft is left unclear.

But the same applies to denizens of the deep, whether whales, or fish. If they are owned privately, their continuation is assured. Under present institutional arrangements, they are greatly endangered, by the same tragedy of the commons that prevails in the barnyard.

Klein (2014) points to yet another failure of the bureaucrats now in charge of this sector of the economy:

> "This year's silly Copenhagen Zoo controversy reminded us that, when it comes to animal care, people have difficulty thinking clearly. NPR's *Planet Money* ran an interesting piece this morning about animal barter among zoos. The US Endangered Species Act and global treaties such as the Convention on

International Trade of Endangered Species of Wild Fauna and Flora make it a crime to buy and sell zoo animals like other commodities. This makes it difficult for zoos not only to obtain new animals, but also to get rid of existing, unwanted ones. (Hence the fate of poor Marius the giraffe.)

"To get around these rules, zoos have adopted a complex and cumbersome barter system. Zoos are, under the law, allowed to make animal-for-animal swaps. But, as economists such as Carl Menger explained more than a century ago, barter is hampered by the double coincidence of wants: to trade with you, it's not enough that I want what you have; you also have to want what I have. Money eliminates the double coincidence of wants by introducing a third commodity that serves as a generally accepted medium of exchange. Unfortunately for the zoos, money is off the table. And hence:

"The New England Aquarium in Boston was recently in the market for some lookdown fish, and they knew of an aquarium in North Carolina that was willing to trade some.

"The folks in North Carolina wanted jellyfish and snipe fish. The New England Aquarium had plenty of jellyfish—but no snipe fish.

"Steve Bailey, the curator of fish at the New England Aquarium, wound up making a deal to get snipe fish from an aquarium in Japan, in exchange for lumpfish. Then he sent the snipe fish and some jellyfish to North Carolina. In exchange, he finally got his lookdown fish."

Allowing zoos to buy and sell animals using money, rather than complex and inefficient barter arrangements—why, that would be SO inhumane!

THE UNITED NATIONS
CONVENTION ON THE LAW OF THE SEA

What is the U.N. Law of the Sea Treaty? "The United Nations Convention on the Law of the Sea (UNCLOS), also called the Law of the Sea Convention or the Law of the Sea Treaty, is the international agreement that resulted from the third United Nations Conference on the Law of the Sea (UNCLOS III), which took place between 1973 and 1982" (Law of the Sea, Undated). And what, pray tell, does this agreement provide? Its main provision, in terms of the interests of the present book is the following: ". . . the General Assembly of the United Nations solemnly declared *inter alia* that the area of the seabed and ocean floor and the subsoil thereof, beyond the limits of national juris-diction, as well as its resources, are the common heritage of mankind, the exploration and exploitation of which shall be carried out for the benefit of mankind as a whole, irrespective of the geographical location of States. . . ." This is more than passingly curious. It claims (partial) ownership status in the oceans for landlocked countries.[7] But, what did these countries do to deserve such wealth? To be sure, if any of the citizens of these nations *did* something to buttress such a claim, that would be one thing. But this sea convention asserts they have a right to such largesse merely by existing; this requires absolutely no effort on their part.

Suppose this doctrine were applied to other arenas. Consider the situation should all the oil wealth, or all the violins on the planet, be the "common heritage" of all mankind. That is, that an aliquot share of these goods was to be owned by each and every one of the some seven billion people now alive. What would be the implication of such a policy? As with any commons, the incentives to protect, develop, create, and defend oil and/or violins would be seriously atrophied. It would be a heroic assumption to posit any other result with regard to the oceans and their riches. Namely, this "common owner-ship" would sound the death knell for that which would putatively be "owned." It would disappear. This is not to say that if the entirety of mankind owned the oceans all the water would vanish, but if this disastrous U.N. policy were ever implemented, much of its value certainly would be dimin-ished.

In addition to the economic inefficiency, there is also the matter of sheer justice. Why should people get to own shares in property—whether violins, oil, or water—with no connection to them whatsoever? In due course, the progeny in each of these places will come to control the acreage in his own area, but not that in the other. The U.N. policy sets all of this asunder, with its pronunciamentos to the contrary.

GREENPEACE

Greenpeace is an organization that supposedly advocates "on behalf" of the world for the health of oceans. It fancies itself as a forward thinking and radical party of activists using "peaceful protest and creative communica-tion" (Greenpeace, 2014) to achieve its goals. Yet their tactics often seem to more closely resemble those of John Paul Jones and his craving for fast boats to ram fishing ships as opposed to Henry David Thoreau living peaceably on Walden Pond. As shown herein, Greenpeace is really a rather commonplace and mainstream, though quixotic, purveyor of a criminal philosophy. It has been known to commit felonious acts on the high seas. On its web site, the following mission statement is proclaimed. With a couple of notable excep-tions, it recommends the standard failed aquasocialist agenda to which virtu-ally all powerbrokers subscribe:

> "Ocean health is central to our mission . . . And despite the many threats and challenges our ocean faces, we know that change is possible. But change will only come if people come together, bravely and loudly, and demand change from their governments, retailers, and neighbors.

- "We can end overfishing by putting limits . . . on the methods and practices of industrial fishing companies and factory fishing vessels.READ MORE about overfishing
- "We can . . . start to rebuild fish and whale populations by pushing the international community to set aside marine reserves . . . , particularly in the high seas, waters not part of any country's territory. READ MORE about marine reserves
- "If consumers are aware of the impact of their shopping practices, they can join us to force change through seafood markets. We can foster a vigorous market for sustainable seafood by pushing our retailers and producers. READ MORE about sustainable seafood
- ". . . we can demand that our governments . . . pursue national and international policies that make outdated, unnecessary practices like whaling and overfishing of tuna illegal. READ MORE about whaling
- "We can preserve vital ocean habitats teeming with life, keeping those places safe from destructive fishing practices. At Greenpeace USA, we are starting with the Bering Sea's Zhemchug and Pribilof canyons, massive underwater canyons home to countless critical species.READ MORE about the Bering Sea

"All of these individual campaigns are united by one core goal: . . . It is time the global community makes a good faith effort to set aside a large portion of the oceans as marine reserves . . . Marine reserves are places where destructive or extractive practices, like fishing, dumping, whaling, and other industrial activities, are forbidden.

"Currently only one percent of the world's oceans are set aside as marine reserves. Consider that 70 percent of the planet is covered by oceans. Consider also that a full 13 percent of land is under protection. We have exploited the oceans so fully that habitats and marine life need time—and above all, space—to recover. One percent is just not enough.

"For too long, we have treated the oceans as a global commons that anybody can exploit [SIC]

"Global oceans deserve our respect and protection.

"That is why . . . we are advocating for a series of connected marine reserves comprising up to 40 percent of ocean area. . . . That includes connected areas in countries' exclusive economic zones, as well as areas in the high seas, which no nation can claim."

First the good news: Greenpeace acknowledges that the deep waters have been treated as a "global commons," and they furthermore imply that this has led to a lack of respect and protection. Your present authors heartily agree that "oceans deserve our respect and protection."

Unfortunately, the good news ends right there. For their prescriptions to improve the status of these bodies of water are entirely wrongheaded. Even as they complain that "we"[8] have treated the high seas as a commons, they advocate making 40 percent of the ocean, wait for it

..., a "commons" in the form of marine reserves. As is all too typical of statists; their customary answer is to initiate force against the innocent. Like the average bureaucrat (Mises, 1969), the leaders of this body see the population of this planet as a group of static entities unable or unwilling to react to an intrusion against their freedom. Throughout all of history, when the powers that be have set aside preserves, poachers have overcome those initiatives.

The fact of the matter is that such approaches as Greenpeace promotes create artificial shortages. For example, their tract refers to the "overfishing of tuna." Rather than advocating profit-based businesses that rely on a healthy school of fish for their livelihood to husband this fish, they want to restrict by 40 percent the areas of the earth's surface where they can be caught (as if that would not predictably increase the pressure in the other 60 percent to compensate). Assuming in defiance of logic that their actions were in fact successful in limiting the global take of this tasty species, the price can be expected to rise, and if wildly effective catapult to a level similar to, say, heroin. As with any other prohibited or severely limited substance, illegal activity would abound. Police would be corrupted. Violence would become endemic.

On the contrary, private owners of tuna would cherish their asset and be well motivated to keep the population healthy.[9] Unlike bureaucrats with no personal stake, maguro[10] harvesters would protect their charges as though their very lives depended of it, because they would.

NOTES

1. For the full convention, see, Cites, 1973.
2. "Trade" and private ownership are diametrically opposed to theft and commons.
3. Socialism is about cooperation "or else." In the end, the person who demands the freedom to own an elephant must, like the victim of the Inquisition, recant or be killed. What Cites proposes is, as Doug Casey frequently says, not just the wrong thing to do, but the exact opposite of the right thing. Refer to Anderson and Hill, 1995; French, 2012; Lora, 2007; Kreuter and Platts, 1996; Simmons and Kreuter, 1989; U.S. Fish, 2013.
4. Anderson and Hill, 1995; Benjamin, 2012; DiLorenzo, 1998; Malek, 2007; Simon, 1981, 1996.
5. No price other than the bullet and related costs of hunting.
6. The reference is to Rudyard Kipling's *Just So Stories*; "The Elephant's Child," a mythical account of a crocodile giving a young animal (similar in many respects to a buffalo) a long funny nose.
7. Included are such landlocked countries as Andorra, Armenia, Austria, Belarus, Czech Republic, Hungary, Kazakhstan, Liechtenstein, Luxembourg, Macedonia, Moldova, San Marino, Serbia, Slovakia, Switzerland and Vatican City in Europe; Armenia, Afghanistan, Kazakhstan, Kyrgyzstan, Tajikistan, Turkmenistan, Uzbekistan, Nepal, Bhutan, Laos, and Mongolia in Asia; Botswana, Burkina Faso, Burundi, South Sudan, Chad, Central Africa Republic, Ethiopia, Lesotho, Malawi, Mali, Niger, Rwanda, Swaziland, Uganda, Zambia, and Zimbabwe in Africa; and Paraguay and Bolivia in South America.

8. This is an example of the infamous WE, an indefinite appellation intended to draw everyone in to a feeling of guilt and a sense that "something must be done." That something inevitably entails violence against those who have violated no rights.

9. For more on the means and methods for proprietorship of aqueous species, refer to Chapter 7, "Ocean–Concepts of Oceanological Ownership."

10. Maguro is the Japanese term for bluefin tuna. Ahi (yellow fin) and albacore are other popular tunas. Toro, especially otoro from the belly of maguro, is the most prized for sushi as it melts in the mouth like butter. At one time, the samurai of Japan would not eat tuna as it was considered unclean. My, my, how things change!

Chapter Twelve

Piracy

"But when he disposes of his outside enemies by coming to terms with some, and killing others, and has nothing to fear from them, then, I suppose, his first measure is to be constantly stirring up wars, so that the people may require a general." —Plato, *Republic*

A BRIEF HISTORY

An unfortunate reality of life in this world means thieves will inflict harm on the innocent, especially those who are perceived as wealthy. The ocean is no different than the continents in this respect. And what target of opportunity exceeds a huge ship plying the seven seas? These behemoths transport a giddy array of highly valued goods that are already loaded on single self-portable vessels in which a raider can sail away. The word for these robbers is "pirate," and piracy is their "trade."[1]

In the days of the Greek merchant fleet 25 centuries ago, sea robbers would lie in wait for traders sailing the Mediterranean Sea with olive oil, grain, papyrus, spices, wine, linen, and other valued commodities. Capturing a Greek cargo vessel would yield much value to the perpetrators. Defensive measures included the Greek light trireme which had the speed and power to catch and dispatch these pirates. Navies are discussed below.

Through the ages, many local cultures, from the Vikings of Scandinavia and the buccaneers of the Caribbean through the corsairs of Tripoli, were based on such thievery. Most frequently in ancient times, the cargo would be stolen and either used or sold. More recently, pirates would demand ransom to return the ship, cargo, and crew.

Modern Pirates

Pirates continue to attack merchant vessels on the high seas. They attack their prey from simple, fast, small, low-cost boats. They are armed with weapons from machine guns to machetes. They are equipped with grappling hooks and ladders with which to board a large ship.

The typical object of these modern buccaneers is ransom.[2] The victims and their boat are interned in port until payment is received. Of course certain objects such as guns and ammunition would be highly prized for their own sake. The real question is this: In this day and age why is piracy still a problem? When looking at a massive, mobile container in comparison to a small wooden craft of doubtful seaworthiness, we must ask: Why? How can this happen? The answer is that merchantmen are out in a watery wilderness with no protection. Granted there are naval vessels around that could overcome the typical pirate vessel with a single shot. But they cannot be everywhere and all too often are not nearly fast enough to arrive at an altercation until it is too late. Of course that has been the reason this most contemptible occupation has paid well in all eras from the trireme to the guided missile frigate.

RESPONSES TO PIRACY

Navy, as a State Run Entity

One approach to piracy, the predominant one in the world today, is the state-run navy. In general, pirates cannot compete with the sea-going armed force of a major super power. They cannot outrun these armies of the world's waters. Likewise in ancient times, the light trireme (without a deck) was the fastest ship on the ocean in its day. But, like the "policeman who is never there when you need him," these vessels could not be everywhere.

Neither can these reprobates[3] out-gun government forces, though as this book is being written, there is a rumor that a terrorist group, al-Qaeda or ISIL, may be able to take possession of some nuclear weapons (Cefaratti, 2014; Dalrymple, 2014; Carroll, 2014). Those are very powerful and could easily be used in piracy. Although usually pirates like to keep their prey intact so they can enjoy the value of what they steal. This weapon or its threat would enable ocean robbers to battle on somewhat more even terms with even strong nation states.

For the libertarian, the state navy will not do. The sailors and their political bosses have no real interest in safe-guarding the property of merchant ship owners. They exist to protect the state and enhance its power. So, yes, it will respond if a citizen is being attacked; and, more to the point, if it is convenient for the navy. But its main functions are to resist or prevent an invasion of the territory of the state and to bring more *lebensraum*[4] and victims under its tutelage.

Its activities are often ethically dubious. It may, and frequently does, turn its guns on its own citizens if they are conducting disapproved business. Even aircraft carriers have been used to interdict merchantmen carrying disallowed plant materials (Salonia, 1990; Ahart, 1991). The sailors on board frigates and cutters will be more than willing to launch an unprovoked attack on passenger ships transporting people without the "proper" (read state approved) documentation.

Then there is the financing. State navies are supported by conscripted funds, or "money" that is created out of thin air by government fiat. So a person living in the middle of Nebraska who has never seen the sea, is forced against his will to pay for a bunch of excessively expensive floating weapons of war. The libertarian disapproves this kind of violence. Others should too.

As if that were not bad enough there is also the question of personnel. A state navy is manned by either slaves or mercenaries. Conscripted sailors fall into the former category. They "serve" under threat of sanctions like fines, jail, or worse. Libertarians call it involuntary servitude. In the United States it is supposed to be prohibited by the 14th Amendment to the Constitution, though that corrupted arbiter known as the Supreme Court, disagrees.[5] What else would it say since it is an arm of the state?

Often times, conscripts are kidnap victims. Prior to the War of 1812, British naval vessels would detain American ships and press the mariners into their crew. Press gangs would roam the streets of London kidnapping people without notice. Why are navies corrupt? They are often manned by slaves, and people in that wretched condition do as they are told or suffer violent consequences.

If the state navy is not manned by slaves, then it is a mercenary armed force. However, even when there appears to be a voluntary aspect to paid service, that may not be entirely so. During the Vietnam War, many sailors were there because it was preferable to toting an M-16 through the steaming jungle where snipers were waiting to take pot shots at them. If the poor bloke's only choices are slavery in the infantry or "service" in the navy, what kind of mercenary is that? Simply, it is not. It is slavery disguised.

Mercenaries are sellouts to the state. They are distinguished from volunteers and honest providers of protection. The former provide enforcement to the government's edicts. Sailors of fortune do not limit their violence to the pirates who attack innocent traders; they go after whoever has incurred the wrath of the state. When transporters of unapproved arms, chemicals, or persons are set upon by protection squads of sailors, the mercenaries effectively become pirates.

Privateers

Privateers are a form of private navy contracted to the state. They offer one layer of separation from direct state employee status. But they are still beholden to the state. Perhaps it is because of the relative freedom and departure from straight government regulation that the Constitution of the United States allowed for Letters of Mark and Reprisal.[6]

As shown in the Fig. 12.1, the Brig Prince Neufchatel captained by Nicholas Millin, was granted a Letter of Marque by President James Madison on December 12, 1814 to subdue and seize "any armed or unarmed British vessel public or private…" That is to say a person who has nothing to do with the war, who, indeed, may oppose the war, but who happens to be flying the "wrong" flag, is susceptible to attack according to this document. In libertarian terms, Captain Millin would be an aggressor, and James Madison would be a conspirator before the fact. This is not just.

As with state navies, privateers are motivated to launch unprovoked attacks on innocent victims who are conducting business activities not approved by the host country. When they are hired by the state, they must, like the navy, do as they are contracted to do. That might include the same

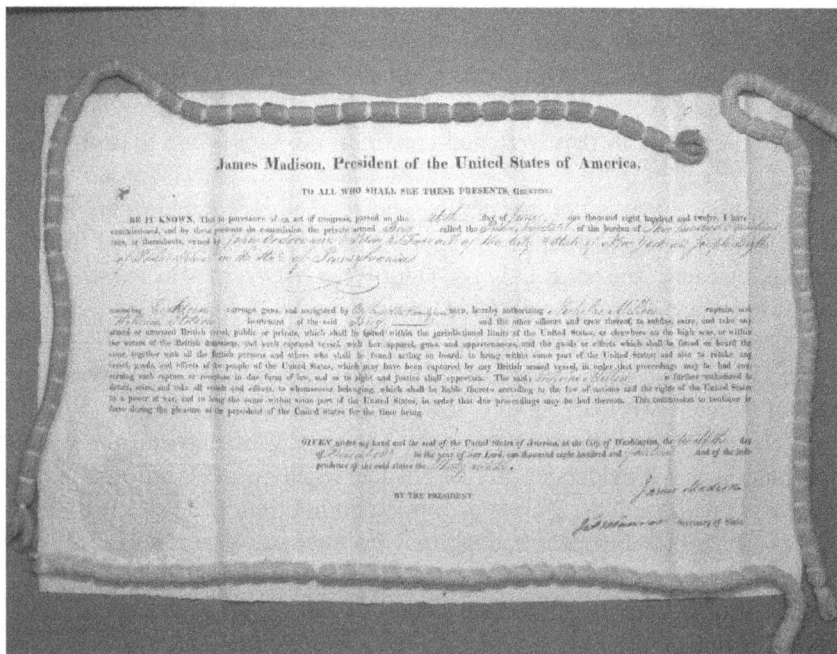

Figure 12.1.   Facsimile Letter of Marque and Reprisal

depredations listed above: the oppression of transporters of arms, chemicals, or persons, etc.

However, it is conceivable that letters could be issued by private victims of piracy. Say Smith was attacked on the high seas by Jones. Could not Smith hire Williams to recover his losses? Yes he could! Here the relationship is one that is directed at the specific act of theft or assault against a specific perpetrator. Smith has no interest in attacking third party passengers because of their documentation or lack thereof. Should Williams go off and attack Johnson, then he would be a criminal and would have deficient authorization. This is in stark contrast to a government issued license wherein a general category of people can fall victim to unprovoked attacks or where a rogue ruler can issue licensure to actual pirates seeking a cover of legitimacy.

World Government

Perhaps the reason piracy exists despite the best efforts of national governments is that they are not sufficiently well-coordinated. That is, no one state can patrol the entire oceans of the world.[7] Yes, they can focus on given trouble spots, Somalia in the present day, the Barbary pirates and Caribbean buccaneers of yesteryear, but if they do so, they leave vast other areas undefended. Perhaps centralism is the answer? Were there a world government,[8] presumably, it could better coordinate the efforts of its entire navy. "Pirates beware: the world government is now on your trail" might be the motto of such institutional arrangements.

But difficulties proliferate. Rothbard (1962) demonstrates with his analysis of the "one big firm" that even under private enterprise, large size is no guarantee of economic efficiency; indeed, the very opposite is sometimes the case. "The bigger they are the harder they fall" in terms of productivity, might summarize this lesson. If so, if there is a ceiling in terms of efficiency for even marketplace participants, then this applies, in spades, to government. It is likely that present efforts to eradicate piracy would be reduced, not enhanced, with this option.

Then, too, if this world government were in any way democratic, a one man one vote policy would place China and India at its forefront. Given the move toward welfare policies in many countries, if this virus affected the world government, much of the goods and services produced elsewhere would be shipped to those two countries. Perhaps, even a relatively small amount of piracy would be preferable to such a situation?

Private Navy

More acceptable is a navy financed and owned by one or more entrepreneurial parties. A shipping company could own warships as well as merchantmen.

They could patrol their routes on a regular basis or they could escort or convoy their merchant ships. Such boats would only be the size necessary for their task. They would tend to be small, fast, and well-armed. Any pirate would want to stay clear, knowing that one of these patrol craft would come calling should he try to ply his cruel and usual practice. We expect such ships would be bristling with sufficient weapons to devastate thieves.

Besides the trading firm, a sea police company could provide constabulary services on a fee basis. There are at least two plausible fee structures: subscription, and fee for service. The former would work like the shipping company's warships. They would escort the shippers. The latter, would act more like the patrols. Upon receiving a distress call, they would respond.

The point of a private navy is that they would be equipped to provide the services required. There would be no aircraft carriers sporting planes with nuclear tipped rockets.[9] Rather, they would have low cost but very fast boats equipped with something like an MK 75, 3-inch cannon and an array of smaller machine guns. Only the most dedicated pirate would tangle with that, and would experience less than satisfactory results.

Alternatively, or additionally, given the vast reaches of the oceans and improvements in modern communications technology, it would be airplanes, not ships, that would be employed by the private sea-police. Even the fastest boats cannot travel at air speeds. Merchantmen would be fitted with the best possible means of communicating with these air-borne private protection services, and piracy might be radically reduced. We can extrapolate from the relative efficiency of private vis a vis state services in a myriad of fields from garbage removal to post offices to policing, and infer that market oriented protection services at sea would also far outstrip their governmental counterparts. Further, it is difficult to see how airplanes could be as effectively used by the pirates as by the private police. How could a pirate plane force a boat to surrender? It could be done, by threatening to blow up the entire ship. But this would defeat the goal of the pirate. Besides, if that were a viable threat, the constabulary entrepreneurs would be equipped to deal with it.

Self-Protection

Finally, the Libertarian would have no objection to self-protection. In a truly free market, it is impossible to predict what defensive programs would be devised. However, it is not difficult to suggest a few countermeasures based on historic or even existing systems.

One form of defense would be to arm the merchant vessels themselves a la the East India Company ships of old.[10] Not many pirates in the sixteenth century could prevail against a 38 gun merchantman. In the same way, they could not hope to triumph over a modern commercial vessel mounting a couple of 3-inch guns along with a couple of Phalanx Gatling guns.

What about a pirate armed with torpedoes? Remember that the thieves want to take possession of the ship, not destroy it.

One other method for protection is often overlooked because of the sorry experiences of the past. When faced with a criminal protection racket, a store owner can pay the protection fee and avoid having his business trashed. In the same way, a trading corporation may pay off would-be pirates in advance. Yes, this would be another form of payment that supports criminal activity. But as a private enterprise, such a firm has the freedom to take the actions it believes most advantageous. Furthermore, the pirates must keep in mind that if, like governments, they become too greedy; then, unlike states, [11] the victim will hire a military organization to put them out of business.

NOTES

1. For an economic analysis of piracy, see Leeson, 2007, 2011.

2. For a libertarian analysis of this problem, see Block and Tinsley, 2008.

3. We make an exception for one "pirate": Ragnar Danneskjold, a fictional character in Rand (1957).

4. German for "living space."

5. "Finally, as we are unable to conceive upon what theory the exaction by government from the citizen of the performance of his supreme and noble duty of contributing to the defense of the rights and honor of the nation as the result of a war declared by the great representative body of the people can be said to be the imposition of involuntary servitude in violation of the prohibitions of the Thirteenth Amendment, we are constrained to the conclusion that the contention to that effect is refuted by its mere statement." —ARVER v. U.S., 245 U.S. 366 (1918).

6. "[The Congress shall have Power...] To declare War, grant Letters of Marque and Reprisal, and make Rules concerning Captures on Land and Water." —Article I, Section 8, Paragraph 11. Ron Paul has called for the use of this solution upon numerous occasions (Foldvary, 2002; Lovley, 2009).

7. Though it often appears that some in the service of the U.S. government believe they have a mandate and right to do just that.

8. The United States seems to be heading in that direction.

9. That is unless their foes were so powerful that only atom bombs could deter them.

10. See for example the Red Dragon discussed in Pitney (2014, p. 8).

11. This, of course, occurs. But, more rarely because of the legitimacy that governments enjoy, courtesy of their buying off the intellectuals, who sing their praises and inevitability. See on this Hayek, 1990; Hoppe, 2006A; Klein, 2006; Rothbard, 1965, 1989B.

Chapter Thirteen

Case Studies

CASE STUDY A—HOW PROPERTY RIGHTS AND A FREE
MARKET WOULD SOLVE FLOODING AND POLLUTION
PROBLEMS IN SOUTH FLORIDA

"Auferre, trucidare, rapere, falsis nominibus imperium; atque, ubi solitudinem
faciunt, pacem appellant." (To kidnap, massacre, and snatch, they falsely name
empire; and when they make a desert, they call it peace.) —Tacitus, *De Vita et
Moribus Iulii Agricolae*, (98)

Alvarez (2013) expresses concern for a potential man-made disaster in South
Florida (Figure 0.4). According to her article, threats portending "a giant
environmental problem" include:

- Breaching the levees that constitute the Hoover Dike, leading to catastrophic flooding of farms south of Lake Okeechobee.
- Devastation of three major estuaries [1] (this already occurred in May 2013).
- Release of billions of gallons of polluted water into the three estuaries.
- Devastation of aquatic populations of oysters, manatees, sea grasses, reefs, and shellfish.
- Reduction of flow to the Everglades National Park thereby damaging native wildlife.

The tenor of the case study suggests that the current conditions, prior to
recent flooding of the estuaries, are ordinary and that the problems listed
above threaten to create a disastrous deviation from the historic, unobjectionable patterns of flow. According to Alvarez, Republican governor of Florida,
Rick Scott, has proposed two projects to help mitigate the problems: (1) to
relieve the stress on the Hoover Dike by diverting more water to the Ever-

glades, and (2) to add stormwater treatment for runoff entering the St. Lucie River Basin.

The failure to respect property rights is shown below to be the real source of the imminent dangers listed above, and the strict application of and adherence to private property and free market principles are presented as the better way to solve these difficulties. However, before showing how the unfettered market would work, an understanding of the challenges to be solved necessitates a review of the current situation and its history.

Historic Conditions Prior to Manmade Works

Prior to man-made (e.g., governmental) flood control efforts, regular storm runoff traversed the lower Florida peninsula from north to south. It is this natural flow that enabled the evolution of Lake Okeechobee, the Everglades downstream, and the estuaries discussed herein. Because of the natural flow patterns, the areas now occupied by farms to the south of the Lake and the bays were always subject to flooding—from time immemorial.

In addition to normal rainwater runoff, the ground south of Lake Okeechobee experienced occasional devastating floods. The Great Miami Hurricane of 1926 brought a high storm surge to the Lake and created much havoc including the breaching of those man-made dikes that had been built in 1910. Over 2,500 deaths occurred during the Okeechobee Hurricane of 1928, the second deadliest in the United States. [2]

Regular and historic large flood events mean that the St. Lucie River and other estuaries always experienced large changes in salinity incompatible with stable aquatic populations. The types of fish and aquatic species that inhabit south Florida inlets need brackish water: a mixture of fresh and ocean water. Large floods can, and do, flush the estuaries with fresh water and thereby damage the wildlife.

Flood volumes[3] are unpredictable except on a stochastic, or probabilistic, basis and even then can change over time. For example, the "Probable Maximum Flood," the largest theoretical event used in this type of design, includes the word "Probable." This potential disaster is estimated by accounting for temperature extremes, elevation, the Corioles[4] effect, etc. to come up with the greatest amount of water which can be supported by the atmosphere over the drainage basin of interest and the maximum rate it can condense and fall as precipitation. The flood resulting from such a storm would far exceed the more commonly used 100- or 500-year[5] events. There is never anything like a full accounting for an "improbable" maximum flood. An example of an improbable episode would be the Italian Vaiont Dam failure which in 1963 resulted from a landslide that suddenly displaced a large portion of the water in the reservoir and breached the dam (Ward, 2011).

Infrequent but large floods (10-, 50-, 100-year, probable maximum, or beyond) fill reservoirs such as Okeechobee Lake and, when large enough, inundate ground not normally affected. Large storm flows flush brackish estuaries with fresh water. Any prehistoric flood with a volume nearly equal to or greater than that of the estuary would have converted it temporarily to fresh water. Even much smaller floods would have reduced their salinity.

Property rights are an important part of the analysis. An integral feature of any parcel, especially that near a lake or waterway, is that it can flood. Though unlikely, that applies even to the top of a hill where a massive rain event could cover the hilltop with water faster than it could run off. Steps, discussed below, can be taken to mitigate the risk; but since an "improbable" maximum flood cannot be ruled out or assessed, and since the frequency of large storms can only be roughly estimated on a stochastic basis, the risk can never be entirely prevented or even fully understood.[6]

Particularly for lakes and reservoirs that store water for an extended time period, a series consisting of many moderate sized floods will have a similar effect as a single large storm. With a lot of rainwater arriving at the storage facility, uncontrolled overflow and flooding will occur. Mitigation efforts have been implemented in south Florida.

Flood Mitigation around Lake Okeechobee

To control the flooding, reduce the resultant loss of human life, increase the value of land for farming, and stabilize the saline level in the estuaries, levees were built to contain and store storm water in the Lake. The current structure built during and after the Hoover Administration is called the Hoover Dike.

In pursuance of those goals, the United States Army Corps of Engineers (COE) completed the Dike in 1937 and strengthened it in the 1960s. As of 2014 it was about 30-feet high which enables Lake Okeechobee to store up to about 14 million acre-feet of water.[7] The project was justified in the minds of its builders by the expectation of a reduction of flood risk.[8] As indicated by the apparent health of the farms to the south of the Lake completion of the Hoover Dike has excluded this threat—and promoted their prosperity. In terms of these stated goals, this Dike has been successful—that is: so far.

To reduce salinity fluctuations in the St. Lucie River and nearby estuaries, the Hoover Dike includes control structures that allow the COE to control discharge to the estuaries. Thus, the COE balances the flow to stabilize the salinity by increasing the inflow of fresh water when the saltiness intensifies and reducing it if too fresh. A steady salt content enables the development of healthy and stable aquatic populations. An unchanging density of wildlife, in the minds of the COE and its supporters, provided a further justification for the project.

Problems Remain after Mitigation

The basic problems with the existing and proposed flood mitigation facilities amount to unintended consequences, such as the four discussed below, resulting from a failure to honor property rights and from subsidies to certain interested parties at the expense of others.

1. Since flood volumes are unpredictable, the Hoover Dike does not guarantee there will be no flooding of the downstream farms. Someday a sufficiently large event will[9] breech the Dike and thereby cause a large, rapid release of storm water exceeding 14-million acre-feet, greater than ever experienced in the past, prehistoric or historic. It is not that a flood large enough to overtop and breach the Dike *could* occur. Such an event *will* occur someday. With the COE mitigation, farmers and other property owners are still subject to flooding but are now deluded into thinking they are protected and that they have a right to that protection.

2. The Dike and its control facilities cannot guarantee a stable salinity or aquatic population. Due to pressure on the Dike, any sufficiently large flood or a proliferation of smaller ones will presumably lead the COE to release too much fresh water to the estuaries. No matter how large and sophisticated the system, such large events will occur. From time to time, one or more of these valuable assets will be flushed of brackish water and many aquatic animals and fisheries will be wiped out. With the current control structures, or even with the proposed enhanced facilities, the estuaries are still subject to salinity variations; but fishermen are deluded into thinking their fisheries are and ought to be protected by law.

3. Furthermore, other property owners such as residents near the estuaries are subject to flooding. Due to the long history of control, most of these homeowners have been deluded into thinking they are not subject to damage; but many if not all of them are so threatened (Alvarez, paragraph 2; Alvarez and Robertson, 2013).

4. Control of the discharge from Lake Okeechobee, as well as other facilities such as I-75 and the Tamiami Trail, upset the flow patterns to the Everglades. By making farms less subject to flooding, those properties are now far more valuable. Water that historically went to the Everglades has been diverted to irrigate this increasingly valuable farm land. Since storm water on adjacent land flows towards rivers and lakes, it is natural that pollution would follow along with the water. Being public, that is un-owned, facilities, there is no one with an interest in the water quality of the Lake and estuaries who will sustain a personal loss due to failure.[10] As a result, despite oppressive

attempts to control pollution, it continually increases especially if it is regarded as in the public interest. This pollution harms irrigated crops, aquatic wildlife, the Everglades, etc.

Water Rights in Florida

To understand how a strict observance of property rights can solve these problems, it is necessary to understand water rights: a subset of property rights. In the first place, most people understand ownership with regard to a static system. A plot of land can be surveyed and pins or markers can be placed in the ground or on a map that defines the territory that constitutes the domain. Unlike land, some assets, such as cars, move. An automobile is a distinct object owned discretely and, hence, even though it is mobile, is static in the sense that it tends to remain unchanged over an extensive time period. To the contrary, water in a river is a dynamic resource. It cannot be surveyed like land. Neither can it be enclosed as a discrete object like a vehicle, at least not in a wholesale sense, and still retain its essential properties as a free-flowing, life-sustaining fluid.

In Florida, water rights are predominately predicated on the riparian system which is based on proximity of the user to a river or other body of water. Under a pure riparian system, if the user is located adjacent to the river, including part of the river bed, the water is his. However, in Florida, the riparian system is modified in at least three ways. 1. Prior appropriation is based on the concept of first in use, first in right. Prior appropriation is used to help settle disputes among riparian right users and to delimit their rights. 2. Rights are subject to beneficial use. No "unreasonable" use may interfere with the use of other users. 3. The water right must be consistent with the public interest (Fletcher, Undated).

In other states, the Prior Appropriation Systems or Public Trust Systems have been adopted. Colorado uses the former while Montana uses the latter.[11] With the Prior Appropriation System, the owner has a right to divert and use a given amount of water from a natural stream if available. As with other types of property, this asset can be bought and sold. The resource is associated with a specific use, e.g. irrigation. The water is owned as a flow rate for the designated beneficial use, not as individual molecules of H_2O. The user diverts flow from a source such as a river, uses it, and releases it through evapotranspiration or back to the source. His right to divert and use is subject only to the water being actually available after more senior right-holders have received theirs.

With the Public Trust System, the State owns the water. It is socialism pure and simple. Users have the right to water only by permit or license (Montana, 2012, p. 1). While Florida water law is centrally based upon the riparian concept, it also includes aspects of the public trust concept, to wit: the "right must be consistent with the public interest."

Traditionally, neither the riparian nor the prior appropriation systems of water rights have adequately acknowledged in-stream use. This is why the Everglades receive short shrift. No private person associated with the Everglades has been acknowledged as a user with water rights. For example hunters of wildlife who depend on the water regime in the Everglades never "removed" water from the system and were, therefore, not regarded as water users. Even worse off have been nature lovers who simply enjoyed viewing wild scenery.[12] Even though a private park owner who provided a natural environment to his nature-loving customers relied on water, he never removed water from the system. He was, therefore, never regarded as establishing a water right. To get water, in-stream users have traditionally, and unjustly, had to become beggars. Even when they were first in use, they have tended to be viewed by other water users, and by the law, as akin to thieves.

Water rights include the presumption of usable water. Activities that pollute rivers and lakes amount to a form of trespass that harms the rightful owners (Rothbard, 1982).

Before moving on from water rights, it is important to acknowledge that in a prior appropriation system, large floods can sometimes provide a benefit. If someone without rights to this substance needs water, he has two options. First he could purchase a right which would meet his needs with a high a degree of reliability. That is to say that if his newly obtained entitlement was reliable and of high quality, it would *be in priority*[13] whenever he needed water. The second way is called augmentation. The prospective user could buy a cheaper, less reliable right and combine it with storage in a reservoir. His containment would fill during floods, and he could put a call[14] for delivery during dryer periods when needed.

Intractability of Those Problems

Why do these problems persist? This is because those with a firsthand interest have been separated from control over the situation and from the associated costs and liabilities. The building of the Hoover Dike amounted to a subsidy to its beneficiaries: farmers, residents, fishermen, etc. The balance between the real benefits of the Dike against the real costs was hidden from the beneficiaries. They were likewise hidden from the taxpayers.

Most beneficiaries were presumably in favor of flood mitigation projects because they were not to be fully charged for the costs. Furthermore, the beneficiaries were not fully informed of the remaining flood risk or of the increased severity of the risk in the event of a failure of the Dike. Payers, on-the-other-hand, were spread out nationwide so that the personal cost to each person was not noticeable; strong opposition was thus muted.[15]

One set of beneficiaries tend not to be acknowledged: sponsors of the project. They gain political brownie points because while they too do not pay the costs, they can "demonstrate" to the perceived beneficiaries that they have done them a great favor and "saved" them from future flood damage. The sponsors become popular, well liked, and most importantly—re-elected. One of the ensuing problems is that neither those who foot the bill nor the sponsors have an interest in the project after the initial accolades. As the Dike ages, it wears out. Money and resources are required to maintain and restore it. The proclaimed beneficiaries want it preserved or even upgraded, but as a small minority, convincing the sponsors of the need to provide funds for upkeep year after year is a never-ending challenge. They become just one more small and disliked pressure group among the many who are seeking handouts.

The Hoover Dike amounted to a hidden tax on those who were harmed. For example, hunters, recreation seekers, and environmentalists in the Everglades faced damage in the form of reduced utility of this amenity. Likewise, pollution amounts to a concealed levy on those who are harmed.[16] By inadequate supervision stemming from the lack of direct injury of the facility managers, contamination increases and negatively impacts water users. The latter want the polluters stopped, but they have no control over the system and must join the line of the needy seeking aid.

Solutions that Work

The first thing to acknowledge is that regardless of how the current situation evolved and the injustice of that process, it is in fact the reality that does exist. Large floods will continue no matter how many protection devices are installed.[17] An integral facet of virtually all property abutting streams and rivers is that they will be flooded. Farms will be inundated and fisheries wiped out as always happened in the past, albeit less frequently today.

To solve those problems while avoiding the difficulties stemming from public ownership, Lake Okeechobee should now be transferred to private ownership and administration. One viable process to enable that transfer is to find out who are the homesteaders of this amenity, and give them proportionate shares of stock in a new firm that owns the entire premises. Alternatively, the Dike and Lake could be sold to a private party. Another way is to grant the rightful owners an outright gift of the assets.[18] The new owners can be a single entity or a consortium. There can be separate owners of the physical Lake and Dike (similar to an office building owner) and another owner of the water in storage (analogous to a tenant in the building). Alternatively, the farmers and fishermen could jointly buy the facilities. No specific recommendations for ownership are made herein. The point is to transfer it to private ownership, whether by gift to the rightful (homesteading) owners or by sale.

The fact that private ownership makes the owners directly interested in water quantity and quality, as well as in liability for flood risk, trumps the assertions of controlling power seekers. The owners will be legally able to demand any interloping polluter to immediately cease and desist from such trespassing.[19]

The privatization of the facilities would require distribution of liabilities going forward to the new owners. This transfer would provide a clear responsibility for maintenance.[20] The new owners would have the interest in their newly acquired resource to enhance its value by keeping it in good repair. There would be no need to convince a politician that sustaining the Dike is more important than building his new pet expressway or whatever.[21]

Farmers, fishermen, and other property owners may seek flood insurance. To be effective, this protection must be free from public management and the associated politics. Properties subject to frequent flooding could only obtain such benefits if the insurance company saw the venture as profitable. Either the premiums would be high enough to defray the risk, or insurance would be unavailable. To reduce the risk, and thereby the premiums, the beneficiaries could maintain the Hoover Dike or could pay an organization to do so.[22]

Likewise, an insurance company could use premiums to pay for maintenance. If there were an insufficient number of participants, administration of the Dike and Lake would be minimal or non-existent. In that case, the insured would be compensated for damages from large flood events. The uninsured would not.

Facing real personal damages, many uninsured would learn to obtain insurance and/or take steps to reduce their own risk. With increasing revenues and liabilities, the companies offering financial protection would be motivated to call and pay for improved administration of the Dike.

Those who are currently receiving short shrift would be free to address their own needs. For example, those interested in the Everglades could buy water rights and/or storage in the Lake and call for water releases as needed and as available from their containment. In buying water and storage, they would compete with other users bidding for these amenities. If the price of reservoir capacity became high enough, the funds for building greater volume to collect more water from the truly large floods would likely be available, given the usual profit and loss incentives involved in all other private industries.

Conclusion

The failure to recognize property rights led to intractable problems in south Florida. On the contrary, while unsatisfactory to statists, power seekers, and control freaks, strict observance of property rights solves those problems.

A policy of strict property rights renders facilities such as Lake Okeechobee and the Hoover Dike self-financing; or else it demonstrates that the facilities should not exist. The most difficult part of the solution is to bring to an end the injustice that caused the problem in the first place. That injustice consisted mainly of the forcible transfer of resources from some to build facilities to be enjoyed by others. The solution is difficult because in the intervening time from the original injustice, relatively innocent people have adapted to the status-quo and would be damaged by the end of the subsidy real or implied by the existing man-made flood control.[23] In the interest of ending the injustice, an analysis of the current de facto property rights and their formalization through the market methods discussed herein leads towards a more just state of affairs.[24] Then the property owners can bid for benefits according to the most valuable use as in the case of all other goods and services under free enterprise. Rather than being relegated to beggar status, those currently in need can bid for resources with which to resolve their problems.

CASE STUDY B—SACRAMENTO RIVER—
HOW THE STATE HAS PREVENTED SPONTANEOUS
PROVISION OF FLOOD PROTECTION AND
INSURANCE AND HAS INJURED PEOPLE IN THE PROCESS

"Être GOUVERNÉ, c'est être gardé à vue, inspecté, espionné, dirigé, légiféré, réglementé, parqué, endoctriné, prêché, contrôlé, estimé, apprécié, censuré, commandé, par des êtres qui n'ont ni le titre, ni la science, ni la vertu." (To be RULED is to be observed, inspected, spied on, directed, legislated, regulated, parked, indoctrinated, sermonized, controlled, estimated, valued, censured, commanded, by persons who have neither merit, wisdom, nor virtue.) —P. J. Proudhon, *Idée Générale de la Révolution au XIXe Siécle*, (1851, p. 341)

Floods have a devastating impact on people. Homes, businesses, and farms have been wiped out. Yet, people continue to live and work in floodplains for economic opportunity and for sheer enjoyment. The losses have been aggravated by the activities of governments at the local, state, and federal level. Particularly harmful is the National Flood Insurance Program (2012). This inquiry lays out a libertarian approach to flood protection and insurance. A little history will show how flood management has evolved and repeatedly failed under statism. Northern California provides an excellent case study.

History of Floods and Physical Flood Control Measures in California's Central Valley

The Central Valley is a low lying and very flat basin. A map of this area can be viewed on in Figure 0.2, the Central California Watersheds. The elevation of Marysville/Yuba City, on the Feather River[25] about 50-miles north of Sacramento and about two hundred river miles north of San Francisco/San Pablo Bay, is 62-feet above mean sea level. That comprises a gradient along the river of less than 4-inches of fall per mile on average. In general the rivers of the Valley are higher than the lowest point of the surrounding country. The elevation of Knights Landing, immediately adjacent to the Sacramento River,[26] is 36-feet above mean sea level while that of Robins is 23-feet. Robins is 5-miles north of Knights Landing, farther from the Bay, and inland from the rivers surrounding the Sutter Basin.[27]

The Valley is surrounded by mountains that collect copious amounts of precipitation from moisture-laden marine winds. In the 1840s and earlier, much of the Central Valley was swamp land.[28] Early developers found the acreage to be very productive, particularly within about half a mile of the rivers, where the elevation was relatively high, and dry enough to cultivate. Farmers found that by building drainage canals, territory even further away from the rivers could be brought into production.

They also discovered that following large storms, the rivers overflowed their banks. Frequent, seasonal, and extreme flooding became a major problem. In 1862 and again in 1907–09 large floods covered much of the Sacramento Valley (Garone, 2011; Leclerc, 2012; Smith, 2012). The flow rate at Suisun Bay[29] in 1907 was estimated at 600,000 cubic feet per second.[30] That is about half the rate of the spring of 1973 Mississippi River flood at New Orleans, one of the largest on record (NOAA, 2011).

The activities of gold miners along the Mother Lode in the Sierra Nevada Mountains intensified the potential for serious inundation of the Valley. Hydraulic mining is a process wherein water is diverted from a stream to operate a monitor (water cannon) that shoots a torrent against the hillside to wash the soil into a grizzly/sluice box that separates gold-rich material from debris. The mud generated by the process flows downstream. As a result, it accumulates in the Valley river bottoms. The sediment reduces the capacity of the floodway and raises the elevation of the riverbed thereby increasing flood risk.

By the 1880s, the frequency and severity of flooding in the Valley had reached intolerable levels. A lawsuit was brought against the mining companies to cease and desist. "On January 7, 1884, after two years of litigation in the case of Woodruff vs. North Bloomfield Gravel Mining Company," (Malakoff, Undated) the Sawyer Decision effectively brought an end to the practice. Sediment already washed into the mountain streams continued to move downhill and accumulate in the rivers of the Valley at an elevated rate until about 1920 when the sediment load had declined to normal.

The 1907 flood, followed soon after by another in 1909, convinced the politicians of the state that physical protection structures were required. In the Flood Control Act of 1917, the so called Jackson Plan (U.S. Corps, 1999, pp. 2–4) was adopted. It proposed a bypass to divert overflows from the Sacramento River. Today, the Sacramento and Feather Rivers carry their normal flows; but the Sutter and Yolo (Russo, 2010) bypasses, through the middle of the respective valley basins, convey much more flood water than the rivers. The Yolo Bypass at highway I-80 opposite the City of Sacramento is about 2-miles wide with levees up to 24-feet high (Figure 0.2).

In addition, dams with a flood control function have been added. The First was Shasta Dam with capacity of 4.5 million acre-feet (U.S. Corps, 1992, p. 7), of which 1.3 million are reserved for flood control. As of 2015, dams surround the Sacramento Valley.[31] Nevertheless, it appears that a major flood causes one levee or another somewhere in the Valley to breach approximately once every 15-years on average.[32]

While the purpose of this study is to discuss floods and related insurance, here is a good place to remind the reader that central California also regularly experiences extremely dry periods. The drought of 2013–15 is only at the time of this writing approaching the worst experienced time and again since the early 19th century in terms of severity and duration.

Flood Insurance

Early in the morning of Christmas Eve 1955 while still dark, Henry Delamere, late Historian of the City of Marysville and, in that year, a volunteer for Reclamation District 10 (Madwin, Undated), was on the levee north of town. He and other volunteers were working on a boil[33] that had developed. Mr. Delamere stated that suddenly the water in the river began to recede rapidly. After the Feather no longer posed a threat to District 10, the volunteers packed up and headed home wondering what had happened.

As it turned out, Yuba City was flooded. The deluge was serious and overwhelmed residences and business up to the eves of houses. 38 people lost their lives (two more died a few weeks later while the water was still high) and 100,000 acres of the Sutter Basin were inundated (Sutter Butte Flood, 2010). Over 6200 homes were lost or damaged and property damage exceeded $65 million in 1955 dollars.

Flood insurance in 1955 was in a state of flux. Prior to 1950, a standard homeowner's insurance policy covered flood damage. The National Flood Insurance Program did not yet exist. Floods such as that in Yuba City and in other parts of the country were becoming more devastating. Despite the levees, bypasses and dams, breaches in the Sacramento Valley continued to occur. Insurance companies dropped this type of protection from their standard policies.

One effect of the current institutional arrangements is that risk is nearly impossible to assess. If the system is simply taken at face value, one can study rainfall and river gauges to develop probabilities for the various discharge stages. The gradients, cross sectional areas, and roughness of the many rivers and channels can be measured.[34] Finally, the probability for the overtopping of a levee can be calculated at any point in the system. However, what is the probability that a levee breach will occur prior to overtopping somewhere in a basin where the homeowner seeking flood insurance has located his house? What is the likelihood that a ground squirrel has burrowed through the levee? How can we know the location of all of the sand and gravel lenses[35] under the levees from pre-historic river alignments? The losses from any single levee failure are extensive and catastrophic. The devastation from the failure of a dam such as Shasta would be nearly total for the entire Valley. Due to these and many other imponderables, insurance companies facing extreme flood-related losses in the middle of the 20th century began to restrict this type of product[36] in the 1950s and 1960s. These losses were not limited to the Sacramento Valley. Extreme floods occurred during this time period in the San Joaquin Valley, the Central California Delta, the Los Angeles Basin, the Colorado River, the Mississippi River, the Ohio River, and even the Potomac River as well as innumerable other rivers and streams throughout the country.

In addition to rivers, coastal flooding from tropical storms resulted in devastating floods. Hurricane Betsy (*Times-Picayune.* 2011) struck first southern Florida and then Louisiana as a category 4 in September, 1965. Damage from Betsy, which tracked up the Mississippi and Ohio valleys, was unprecedented, exceeding $1.2 billion in 1965 dollars. According to the Hurricane Severity Index (Chambers, 2008), Betsy remains tied with Hugo, after Carla, as the second most severe hurricane to make landfall in the U.S. The Hurricane Protection Program was instituted in response to Betsy and other such incidents. Among the projects proceeding from that program was the levee system around New Orleans. Predictably, those levees failed when Katrina came ashore in 2005.[37]

Prior to 1968 the central government of the U.S. frequently stepped in to "help" with disaster recovery. These efforts often involved constructing new hard facilities such as the levees in California and New Orleans. In an effort to mitigate this risk, the National Flood Insurance Program (NFIP) was enacted. The idea was to encourage local communities to enhance the level of protection and to discourage development in floodplains. Higher rates for flood prone lowlands were to provide the discouragement, but not enough people signed up for the insurance.[38] By the time Agnes (Kentucky, 2011) struck in 1972 only 1,200 communities participated in the program, and only

95,000 homeowner policies were outstanding. Damages exceeded $4 billion, but only $5 million was paid out in NFIP claims.

The plan was amended several times over the years to mandate more comprehensive coverage. Today, any mortgaged house in a designated flood zone must, by law, have insurance. *The program works against its own stated objectives* because it reduces the costs to a flood victim. This government initiative regularly pays out more in benefits than it collects in premiums. It amounts to a subsidy for people to live in these districts. Since it only mandates insurance for mortgages, seniors who have paid off these debts, and who are less able to deal with a flood, are less likely to purchase protection. Caps on payouts and remaining risks to occupants skew the program against low income people who lack the means to defend themselves.

The biggest failure of NFIP stems from its nature as a subsidy. If someone lives or does business on a low-lying property and has cheap insurance, the expected benefits will outweigh the costs. If a resident experiences a flood, he will be motivated to rebuild in the same spot since his losses are covered. In short, the activities of governments at all levels: local, state, and central, have created a moral hazard wherein people are effectively paid to live in high risk areas. That applies whether the activities consist of subsidized hard infrastructure facilities such as levees and dams or insurance schemes such as the NFIP.

Government sponsored programs also fail because they dissociate the victims of flooding from the costs and risks of protective infrastructure. The designers, builders, and financiers of dams and levees do not face the same risks as the people who live behind these artificial shields. The beneficiaries will tend to support these projects because the costs are spread over the entire tax-paying populace. Since those in charge tend not to suffer as much from failure, protection is reduced sometimes to the level where flood risk is actually higher than it would be without the program (Hanscom, 2014).

The Libertarian Approach

The libertarian approach starts with an acknowledgement that flood risk is real. People and their property can and will be devastated by dangerous high water if they allow themselves to be. And that is the key factor: "If they allow themselves to be." Libertarians consider people as responsible individual actors. As such, they can choose whether or not to live in a risky area. The desire to live in beautiful riverine surroundings and take advantage of economic opportunities motivates people to devise methods of coping with the dangers. If they choose to do so, they can simultaneously take measures to protect themselves whether through hard structures or insurance. As individual actors, they can choose to freely work together, contractually for example, to embark on large projects. No state-run programs are acceptable because (a.) they will create a moral hazard encouraging risky behavior and (b.) relatively innocent people will be forced to bear the costs. In turn when statist theory prevails, these risks encourage the bureaucratic oppression that discourages audacious creativity. There are plenty of reasons to live on flood-prone land. Life next to a stream is generally pleasant most of the time.

- The land in the Central Valley of California is extremely productive and valuable.
- New Orleans is mightily treasured as a major shipping and transportation hub, to say nothing of its tourism.
- Would it not be a shame if the daring ingenuity of Fallingwater (1997)[39] had never been built because of fear of flooding?

In other words, whether people need to live and work on high risk land or just want to locate there because they like it, they should be able to do so. They also should not be subjected to unusual punishments or cruel and arbitrary regulations. Rather, they would ideally conduct their own due diligence and calculate the risk they face to farm in a floodplain, ship containers from a hurricane district, or live for pleasure's sake next to a mountain stream. Then according to their own risk tolerance, such people can devise appropriate and personal protection measures. Nor should they be subsidized by others in support of their risky decisions. Those who build in such places should pay their own way and accept the consequences without expecting a bailout.

How might Northern Californians in the Central Valley deal with the reality that huge floods will certainly reoccur?[40] A farmer or an owner of a farm service company could live in the foothills and commute to his place of work; but if he wishes to live in the endangered area, he will have to provide solutions to mitigate the risk he is undertaking. Many people ask libertarians how they would solve this or that problem. Such questions miss the point. The essence of libertarianism is that people are free to devise their own solutions and, if helpful, collaborate with others but may not force other individuals or groups to provide for their protection. In addition to traditional devices, the result of private enterprise, not possible under governmental regulation, is creative innovation of new safeguards never before imagined. Therefore, what steps will be taken cannot be predicted in the free society. The freedom philosophy precludes using the violence of the state to impose on others one's own vision for safety.

However, we can speculate as to what plans might be implemented by private actors. The current system of dams and levees are quite possible in a libertarian society, only the current financing methodology would be very different. A farmer can buy insurance (if there is a willing insurance provider[41]). In an effort to reduce risk, the insurance company (or a consortium of farmers if insurance is not available) can finance levee and dam construction or hire companies to construct and then own these safeguards. The insurance provider does not need to be the sole financier. Irrigation companies might well have an interest in water storage reservoirs. So, likely, would recreation providers, fishing enterprises, transporters, and the list goes-on to the extent of human imagination.

With statist financing, in sharp contrast, the provider of a levee has no personal stake in the protection provided by it and, most importantly, no liability. A private owner of a flood protection device would be personally responsible and liable for the efficacy of his service. It is quite possible to design a levee that if properly maintained will in all likelihood not fail.

Can we guarantee this? Of course not. Human beings are fallible creatures, and nothing, but *nothing*, we ever do is beyond error. The real question is a comparative one: are dams and levees more likely to fail under private or public ownership? And here, the answer readily appears: the latter. That is because there is a weeding out process that takes place under free enterprise (Hazlitt, 1946): entrepreneurs who fail lose money and eventually go broke; bureaucrats who do so suffer no such automatic penalties.

Some will object that such a levee would be expensive. It would indeed, but that is the argument of one who is concerned with public financing and, more to the point, will not suffer the consequences of failure. A private company would immediately lose profits and customers and court bankruptcy if it acted like the Army Corps of Engineers. The public financing mindset results in a system that feigns "safety" but fails to provide real protection because of the shortcuts taken by those with nothing to lose. The fact is that private enterprises are generally more efficient than public; this is well documented.[42]

It might be argued that public officials risk losing the next election if they spend too much, and that therefore we may expect some rationality from their behavior as well. Based on this objection, there seems to be little difference between the public and private spheres: in both cases, not just the latter, powerful forces tend to bring about reasonable behavior. This sounds superficially plausible, but it cannot withstand serious analysis. First of all, the dollar vote[43] occurs every day, every hour, every second. It serves as a leash the consumer uses to guide the entrepreneur. In contrast, the political vote takes place only every two, four, or six years. Thus, the politician has far more leeway to ignore the wishes of the electorate than does the entrepreneur the customer. Second, in the market, one can narrowly focus his likes and dislikes. He can "vote" for peach ice cream, or blue suede shoes, or a silver flute. In the political sphere, all one is offered is a package deal between candidate A and B. But suppose a citizen likes A's views on policies 1, 3, 5, and 7 and B's on 2, 4, 6, and 8. He is then powerless to express himself. He must accept the "package deal" of one or the other; he cannot pick and choose as can his consumer counterpart. Third, in the market, everyone wins.

Every time a purchase, sale, rental, borrowing, or lending takes place, both parties gain in the *ex-ante* sense, or they would not engage in the commercial activity at all.[44] In politics, the majority wins and the minority loses. Fourth, there is rational ignorance (Caplan, 2007) as far as the ballot box is concerned, but this is literally unheard of in the market. A professor of political science, who has intelligently and systematically studied the candidates and their policies for years, gets exactly as many ballot box votes as the "low information" voter: namely, one. Sixth, those who contribute more to society have more dollar votes than those who do not; thus, the system promotes wealth and prosperity. This does not occur in the political system.

What if the cost of a reliable levee is so expensive that the owner cannot make a profit? A flood protection company will be motivated to develop a better, more effective, safer, and less costly system. One idea would be to build such large dams that water in excess of the natural river's capacity could be stored. Then levees are not required at all. Of course such large dams would have their own problems, but the point is that innovative people with an ownership interest will be well-motivated and far more likely to solve them.

What if no one is able to develop a hard structure solution at a price people can afford? This means that the long term productivity of the land is not expected to be as high as was originally thought, certainly not more than the costs[45] of the investment. In that case, farmers, other businesses, and residents would design their facilities so as to sustain occasional flooding. The farmland would be less productive because in some seasons or years, fruits and vegetables, etc., would be washed out. If say 10 percent of the years had a crop loss, then the land would be only 90-percent productive. One advantage to periodic river overflows is that soil nutrients tend to be replaced. With healthier land, productivity losses might not be so bad.

Softer solutions in the form of wider river banks and beaches can be used to mitigate the power of damaging high water. The same concepts of adaptation apply to other occupants. Businesses and houses can be built on stilts and/or on natural and artificial berms.[46] Short levees can be built around towns rather than long ones along rivers.

There is also the possibility that if the costs outweigh the benefits by an even greater degree, that under present technology this land is thus submarginal. It does not pay to build on each and every acre, at present: not on Mars, not on the moon, not at the top of Mount Everest, and, perhaps, not near bodies of water that inundate us whenever the weather brings torrential storms. All this of course should be determined by the economic actors themselves, and not by a one-size-fits-all government in Washington D.C.

Conclusion

The current systems of flood protection in areas such as the Central Valley of Northern California, New Orleans, and the Gulf Coast have been built as public works projects. As such, they suffer from inadequate structures and deceptive promises for protection that cannot be provided. These systems have frequently suffered catastrophic failures with loss of life and extreme property losses. Solutions are elusive because the designers and "owners" of these facilities do not share personal responsibility for the losses.

Likewise, public insurance is set up in such a way as to subsidize the occupants of flood zones. People are encouraged to live in risky places thus increasing losses. These individuals are often deceived into thinking they are protected from the risk, but they are not.

A private system will provide a defined level of protection with engineered facilities so that insurance companies and other interested folks can calculate and address their risks. Only people who find sufficient economic or cultural advantage to living in floodable environments will do so. Others will eschew the danger and expense by choosing to live and work elsewhere. But the main point is that those who must will develop a wide variety of innovative approaches to limit risk and live with the consequences of occupying floodplains.

CASE STUDY C — ACCIDENT ON THE ELK RIVER

"Whose property is my body? Probably mine. I so regard it. If I experiment with it, who must be answerable? I, not the State. If I choose injudiciously, does the State die? Oh no." —Mark Twain, "Osteopathy" (1901, p. 253)

On January 9, 2014, Freedom Industries announced that the chemical 4-methylcyclohexylmethanol (MCHM) had spilled into the Elk River from its Charleston, West Virginia facility (Berzon, 2014). The location of the leak was upstream of the principal river intake for West Virginia American Water, a division of American Water. About 7500 gallons of MCHM were released. The failure was twofold: a storage tank developed a one inch hole, and the secondary containment wall or berm was non-functional. The contaminant passed through the treatment plant and temporarily rendered the entire drinking water system non-potable, featuring highly turbid water—disgusting in appearance and odor. In addition, the contaminant was predicted to travel down the Ohio and Mississippi Rivers fouling water systems all along the way.[47] Because of the unknown risks, a no-use advisory (stricter than a do-not-drink advisory) was issued by West Virginia American Water for nine counties in the western part of the state. The free enterprise system, and paucity of government regulations, was widely blamed. Improperly so.[48]

In a truly free society, there would be property rights in bodies of water such as rivers, lakes, and oceans. They would all be privately owned. This will strike most people as delusional. That is because they have been unknowingly victimized by their statist educators who taught them the concepts of aquasocialism. This applies to even otherwise free enterprise supporters. But there is no reason why privatization, which has proven itself time and time again on the land, should not be applied, also, to water resources.

Would the leak have happened in the first place in a libertarian society? The answer is maybe, but far less likely. Humans are not omniscient; so, mistakes occur. However, when people are fully liable for their actions as they would be in a purely free market world, they tend to be very alert to anything that might destroy their livelihood. This attentiveness proceeds from the knowledge that a viable backup to an existing livelihood is not usually an option, at least not an appealing one. Besides the challenge of earning a living in a new field, there is the debt to be repaid to those who were damaged by negligence. Worse, the corporation, Freedom Industries, cannot just skip town. It has major facilities at a particular location that cannot be effortlessly packed up and relocated. They will remain at their location unless the company decides at some time in the future to demolish them.

Imagine an "Elk River Corporation," owners of the river—they would likely have been more diligent monitors than the government. Why? Because only those who stand to lose all or part of their investment in addition to their livelihood will constantly monitor the facilities and meticulously work to anticipate potential disasters before they have a chance to materialize. It is the proprietors who assiduously sustain potentially dangerous tanks and pipelines in good repair, not public "servants."

Statists should ask, where is the consumer more secure? People are quite safe in a privately owned amusement park or private mall where the owners pay a steep price if a rape or theft occurs on their premises. They are at much greater risk in Central Park, where no one in a position to stop such crimes pays any penalty when such barbarism takes place. All too often their position turns absolutely dire on the city streets when those charged with controlling crime mug or kill innocent bystanders.[49] It would be the same with rivers.

Nevertheless failures of this sort would happen occasionally. Then what?

In a free society, several layers of protection are encouraged and would exist. First, the wise economic actor anticipates the possibility of crises. He would be ready beforehand with stored water rather than waiting for state sponsored salvation. This applies at the individual as well as at the industrial or commercial level. Individual businesses and homeowners would keep an emergency supply of safe water, even as they should right now (Brouhard, 2014). Who knows what is going to happen in the next 10-minutes let alone the next few years? Knowing that no bailout was coming, a commercial enterprise like Freedom Industries would maintain a reservoir to enable their business to continue at least on a marginal basis until the crisis was resolved.

Second, the river's proprietor would face revenue losses. With filthy water, he would not be able to sell his product to the water company. He would lose still more from the destruction of fishing, carrier traffic, recreational boating, swimming, and any number of other uses. He would not be able to deliver clean irrigation water for crops. As with any property owner, the river corporation would have precautions already in place to protect against the unexpected. The firm would install alarms to signal a problem and cleanup machinery at the ready. Entrepreneurs would have emergency containment ready to go. Finally, as a personally interested owner, he would monitor all possible abusers of his river to ensure they were operating safely and not trespassing on his domain.

In contrast, under statism, an inspection by a government official is deemed "good enough." After all, it wasn't leaking yesterday and nothing has changed; so, it must be safe today, right? In fact no governmental bureaucrat or socialist has an ownership interest in this body of water; so, no one is ready, willing, and able to quickly contain a problem. The water company has no competition; thus, while their facilities would be damaged and they would certainly lose revenue, they could expect to stay in business. As a quasi-governmentally approved monopoly, they could expect to be bailed-out financially.[50] Individual users are quite sure that their "surrogate parent," the state, will protect them; so, they tend to neglect prudent preparation. As a result, the system is shaky at best with each potential layer of protection either non-existent or requiring a long response time to implement. Said Clint Eastwood, "If you want a guarantee, buy a toaster."[51] Each player looks to someone else to solve his problems.

Private river ownership is not delusional, after all.

CASE STUDY D—CALIFORNIA'S CENTRAL VALLEY AQUIFER

"Liberty, Sancho, is one of the most precious gifts which Heaven has bestowed on man. With it no treasures can be compared which the earth contains or the sea conceals. For liberty, as for honour, one can and should adventure life. . . ." —Miguel de Cervantes Saavedra, *Don Quixote* (Cervantes, 1895)

Campbell (2013) writes about the Central Valley Aquifer and the effects on the San Joaquin Valley of over pumping. She reports "a federal study"[52] and several authorities[53] who maintain that the aquifer levels are in decline due to over pumping of groundwater. As a result of the excessive use of underground supplies, the surface is subsiding and damaging infrastructure including "dams, canals, roads, bridges, rail lines, power transmission structures and flood control systems."

Harms such as these are the natural effects of inadequate recognition of property rights. In this case, the Central Valley Aquifer is not owned by private and responsible people. Rather, in California, "land ownership does not imply any limits on groundwater pumping"; though, by experience, when withdrawal from an aquifer threatens depletion, adjudication can assign limits (Pasadena, 1949).

Ownership of land that carries with it unlimited privileges to withdraw conflicts with the nature of limited supplies. As a free flowing liquid, water seeks a level surface. Since pumping creates a drawdown cone, an underground current from adjacent properties develops. That is to say the water user in effect "steals" from his neighbors. Thus, without clear title, everyone is motivated to extract this life-giving fluid as fast as possible lest someone else gets it first (this is not the first time we have had occasion to mention the tragedy of the commons, and, unfortunately, it will not be the last).

For these reasons, a more sensible regime involves ownership of the actual water in the reservoir. This chapter explores how private ownership would address subsidence, damage to infrastructure, and salt water intrusion (another problem occurring in the Valley).

Pre-Historic Evolution in California's Central Valley

California's Central Valley Aquifer is an underground reservoir extending under ground between the mountains from north of Redding to south of Bakersfield. Figure 0.2, provides an aid to help the reader get their bearings. It lies atop a sloping granitic basement which is an extension of the western slope of the Sierra Nevada Mountains. It is thickest in the west-central portion of the valley (Faunt, 2009, p. 21–22).

The granitic slope was created by tectonic forces which caused the uplift of the Sierras. In the meantime, faulting along the west valley occurred with the rise of the Coast Range. An extension of the Pacific Ocean occupied the space between these two ridges. Over eons of time, material eroded from the mountains filled the inland gulf until the Central Valley was created.

The deposited material includes layers with a variety of grain sizes [54] and a variety of consolidation. [55] Due to the heavy rainfall, particularly in the Sierras, fresh water flows through the valley soils from its extremities towards the Carquinez Strait. In more recent times, large scale pumping of groundwater has reduced this flow so that saltwater intrusion from San Francisco Bay and the Pacific has occurred.

Mining of Groundwater—Subsidence

In general for the California Aquifer, the groundwater surface is higher on the east side of the Valley next to the Sierras and lower near to the major rivers to the west: the San Joaquin and the Sacramento.[56] Groundwater flows towards the lower elevations. Mining[57] causes a lowering of the water table at the well with movement in that direction.[58]

"In the Central Valley, because of the typically slow process of draining fine-grained deposits, pumping has caused the permanent and irreversible compression or consolidation of fine-grained deposits. This consolidation has resulted in extensive land subsidence, particularly in the San Joaquin Valley (Faunt, 98)."

In the more southerly two thirds of the Valley, particularly along the central portion of the California Aqueduct[59] and south of the Delta-Mendota Canal[60] (the Los Banos to Mendota area), the ground has subsided up to 30-feet or more.[61] Most of the pumping has been for irrigation. The San Joaquin Valley receives about 5- to 15-inches per year of rainfall (Galloway and Riley, 1999, p. 25) and yet is one of the most productive agricultural regions of the world.[62] The irrigation enables this amazing productivity. Most of the water comes from mountain snowmelt that discharges to the local rivers. A lot of it comes from the Sacramento River via the Delta. But a significant amount, especially in draught years, has as its source the Aquifer.

The amount being pumped far exceeds the natural recharge rate. Where the drawdown cone is too steep, especially where it does not touch the bottom of the well, suction will literally shrink the soil matrix like sucking air out of a balloon.

The reduction of soil volume manifests in a lower elevation of the surface. Any structures on or near the surface are thereby damaged with tipping and cracking. Highways, water transmission canals, pipelines, and buildings are all susceptible to damage. Over longer distances, elevation changes alter the natural land slopes which in turn cause deviations of the drainage patterns. Some areas will receive less than in the past while an increase in flood potential may occur in others.

Mining of Groundwater—Saltwater Intrusion

Normally the aquifer discharges into the Delta[63] and through the Carquinez Strait to the ocean. This aqueous area stretching out into the Gulf of Farallones northwest of San Francisco is the largest estuary system on the eastern shore of the Pacific Ocean. The riverine and hydrogeological discharge provided positive pressure that kept saltwater at bay.[64] The increase of pumping from the aquifer, combined with the diversion of surface water, reduces the flow of fresh groundwater to the Delta. As a result saltwater intrusion increases[65] and effectively pollutes inland streams. Thus less suitable H_2O is available.

The increasing salt content harms fisheries in the Delta which rely on freshwater. Certain species are endangered by the change. "So much fresh water is diverted upstream and in the Delta that what remains is not sufficient to support the needs of fish and wildlife" (Delta Crisis, Undated). In fact due to the repeated recycling, the salt content of the rivers entering the region is higher than normal and much warmer. The discharge from the aquifer is in 2014 mostly artificial via wells rather than directly to the estuary. What is not lost through evapo/transpiration enters the rivers and is heated through exposure to direct sunlight. Thus the habitat has changed to a warmer condition that enables more warm water predators. These apply further pressure on native aquatic populations such as salmonids.[66]

Which public policy recommendations emanate from the powers that be, the ones responsible for the poor state of affairs depicted above, in the first place? Relying on a first-glance overview, statists would call for the government to step in and forbid those evil "Capitalists" from defiling the natural environment. What they would fail to notice is that property rights have not been respected and that is why the deterioration proceeds. Indeed, many of the assets discussed above are not even allowed to be owned. No one possesses on his personal account the salmonid fisheries, the abalone, or any other aquatic animals. No one has ownership interest in the estuary: not the Delta, not San Francisco Bay, and not the Gulf of Farallones. No one has a direct proprietary interest in protecting any of these resources.

Another "solution" springing from that source is to throw more money at the problem. Toss a few federal billions, maybe tens of billions, in the direction of California's water crisis, and all difficulties will supposedly disappear, or so the theory goes. It is an argument popular amongst the "regressives."[67] Well, perhaps, with a large enough lever, and a big steady fulcrum, this is even within the bounds of possibility. Maybe we can float some icebergs down from one or both poles. But this will not really address the causes of the difficulties; it is more like placing a very expensive Band-Aid on a cancer patient. What, then, will work? It is a real solution to which we now turn.

Libertarian Approach

The libertarian approach is to align the interests of people with the protection of valuables. This is done not with discouraging, pejorative words, but by allowing people to prosper. Capitalists and business owners are just folks like the rest of us. But they are people who care for their possessions especially when those assets are the source of their livelihood. The owner of the salmonid fishery upon finding that he was being damaged would enjoin those who were creating that damage to cease and desist. He would also manage his own stock to maximize his returns on a present discounted value basis.

But who can prevail if the farmer near Mendota needs more fresh water while the fisherman in the Bay does also? That question is answered according to homesteading priority. In the case of the Central Valley aquifer, owners with interests in the property will in the first place have an interest in its preservation. With secure title, they will not pump it dry. Why? Because as owners (rather than dependents of the state), they want their livelihood to remain viable for the long term. Extraction will tend to be limited to a sustainable level. They will understand that they have an interest in a reservoir. Yes, during dry years they can pump at a higher rate than recharge so long as during wet years their reservoir is allowed to fill and as long as they do not create suction sufficient to collapse it. They will quickly learn that the compression of fine grained soils damages their capacity and thus the value of their property. Owners do not act to destroy their own possessions. That concern alone would stop the subsidence in its tracks. And, if perchance they do not learn these lessons, at the very least they will earn less profit than would otherwise be the case and more likely will be driven out of business. The tendency, then, will be for the market to reward with profits those who act in a rational manner, and penalize with losses and eventual bankruptcy those who do not. This is in sharp contrast with governmental bureaucratic statist managers of water resources who cannot financially benefit if they do a good job,[68] nor do they suffer automatic financial setbacks if in the far more likely case they bollix up the works.

In the event of a conflict, a person with ownership in surface property will enjoin the aquifer owners from damaging his land by causing settlement. A farmer will not tolerate activities of others who change the drainage patterns upon which he relies.

In like manner, those with interests in the Delta will insist on receiving their historic and homesteaded discharge from the aquifer. The fishery owner will demand the cool fresh groundwater upon which his stock depends.

Does this mean that the proprietor of the aquifer is hamstrung and unable to extract any fluid whatsoever? By no means! It implies rather that the rights of prior homesteaders are honored. The owner may extract water any time he wants. However, he cannot legally access so much that it destroys or damages the formerly established farm, the previously settled town, or the earlier homesteaded fishery. Finally, a late arriving user of groundwater may not steal it from previous occupants.

With secure titles, there is no fear of neighbors and no need to remove the water as fast as possible. None of the irreparable damages discussed above or in the cited references can occur without rapid rectification of the issue. In one fell swoop, with the "magic" of private property rights, the tragedy of the commons is banished. It may no longer wreak havoc in the California water community, or anywhere else it is employed.

CASE STUDY E—CANADIAN WATERS

וְאֵין כָּל־חָדָשׁ תַּחַת הַשָּׁמֶשׁ: (There is no new thing under the sun.)[69] —King Solomon, *Ecclesiastes*

"Water, water, everywhere, but not a drop to trade."[70] Canada is a case in point for everything wrong about how we treat the precious resource, water. That, except perhaps for water in plastic bottle containers, seems to be a common Canadian attitude on the matter, and not just official Canadian policy. This attitude infests the entire Canadian culture. For example, consider the following statements:

- If the government let a giant foreign corporation buy up half of Canada's water, you would be outraged."[71, 72]
- Proposals have been made for the export of Canadian water for half a century. There is an emotional, often strident, debate between strong proponents and opponents over this controversial issue... Many of the complexities lie in the fact that water is unlike any other natural resource, as it is essential to life and has no functional substitute. It is, therefore, difficult for many to conceive of water as a commodity. On the other hand, the reliance on water for industrial processing, irrigation, electricity generation, and other economic uses suggests that a monetary value could be established for water (as opposed to being free of charge as it is in Canada) allowing for the possibility of profitable exports" (Thompson, 2013).
- Paul Celucci, Canadian Ambassador to the US, says: "Canada has probably one of the largest resources of fresh water in the world. Water is going to be—already is—a very valuable commodity and I've always found it odd that Canada is so willing to sell oil and natural gas and uranium and coal, which are by their nature finite. But talking about water is off the table, yet water is renewable" (Campbell, 2006, p.95).
- Former Minister of the Environment, David Anderson bluntly said: "We're absolutely not going to export water, period" (Campbell, 2006, p.95).
- Water is an economic good, but it is so much more than that: It is the basis of all life, not just human. It is integral to the health and beauty of Canada's landscape. It is the key to our past and future. If this, the last and greatest natural resource still in Canadian hands is traded away, we are a lesser people, sovereign in name only" Frank Quinn, leading Canadian water expert (Bauch, 2007).

Nor is this strategy a partisan one. On the contrary, to the extent that Canadians are unified on anything, this would seem to apply to this one issue. Then Liberal Leader John Turner has been peppering the Tories for assurances that large scale diversions of fresh water not be allowed, and New Democratic Party (NDP) trade critic Steven Langdon has gone so far as to call for emergency legislation on this matter.

As can be expected, this sentiment is highly popular, too, in the left wing[73] environmentalist community. In the view of Johansen (2002):

> Canada is the largest single owner of fresh water resources in the world. This vast abundance of water has prompted some to advocate its export to water-poor regions, primarily the southwestern region of the United States. The debate over whether to export water from Canada has continued over the past three decades. Although the federal government's policy officially opposing large-scale exports has been in place since 1987, public fears nevertheless continue.

States Rubin (2010):

> With over one million lakes, including part ownership of the Great Lakes, and massive ice fields, Canada is home to nearly nine per cent of the world's supply of fresh water. But with a population of less than one per cent of the world's total, Canada has a lot of room for water exports. In time, those exports might be more valuable than the 170 billion barrels of oil that are trapped in the country's oil sands. The notion of exporting water is still a taboo subject in Canadian policy circles; the country took great pains to keep water out of the North American free-trade agreement.

According to Alexander (2008), "A group of American Indians has been walking around most of Lake Michigan this spring to focus public attention on the intrinsic value of water. The sixth annual Mother Earth Water Walk continues through May 12. 'The important thing we want to tell people is that our water is not for sale, it's for us to use respectfully,' said Josephine Mandamin, an Ojibway Indian from Ontario who co-founded the walk. 'It is important to keep our waters clean to ensure the everlasting use for our grandchildren and their grandchildren.'"

Most Canadians are bitterly opposed to the exportation of water. Virtual unanimity of opinion, however, hardly guarantees common sense.[74] It may only indicate that people tend to think in the same tired ruts. And this, unfortunately, applies to the present case.

What are the problems that Canadians suffer due to this protectionist attitude? They suffer from the difficulties that all refusals to trade create: reduction in their standards of living.[75] Canada is up to its armpits in water. There is more water per capita in this country than in practically any other nation in the world.

Among the disquieting elements in this discussion is that it does not seem to have occurred to anyone to determine the price Canadians might be offered in return for their precious, but renewable, water resources. All participants act almost as if the question were one of giving this asset away, for free. But trade is precisely the opposite. It is not the unilateral making of a gift; it is, rather, an *exchange* of commodities. And under voluntary commercial interaction, the presumption is that both parties gain; if they did not, there would hardly be mutual agreement to engage in it.

The feeling, that selling water amounts to giving it away, suggests confusion about the meaning of ownership. The sentiment is typically phrased as "We shouldn't sell OUR water," or, "We cannot let some foreign corporation buy up half of CANADA's resources." However, it is not "our" water; nor is it "Canada's." Or if it is Canada's, then it is so only because it was stolen. It properly belongs to whoever homesteaded it. This commodity, as with all natural material, has categorically no value until an individual or consortium of people finds a use for it and puts it to beneficial use. Only then does it become a resource. Through mixing his own labor with the water, the entrepreneur makes it valuable and converts this otherwise slippery nuisance into his properly prized possession. In short, the water is *his*—not ours. To make it "ours" by aggression without payment is no different than pulling out a gun and forcing a child to hand over his lollypop.

Suppose, then, that Canada's neighbors to the south were to offer the northerners $10.00 per quart for H_2O. Is there any Canadian who would not be deliriously happy to sell water to the U.S. on these conditions? Why, by sending them a few trillion gallons under these conditions—a mere pittance in terms of the astronomical availabilities—Canadians could all be rich beyond their wildest dreams.

Naturally, no one would rationally offer such an exalted price under today's conditions.[76] But the point still holds: crucial to a determination of whether it is in the interest of Canadians to sell water is what they would be offered in return. Without knowing that, members of that country are not in a position to accept or decline such an offer. Especially, bureaucrats of the state cannot legitimately forbid a water holder from selling his property to whomever he wishes, at any mutually agreeable price.

What if the price offered were more reasonable? Say, one penny per barrel? Then, the advantages and disadvantages might be more evenly balanced. Perhaps the best result under these stipulated conditions would be to meet part of the demand in an attempt to obtain still more advantageous terms of trade.

There is a great difficulty, however, in any such scenario. Water in Canada, unlike other natural resources, is not privately owned.[77] Rather, it is possessed on much the same basis as were commodities in the pre-perestroika Soviet Union. That is, the government owns them.[78]

It will not be easy to privatize water resources. Indeed, the very idea will appear ludicrous to many. But if Canadians are to put water exports on a business basis, if they are to become international "drawers of water" at a time of drought, no less must be undertaken.

How would private property in water help alleviate these problems? There is of course no guarantee that private ownership of bodies of water would address them. If the government remained obdurate, and absolutely refused to allow one drop of this precious fluid[79] to be exported to any other country, then, it might readily be argued, privatization would not help at all. (Though what kind of privatization is it that does not allow the owner to dispose of his property?)[80] However, we can consider a more realistic scenario, where water is placed on an equal legal footing with other liquids such as oil and milk. While the Canadian government cannot be considered a pure free trader with regard to either of these latter commodities, it is also not the case that they have placed insuperable barriers against international commercial activity with regard to them. Thus, there is some hope that if water were considered more in line with these other liquids, there might well be some movement in the direction of free trade with regard to it.

What is it about water that removes it from the commercial realm, at least in the minds of not only Canadians, but most people? It is purely speculative, but perhaps there is a kinship between it and yet another liquid, this time, blood, which shares with water an aversion for treating it as a commercial product. Why oil, milk, orange juice, soda, and dozens of other liquids, but not blood[81] and water? The human body, of course, is made up, mainly, of water, and blood is in our circulatory system. This is a mystery beyond the powers of the present authors to solve. Perhaps there is some sort of atavistic or biological explanation. The puzzle is that milk, too, is part of the human makeup, at least for women.[82] But our warrant here is not to solve the problem of why some fluids are widely acceptable for trade, and others not. We are looking at the problem from an economic point of view, not a psychological one. And from the perspective of economic science, there is a clear answer to the question of "What are the problems that Canadians and most others suffer due to this refusal to allow water to enter the commercial realm?" They suffer from having a less prosperous economy than would otherwise be the case. In the extreme, this can cause actual death, due to shortages of the precious fluid.

CASE STUDY F — THE GULF OF ADEN, HOW PROPERTY RIGHTS AND A FREE MARKET WOULD SOLVE CONFLICTS ON THE OCEAN

"Δὶς ἐς τὸν αὐτὸν ποταμὸν οὐκ ἂν ἐμβαίης." (You could not step twice into the same river.) —Heraclitus of Ephesus (1921)

With the background of an unowned sea and immorality in the context of the all-powerful state, The Gulf of Aden, otherwise known as the Gulf of Berbera, is a troubled patch of ocean located between the Horn of Africa (Cape Guardafui) and the Arabian Peninsula. Refer to Figure 0.3 in the Map section. To the south is the Federal Republic of Somalia and to the North is the Republic of Yemen (are either of these real "republics"?). At its western end the Gulf narrows to a straight, Bab-el-Mandeb, connecting to the Red Sea. At the other end of which is the Suez Canal. The Republic of Djibouti (ditto) occupies the peninsula of Ras Siyyan while the peninsula of Ras Menheli on the opposite shore lies within Yemen. The eastern end opens up to the Arabian Sea and the Indian Ocean. The general shape is influenced by an extension of the Indian Ocean Ridge rift zone. The greatest depth exceeds 17,000-feet.[83]

The Gulf lies in the vicinity of 13 degrees north latitude in the zone of northeast trade winds. Tropical weather dominates the area, and monsoons and typhoons are not unknown. The surrounding land tends towards desert. The sound is a major shipping route connecting the Mediterranean and the Red Seas to all points east. That includes the oil rich Persian Gulf countries as well as India, Indonesia, China, Japan and numerous other locations, in Southeast Asia and beyond.

In general the people of Somalia are desperately poor. Many in Yemen and Somalia hold the countries on the north shore of the Mediterranean in low regard. As is well-known, shipping in this corner of the world is subjected to high risk. The Indian Navy usually maintains a warship in the area to escort vessels leaving and approaching India. In addition other countries including the United States provide patrols. China has sent a submarine as a counter terrorism measure (LaGrone, 2014).[84] These are credited with the touted decline in piratical activity over the last decade (Sterio, 2013; Piracy statistics, 2013).

The Gulf enjoys a rich diversity of aquatic life. Significant populations of rock lobsters, sea turtles, sardines, mackerel, dolphin, tuna, billfish, and sharks occupy these waters. Even whales are frequently sighted. While fishing for these and other species occurs among the local peoples, there is little large scale commercial activity in this regard.

To understand how terrorism and piracy have come to be endemic in the region, a brief review of the history is helpful. Prior to attempting to describe Yemen and Somalia, it is important to remember that the people occupying in these countries live ordinary day to day lives. Most of the time, it is peaceful. There are nice buildings and consumer supplies are available. Flowers bloom, and the skies are blue. People have friends and neighbors. The western media and other propagandists frequently forget to mention these things.[85] What follows exists within that context.

Yemen

Yemen lies in the southern Arabian Peninsula. It was at one time part of the Ottoman Empire.[86] In the early 19th century, Britain took an interest in the City of Aden as a possible coaling station on the route to India.[87] In 1839, they bombarded the City after a pirate attack by Arab tribesmen.[88] For several decades, the British maintained protectorate agreements with several of the local tribes. Jealous of what they claimed to be incursions into their sphere of influence, the Ottomans returned to the area. Imam Yahya hamid ed-Din al-Mutawakkil, who ruled the northwestern part of what is now Yemen, moved into the areas abandoned by the Ottomans in 1918 in competition with the British who were in support of the Idrsids, which occupied southeastern Yemen. Using aircraft, the Brits continued to fight Yahya to a standstill. The Italians recognized Yahya as king of Yemen in 1926. The British remained involved because the Sauds, who supported the Idrsids, appealed to them for aid against Yahya.

South Yemen (in the east) gained independence from England in 1967. By 1979 it had joined the Soviet Bloc and adopted Marxist practices though the decline of the Soviet Union and resistance to rivalries with North Yemen resulted in a short-lived government. It was not until 1990 that the two regimes were brought together. Former North Yemeni, Ali Abdallah Saleh became president of the then united Yemen. Despite this richly convoluted history, or maybe because of it, Yemen compared to Somalia is a relatively integrated country and fiercely independent.[89] The rivalries and ingrained anger are intense. The tendency towards rage was intensified by Saleh's imposition of rather severe controls, the murder of rivals, obtaining a term extension from Parliament, etc. The people have good reason to hate outsiders. This justifiable opposition to the west is manifested in violent attacks.[90]

This fighting continues as one Abdulmalik AlHouthi has taken possession of large portions of North Yemen (*Gedab News*, 2014). In the meantime "On October 14, 2014, in a rally commemorating the 1963 revolution of South Yemen, politicians made clear calls for secession from the Yemeni union which a politician called, 'The barbaric occupation of North Yemen.'"

Somalia

Why in such a rich environment has the outright theft that is piracy taken hold in Somalia? It goes back to the 1970s and 80s and earlier.[91] In the early 20th century, the country was divided between British (along the Gulf of Aden) and Italian (along the Indian Ocean coast) Somaliland. Following World War II, Britain took control of both portions. After independence, Somalia had a democratic government. That means that rival groups were seeking majority status and hence power over other clans. And clans were the locus of personal identity. Mohamed Siad Barre took power as a military dictator with absolute power. One of his first moves to cement control was to institute a mandatory language: *Af Soomaali* (Somali). Schools were required to teach and conduct classes in this dialect. Students were sent out to "educate" nomads.

Nationalism was promoted. It was made illegal to inquire about or even consider a person's clan.[92] Informers were used to report such "criminals" who continued to employ clanism ("see something—say something"). Such reports could lead to arrest and imprisonment.

The military was used to bring Somali people into a greater Somalia which included Djibouti and parts of Ethiopia and Kenya. This went so far as an invasion and attempted annexation of the Ogaden region of Ethiopia. Unfortunately for Seeydi[93] Barre, his ally, the Soviet Union disapproved this naked aggression and withdrew its support. Cuban troops were sent in to aid Somalia's western neighbor. Need we doubt the result? In the late 70s the United States then became a Barre supporter.

After the failure of the Ogaden campaign, Barre suffered loss of support among the local population. Rebellions were put down with summary executions. Several governments in exile were formed. Barre attempted to increase his totalitarian control over the country.[94] Civil war broke out in 1991 based on the historical clans attempting to assert power.[95]

Activities undertaken by the United States, and Presidents Bush and Obama[96] even dating back into the Clinton years, have not helped. In the traditional style of previous imperial powers, the United States and the United Nations[97] have stationed military troops in the Horn of Africa. These soldiers had pulled out in 1994 following the First Battle of Mogadishu[98] in 1993 (Scahill, 2013). Starting in 2003, with a meeting with Mohamed Afrah Qanyare, US fighters in the Global War on Terror began working with Somali warlords to track down and kill Al-Qaida members.[99] The CIA and the JSOC[100] set up a base, Camp Lemonnier, in Djibouti to watch over Yemen and Somalia (Scahill, 2013, p. 122). Far from limiting the power of terrorists, Washington's meddling and use of ill-advised "snatch and grab" tactics caused a sweeping backlash which enabled the entry of Al-Qaida (Scahill, 2013, pp. 121 and 123).

Why Piracy?

How does piracy fit into this sad situation? Most Somalis view their problems as stemming at least in part from foreign intervention: first from colonial masters, Britain and Italy, then from Russia, and finally from America and the U.N., Somalis, speaking in generalization, view all of these as well as current interventionists, India, Italy, the United States, France, the United Nations, etc. as booty seekers[101] attempting to steal resources from their country. Fishermen feel threatened, and have suffered attack by international naval forces (Appleton 2012).

The pirates are viewed locally as protectors of the waters around their land and enjoy a legitimacy based on that perception. In other words, those who are regarded by international communities as pirates are more akin to privateers[102] from the Somali viewpoint. For the benefit of their economy, these adventurers, especially western trespassers, are looked upon as violent invaders who are seen as intent on subjugating the local population to facilitate carting away resources.

The local stationing of powerful modern destroyers and guided missile frigates only intensifies the suspicion of the native denizens. Since there is no way for them to contend directly with such military might, they must wage asymmetric warfare (Rand Corp. 2013). By posing as fishing boats, which they are when not in attack mode, they can inspect unarmed merchant ships; and when no one is looking, they will strike. They assault their enemy where he is weakest and thus gain strength even as their opponent is most feeble.

The competing programs of Somalis protecting their natural resources via "privateering" and the west defending its shipping via modern navies enables the issues and the violence. Both sides have "right on their side," of course.

Somaliland,[103] the western portion of the north extension along the gulf, differs from the rest of Somalia. There a desire for recognition by the larger international community has added legitimacy to the counter piracy initiatives. However, because of the overlap between the objectives of pirates and entrepreneurs, both piracy and countermeasures can damage the people and their economic well-being. The rest of Somalia including Puntland, the United Islamic Courts (UIC), and areas allied with UIC are not seeking independent recognition, so the same dynamics do not apply. There is a Federal Government of Somalia which has its capital in Mogadishu and is recognized internationally but which faces widespread approbation and armed resistance.[104]

Private Ownership of the Gulf of Aden

This book advocates private ownership of bodies of water. How could privatization solve such deeply rooted issues, and how could it be implemented? The suspicion of all external (foreign) initiatives is rampant because a long history of exploitation, murder, and theft continuing to the present, 2015, has led to terrorism from the north, Yemen, and piracy (privateering) from the south, Somalia.

Implementation

Implementation of private ownership is undoubtedly the most difficult subject because each player is convinced of its righteousness and will not take no for an answer. Each will kill to protect these supposed rights. The libertarian answer is to analyze this situation via the prism of property rights. They go back a long way.

Fishermen from Somalia and Yemen first "homesteaded" the Gulf of Aden millennia ago. Today, their successors continue to fish these waters. Formalization of such assets as legally defendable in courts[105] would go a long way towards mollifying Somali and Yemeni combatants. Fishing rights would necessarily include the legitimate ability to follow, husband, and/or fence off their fisheries as most beneficial to themselves.[106] The point is, if Somali/Yemeni assets are universally recognized and legitimately unassailable, the need for alternative defenses such as privateers (pirates and terrorists) disappears.

The use of the Gulf as a transportation route goes back at least a couple of hundred years, maybe more. No reason exists why shipping across the Gulf must impinge fishing rights which are much older by millennia. However, the local citizens may not see it that way. If the relatively late arriving carriers and their successors are perceived as invaders, it becomes a libertarian court case. The fishermen would sue the perceived trespassers who would defend their actions by attempting to prove their activities justified. Win or lose, both sides are honored in that their case is heard in a fair venue. Should the fishing interests prevail the shippers would then have to cease and desist in their activities. But that does not mean they are shut down and forever barred from plying these waters. They could find alternative routes; they could purchase or rent shipping lanes. Once again, all sides are honored as owners of their particular assets. What they would not be allowed to do is bribe some state run navy to shoot down the locals.

Private Ownership

How would private ownership work? The implementation described above suggests longer term mechanisms for solving these problems. In previous chapters, a wide variety of enterprises have been discussed. Should a valuable resource be discovered that is currently unknown, entrepreneurs would seek to exploit it. To do so, they would establish a homestead. If current interested parties saw this new establishment as a threat, they would issue a challenge. Either the newcomer would demonstrate no damage, or he would have to purchase access, or maybe abandon his project. Private proprietorships provide the means to solve conflicts and to implement those institutions.

Would private ownership of the oceans solve the problem of piracy? Yes and no. Yes, if private property rights, along with private courts, were allowed to prevail. No, if not. But the same may be said of any issue.[107] The point is, do not blame private property rights for piracy, or the tragedy of the commons, or shortages of toilet paper, if this institution is not allowed to fully function.

NOTES

1. An estuary is the wide channel of a river as it approaches an ocean or small bay, with tidal mixing of fresh and salt water and including the mixing zone extending into the receiving body.

2. The 10 Deadliest Hurricanes (CNN, 2014) in the United States—1851–2010—in terms of number of deaths. This measure is not the same as "most severe" according to the Hurricane Severity Index (2008).

	Name and/or Place	Year	Category	Deaths
1.	Galveston, TX	1900	4	8,000+
2.	Southeastern FL	1928	4	2,500
3.	Hurricane Katrina	2005	3	1,723
4.	Louisiana	1893	4	1100–1400
5.	South Carolina/Georgia	1893	3	1000–1200
6.	Georgia/South Carolina	1881	2	700
7.	Hurricane Audrey	1957	4	416
8.	Florida Keys	1935	5	408
9.	Louisiana	1856	4	400
10.	Florida	1926	4	372

3. The volume of a flood is the sum of the products of the average flow rate over each time interval and the length of the respective time interval for the entire duration of the flood. Alternatively, it is the area under the hydrograph normally shown with the time on the horizontal axis and the flow rate on the vertical axis.

4. The Corioles effect, with respect to weather, refers to the movement of the atmosphere resulting from the rotation of the earth and the momentum of the atmosphere. It is responsible for the trend wherein weather patterns move from west to east and, in the northern hemisphere, for the tendency of south winds to curve towards the east (i.e. become west winds). It is also responsible for the direction of circular movement of water flowing into a drain.

5. The return period of a flood (e.g. 100-year) is the inverse of the probability during each year that a given flow rate will be exceeded based on discharge statistics. Thus, a 100-year event is a theoretical flow that has a 1-percent chance of being surpassed by one or more larger floods in any given year.

6. That is, at our present level of competence. However, if the public policy recommendations of the present book are taken up, and private enterprise supplants government mismanagement of water resources, it is to be expected that our understanding of these matters will radically improve.

7. For a very rough calculation of the volume, the area of the lake is 730 sq mi (SFWMD. Dynamic Date) with the height of the levee at 30-feet, the volume is about 14 million acre-feet.

8. The discharge is reduced by storage according to the following formula: $Q_{out} = Q_{in} — \Delta S / \Delta t$; where Q_{out} is the flow rate leaving the storage facility including infiltration, Q_{in} is the discharge of streams tributary to the storage facility (including precipitation), ΔS is the change is storage volume, and Δt is the time interval of analysis. As long as S is increasing, Q will decrease. S increases until the reservoir overflows or until the quantity of Q_{in} drops below Q_{out}.

9. Some might prefer to use "may" rather than "will." The assertion being made is that what may occur will in fact become reality at some time in the indefinite future just as surely as the sun will rise in the morning.

10. States Thomas Sowell (2000): "It is hard to imagine a more stupid or more dangerous way of making decisions than by putting those decisions in the hands of people who pay no price for being wrong."

11. Colorado Constitution; Article XVI—Mining and Irrigation; Section 6—Diverting Unappropriated Water Priority Preferred Uses: The right to divert the unappropriated waters of any natural stream to beneficial uses shall never be denied. Priority of appropriation shall give the better right.

12. Simply observing a scene does not demonstrate sufficient labor or commitment to establish a property right. Furthermore, absconding with the land and water of private owners by force of arms, using resources stolen from other people, a la the state, establishes no property right. Only a private person who is willing to dedicate his own effort and resources to create and maintain a park or nature preserve can establish a legitimate right. If he wishes, once established, the owner may charge fees for hunters, tourists, nature lovers, etc. to visit his facility (Nelson, 2015A; Nelson, 2015B; Block, 2012).

13. "To be in priority" is a common term used in the prior appropriation system. It means that the water source has sufficient water to fill the call for water at least up to the right under consideration as well as all prior rights.

14. The word "call" has special meaning in the industry. A typical expression might be as follows, "A farmer who wants water puts a *call* on the river, but he receives it only if his right is *in priority.*"

15. Friedman (1962) explains much of what would now be called crony capitalism on the basis of this phenomenon: benefits are concentrated, costs are diffuse.

16. In terms of Rothbard's (1982) analysis, pollution is a trespass, a violation of private property rights.

17. At least for the foreseeable future, assuming present technological ability on the part of prospective owners.

18. No one is omniscient, and a *perfect* resolution for a complex system with a long history of injustice falls between very difficult and impossible. Selling the Dike is inferior because the state, the despoiler of this resource in the first place, would unjustly end up with the proceeds of the sale and it already has far too much ill-gotten money at its disposal. Likewise, a gift to a previous owner (homesteader) would fall short of justice because the previous owner was probably well paid-off with money stolen from taxpayers. The current managers and personnel maintaining the system are employees of the state and, if anything, deserve to be charged to recompense taxpayers, not granted a gift. (In this case, the term "homesteaders" includes those who have purchased a property from original homesteaders.)

19. For a discussion on enforcement of liability in a libertarian society refer to: Rothbard, 1973. See also Epstein, 1980; Hoppe, 2004; Kinsella, 2009E; Lewin, 1982; Rizzo, 1980A; Rothbard, 1979, 1982.

20. Suppose it is the case that "nature" is responsible for 100x acre feet of flooding, and that due to the efforts of the private owner, only 90x units harm other people's property. Then, the owner would not be responsible for any damages, as they would have occurred in any case, and, indeed, have been reduced due to his efforts. On the other hand, if the damage is in the amount of 120x units, then the owner would be responsible for the damage, but only to the extent of 20x units. The burden of proof, of course, as always, would rest with the plaintiff, not the defendant.

21. For bridges to nowhere, see Utt (2005).

22. In the free society, there would be no more subsidization of building on beaches subject to the depredations of storms.

23. A similar challenge occurs with the repeal of many other statist interferences with the free enterprise system, such as ending rent control, or taxi medallions, or farm subsidies, etc.

24. We are on the wrong side of the Garden of Eden to achieve anything like full justice. But, the enemy of the good is the perfect. *"Le mieux est l'ennemi du bien."* —Voltaire (2010).

25. The Feather River is an Anglicization of *Rio de las Plumas*.

26. The Sacramento River is an Anglicization of *Rio del Santissimo Sacramento*.

27. The Sacramento and San Joaquin (Saint Joachim in English, the river was earlier called: *Rio de San Francisco*) Valleys are divided into "basins" by the rivers which are relatively higher in elevation than the floors of the respective basins. For example, the Colusa Basin is separated from the Sutter Basin by the Sacramento River.

28. Political correctness mandates that we call these bodies of water wetlands, but in our view a swamp is a swamp is a swamp.

29. Suisun Bay is really a tidal lake (an inland freshwater lake at a low enough elevation that the twice daily rise and fall of the surface can be measured) on the east side of the Coast Range connected to San Francisco Bay via San Pablo Bay and the Carquinez Strait.

30. Imagine a bathtub 1-square mile in size. 600,000 cubic feet per second (cfs) would fill the tub to a depth of 1-foot in less than a minute.

31. Some of the larger dams include Shasta Dam, Folsom Dam, Oroville Dam, New Bullards Bar Dam, Monticello Dam, East Park, Stoney Gorge, Black Butte, Whiskeytown, Collins, Englebright, Camp Far West, Nimbus, and Camanche.

32. Recent levee failures accompanied by major flooding include: 1955—Feather River—Yuba City, Sutter County; 1972—Sacramento/San Joaquin River Delta—Andrus and Brannon Islands; 1986—Yuba and Feather Rivers—Linda, Oliverhurst, Yuba County; 1997—Sacramento, Feather, and Cosumnes Rivers—Oliverhust, Arboga, Wilton, Sacramento County, Yuba County (Roos, 2007; Pezzaglia, Phil. 2011).

33. A boil occurs where the hydraulic head between the river side and the landward side of a levee is sufficient to cause an increase in the velocity of groundwater adequate to wash out the soil. Unless staunched, a "pipe," or passageway through the ground, will develop rapidly and cause the levee to collapse. It is called this because the soil appears to boil.

34. Cross section: a shape that would be exposed by cutting straight through something as a river, generally perpendicular to the centerline. Roughness: an estimated measure of the irregularities in a surface such as a river bed; for example a concrete channel has low roughness or is smooth while a jagged rock channel with many bushes and trees has high roughness.

35. Sand and gravel lens: a pocket, usually convex lens shaped, of relatively permeable sand and gravel within a larger soil matrix. A permeable soil allows fluid to flow rapidly and often increases the danger of levee failure.

36. For a splendid Austro-libertarian analysis of insurance, and its relation to the free society, see Hoppe, 2006B.

37. See on this Block, 2005A, 2005B, 2005C, 2005D, 2006B; Block and Rockwell, 2007; Rockwell and Block, 2010.

38. FEMA backs up this claim. Does this sound familiar with respect to Obamacare?

39. Yes, Fallingwater, located in Pennsylvania, has been flooded.

40. An interesting anecdote on how huge these floods can be is the filling of Folsom Reservoir. Though it was predicted to take a year to fill, in 1956 when the dam was nearly complete, the second largest storm recorded up to that time on the American River filled the reservoir in a week. The City of Sacramento was saved from major inundation (SAFCA, 2008).

41. Presumably, there would be, at least at a premium high enough to incorporate the full risks.

42. See on this Adie, 1990; Ahlbrandt, 1973; Alston, 2007; Anderson and Hill, 1996; Bennett, 1980; Bennett and Johnson, 1980; Boardman and Vining, 1989; Borcherding, 1977; Borcherding, Burnaby, Pommerehne, and Schneider, 1982; Butler, 1985, 1986; Chapman, 2008; Davies, 1971; De Alessi, 1982; Dewenter, and Malatesta, 2000; Fitzgerald, 1989; Frech, 1976; Hanke, 1987; Lindsay, 1976; Megginson and Netter, 2000, 2001; Moore, S., 1987; Moore, T., 1990; Poole, 1976; Priest, 1975; Savas, 1979; Vining and Boardman, 1992; White, 1978. Some of these publications argue in favor of contracting out: the government awards contracts to private firms to implement so-called public sector jobs. The present authors are not proponents

of "better government at half the price" or pseudo-privatization wherein tax dollars are used to hire private companies to do "public works" jobs. We prefer that fully free market firms undertake these projects. Entrepreneurial organizations that sink or swim on their own generate better outcomes without state intermediation. Of course we see some relatively second-rate benefits to the public when private companies work for tax dollars, when compared to outright government employees. We refer to these publications only for their empirical findings that private enterprise is more efficient than government.

43. The "dollar vote" refers to the fact that every dollar spent by free agents expresses non-ignorable preferences.

44. In most cases, they benefit *ex post* also. That is, they do not regret their trade after the fact.

45. All such calculations are always in terms of present discounted values.

46. The streets of Old Town Sacramento have been filled, in some places as much as 14-feet, so that they and the adjacent buildings are protected from floods (SAFCA, 2008). This is something that perhaps should happen to the Lower 9th Ward in New Orleans. Of course, in the free society, this would be determined by the owners of the relevant properties.

47. The authors note that after a few days, we heard no more about it. Apparently these dire catastrophes evaporated into the ether.

48. We admit, the perpetrator's name, "Freedom Industries," is embarrassing to the libertarian case.

49. In a statist society, the police, who are supposed to protect the public, are all too often manned by excitable personnel with the machismo to feel free to shoot innocents because they do not cower sufficiently. Almost daily somewhere in the US, "on duty" police shoot or beat unarmed people and/or lodge false charges in order to enhance their reputation as committed crime fighters. They are themselves criminals. How often does a private security guard shoot someone?

50. It might not be "too big" to fail, but it would be too "wet" to be allowed to do so. That is, we need more than private ownership of rivers to attain free enterprise in this regard. Also required is that government not bail out any private river owner.

51. While playing Nick Pulovski in "The Rookie." After all, toasters are manufactured by private concerns with much to lose if they get it wrong.

52. The study is not identified in the article but is likely Galloway and Riley (1999, p. 25).

53. In the order referenced in the article these authorities include: "Michelle Sneed, USGS Hydrologist; Chris Scheuring, California Farm Bureau Federation environmental attorney; Andrew Stone, American Ground Water Trust executive director; Mark Larson, the conservation district general manager; and Chase Hurley, manager of the San Luis Canal Co.

54. Water capacity is related to grain size. Courser material has more storage because the pores between the grains are larger.

55. Unconsolidated soil has a higher capacity, again because of larger pore volume. This type of formation (a geological term referring to a structure with similar properties laid down within a geological time frame) is compressible and will condense upon pumping of water because the pore pressure declines and in extreme cases can become negative; that is, suction may develop which pulls the material tighter.

56. The Central Valley has a northern portion drained by the Sacramento River which generally flows southward and a southern portion drained by the San Joaquin River, flowing northwesterly. The two join in the "Delta" and discharge through the Carquinez Strait to San Pablo Bay, San Francisco Bay, and finally the Pacific Ocean. The most southerly extremity of the Valley does not drain to the Pacific but rather to Tulare Lake, Kern "Lake" and Buena Vista "Lake" near Bakersfield (McDonnell, 1962). The latter lakes are frequently dry. Nevertheless, the moisture does drain via the aquifer as above.

57. Mining refers to the extraction of a natural resource, in this case water. To use the term "mining" in this application emphasizes the fact that the resource is being removed faster than it replenishes and, like a mine, will become depleted until the resource ceases to exist.

58. Another cause of subsidence in California, beyond the scope of this chapter is oxidation of peat in the soils of the Sacramento-San Joaquin Delta.

59. The headwork of the Aqueduct near Tracy, CA lifts water about 240-feet. With additional lift stations along the way, the project takes northern CA water as far south as the Los Angeles basin.

60. The headwork of the Canal also near Tracy, CA raises water from the Delta by about 200-feet from which it flows southeast (upstream relative to the San Joaquin) to Mendota.

61. For reference, the elevation of Mendota, CA is about 174-feet above mean sea level and 115 miles from the Delta for an overall gradient of 0.029-percent (that is, as the crow flies; along the San Joaquin River it is much flatter).

62. "The Central Valley of California, which includes the San Joaquin Valley, the Sacramento Valley, and the Sacramento-San Joaquin Delta, produces about 25 percent of the nation's table food on only 1 percent of the country's farmland" (Galloway and Riley, p. 1).

63. The description of saltwater intrusion is greatly simplified in these paragraphs. The intent is to simply highlight a few of the effects of diverting water, including groundwater, from the natural waterways. For a map of the Sacramento/San Joaquin Delta refer to this site: http://www.ppic.org/content/pubs/report/R_207JLMap1_1.pdf, accessed on 5-4-2015.

64. "An artificial balance is maintained in the water exchanged between the Delta and the San Francisco Bay. Freshwater inflows regulated by upstream dams and diversions supply water to the Delta ecosystems and to farms and cities in central and southern California. Subsidence of Delta islands threatens the stability of island levees and the quality of Delta water. Delta levee failures would tip the water-exchange balance in favor of more saltwater intrusion, which can ruin the water for agriculture and domestic uses" (Ingebritsen, 1999, p. 92).

65. Another cause increasing salinity of San Joaquin Valley soils is mismanagement of irrigation. All naturally occurring water contains at least some salt. If a field is irrigated to minimize discharge, salt will be left behind as the moisture is evapo/transpired to the atmosphere. To prevent this effect, enough water must be applied to carry away the salts. The temptation, of course, is to use every drop in order to increase crop yield in the short term.

66. Salmonidae is a family of fish that includes such species as salmon, chars, trout, and others.

67. Those who like to picture themselves as *pro*gressives, but who are in fact *re*gressives that harken back to ancient regimes based on violent control.

68. This is called graft and is illegal: but what statist bureaucrat ever let that stop him?

69. Ecclesiastes 1:9, King James Version.

70. The paraphrase is based on Samuel Taylor Coleridge, *The Rime of the Ancyent Marinere*.

71. The rest of this advertisement asks in effect, then why allow foreigners to buy up Canadian airwaves, which are also precious, and limited, and thus should not be sold, either?

72. For further evidence regarding Canada's policy against exporting water, see: Environment Canada, 2013 Johansen, 2002, 2010; D'Aliesio, 2012; Rubin, 2010; Scarpeleggia, 2012.

73. There is indeed such a thing as free market environmentalism, in sharp contrast to that expressed by these Canadians, and the present book is an example of that. By the way, we might want to be aware that The Heritage Foundation's 2014 Trade Freedom Score for Canada is 88.3 (a rank of 9th worldwide) while that of the US is 86.8 (a tie for 39th place) (Riley, 2014).

74. "The majority never has right on its side." —Henrik Johan Ibsen, *An Enemy of the People*, Act IV.

75. It would take us too far afield to defend the claim that free trade is the most economically efficient system known to man, and that all interferences with it—tariffs, quotas, discriminatory practices, buy local provisions—are wealth destroying. The seminal literature on this is Smith, 1776. See also: Block, Horton and Walker, 1998; Brandly, 2002; Brown, 1987; Friedman and Friedman, 1997; Johnsson, 2004; Landsburg, 2008; Murphy, 2004; Ricardo, 1821.

76. Perhaps this high price could occur on the moon or Mars one day far in the future, but not here and now.

77. This is true of every nation on earth. Why pick on Canada? We are not, here, inspired by the South Park movie "Blame Canada." Rather, it is that this country is up to its armpits in water, unlike few others on the planet, and yet acts as if drought is right around the corner.

78. Under the inspired leadership of Chairman Gorbachev, the Russians battled valiantly to overthrow almost a century-long dependence on central economic planning. Unfortunately, at the very time the Communists seem to be embracing the teachings of Adam Smith, politicians, pundits, and professors in the West are urging a move to embrace the teachings of Karl Marx, in the very opposite direction. The reactions against free trade, privatization, and deregulation are all cases in point.

79. The phrase "precious bodily fluid" played an important role in the movie "Dr. Strange-love" (1964).

80. It would be private in the sense it could be used as the owner wishes *within* the country, but exports would be prohibited. At best, this could be considered a "semi-privatization." But this arrangement is hardly unique. When a country forbids exports of a good, its status as a private good is severely truncated, but does not disappear entirely.

81. For the case in favor of free markets in blood, allowing it to be bought and sold like any other valuable commodity, see Blundell, 2003; Healy, 2006; Seldon, 1968.

82. Says Dutton (2011): "Most body fluids, tissues, and organs—semen, blood, livers, kidneys—are highly regulated by government authorities. But not breast milk." See also (Block, 2013B, pp. 103–108).

83. For general information on the Gulf of Aden refer to Encyclopædia Britannica, 2014 and World Atlas.com, Undated.

84. One must wonder exactly how a submarine is the most effective counter-terrorism tool.

85. Life in Somalia is often compared with that of more advanced countries such as the U.S., Japan, France, Canada, to the great detriment of the former. But when more of a *ceteris paribus* viewpoint contrasts this beleaguered nation with its immediate neighbors, a very different and more positive picture emerges. See on this Leeson, 2007; Powell, Ford and Nowrasteh, 2008; Powell, 2009; Coyne, 2006; Little, 2003; Menkhaus, 2003; Mubarak, 1997, 2002; Nenova, 2004; Van Notten, 2005.

86. A more full description of Yemen can be found at these sources: CIA, 2015; BBC, 2015A; Alcock, Undated; Times, Various dates; World Bank, 1979; YemenWeb.com, 2011; Almadhagi, 1996; IWM, 2014; Polynational, 2014; and Peterson, 2009.

87. The Suez Canal did not open until 1869 though freight was carried overland prior to the canal where ships would continue the journey to India (Suez, 2008).

88. Apparently, with regard to piracy in this region, there is no new thing under the sun.

89. Recently, this decades long apparent stability has proved deceptive (BBC, 2015E).

90. For reasons stemming from Turkish, British, Soviet, and American incursions and foreign attempts to control the people of Yemen, your authors view these attacks by Yemenis as defensive in nature. The attack on the USS Cole is but one example (FBI, Undated). We fully realize this will be a rather unpopular stance in some quarters. But, imagine the shoe was on the other foot. Let us assume that Yemen was a gigantic country which had long interfered with America. The Yemeni navy had a ship stationed off the coast of Virginia. Some U.S. patriots, perhaps Tea Party members, attacked this vessel. The Yeminis would have been apoplectic that a boat of theirs was partially destroyed, and some of its sailors killed. What would have been the response of Patriotic Americans? To ask this is to answer it. What was the USS Cole doing there in the first place? Surely, its location there was not compatible with this statement of one of our early presidents John Quincy Adams: "America . . . goes not abroad seeking monsters to destroy. . . . We favor the freedom of all nations, but will fight, only, to protect our own." For cites on this see Vance, 2012; Congressional Record, 2005, p. 4864; and https://www.google.ca/?gfe_rd=cr&ei=elpaVaCCGLE8geU2IGwDg&gws_rd=ssl#q=%22goes+not+abroad+seeking+monsters+to+destroy%22.

91. On Somalia refer to the following sources: CIA, 2015; Goodwin, 2006; BBC, 2015B; BBC, 2015C; BBC, 2015D; Reno, 2011; Hanson, 2008; James, 1995; RBC Radio, 2014; Dalsan, 2015; Plaut, Martin, 2013.

92. Other than changing a few names and places, how does this Somali version of political correctness differ from other PC programs such as that currently promulgated in the United States where even common language usage becomes verboten?

93. Somali title for "Sir" used here sarcastically.

94. Once again, the usual and classic moves of desperation were used in Somalia to maintain power despite the loss of moral support for the regime.

95. Many regard Somalia as being in a state of anarchy. This perception completely misreads the current situation (as of 2015). Granted it is a "failed state," but it is actually a region of competing states with each clan striving to wrest control from the others and exercising unmitigated power over their subjects. In the words of von Clausewitz (1976, Chapter 1, Section 24): "War is the continuation of policy by other means." Virtually all Somalis believe heart and soul in the efficacy of government, that is to say in *their* clan's government. It is just that none of the competing states has sufficient power to decisively defeat the others. This condition, many governments, is as opposite as possible for it to be from anarchy, which is a situation where NO state exists. Thus it is chaos, not anarchy, that reigns. Nevertheless, multiple governments do leave open opportunities for entrepreneurs to step up and provide services unavailable elsewhere. Should one particular warlord become too oppressive, the more adventurous, open-minded people will start migrating to freer zones.

96. Otherwise known as OBushama.

97. UNOSOM II or United Nations Operations Somalia II.

98. The "Black Hawk Down" incident.

99. "… they started cooperating with the warlords, thinking that the best way to combat terrorism was to help the warlords become stronger, and chase away the fundamentalist from Somalia. That backfired" (Scahill, 2013, page 121).

100. Central Intelligence Agency and the Joint Special Operations Command.

101. Members of the Public Choice school would characterize this as "rent seeking." For a critique of such verbiage see Block 2000, 2002.

102. For more on privateers, refer to Chapter 12.

103. The term "Somaliland" currently refers only to the northwestern portion of Somalia even though in the past it referred to British Somaliland and Italian Somaliland which together encompassed the entire territory as currently configured.

104. As examples: in June 2014, US and EU officials met President Hassan Sheikh Mohamud to discuss the deteriorating political situation in Somalia. They met on a warship off Mogadishu for security reasons. In June 2013, a spike in violence transpired with various attacks by Al-Shabab, including on presidential palace and UNDP compound in Mogadishu (BBC. 2015D).

105. Your authors advocate courts run by private adjudicating organizations.

106. For more on proprietorship of wildlife, the reader is referred to Chapter 7.

107. Would private ownership of land or animals solve the tragedy of the commons? Yes and no. Yes, if private property rights, along with private courts, were allowed to prevail. No, if not. Would private ownership of toilet paper solve the problem of the lack of this good in Venezuela? Yes, if private asset possession carries the day. No, if not.

Chapter Fourteen

Debate—Technological Viewpoints that Inform Homesteading, Technological Units

"It is not he who gains the exact point in dispute who scores most in controversy, but he who has shown the most forbearance and better temper." —Samuel Butler, "Reconciliation," (1917, p. 348)

TWO WORKABLE AQUEOUS OWNERSHIP CONCEPTS—A DEBATE

Until man learns to manufacture fresh water and distribute it across continents in teralitres and petalitres with little or no expenditure of energy, it will remain a limited resource. Markets, i.e. *free* markets without cronyism, provide the fairest distribution of scarce commodities. After dismissing the riparian theory as laughable for the reasons exhumed in Chapter 4, we authors recognize two viable alternatives. While not perfectly aligned to their traditional meanings, these could be labeled the "Prior Appropriation" and the "In-Toto" models.

It is rare for a book, any book, to feature a debate between the two coauthors. Scholars ordinarily undertake to coauthor a publication because they agree, entirely, with each other; at least this would be a necessary albeit not sufficient condition. The present case is an exception to this general rule. We two discovered, after we had done more than just a little bit on this undertaking, that we had a serious disagreement with each other on one not unimportant issue: Prior Appropriation versus In Toto ownership. What to do? Stop writing and give up our present efforts as a waste of time? Here, the two of us are in enthusiastic agreement, shocking as it may sound: we both think what we have written to this date makes an important contribution to economics, ecology, intellectual letters, etc. Furthermore, we remain in complete agreement on the radical and most important point of this book: that bodies of water should be privately owned. Therefore, ending our collaboration on this book was not an option. Should we then ignore our disagreements as if they did not exist? This, we both discovered, is not congruent with the intellectual style of either of us. Indeed, we are both committed to truth seeking: "For the sake of truth we are not only permitted to make a quarrel, we are obligated to make a quarrel" (Schick, 2015).

Despite the fact that there are apparently two ways to own naturally occurring fluids, we believe that this essential element of privatization should be advocated most vehemently. It is the ideal that is far more important than the mere operational mechanisms, as important as practicality may be. Thus, we decided upon perhaps an unusual solution to our difficulty: let us have "at" it in print with each other on this topic. Hence: the following debate. There is one more justification for this decision. As we claim in the literature review appendix, this is a unique book. While a few other volumes are entitled as if they favor the complete privatization of all bodies of water, none actually attempt, let alone succeed in, making this case.

Both concepts are based on the Lockean principle of mixing one's labor with a resource to register or enact a homestead (i.e. absent the notorious Lockean proviso, of course). We recognize that "There are continuum problems in political economy. There are no objective non-debatable solutions to any of them. All answers to them are arbitrary. Responding to these challenges are [sic], ideally, the responsibility of courts, juries, etc"[1] (Block, 2011C). A debate, then, there shall be! In the inestimable tradition of the prep-school classroom, of Hayek and Keynes, Stalin and Trotsky, and yes, even the eminent Lucy and Desi, your authors herein duke it out between those different viewpoints (our weapons of choice: 5-gallon water balloons).

Nelson's Initial Position

The Prior Appropriation model is superior to In Toto. "Appropriation" refers to taking a rate of flow and putting it to use. That is, any volume of water used or consumed divided by a period of time. The water right maybe held in fee simple similar to any other real estate with the prerogative to sell or lease at will. "Prior" refers to seniority: the first in use is the first in right. A late arriving interloper, regardless of whether he is upstream or not, who takes this liquid from a historical proprietor is a thief. The flawless Prior Appropriation recognizes that H_2O is finely divisible. As with land whereon parcels are spread across many proprietors varying from minuscule to immense, Prior Appropriation countenances many owners: each with an inviolable property in his pet wet asset.

Block's Initial Position

The technological unit is a key element in setting up private property rights. According to that parable of the blind men and the elephant, one of them touches its leg and thinks he has got hold of a tree. Another reaches for the tusk, and opines what he has in his hand is a metal bar. A third takes hold of the trunk, and fourth of the tail, a fifth of the belly, and sixth of the back, and each one determines there is a different object at hand.

Suppose each of them claimed, as his property right, his own vision of what he had in effect homesteaded. Would this be a viable way to determine ownership? No, it would not. The difficulty would be that the elephant is a technological unit, and must be owned by a single legal entity, not by some half dozen parties, each owning a different aspect of this creature. If the latter were the ownership pattern, each proprietor would pull in a different direction, and that which they claimed would soon be vitiated. Here is what Rothbard (1982, footnotes deleted) says of the technological unit:

> In our discussion of homesteading, we did not stress the problem of the size of the area to be homesteaded. If A uses a certain amount of a resource, how much of that resource is to accrue to his ownership? Our answer is that he owns the technological unit of the resource. The size of that unit depends on the type of good or resource in question, and must be determined by judges, juries, or arbitrators who are expert in the particular resource or industry in question. If resource X is owned by A, then A must own enough of it so as to include necessary appurtenances. For example, in the courts' determination of radio frequency ownership in the 1920s, the extent of ownership depended on the technological unit of the radio wave — its width on the electromagnetic spectrum so that another wave would not interfere with the signal, and its length over space. The ownership of the frequency then was determined by width, length, and location.
>
> American land settlement is a history of grappling, often unsuccessfully, with the size of the homestead unit. Thus, the homesteading provision in the federal land law of 1861 provided a unit of 160 acres, the clearing and use of which over a certain term would convey ownership to the homesteader. Unfortunately, in a few years, when the dry prairie began to be settled, 160 acres was much too low for any viable land use (generally ranching and grazing). As a result, very little Western land came into private ownership for several decades. The resulting overuse of the land caused the destruction of Western grass cover and much of the timberland.
>
> With the importance of analyzing the technological unit in mind, let us examine the ownership of airspace. Can there be private ownership of the air, and if so, to what extent?
>
> The common-law principle is that every landowner owns all the airspace above him upward indefinitely unto the heavens and downward into the center of the earth. In Lord Coke's famous dictum: *cujus est solum ejus est usque ad coelum;* that is, he who owns the soil owns upward unto heaven, and, by analogy, downward to Hades. While this is a time-honored rule, it was, of

course, designed before planes were invented. A literal application of the rule would in effect outlaw all aviation, as well as rockets and satellites.

But is the practical problem of aviation the only thing wrong with the *ad coelum* rule? Using the homesteading principle, the *ad coelum* rule never made any sense, and is therefore overdue in the dustbin of legal history. If one homesteads and uses the soil, in what sense is he also using all the sky above him up into heaven? Clearly, he isn't.

The *ad coelum* rule unfortunately lingered on in the *Restatement of Torts* (1939), adopted by the Uniform State Law for Aeronautics and enacted in 22 states during the 1930s and 1940s. This variant continued to recognize unlimited ownership of upward space, but added a superior public privilege to invade the right. Aviators and satellite owners would still bear the burden of proof that they possessed this rather vague privilege to invade private property in airspace. Fortunately, the Uniform Act was withdrawn by the Commissioners on Uniform State Laws in 1943, and is now on the way out.

A second solution, adopted by the Ninth Circuit Federal Court in 1936, scrapped private property in airspace altogether and even allowed planes to buzz land close to the surface. Only actual interference with present enjoyment of land would constitute a tort. The most popular nuisance theory simply outlaws interference with land use, but is unsatisfactory because it scraps any discussion whatever of ownership of airspace.

The best judicial theory is the "zone," which asserts that only the lower part of the airspace above one's land is owned; this zone is the limit of the owner's "effective possession." As Prosser defines it, "effective possession" is "so much of the space above him as is essential to the complete use and enjoyment of the land." The height of the owned airspace will vary according to the facts of the case and therefore according to the "technological unit." Thus, Prosser writes: "This was the rule applied in the early case of *Smith* v. *New England Aircraft Co.*, where flights at the level of one hundred feet were held to be trespass, since the land was used for cultivation of trees which reached that height. A few other cases have adopted the same view."

"The height of the zone of ownership must vary according to the facts of each case."

On the other hand, the nuisance theory should be added to the strict zone of ownership for cases such as where excess aircraft noise injures people or activities in an adjoining area, not directly underneath the plane. At first, the federal courts ruled that only low flights overhead could constitute a tort against private landowners, but the excessive noise case of *Thornburg* v. *Port of Portland* (1962) corrected that view. The court properly reasoned in *Thornburg:* "If we accept . . . the validity of the propositions that a noise can be a nuisance; that a nuisance can give rise to an easement; and that a noise coming straight down from above one's land can ripen into a taking if it is persistent enough and aggravated enough, then logically the same kind and degree of interference with the use and enjoyment of one's land can also be a taking even though the noise vector may come from some direction other than the perpendicular."

What would Rothbard have made of the elephant case? Obviously, that the entire elephant was one technological unit, and if anyone thought he could homestead one part of this creature all on his own, and ignore the equally valid property rights all of the other homesteaders, his claim would be invalid. Why so? Because the elephant in its entirety is a single technological unit, and therefore must be owned by one and only one legal entity; and this would be, presumably, an individual or a partnership. If all the blind men "homesteaded" the different parts of the elephant at the same time,[2] then they would all be partners in the ownership of this animal. And this would hold true whether or not the different men knew each other, or liked each other, or were bitter enemies.[3]

Let us now consider another example (Block, 2007). We are going to privatize Elm Street in Anytown, USA. We shall do so via the riparian doctrine: we split the road in half, and then award the territory from the sidewalk to the center line of this thoroughfare in front of each home. If the houses have frontage of 50 feet, then each owner now takes over half the street in front of his home. Every homeowner with property abutting Elm Street now owns, in its entirety, 500 square feet of road, assuming that Elm Street is 20 feet wide, and thus half of its width is 10 feet.

If this is not a recipe for utter and total disaster then nothing is. If there are 300 properties contiguous to Elm Street, there are now 150 owners of half the road in front of their homes. Some of the new property owners may decide to allow motorists to travel for free. But others may charge a price by setting up a coin machine: deposit $1 in the kitty, and move on along Elm Street to that part of the road owned by the next homeowner. However, others may decide they do not want traffic whizzing by in front of their homes and plant petunia flowers where once Elm Street stood. Motorists, of course, could no longer use Elm Street as a thoroughfare even if as many as one person acted in any such manner.

Again extrapolating from the Rothbardian analysis: Elm Street is a technological unit. It simply cannot be owned, in constituent parts, by 300 different capitalists. Rather, these 300 must be considered partners in the ownership of Elm Street. Alternatively, a corporation may be set up with 300 shares in it, each one of them owned by someone with an Elm Street address. In either case, one single entity, the chairman of the partnership or the president of the corporation, will make the rules of the road. We posit that the value of this terrain can be maximized by leaving it as a roadway; not allowing each owner to set up a toll booth, or to start planting flowers in "his" portion of the road, and forbidding traffic. Then, presumably, there will be but one toll booth for the entire roadway and each owner will get an equal share of the proceeds (assuming no technology has yet been invented to allow for electronic methods of collecting revenues).

Would the I-10 highway, stretching from Florida to California be considered a single technological unit? This is unclear. Rothbard states: "The size of that unit depends on the type of good or resource in question, and must be determined by judges, juries, or arbitrators who are expert in the particular resource or industry in question. If resource X is owned by A, then A must own enough of it so as to include necessary appurtenances." Most reasonably, the entire I-10 highway would indeed constitute a single technological unit, even though it would be the rare motorist who would travel its entire length.[4]

We now arrive at the subject of our book: waterways. Is the entire Mississippi River, with all of its tributaries, a single technological unit? What of the Atlantic Ocean, or Lake Superior? The opponent of the Prior Appropriation doctrine need not commit to any of these options. It is enough to be open to the possibility that these large bodies of water are indeed technological units. As Rothbard says, this determination must be made by experts in the field.

What is the difficulty with Prior Appropriation from the point of view of the In Toto doctrine defended in the present chapter? Consider a small lake with 100 homes surrounding it. Assume that all owners of these cottages homesteaded 1 percent of the lake at the same time. Some did so for fishing, some for boating, others used this body of water for drinking and watering their lawns, still others for swimming. The problem is conflicts are all too likely to arise with no one single entity able to speak for the entire lake. Should motor boats be allowed? The boaters say "yea" while the swimmers, "nay." Should someone spray for mosquitos? Should the lake be emptied to deal with a crisis that has arisen?[5] If each of these 100 people has complete and total ownership over his 1 percent of the lake, it is difficult to see how these problems can be addressed. It will be as if the 10 people who each own different parts of the elephant are faced with the issue of whether or not to bring their property to a veterinarian, and if so, which one. It will be as if the 300 owners of Elm Street had to deal with issues affecting them all.

Similar issues arise with regard to ownership of any other water resource that is really a single technological unit. Suppose there to be 10 different owners of the Atlantic Ocean, and that this body of water is unified property. How will the following challenges be confronted? The water level rises, and inundates shoreline cities: should steps be taken to mitigate this situation? By whom? What policies should be pursued to overcome this problem? Who pays damages? Suppose the 10 owners cannot agree on any of this, any more than can the 300 owners of Elm Street nor the dozen owners of the elephant. What then?

It cannot be denied that there are difficulties, too, with the In Toto doctrine. For example, there is a water cycle: from the ocean to the clouds in the form of evaporation, then to rain in the mountains, then to small brooks, which feed into larger tributaries, then to mighty rivers, and, to complete the cycle, back into the seas (refer to chapter 7). Water molecules make this "trip" over and over again. Where, then, to apply the cut-off point between lakes, rivers and oceans which, we contend, should and can be privatized, on the one hand, and on the other, the clouds, for which we make no such claim. Any cut off point in this process runs the serious risk of being arbitrary. But, this is not really an argument in favor of Prior Appropriation and against In Toto ownership. Rather, it is aimed at both, equally, so neither side of the present debate gains any points from this difficulty.

Here is another challenge. Posit that the Mississippi is one technological unit. Settler, A homesteads part of this river in the far north, B does so in the far south, near New Orleans. Stipulate that they did so at the same exact time, so that the claim of neither of them has any obvious preference over that of the other. What happens when, due to some issue that affects the both of them, they discover each other? Why, according to In Toto ownership, they each take a 50%-50% position in the corporation or partnership that owns the totality of each of their holdings. If instead of merely two owners, A and B, 100 homesteaders now discover each other, then each can own one percent of the entire river. Problem solved. With prior ownership, matters are much more complicated. If all 100 began homesteading at the same time, the difficulties may well be enormous. But even in the more likely case of serial homesteading, with the property rights being shared in accordance with priority in time, there are the vast obstacles mentioned above as regards issues that affect all owners. Why? Because the river is a single technological unit.

Nelson Responds

The key to private property is the humanity of the property holder. An asset has value precisely because a real person finds it desirable. More importantly, the proprietor, out of his innate need for self-preservation, wants to improve the environment in which he lives. When he does so, he changes that environment and makes it his own. That is the basis of privately held possessions. An individual's valuation backed up by personal labor is the central element.

However, except for the use of the word "key," my esteemed colleague is most certainly correct when he writes: "The technological unit is a key element in setting up private property rights." He and Rothbard have a good point about the idea of the Technological Unit. Clearly the separate owners[6] of an elephant divide their possession only at the peril of losing most of its value. Then they would have nothing but skin, meat, and ivory. In order to remain essentially a living, breathing animal, it cannot be partitioned.

However, while it is true that many assets, such as the elephant, are indivisible technological units, others are not. Take for example a lump of gold. Multiple owners can divide a chunk into several pieces without any

harm to the precious metal. It is exactly what it was before. Is there a technological unit for a divisible substance? Well, it certainly cannot be divided
smaller than one atom; for then the respective parts would be different, less
valuable chemical elements. However, how convenient would it be to possess one atom of anything, even gold? Not very. Is there a definitive size, say
one hundredth of an ounce, a tenth of a gram maybe, which would constitute
a technological unit for the metal? There is no size that is clearly definable
beforehand that cannot be divided. The smallest technological unit for gold,
if we assume such is larger than an atom, is dependent on the individual and
what he desires to hold.

With regard to the example of the division of Elm Street, the concept of
the various owners effectually prohibiting traffic is a straw man.[7] The illustration is said to follow the "riparian" theory. That is a misconception. "Riparian" refers specifically to rivers and has over time come to include certain
other water bodies such as lakes, and derives the centerline principle by
analogy from common law prescriptive rights theory. My learned opponent
in this discussion goes on to refer to an award to the existing home owners.
This is not an award; it is rather an acknowledgment of the fact that those
farther afield always traveled along the property lines. Referring to those
ancient times from which common law derived, was it not the case that the
right of way was established first and the definitional centerline only came
afterward? Was it not that a prehistoric foot path existed from before the
dawn of civilization and that people then settled along the trail? Only long
after this reality was well established, the common law posited the property
limits as the centerline of this road existing from the earliest memory. In the
case of rivers, the waterway certainly came first and the middle boundary
concept a long time later.

The modern Elm Street example is not a fair extrapolation from Rothbard.
Each of the homeowners has always had the right of access to his property.
The thoroughfare existed prior to the first house being built (otherwise, how
would have a builder have approached the property to build the house?).
Should libertarian principles overtake society, theft of currently enjoyed
paths of travel could in no way be part of the change. More likely, the
common law principle of prescriptive right of way would hold sway. In other
words, no one could charge a toll or shut off access for the sake of petunias
since the right to travel was already theirs before the *revol*ution. (Emphasis
added.) That would be a commons in the sense that none of the owners would
be motivated to care for their portion of the street. Nevertheless, everyone
would have the right of entry: free access.

That free access is fraught with difficulties is axiomatic. The homeowners
would have several options. They could live with poor entry facilities. Inci-
dentally, there are some benefits to that approach. (1.) By definition, it would
be cheap. (2.) Would-be trespassers would be driven to find alternative

routes; so, the neighborhood would tend to be quiet, peaceable, rural in appearance, and exclusive in its own way: demanding four wheel drive with tundra tires.[8]

Alternatively, they could negotiate a maintenance or sales agreement wherein a road company would contract to keep the whole of Elm Street in good repair. With respect to the upkeep contract, the homeowners remain and the contractor works for them. In the latter case, a new street proprietor would agree to provide access for a fee. Then the thoroughfare would be a technological unit but not by virtue of the essential properties of the trail. It would be a single entity by design of the residents. It is safe to say that different neighborhoods would develop their own solutions. Some would feature rutted unpaved mud pits open to the travelling public for no charge. Others would have beautifully manicured parkways inside of gated communities. What if all 300 residents could not agree? The default position of a mud pit would remain in effect.

The endless possibilities (some of which could provide a source of income to the residents) need not be expounded upon in this debate. The points of this discussion are that all of the existing residents would have access and that no predetermined size of unit exists.

Could the same ideas apply to controlled access highways like I-10? A freeway seems like a better candidate for being a clear-cut technological unit than a few city blocks. However, even here division need not alter the nature of a passage way. Sure, a single unit for a long distance appears logical at first glance. While few do it, a driver could travel from California to Florida and pay only one toll in the process. What could be better than that?

Like the lump of gold, however, a portion of this trail is still a passageway. *Would* someone want to own say 100-feet of I-10? Probably not. But that is not the question. *Could* someone own 100-feet? The answer to that is *absolutely*. There may be genuine benefits to the traveling public. Why? Because the proprietor has an extremely powerful need to keep two groups of people happy. First he must relate well to his customers. If he has a toll booth for his small portion, drivers will be upset and go elsewhere. Therefore, he will negotiate an innovative and painless joint toll collection system with his neighbors so that customers may travel great distances while only paying a toll once. They should be ecstatic. In addition, he will want to attract people to his road. How does he do that? He must make his little plot a draw to fascinate patrons. He will want drivers to go out of their way in order to see his wonder of engineering excellence.

In addition, he must satisfy his neighbors. If he causes disgruntled motorists, his co-highway purveyors would find a way to bypass his reach. Then he would be left with an isolated 100-feet of expensive but useless asset. Who wants that?

Prior Appropriation of waterways shines regarding ownership of techno-logical units. Certainly, one can make the case that ownership of 100-feet of interstate highway is a stretch (so to speak). But, water naturally divides and can be very finely cut in the same sense as the lump of gold. The preceding examples are by way of analogy intended to show that the determination of a technological unit is not so easy and that the unit can be quite flexible because society is unconstrained to reckon all property in terms of some sort of geometrical shape. As Rothbard (1982) truly said, "The size of that unit ... must be determined by judges, juries, or arbitrators who are expert in the particular resource or industry in question." Rothbard discussed radio fre-quency ranges as a proper subject for ownership. That has almost no relation-ship to a traditional understanding of geometrical shapes.[9]

Ideally, people would tend not to own water in the same sense as an elephant or a lump of gold. Water can only be owned in a usufructuary sense.[10] Even when it is ingested or "integrated" into the body of a person, it passes through and goes back into the environment. There is no more inti-mate mixing of a material with oneself than making it a part of the body. Yet, despite that intimacy, this most precious of fluids merely passes through. All possession of this liquid is thus time limited. That is to say it is only for a period of time. Conceptually, the ownership of water must take this time element into account. Just like the radio wave is watts divided by time, so the water right is volume divided by time. For good health, a person must drink so much H_2O *per day*. That is a rate.

The technological unit of water must fit a definition in the form of volume divided by time: something like gallons per minute or cubic meters per day. Even when there is "no flow," such as the case where one holds a bottle of water, it will most likely eventually be consumed and passed back to the environment. In other words, it will still be a volume held over a time period.

Of course, it may be stored, as in the instance of the bottle, in which case a straight volume is the appropriate technological unit. But, still, most stor-age experiences losses, such as from evaporation, over time and is intended to be consumed eventually.

An aquatic technical unit that does not involve time is a fiction. The In Toto notion really discusses containers while not seriously accounting for the water. In fact, except for scale, the In Toto concept of ownership appears to be precisely the same as the riparian theory roundly criticized in Chapter 4. Referring to Fig. 14.1 the south property line of parcel B is the centerline of the river for a defined length, to wit the extent of its lot along the river B controls whatever liquid lies within his plot. On the other hand, the In Toto concept is larger in scale in that it extends for a long distance (perhaps the entire length of the river and maybe the tributaries also) and because, like tract A, it is on both sides under single ownership.

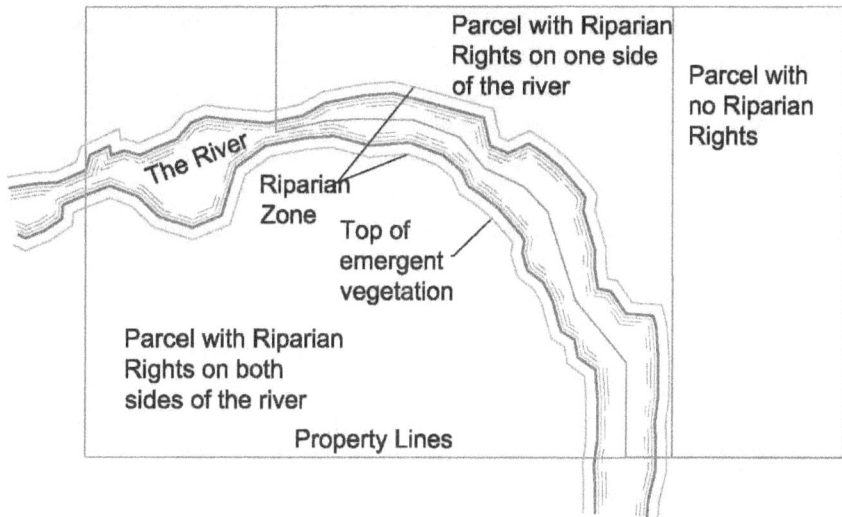

Figure 14.1. Illustration of Riparian Rights

Classic riparian notions apply because ownership includes whatever water is in the river at any given time regardless of how much or how it got there, "In Toto" so to speak, i.e. except for scale (and the usual practice of state imposed regulations which diverge from a purely riparian concept), it's exactly the same. The identical problem as described in Chapter 4 of stealing fluid from the neighbors because it flows towards a diversion point is shared by the In Toto model. There can be no property lines where this theft will not occur.

Surely In Toto ownership sounds as enticing as any erroneous idea does; the fact is that the real value, the water, is not defined. Since the fluid volume itself is indefinite, there can be no clear title when we limit our discussion to containers. The liquid flows where it will as deep as it will. The landlubber likes the idea of a vessel because it resembles a circumscribed parcel. All owners (barring the case where there is only one owner in the entire watershed) are highly motivated to get all water possible before it is taken by others. Thus it becomes a (tragedy of the) commons with all of those attendant war-inducing problems. In the end the In Toto concept becomes indistinguishable from riparian rights despite the scope, or else it requires one single proprietor of an asset that cannot be traded in parts. It can only be exchanged as a single lump. This is to say: it becomes a lump in the throat rather like the elephant in the room that no one is willing to acknowledge.

Rather than locking ownership of a fluid to some arbitrarily large container such as a river, an ocean, or a parcel of land through which water flows, Prior Appropriation looks at the H_2O itself as the asset of concern. It recognizes that the very current has an essential characteristic that makes it a desired asset in the first place. To the contrary, the owner of a cylindrical object, for example a tank of oil, has a storage device. He does possess a geometric shape and, very likely, the material contained therein. He can rent out his vat, if he wishes, to another fluid owner; or he can use it exclusively for his own purposes.

Unlike the tank and the static fluid in it, the water in a river, ocean, aquifer, or even a lake is dynamic. Those objects are primarily conveyance devices.[11] To compare storage and conveyance is to confuse apples and oranges. The storage company may at will prevent oil from being poured into or removed from its tank. A river is different because fluid will move through it irresistibly. Similarly, a road holder can shut off access and absolutely forbid a truck to use his property until the toll is paid. With a flowing stream, like the Sorcerer's Apprentice,[12] good luck with that!

Whether owned or not, like it or not, water is coming down the river. Even with a dam, the reservoir will fill up and then overflow and come through as before. An aspect of a river is that fluid runs; it cannot be avoided (even if the Sorcerer's brooms are chopped to bits).

The results of ownership of the valued resource itself implicit with Prior Appropriation enables a much more vibrant and dynamic arrangement. Containerization is not a concern for the water, as it will take whatever shape is available. The key is that it is not associated with the land. An appropriated right can be sold. Thus waste is not prevented by government regulation but by the interests of the owner. If proprietor A is wasting water, it is as though he were burning his own money. Instead of wasting it, he could sell it on the open market.[13] Unlike the In Toto holder who could divert and sell without limit until the river was dry to the detriment of downstream victims, the priority vender can only sell what is his.

Furthermore, priority ownership of the substance enables fine division of the flow. Rather than requiring massively large "technological units," ownership is divisible into as small a holding as convenience dictates.[14] The technological unit is that flow through such a small orifice that were it any smaller H_2O could no longer pass. (Even then, a still smaller division could be accomplished with a valve that causes intermittent flow.) For example, an opening smaller than the diameter of a water molecule will not permit flow. In short, the technological unit is the smallest imaginable fluid stream.

In this section so far, most of the emphasis has been on rivers since the issues are relatively easier to visualize where flow is narrow and rapid. However, the priority system applies to every type of water body: oceans, lakes, and aquifers as well as fast, skinny waterways or even slow, wide ones.

My treasured co-author posits other dilemmas regarding bodies of water, specifically lakes. These supposed problems are eminently simple to address with the Prior Appropriation model. The idea that 100 persons homesteaded a lake at the same time is extreme. As we say (chapter 5), "Extreme cases make bad law." No, the residents would arrive one by one, and whatever asset the senior owner homesteaded would take precedence (Block has introduced yet another straw man). Another likely scenario is that a developer had possession of the entire Lake in the past. He would have created contractual agreements to which buyers would have to affix their signatures as a part of their purchase contract.

There is every reason to suspect that multiple owners, similar to those in a condominium, would employ a manager to perform necessary maintenance functions. His duties would be spelled out in the contract. So, what about draining Lake Conway? This is not a difficult problem. Why? Because all of the users want a healthy lake. The fishermen want vital fish; sail boaters want clear water not choked with invasive plants; motor boaters want the same thing and also to be able to race at high speeds. Some wish to extract H_2O for drinking and irrigating their lawns, while still others want to swim. All wish for pure clean copious water. They all (except maybe the fishermen) want mosquitos limited; but even the latter want insects restricted; they just want their fish to do the controlling. Could the lake be emptied to deal with a crisis that has arisen? All these wants and needs would be addressed by contract. Granted that all will be disaccommodated during the period the lake is emptied. But since everyone ultimately desires vigorous aquatic species which depend on healthy lake water, they will happily include the operations of lake maintenance in their planning. The same applies to other types of water bodies including oceans and aquifers.

What of the two persons who homesteaded the Mississippi in the north and the south respectively? In the same sense that the homesteader of the land did not in any way mix his labor with the atmosphere and thus has no legitimate claim; so, A in the north did not mix his labor with the south and thus has no claim. Such a supposed conundrum is resolved with Prior Appropriation because what A does has no negative consequences for B.

My worthy opponent concedes the fact that In Toto risks being arbitrary with respect to "any cut off point" (i.e. property line). That is exactly the case as explained above. It is the fact that Prior Appropriation deals with the water per-se that is precisely what enables it to avoid the arbitrariness implicit with In Toto.

Block Responds

The problem with the term "Prior Appropriation" is that it actually constitutes not one but two entirely different concepts.[15] First, it applies to the method of homesteading: first come, first served, or, he who first mixes his labor with the resource, whether on land or in our case regarding water, becomes the legitimate owner. Second, it is a violation of Rothbard's "technological unit" concept in that it divides into several or more different ownerships what is really something that in its very nature ideally can be owned only by one person, corporation, group or entity (the elephant example). With regard to the first of these very different concepts, I am in full, enthusiastic agreement. I am a strong supporter of awarding the first homesteader the property in question. Not so for the very distinct second aspect, or meaning, of this concept, the technological unit.

Suppose there is a developer who will build 640 houses on a square mile of land, one acre each. Would he do well to first install "long thin things" such as water and sewer pipes, telephone wires (before the advent of cell phones), electrical connections, streets, sidewalks and roads, etc.? Or would he be better off just erecting the buildings, and allow those who purchase them to make their own arrangements in this regard? Should he arrange a contract with a sanitation company to collect the garbage, and with a single post office to deliver the mail (we now assume no government provision, and that we have not yet reached the era of the Internet)?

The answer to these questions is pretty obvious. If he tries to sell the homes without any of these provisions, they will be worth a small fraction of their value fully connected to all these "long thin" services. Why? In a word, well, two words: "transactions costs" (Coase, 1960). It is difficult in the extreme for 640 people to agree to much of anything. Yes, they all want roads, water, sewer, telephone, garbage collection, postal service, but unanimity is a rare and precious flower. Even if it could somehow be achieved, the transactions costs of making all these arrangements would be devastating. When five friends get together for a movie and a dinner, it takes quite a while for them to agree to the same package, let alone the timing. To think that 640 people could easily reach accord on all these contractual obligations boggles the mind. Even with the best will in the world, they would diverge as to which particular providers to engage, the length and specifics of the contracts, etc. A far better practice would be for the builder to offer these homes already connected, contractually, with such service providers, along with a codicil to the effect that after a few years the entire group could vote as to whether or not to bring in other firms for these services.

Now imagine that there is a big lake with 640 homes on its sides, and each one owns an equal proportion of this body of water. Assume they each have property rights over a sliver of it, resembling the slices of a pizza. The difficulties of coordination in this case would be at least as monumental as in the case of the 640 houses on that square mile of land. It would be difficult in the extreme to come up with any unanimous agreement as concerns boating, fishing, whether or not and when and how to drain the lake,[16] deal with algae, fish diseases, etc. The transactions costs alone would render such ownership virtually worthless. There is no problem whatsoever with the homesteading part of Prior Appropriation; the difficulty lies with the fact that each proprietor owns a small slice of the lake, and getting them to unanimously agreeing to anything at all would be well-nigh impossible. Yes, it cannot be denied, they all have similar interests. But promoting full agreement amongst so many people is worse than herding cats. And this is to say nothing of the holdout, who is just plain persnickety. My favorite example of this is Eric Cartman of *South Park* fame, whose signature statement is "Screw you guys, screw you guys, screw you guys."

No, the only reasonable manner of ownership is to respect Rothbard's technological unit. This means at least starting out with some sort of condominium association of the 640 residents of that one square mile of land and a similar arrangement for an equal number of lake owners.

Now, let us consider in some detail the arguments my eminently reasonable and distinguished co-author puts forth in his rejection of this In Toto thesis.

My brother libertarian is in accord with Rothbard's concept of the technological unit. That is a good start in a possible reconciliation between us. For example, both he and I would apply it to the elephant and presumably to many, many other things (cars, cows, computers, clothing, catapults, and crowns). However, he does not follow me in its application to bodies of water. I also agree with him, enthusiastically so, when he says: "The key to private property is the humanity of the property holder. An asset has value precisely because a real person finds it desirable." Perhaps we are not so far apart after all.

My wise co-author is also on quite solid ground when he points to the fact that gold is not comprised of indivisible units; rather, this mineral is divisible almost without end. Diamonds, too, are physically divisible to the same degree, at least when and if science progresses to the degree necessary with regard to cutting implements. But diamonds are not *economically* divisible, in that when they are cut, the constituent parts are worth far less than beforehand. Water, like gold, and unlike diamonds (at present) is easily divisible in the physical sense. But my contention is, with the example I use of the (pizza) lake owned by 640 different proprietors, is that it is not *economically* divisible, in that the Cartmans of the world, the hold outs, very high transactions costs, make such a configuration untenable.

My gifted co-author is quite right when he dismisses my breaking up of Elm Street into little bitty bits as a straw man argument. It is precisely that— from any realistic perspective. As he very perceptively says "Should libertarian principles overtake society, theft of currently enjoyed paths of travel could in no way be part of the change." Further, his analysis of the history of the matter is dead-on, too: "Riparian" refers specifically to rivers and has over time come to include certain other water bodies such as lakes" but *not* to roads or highways.

However, from a rather different point of view this Elm Street example is not a straw man at all but rather a reductio ad absurdum[17] of the Prior Appropriation doctrine. For *if* a street could be divided up in any such way, contrary to fact conditional here, it would be an utter disaster. If, arguendo, streets, or rivers, or lakes or anything else owned separately by more than a few people, and assuming Cartmanian holdouts too, this scheme would be unworkable for anything that could be considered a technological unit.

My treasured intellectual opponent equated my In Toto scenario with the Riparian doctrine that we both reject: ". . . except for scale, the In Toto concept of ownership appears to be precisely the same as the riparian theory roundly criticized in Chapter 4." It is now my turn to return the favor; I claim that his Prior Appropriation may be reduced to that very format. How so? Consider the Mississippi River before there were many people located along its banks. Then, at roughly the same time, but fifty miles apart from each other so that they are unaware of their far-away neighbors, people begin homesteading this body of water. That river is 2,340 miles long. I assume that each owns a patch of this waterway 50 miles north and south, and half the entire width, exactly the format of my Elm Street format. After this process is over, there are thus some 92 separate owners of this watery thoroughfare. Now consider a boat owner who wants to traverse its entire length. If there is but one pair of owners who will not allow this (think two Cartmans side by side), the Mississippi cannot be used as the type of transport artery as it is at present. Think Petunias. Simply put, my claim is that Nelson gives insufficient weight to transactions costs and to the possibility of Cartman-like hold outs.

My eminent co-author states that the "Elm Street example is not a fair extrapolation from Rothbard. Each of the homeowners has always had the right of access to his property." Fair enough. But this *does* apply to that river that runs through the center of the U.S. Each proprietor indeed has access to his small bit of the river, homesteaded by him from the land he owns. But, with the hold out, or with lack of full cooperation from all owners, this body of water cannot be used as a liquid highway from Minnesota to Louisiana. That would be at the very least a gigantic economic loss.

My logical friend states: ". . . they could negotiate a maintenance or sales agreement wherein a road company would contract to keep the whole of Elm Street in good repair." Similarly, all of these owners of the 92 bits of the Mississippi could make similar arrangements. "Could" is the key word here. Yes, they *could*. But is it likely? Not very, given the omnipresent threat of a hold out, and the actual high transactions costs involved. In contrast, if In Toto is adopted, then this *necessarily* occurs.

The scholar I am fortunate enough to have as my co-author tries to deal with this very point: "What if all 300 residents cannot agree? The default position of a mud pit would remain in effect." But this is not very salutary. Translated from "mud pit" to river implies it cannot be used for transport, tremendous loss. Translated from "mud pit" to U.S. highway I-10 this implies it cannot be used as a roadway. Those Cartmanian petunias arise yet again.

But Nelson is having none of this. He states: "*Could* someone own 100-feet (of the highway)? The answer to that is *absolutely*. There may be genuine benefits to the traveling public. Why? . . . If he has a toll booth for his small portion, drivers will be upset and go elsewhere. Therefore, he will negotiate an innovative and painless joint toll collection system with his neighbors so that customers may travel great distances while only paying a toll once." The "difficulty" I have with my co-author here is that he is a splendid cooperator. I can attest that it has been a pleasure working with him on this book. He is ever ready to do more than his fair share of the work, way more. I think his middle name, if his parents based it on his personality, should have been "Cooperation." He is so cooperative, and such a nice guy he has difficulty realizing that everyone is not like him. I hate to be repetitive, but there are Cartmans out there. "Therefore, he will negotiate. . . ." Well, my friend Nelson sure would. It is in his DNA. But not everyone, alas, is as generous, kind and, well, *cooperative* as is he.

No truer words were ever said than those penned by my accomplished co-author: ". . . the determination of a technological unit is not so easy." We both agree with Rothbard that "this determination must be made by experts in the field." Nelson is an expert in the fields of hydrology, engineering and hydraulics; I would be the first to admit that I am not. Therefore, when and if In Toto is adopted, it will be people like him, not me, who will be called upon to make the precise determinations of actual technological units.

However, I cannot see my way clear to agree with him that "The technological unit of water must fit a definition in the form of volume divided by time: something like gallons per minute or cubic meters per day." I have in mind something more like the Mississippi River, or Lake Pontchartrain, or the Indian Ocean. My venerated colleague and I diverge on this issue; he says: "An aquatic technical unit that does not involve time is a fiction. The In Toto notion really discusses containers while not seriously accounting for the water." But what is wrong with containers when defined in this manner? Land, too, falls into this category, and there is nothing problematic with ownership in that regard. For example, a mountain is a container. Yet, the property title to it is clear, despite the fact that the wind blows dirt from it, and gravel from elsewhere onto it, as in the case of a body of water. A basic premise of this book is that land and water are not really that different when it comes to property rights. These should apply to both. Land is akin to slow moving (e.g., stagnant) water; water resembles fast moving land (e.g., territory being redistributed by typhoons). Well, which more resembles private property in land: In Toto or Prior Appropriation? To ask this is to answer it: surely, the former. QED.

States my honored intellectual opponent: In "In Toto ownership . . . the real value, the water, is not defined. Since the fluid volume itself is indefinite, there can be no clear title." And here he is entirely correct. Take Lake Pontchartrain, for example. At any given time, there are zillions of molecules of water in it. But, as time goes on, some of these evaporate. They go through the water cycle: into the clouds, then fall as rain into the rivers, and some, but by no means all of it, goes back into this particular lake. Some of the new liquid came from the Gulf of Mexico, etc. So, yes, there is no perfectly clear title, since nailing jelly to a tree is far easier than keeping track of this myriad of H_2O molecules. And yet, and yet. If the Lake Pontchartrain Corporation, a company owned by tens of thousands of shareholders who live in the New Orleans area, wants to hold a boat race at a given time, surely their title would be clear enough such that it could forbid any others from interfering with this sporting event. If the LPC wanted to remove some acre feet of water from its property, its title would be clear enough to accomplish this task as well. The perfect is sometimes the enemy of the merely good.

According to my illustrious colleague ". . . the In Toto concept . . . requires one single proprietor of an asset that cannot be traded in parts. It can only be exchanged as a single lump." Well, yes, at least at the outset. But this is a benefit, not a drawback. The same applies to the elephant, to the I-10 highway, to a pencil, a book, a bell, a candle, a diamond, a gold coin, at least ordinarily. That is because all of these things comprise technological units.

Consider this claim of Nelson's: "Unlike the In Toto holder who could divert and sell without limit until the river was dry to the detriment of downstream victims, the priority vender can only sell what is his." But if the In Toto holder owns the entire river, there is no question of "downstream victims" any more that there would be were a gardener to chop off the top of his tree. He owns the entire thing, and, presumably, will suffer if he makes poor entrepreneurial decisions.

Or this one: "Furthermore, priority ownership of the substance enables fine division of the flow. Rather than requiring massively large 'technological units,' ownership is divisible into as small a holding as convenience dictates." Here we also agree, at least sort of. In Toto, too, allows for a "fine division." It all depends upon the default position. Consider an automobile for example. This would be a paradigm case of a "technological unit." If we *start* with one owner, all is well; he can break it up and sell as many or few parts of it as he wants to willing buyers. He can rent it out by the year, the month, the week, the day, the hour, the minute, or the second, provided, only, that there are others who voluntarily agree to his terms. But, now, imagine that at the beginning of the process 300 people own 300 separate bits of it. In that direction lies utter chaos. In contrast, if there is a firm with 300 shareholders who own that one car, then, again, this is a practical if somewhat unusual situation. ABC Auto Leasing, Inc. may own thousands of automobiles; this creates no problem, since they can dispose of them when they wish through the marketplace.

Or this: "The idea that 100 persons homesteaded a lake at the same time is extreme. . . . No, the residents would arrive one by one, and whatever asset the senior owner homesteaded would take precedence." Let us return to Lake Pontchartrain. No one person could himself homestead even such a relatively small body of water; it is far too gigantic. For the holdout and transactions costs problems to arise it need not be the case that 100 people mixed their labor with this lake all at the exact same time, which, we may readily concede, is unlikely, in the extreme. All that is necessary for economic chaos to ensue is a situation where 100 people, or many more, set up homes around New Orleans' bathtub and start dipping into it without interfering with one another. Then, problems arise when this resource is no longer scarce in the sense that conflicts over its use can occur. If a Lake Pontchartrain Corporation (LPC) ensues, with, for example, all of these homeowners on its periphery taking up shares, e.g., In Toto, then all is well. But if Prior Appropriation is the order of the day, watch out, here comes Cartman and the petunias. Says my brilliant co-author: "There is every reason to suspect that multiple owners, similar to those in a condominium, would employ a manager to perform necessary maintenance functions." Yes, yes, that is precisely the In Toto model, if we *start* from this perspective. But if we do not, there will almost certainly be squabbles; expensive ones.

My courageous colleague does not shrink from considering the case of draining Lake Conway, one of my most powerful arguments. He avers: "This is not a difficult problem. Why? Because all of the users want a healthy lake. The fishermen want vital fish; sail boaters want clear water not choked with invasive plants; motor boaters want the same thing and also to be able to race at high speeds. Some wish to extract H_2O for drinking and irrigating their lawns, while still others want to swim. All wish for pure clean copious water." One answer to this type of Panglossian thinking is: Cartman, Cartman, Cartman. Another is, without one "decider" how are we to settle possible disputes between those who "wish to extract H_2O for drinking and irrigating their lawns, (and those who) want to swim?" Only a condo association, or an LPC, can make such a determination. But Cartman refuses to join. Nelson says: "All these wants and needs would be addressed by contract." I respond that Cartman will refuse to sign any such contract. What then? Chaos. A court could decide? But on what basis? Only by arbitrarily setting up a corporation or a condominium against the will of at least one owner, and, by now, we well know his name. Hint: he is a young fat boy.

Nelson's Turn

With regard to most of the statements above, your authors are in substantial agreement. Right from the outset, however, a problem occurs. Some notions are sufficiently complex to require two or more appellations. "Labor Strike" is indeed one of those institutions. We all know that the two concepts included therein are "labor," meaning the workers themselves and their concerted action on the one hand and the "withholding of labor." It is important not to conflate what is necessary with what is essential. Yes they often if not usually involve violence. But, violence is not essential.

With regard to Prior Appropriation, it is defined above under "Nelson's Initial Position" as a *prioritization* and a *taking*. Technological units have nothing essential to do with it. The only point I wish to stress is that this philosophy is quite compatible with Rothbard's thesis.

Next, my professorial associate launches into a page-long illustration of 640 individual owners within a condominium. However, he failed to notice that the suitability of such organizations has already been accepted. I remain committed to that theory. Still, the setup, though not unusual, is artificial. Valuable items like elephants and diamonds may be units not amenable economically to division, whereas the hallways in a high rise, the "long thin things," are only so by design. In the singular case where a lake is to be divided into residential lots, artificially setting up a technological unit for access routes makes total sense. There is no argument from this quarter on that. The problem is that this unity only becomes desirable when a particular organizational scheme is desired. More to the point, it is only possible within the larger context of a more flexible, fluid understanding of property rights. To wit, what if a non-cooperator, as the worthy professor suggests, wishes to remove the water?

This is where priority comes into play.

I am certainly gratified that my co-author and I are in agreement on "first in use, first in right." In the case of the watery residential community, the developer had better have homesteaded or purchased the rights to the water, or his clients may find their residences sitting on a dry lake bed. Surely a voluntary community may own aquatic assets. But vis a vis those outside of the association, it must *take* (or purchase) possession first.

Before we move on to the subject of what is owned, it is worth discussing the transaction costs that my learned colleague brings up. Why is it that a lump of gold is eminently divisible without loss of value[18] whereas the cutting of a diamond is highly destructive? With very little heat and energy, several small lumps can be melted down and made into one large piece. In contrast, a diamond must be heated under pressure to roughly the temperature of a volcanic tube. This pressure must be on the order of several thousand feet of fluid lava. First, under current and foreseeable conditions, that would be exceedingly expensive. Secondly, diamonds are not uniform. Coming as they do from natural and uncontrolled processes, each individual diamond contains irregularities that add to its attraction. Thus highly uniform products like cubic zirconia or synthetic moissanite cannot hope to compete. They have no individual "personality." Water is even easier to recombine once separated: just pour the separate parts into the same body of water.

Now for the question of what is owned and how it is possessed.

The Elm Street argument fails as a reductio ad absurdum because it is too geometrically oriented for a free flowing fluid. *If* one restricts the conversation to some sort of territorially extensive division, he, as my friend has asserted, will run into the very sort of absurdity he has so ably exposed.

Herein lies the very core of our disagreement. A river (neither an ocean or lake or any other body of water) is not in its essence a geometric form. Granted, at any instance, it may appear to have physical shape, and therein is the apparent though misleading attractiveness in riparian and In Toto ownership perceptions. But the H_2O keeps its economic value in whatever form it takes. Even more than malleable metals, it does so whether it is split, spilt, molded, shaped, or squashed. Why, because the transaction costs to split a current or combine multiple flows are minuscule.

With regard to the Mississippi, if there are "many people located along its banks," consider the description "that each owns a patch of this waterway 50 miles north and south, and half the entire width, exactly the format of my Elm Street format. After this process is over, there are thus some 92 separate owners of this watery thoroughfare." This is nothing other than riparian. That indicates three dimensional thinking with rigid shapes. To understand water requires four dimensional thinking, the usual three plus fluid movement. I remind my learned colleague that he has already agreed that aquatic ownership must include a usufructuary component: "States my honored intellectual opponent: In 'In Toto ownership . . . the real value, the water, is not defined. Since the fluid volume itself is indefinite, there can be no clear title.' And here he is entirely correct."[19] With this statement, my most able co-author reinforces his basic, though unacknowledged, commitment to riparian theory: "Each proprietor indeed has access to his small bit of the river, homesteaded by him from the land he owns." That is a nearly exact description of riparian rights. Granted, he makes this statement as another attempt at reductio ad absurdum, but as before it fails as such because there is nothing in Prior Appropriation that suggests this sort of limited conceptualization. The fact that this is what he offers also reveals faulty three dimensional geometric thinking.

In a way, Prior Appropriation more closely resembles owning shares in a corporation because titles in stock do not specify that this certificate is to a car while another one is to a desk. On the other hand it is unlike a corporation because the use of one's water is not subject to vote. In a joint stock company, if Shareholder A wishes to sell that automobile, the action is submitted to vote (or the selection of a CEO to make such mundane decisions is subjected to the ballot). To the contrary, the proprietor of some H_2O (as a discharge rate) may dispose of his portion without vote, entirely on his own. It is his to do with as he pleases.

What about the holdout who will not cooperate?[20] That is dealt with by precedence. Were the Lake Pontchartrain boat racers the first to homestead that asset? Then a subsequent settler may not interfere with those famed sporting activities. Did the original pilgrim start an alligator farm? Then the sportsmen would be well advised to wear bite-proof suits. The point is no cooperation is needed at all. The so-called holdout only has rights insofar as he takes priority. If he is not "first in line first in time," then he has no standing whatsoever to interfere with the plans of others who come before him in terms of property rights.

My esteemed partner reminds us that we both agree that "A basic premise of this book is that land and water are not really that different when it comes to property rights. These should apply to both. Land is akin to slow moving (e.g., stagnant) water; water resembles fast moving land (e.g., territory being redistributed by typhoons)." However, once again the time element comes into play. How long does it take for an ocean floor to subduct under a continent and then recycle back up to a rift zone?[21] Sorry, but this process takes more time than the human species has existed on earth. In view of our limited time on the planet, we must ignore such slow moving occurrences. Even such relatively rapid events like landslides are so infrequent as to suggest ignoring them until necessary, which we often do through insurance.

My literary companion states: "But if the In Toto holder owns the entire river, there is no question of 'downstream victims' any more than there would be were a gardener to chop off the top of his tree." Here, he seems to "have me." In fact, however, borders always exist. Even if we posit exceedingly extensive holdings, say the entire Mississippi watershed, where is the line to be drawn between the estuary and the Gulf of Mexico? The influence of Old Miss extends hundreds of miles into the Gulf. Or are we supposed to include that in the river ownership? Does he really mean to include the entire watershed? If not, then there are very small tributaries sharing boundaries with Old Man River that are also included.

This sort of massive territorial control starts to resemble a state. In order to avoid government-like control over the entire land surface which contributes water to the river, boundaries must necessarily exist. At each limit with In Toto ownership, mischief will prevail.

Frankly, the following assertion only confuses me: "Let us return to Lake Pontchartrain. No one person could himself homestead even such a relatively small body of water; it is far too gigantic." If that small backwater is too big to homestead, then how is one to do so with the entire Mississippi? So my studious professorial muse asserts that, due to holdouts, were 100 or more persons to "start dipping into it without interfering with one another" chaos would result. That is the same as claiming that they most certainly *would* interfere with each other. To the contrary, primacy of settlement (withdrawal) would mean that when H_2O became short, the late interlopers would not get any because the senior owners would be first to get theirs, unless they had taken steps to ensure their supply through augmentation.[22] Once again, the so-called holdout has no standing with which to make any trouble.

While my brave colleague continues to stick to In Toto and insists that it is not riparian, I find I cannot go along with him on this. While the discussion about technological units has been very valuable, I remain convinced that any geometrical idealization of such is unfounded when the discussion turns to natural free-flowing fluids. Only volumes divided by time will suffice. As with any proprietorship, first in use is essential. Appropriation is also necessary. On that we agree 100-percent. We only disagree with regard to what, precisely, is to be appropriated first in time: the volumetric, shapeless, flowing, and constantly intermixing water. With that understanding, none of his supposed shape-dependent difficulties stand.

Block Responds

I regard Peter Nelson as akin to a chess grandmaster when it comes to technical matters of engineering and physics, particularly with regard to the science of moving liquids. But even the best chess player in the world can lose to a patzer if he spots his opponent a queen and two rooks. Ok, ok, throw in a bishop and a knight too, just to be on the safe side. I fear that my estimable co-author has simply given me way too much material in this little chess match we are now undertaking for his side to prevail.

Consider the Mississippi river. It runs through Minnesota, Iowa, Missouri, Arkansas and Louisiana on the west side, and Wisconsin, Illinois, Tennessee and Mississippi on the east side. That encompasses nine different states. Assume we are back in the days of yore before any of the land on either side of this river was homesteaded, nor the river either. Whereupon, all this changes. Nine different people begin mixing their labor with the riverbanks in each of these states, and also with that body of water which lies nearby. It matters not one whit who was there first; we can assume that they all did so within one given year. But, if it matters, we can posit that the first homesteader was the northernmost one in Minnesota, and the last in southern Louisiana, and that all the rest fall into this north–south order. However, they were all far enough apart from each other that none of them even knew of the existence of any of the others. Each has homesteaded, say, only a two mile stretch of water and abutting land.

Then comes a problem that affects the entire Mississippi. Maybe it is algae, perhaps crocodiles, possibly the water is busily turning into lemonade. At this point they all discover each other. What is to be done to address this situation? They dispute with each other the causes of the problem; there are the algae-ists, the crocodile-ists, and the lemonade-ists. Several of them suggest diverting the water into a different course, until the proposed remedy can take effect; others offer a chemical solution; several maintain that sharks should be introduced into these waters. There are numerous combinations and permutations of causal explanations and would-be solutions. What is to be done if this river is to become, or remain as, an economically viable property? How can there be a reconciliation between these different analyses of the problem, and the very divergent solutions proposed? It will do no good to aver that the owner in Minnesota should decide all this, as my brilliant co-author responds ("This is where priority comes into play."), since this northerner *does not own the entire river*. He is the proprietor of *only the 2 miles of it* that he has homesteaded, as is the equivalent case with all the others. The only thing that all nine can agree upon is that any and all of these solutions will affect the entire river.

My treasured colleague attempts to refute this claim of mine as follows: "What about the holdout who will not cooperate? That is dealt with by precedence. Were the Lake Pontchartrain boat racers the first to homestead that asset? Then a subsequent settler may not interfere with those famed sporting activities. Did the original pilgrim start an alligator farm?" But, I cannot believe he succeeds in this attempt. He is giving away all too many queens and rooks. The point is the first homesteader does not own the entire river, only his itty-bitty small portion of it.

One of these nine owners is, wait for it, Eric Cartman. Even if all eight others agree to any given course of action, he is still the holdout. Based on Prior Appropriation, he will be able to stop any solution to the difficulty. My co-author, I suggest, does not fully appreciate the power of this argument. And the same goes for his lack of recognition of the importance of transactions costs. If instead of nine owners, there are ninety, or nine hundred, or nine thousand or nine million, then even without a Cartman, economic inefficiency will again be gargantuan. The river will cease for all intents and purposes to be a viable economic entity.

Just as no one single person can himself homestead vast tracts of land, for example, owning all of the land in Louisiana based on mixing his labor with it in its entirety, he cannot either do so for relatively large bodies of water. No one person can homestead all of the Mississippi River, nor, even, Lake Pontchartrain. Therefore dozens, scores, hundreds, thousands of people, based on homesteading, will own little bits of each. Nelson's "precedence" simply cannot answer this objection. It matters little that the Minnesotan was the first to homestead his patch of the Mississippi, and the Louisianan was the last. *None* of these nine owners of that body of water can own it *all*, at least not on the basis of homesteading it. Given that, it matters little who was there first. The Minnesotan has precedence over the Louisianan in terms of time, but not insofar as the former may properly give any orders to the latter in terms of what may be done with *his* water property. This objection is also articulated in this manner: ". . . the late interlopers would not get any because the senior owners would be first to get theirs." But this will not do either. To speak of "late interlopers" and "senior owners" is to assume that they are vying for one and the same thing. This is problematic on not one but two grounds. First, it concedes far too much to the notion that the Mississippi River is but one technological unit, the In Toto concept. Second, it violates the concept of homesteading, and the assumption that no one man may mix his labor with gigantic amounts of territory. If each proprietor can claim but two running miles of this river, there can be no such thing as "late interlopers" or "senior owners."

What of my erudite co-author's claim that I am having truck with the riparianism we both reject? At the outset, Nelson seems to have a good case for his claim. He states: "With regard to the Mississippi, if there are 'many people located along its banks,' consider the description 'that each owns a patch of this waterway 50 miles north and south, and half the entire width, exactly the format of my Elm Street format. After this process is over, there are thus some 92 separate owners of this watery thoroughfare.' This is nothing other than riparian." I plead guilty, of course. Fair is fair. However, my guilt consists not in supporting the riparian doctrine, but in failing to make it clear that I was employing this concept as a reductio ad absurdum. I was using it as a foil; as a means of showing its very evident flaws; I was attempting to show that In Toto could rescue this system from its inner contradictions. My writing colleague is to be thanked for eloquently pointing this out. Or, perhaps, I was not that unclear after all, since my learned co-author does state: "Granted, he makes this statement as another attempt at reductio ad absurdum."

Let us now consider my "faulty three dimensional geometric thinking." Who could deny that water flows, particularly in rivers? It does less so in lakes, certainly relatively stagnant ones, but even here, I presume, it does not all obediently stay in one place. But, if we are to take seriously our agreement that land is slow-moving water, water is fast-moving land, then non-aqueous terrain also moves around sometimes more than just a little bit. Think earthquakes, mudslides, volcanoes, dust storms, etc. So there is a difference in degree, albeit a sharp one in most cases, but not one in kind.

My literary companion quotes me thus: "But if the In Toto holder owns the entire river, there is no question of 'downstream victims' any more that there would be were a gardener to chop off the top of his tree." He goes on to say: "Here, he seems to 'have me.' In fact, however, borders always exist.

Even if we posit exceedingly extensive holdings, say the entire Mississippi watershed, where is the line to be drawn between the estuary and the Gulf of Mexico? The influence of Old Miss extends hundreds of miles into the Gulf. Or are we supposed to include that in the river ownership? Does he really mean to include the entire watershed? If not, then there are very small tributaries sharing boundaries with Old Man River that are also included."

This is a scintillatingly brilliant series of questions and challenges. But I do not think they mitigate against In Toto. Rather, as I see matters, the answers to them we provide in the present book are in effect one of its major contributions. To respond very briefly here and now, all bodies of water are connected to each other. Yet, unless we are to conclude that one firm must own all of them put together, we must necessarily provide borders. In the present case, even though "The influence of Old Miss extends hundreds of miles into the Gulf" it seems reasonable, based upon Rothbard's insistence on technological units, to draw a property rights line between them. Similarly, the Atlantic and Pacific Oceans "influence" each other, it would appear cogent to demarcate between them insofar as private property rights are concerned. [23]

My debating partner writes as follows: "Frankly, the following assertion only confuses me: 'Let us return to Lake Pontchartrain. No one person could himself homestead even such a relatively small body of water; it is far too gigantic.' If that small backwater is too big to homestead, then how is one to do so with the entire Mississippi?" I must again apologize for the imprecision of my words. What I meant to say was that *no one single person*, given human limitations, could homestead even a relatively small body of water as Lake Pontchartrain, let alone the Mississippi. But *hundreds or thousands of people*, all of them together, certainly could do so, each of them mixing his labor with a small portion of these gigantic areas. ". . . the so-called holdout has no standing with which to make any trouble?" Au contraire, he has good and sufficient "standing" with which to do so. He is now one of the hundreds or thousands of people who, along with all the others, homesteaded a small part of a large body of water. He may well not have been the very first to lay claim to the Mississippi, but he certainly did so with regard to *his minute part* of this river. If that is not standing, then nothing is standing.

Nelson's Turn

I really do not have much to add. In fact, I tried to end the debate in the last go around. Perhaps the best approach is to repeat the words at the end of my last response:

"We only disagree with regard to what, precisely, is to be appropriated first in time: the volumetric, shapeless, flowing, and constantly intermixing water.

With that understanding, none of his supposed shape-dependent difficulties stand."

For that is the real crux of our disagreement. I applaud my learned professor for he has steadfastly preserved the In Toto position without compromising his libertarian integrity. The concept of technological units is of inestimable power. Nevertheless, from the second paragraph, my partner in this project says: "Nine different people begin mixing their labor with the riverbanks in each of these states, and also with that body of water which lies nearby." Already it is geometrically oriented. For me, much of what follows in his long refutation is non-sequitur because I cannot imagine where I said anything that would indicate that mixing one's labor with a plan view[24] plot of river means anything at all. Rather, the labor that one brings to the watercourse is putting the water to use: to divert and drink, to float on, to traverse. Not one of those uses prevents the other of them from being performed by someone else. Furthermore, take the "divert and drink" example. Can one person drink the entire Mississippi? I think we agree that "No, he could not." So what was not diverted may be used by someone else.

Standing back from the debate that has been put down so eloquently in writing, I wonder whether our difference is not one of personalities. Among other things, I am an airplane pilot.[25] Aloft, it never occurs to me that I am a few thousand feet up with nothing solid below me. No, I feel safe because the physics of air flow around the wings and the momentum of my machine guarantee the craft will remain in flight.

I *sense* (which admittedly is not the same as to *know*) that my able colleague needs to feel a firm foundation. *He* needs an order in which there is no doubt. *He* needs physical, line-in-the-concrete type boundaries. I certainly agree that such demarcations are important where appropriate. However, when the discussion turns to more ephemeral and flexible things, to radio waves or water, *I* find boundaries acceptable, indeed preferable, that are defined otherwise. More than one radio station can send signals because what each station homesteaded was a particular frequency, not the volume of air through which the signal passes.

In a similar way, a rivulet of fluid can be homesteaded by more than one person not by excludable volumes through which the stream has passed from before the time of man; but by flow rates. While in the stream, *your* waters and *my* waters are continually intermixing. That is satisfying to me so long as I may extract my H_2O when I need it or float my boat when I want to do so.[26]

Block Responds

Since my co-author led off this debate, we have agreed it only fair that I end it. However, I have nothing further of a substantive sort to contribute to this joint effort of ours. I will content myself by just congratulating my partner. He gave me an astoundingly strong run for my money, defending a position I thought indefensible at the outset.[27] I congratulate both of us, if I may, for engaging in a real attempt to get to the truth of the matter, and not merely to score points against each other. Indeed, we have each helped the other to strengthen not only his arguments, but have also edited one another's work for lucidity of presentation.

Conclusion, by Block and Nelson

It is time to conclude this debate. We do so by asking two questions, and supplying two answers. First, who won the debate? Our answer: that is for our readers to decide. Second, what have we the authors, and you the readers, learned from this debate? The lesson, we feel, is that we are dealing with *tremendously* complicated issues in this book. That the two of us, who agree with each other on 99.9% of all issues in political economy, with the libertarian political philosophy and Austrian economics, who are both strong followers of Rothbardian anarcho-capitalism, could yet diverge, and sharply so, on In Toto versus Prior Appropriation, is but one evidence in favor of this hypothesis. But this is hardly the only indication that we are swimming in perilous waters, or treading on thin ice, in this book. The very idea that bodies of water should be owned by individuals or companies is per se a shockingly complex hypothesis to contemplate. We hardly needed this debate to exemplify that, although it certainly did not hurt in that regard.

It is, also, time to end this publication. We do so with extreme modesty. As with any first effort to push out the envelope, we are exceedingly likely to have made mistakes in this volume, quite possibly very serious ones. It is our fervent hope that given this lead of ours, others will be encouraged to improve upon our thesis of water privatization, hopefully, not by rejecting it, but by strengthening it, in ways we have neither the wit nor wisdom to do.

NOTES

1. Discussing court and juries would take us too far afield. Suffice it to say that the authors envision private, competitive courts and juries as well as record keeping organizations. Regarding continua peruse Block and Barnett, 2008; for courts and juries see Anderson and Hill, 1979; Benson, 1989, 1990; Block, 2007B, 2010A; de Wolf, 2004; DiLorenzo, 2010; Guillory & Tinsley, 2009; Hasnas, 1995; Higgs, 2009; Hoppe, 2008; King, 2010; Kinsella, 2009C, 2009E; Long, 2004; McKonkey, 2013; Molyneux, undated; Murphy, 2005A; Olson, 1979; Rothbard, 1973, 1977, 1998; Scott, 2009; Stringham, 2007; Tannehill, 1984; Tinsley, 1998–1999; Berman and Dasser, 1990; Marcus, 2009; Popeo, 1988; Tannehill, 2001; Young, 2002.

2. If one of them homesteaded this mammal first, then he would own it in its entirety. We abstract from the issue of how long the mixing of the labor with the unowned property must occur, and also how intensively must be the homesteading. These issues are not relevant to our debate.

3. In the latter case, presumably, one or the other of them could sell "his" share of the elephant to one of the other owners or to a third party. If there were a dispute, it could be settled by a (hopefully) private court.

4. Those large 18-wheeler trucks make this trip, but in the free society, trains, which have been ruined by state imposed regulations, would be a far more efficient means of transporting goods such large distances. There is also the case of the railroads to guide us. Before the spontaneous agreement among railroads to standardize the gauge, when distances between rails were heterogeneous, goods had to be off- and then on-loaded to the next carrier (Puffert, 2000; Missouri Pacific, 2015).

5. In 1999 Lake Conway, located a few miles northwest of Little Rock, Arkansas, was completely emptied due to the Lake Conway Management Plan Evaluation (Fenech, 2003, p. 21; Bly, 2010, p. 11).

6. It is important to note that "touching" a part of an asset is not sufficient for homesteading. In the illustration of an elephant with several owners, they must jointly husband their colossus, understand it, feed it, nurture it, and protect it. Only then may they claim to have made this animal their own. Otherwise, it is only a claim, but one with no merit and no substance.

7. A straw man argument is a logical fallacy where in a situational example is advanced to which one's opponent would not subscribe but which nevertheless is ascribed to him and is in turn criticized. The reason the Elm Street argument is a straw man is that no reasonable person would ever advance a condition wherein motorists would have to pay separate tolls every few feet or in which portions of a traveled way could be converted to petunia gardens.

8. "Tundra tires" is an exaggeration; they are wide, balloon shaped tires that leave a light imprint. That is to say they distribute the vehicle load over a large area so that it does not sink in soft ground.

9. This is not to deny that if we plot power in watts over time on a graph, the radio signal itself will trace out a geometric wave form.

10. All property can be understood in some sense as usufructuary because each of us eventually dies and all of our possessions eventually pass out of our control. The time element is our stay on earth. However, when concerning ourselves with the relation between several persons and their respective assets, private property is inviolable. In addition much property is temporary. A person may have and enjoy a peach. Eventually it will be consumed or, if unconsumed, will rot. Then it becomes a negative or garbage good, something that the owner will pay to get rid of.

11. Even a lake, which has a tranquil appearance and can be used for storage, normally has flow through and currents. The water in it is, therefore, dynamic unlike the oil in a tank.

12. "The Sorcerer's Apprentice" is a musical piece by Paul Dukas. Disney (1940) used it in the movie *Fantasia*. In one scene Mickey Mouse is the apprentice who is tasked with filling a tub with water. The novice decides to put his recently learned magic to good use by empowering a broom to carry two buckets to fill the basin; which it proceeds to do. Mickey then relaxes and falls asleep. He wakes to find the tub full and overflowing into the whole room even as the broom continues its work. He cannot figure out how to stop the disaster from unfolding so he chops the sweeper-turned carrier into tiny bits. Still under the spell, each bit becomes a new broom carrying water and filling the room that much faster.

13. Of course he could also continue to waste it as would be his right to do, but then he would apparently not be looking out for his own best interest. If he is looking out for his own concerns despite appearances to the contrary, then it is *ipso facto* not wasted.

14. On the failures of organizations of excessive size, refer to Rothbard (1962) discussion herein chapter 12.

15. A similar situation exists with regard to labor "strike." This encompasses two very different actions: a mass quit, or a withdrawal of labor services all at one time and in coordination, on the one hand, and on the other hand, something entirely different: using violence to preclude deliveries from the factory of finished goods, to the plant of raw materials, and preventing entry of alternative workers, called "scabs." Another instance is abortion: this, also, includes under one "roof" two entirely different actions: evicting the fetus from the womb,

which may or may not spell death for the infant—depending upon its maturity, on the one hand, and on the other, killing it, which necessarily results in its demise.

16. For an example of this see Arkansas Game and Fish Association, 2010; Brewer, 2010; Courier, 2014; Mosby, 2014.

17. Reductio ad absurdum is a form of argument which attempts to demonstrate the validity of a statement by following to its logical conclusion the denial of that statement.

18. Or at least not much loss. Clearly, cutting a minted coin would entail a loss of value, though not much compared to a diamond.

19. The issues that are discussed following this statement would, under a priority system, be addressed by seniority or contract.

20. By-the-way, the "cooperation" of the 100-foot section of toll road stems not from his generosity or from his cooperative spirit. It stems from his concern for self-preservation.

21. A rift zone is a line of the planet where tectonic plates are moving away from each other and magma is rising to the surface where it hardens to form new crust.

22. Augmentation stores flood water so that it will be available during times of shortage.

23. I faced (Block, 2009C) the identical challenge regarding roads and highways and streets and avenues. They, too, are all connected to one another, at least internal to each continent. Yet, demarcations between them had to be drawn if there were not to be one single owner of them all. See on this Rothbard's (2004) rejection of the "one big firm." I cannot see my way clear to agreeing with my co-author, however, when he maintains "This sort of massive territorial control starts to resemble a state. In order to avoid government-like control over the entire land surface . . ." States are necessarily coercive; large size is not.

24. "Plan view" is the view looking straight down as at a map.

25. Unfortunately, I am no longer active in this regard.

26. Subject of course to the proprietary caveats discussed above.

27. Even though I am well known for "Defending the Undefendable": Block, 2008.

Appendix

Literature Critique

"The danger is not that a particular class is unfit to govern. Every class is unfit to govern." —John Emerich Edward Dalberg- Lord Acton, *Letters of Lord Acton to Mary* (1881)

The present book, as shall by now have been made abundantly clear, is predicated upon the libertarian vision. Some of the important facets of this philosophy are the non-aggression principle and private property rights based upon homesteading. Also, of course, free enterprise, *laissez faire* capitalism, free association and markets unregulated by the regime.[1]

It is now time to compare and contrast the present publication with some literature on the same subject: what are the appropriate institutional arrangements for water? We shall look at only that small part of literature which is devoted to what is called in some circles "free market environmentalism." That is, we eschew as too far afield from our present concerns authors who maintain that water resources are the "common heritage of all mankind." Such calls for socialism are too far removed from the analysis and understanding of the present authors. Also, product differentiation, a goal of ours, need hardly be undertaken with writers who favor water communism.

There is yet another reason to focus attention on the analyses of water markets as brought to bear by free market environmentalists in addition to product differentiation. It is by no means clear that such authors deserve such honorific appellations[2] and it will be the focus of this appendix to determine whether this is so or not, and if so to what degree. The specific publications to be critiqued include:

I. Hannesson, *The Privatization of the Oceans*

201

II. Zetland, *The End of Abundance: Economic Solutions to Water Scarcity*

III. Gardner and Simmons, "The Economic Effects of Using Property Taxes in Lieu of Direct User Fees to Pay for Water"

IV. Goodhue, et al, "The Sacramento-San Joaquin Delta and the Political Economy of California Water Allocation"

V. Anderson and Leal, *Free Market Environmentalism*

VI. Deacon, "Creating marine assets: Property Rights in Ocean Fisheries."

I. HANNESSON, *THE PRIVATIZATION OF THE OCEANS*

We start off with Hannesson (2006). The title of this book, *The Privatization of the Oceans*, (*Privatization*) is one we might readily have chosen for our own monograph. However, had we done so, we would have included as well as those bodies of water, also, rivers, lakes, aquifers, etc. But, judging this book merely by its title, we would have to concede that it is very congruent with our own efforts. Perhaps, even, there was no need for the present volume, in that once the oceans were privatized, very little more work need be done in behalf of applying the institutions of private property to rivers, lakes, aquifers, etc.

In the event, we were greatly disappointed. Apart from the title there is very little overlap between Hannesson's efforts and ours. The title of his book is fraudulent. A fair summary of the so called *Privatization* is that it has nothing whatsoever to do with privatization of the oceans, or any other type or body of water; rather, it is solely concerned with promoting ITQs,[3] a very different kettle of fish (so to speak). We have already criticized ITQs (in Chapter 1), so we tread lightly over that subject at present. Except, we must note there is a world of difference between advocating the privatization of rights to catch fish, on the one hand, with ownership of individual members of the aquatic Chordata[4] itself. There is even more of a gap between calling for markets in fish-catching rights, and privatization of the arena in which the fish themselves exist, namely the ocean. These seem to be basic and elementary distinctions; nevertheless, they were lost on Hannesson.

This, of course, is not to say there are no positive contributions. There are, and they are many. For example, he likens the privatization of bodies of water to the enclosure movement which predated and ushered in the industrial revolution in England (p. 3). His careful analogizing (pp. 14–19) of the pre-industrial revolution enclosure movement and ocean privatization is important and interesting. He (p. 78) clearly sees ". . . that what has made nations wealthy is private property rights and strife for private gain. . . ." He states (p. 169): "The Canadian government poured money into keeping fishermen in Newfoundland until the cod disappeared. That, sad to say, may be the best structural help the Newfoundland economy got for a long time; people have now started to leave this economically depressed province for better opportunities in other Canadian provinces."

While we delight in Hannesson's command of Public Choice theory, alas we learn that fish "cannot be branded and individually monitored by their presumption owners" (p. 3). Branding, it will be remembered, was the lynch-pin of support for private property rights in cattle in the epochs before the advent of barbed wire. Is there no way to emulate this land-based initiative in the water? There is, Hannesson to the contrary notwithstanding. Certainly, this can be done with large sea-creatures such as whales, with modern computer technology.[5] Nor is it even much of a stretch to contemplate electronic tags or biological markers[6] for smaller denizens of the deep. The barrier here is not so much technology, but rather the edicts of various agencies, which at present would not recognize property rights established in any such manner and would punish any entrepreneur who did.

Hannesson avers (p.7) that ". . . societies undergoing the Industrial Revo-lution or having just emerged from it were marred by a skewed distribution of wealth and the class struggle which it generated." It is difficult to see how this quasi-Marxist analysis can withstand real scrutiny.[7] Why is it "skewed" that the industrialists who risked their capital, and sometimes their very lives, became very rich? Did not Hannesson hear of the fact that the market is a positive sum game? That it consists of *nothing* more than voluntary trades, or commercial activities, or employment, which *necessarily* is mutually benefi-cial in the *ex-ante* sense? The point is, each and every decision made in the marketplace by these titans of industry *benefitted* the poor, otherwise they would scarcely have agreed to cooperate with the owners of these firms.

In his view (8–9), ". . . however productive capitalism may be, it will survive in democratic societies only if it succeeds in distributing its fruits reasonably equitably."[8] But *laissez faire* does not "distribute" anything to anyone. Rather, apart from profit and loss, people earn incomes in accor-dance with their discounted marginal revenue productivity. That weasel word "equitably" presumably, implies at least some sort of rough equality. But that is not the way *any* system works, given the heterogeneity of human skills and abilities.

Hannesson (p. 9) blatantly contradicts himself when he maintains, both, that "Pre-industrial societies did not lack private property rights" and, also, that "many (such) societies of the past were rich and produced substantial surplus value, but that value was appropriated by a predatory and unproduc-tive ruling class." How can the former be compatible with the latter?

He ought to be tarred and feathered (figuratively, of course) for saying (p. 11): "Unfettered capitalism is not a pretty sight. The Russia that emerged from the wreckage of the Soviet Union is a warning example." The crony capitalism of Russia after 1991 was an example of *laissez faire* capitalism? We can only read this and weep.[9]

Another oversight is that *Privatization* does not so much as even mention fish farms, not a very radical idea, insofar as they already exist, usually located near coasts. ITQs are, at best, market-*mimicking*. Fish farms in contrast, are the real thing.

It is more than passing curious that an author, who supposedly favors "The Privatization of the Oceans" as indicated by the title he chose for his book, nevertheless supports the United Nations conventions on the sea, where they claim it is the common heritage of all mankind, and thus, presumably, must always remain as a commons, "owned" by all people.[10] States Hannesson (p. 39): "Despite some ambiguities, the Law of the Sea Convention must be hailed as a major achievement. Hopefully, it bodes well for future lawmaking in the international arena..." This is highly problematic. The commons, and private property, are polar opposites. It is difficult to see how any one person can embrace both.

And what are we to make of this: "... some fish stocks migrate out of the 200-mile zone (owned or claimed by national governments) and into the high seas. Property rights to such stocks would be tenuous and of negligible value for the most migratory stocks." To be sure there are anadromous species of fish such as salmon the very survival of which requires mobility over hundreds or thousands of miles of ocean, and of rivers too, and it might prove difficult to "herd" them into smaller ranges of water.[11] But non-anadromous fish are just "waiting" for the introduction of modern equivalents of land-based barbed wire in the oceans. And what might these be? Why, electronic fences of course, something apparently, not in the lexicon of Hannesson.

According to *Privatization* (p. 54): "Private property rights to fish stocks might also be difficult to manage and enforce. Fish stocks typically migrate over large areas so that the rights would have to be geographically extensive." Now, the thesis of the present book is that not only should private property rights apply to fish stocks, but, in addition, to the entire ocean with everything in it included, up to (or down to the sea bottom and below) and certainly including fish. Furthermore, only a lack of imagination regarding the dynamics of people and the markets they create leads to the conclusion that "rights would have to be geographically extensive." We have shown (chapter 7) that sea-steading could take several forms that do not necessitate extensivity. Hannesson, in contrast, balks at applying this essential element of economic freedom, namely private property rights, even to so relatively an insignificant part of the oceans as fish. Here, his argument appears rather weak. Yes, it cannot be denied, *at present* the fish are gadding about all over the place, in virtually all cases without rhyme or reason.[12] But these need not always be the case, especially not when the industry becomes rationalized, under private property rights. Then, with electronic fences, the fish will go where *we* want them to go, not where the vagaries of nature take them.[13] Our motto will become: "no more fish freedom." A similar situation prevails with regard to buffalo. When the former had the run of the place, able to stampede in whatever direction they wished, they were driven close to extinction. Nowadays, there are buffalo ranchers who keep these beasts in their place, and their survival is ensured (Rocky Mountain Buffalo Association, 2015). Similarly, while for their health and economic viability, elephants cannot be confined to an acre or two, expansive barnyards would allow these gigantic creatures the necessary space to roam. In the present direction of unconfined trampling of human habitations lies their disappearance. No, under free enterprise, elephant farms would be bigger than those that cater to buffalo, but would not be all that extensive either.

Hannesson explains not only ITQs, but also TURFs (pp. 63–64): Territorial Use Rights in Fisheries. This involves "exclusive use rights . . . to fish within a given territory." He does not place much emphasis on this type of property, "For stocks (of fish) that migrate in and out of the assigned territory the property rights over the stocks will be diluted or in effect non-existent." Electronic corrals, for example, would (radically?) reduce the extent of the migration patterns. We have shown several of the many possible market oriented solutions to this issue in chapter 7. Thus, we cannot be too sympathetic to Hannesson's denigration of this option.

Hannesson is by no means finished with his attack on private property rights. He sallies forth with the following critique (p. 65):

> One can easily construct theoretical cases where it would make most sense, from an economic point of view, to fish a stock to extinction as quickly as possible, . . . The role of private property rights in that context is highly limited; *private ownership of stocks would not necessarily give them any protection.* (Emphasis added by present authors.)

While if this were to occur it would not imply any logical contradiction, it is exceedingly difficult to accept on any realistic basis. For one thing, as such a species becomes more and more rare, its price will rise. This will mean greater profits than before, but only if there are still some members of this species alive to be sold in the next period. This would not hold true if there were no more units left. Secondly, pharmaceutical companies, and the biology departments of major universities, might likely be interested in preserving a species in danger of extinction, the former in case the species might be useful in curing some disease of the future, the latter for purposes of study. This applies not only to "cuddly" animals such as the giraffe, but also, and perhaps especially, to creepy, crawly disgusting creatures such as bugs or worms.[14] Hannesson is of course correct in pointing out that private property rights will not save *all* species, there might be some so grotesque or uneconomical that it simply does not pay to do so.[15] But this opens up the question of what is the optimal number of species in the first place. According to our friends the "watermelons,"[16] no species whatsoever should ever be allowed to go extinct. Based on a more rational consideration, that number is such that in saving one more the cost is greater than the benefits, to human beings that is, since there is no intrinsic value to our fellow creatures. That is to say, we take a "human-centric" position in this book. The present authors maintain that if no human being, not a single one, wants to keep a species from going extinct[17] then it should be allowed to go by the boards. If a few people want to maintain an innocuous species, e.g., the snail darter, they should be allowed to do so, at their own expense. But it is human beings who should make all such choices. Our author himself would appear to agree when he says (p. 65): "Economically optimal extinction of fish stocks is likely to be an exceptional case . . ."

Hannesson next attacks private property rights since they are not compatible with so-called "collective" goods (p. 66): ". . . (collective) goods which each and every one can enjoy simultaneously without interfering with one another are called collective goods and to ensure a sufficient provision of such goods we need collective institutions such as governments and their agencies, not private property rights which are useful mainly for exploitative values."[18]

We do not accuse this author alone of making these things up as he goes along, since he is but following the mainstream economics profession in doing exactly that.[19] The difficulty here is that it is simply impossible to demonstrate a preference for the very survival of a congeries of bull trout (Rothbard, 1997A). Purchasing a fish will not suffice; that only reveals the buyer values this particular fish more than the asking price. From this act we are not entitled to deduce that the shopper values *the idea of fish existing.*

Another problem is that all sorts of reductios ad absurdum are opened up by this sort of "reasoning." For example, if we can maintain that "you and I can both simultaneously enjoy the knowledge that a fish stock exists," we can also entertain the polar opposite, to wit, that "you and I can both simultaneously enjoy the knowledge that a fish stock *does not* exist;" smelly creatures, those. Therefore, "we need collective institutions such as governments and their agencies" to wipe this pox off the face of the earth. A concept that can lead to conclusion X, and also, with equal validity, demonstrate non-X, lacks intellectual substance.

Nor is Hannesson's attack on private property rights yet concluded. He (p. 72) supports "stinting, an arrangement by which government leases land for grazing, and propose(s) a similar arrangement for the fisheries."[20] Through no fault of his own, this suggestion comes with particular ill grace given Nevada rancher Cliven Bundy's fight with the Bureau of Land Management over precisely this issue: government ownership of land they never came within a million miles of homesteading. It is unclear whether this confrontation will be solved peacefully, or will deteriorate into another Ruby Ridge or Waco.[21] If Nevada Senator Harry Reid has his way, the latter probability will predominate, since he characterizes Bundy supporters as domestic terrorists (Watson, 2014).

One would not expect such naiveté from the author of such as scholarly book as this, but he does actually utter this howler (pp. 73–74): ". . . the National Marine Fisheries Service and the management councils represent the government and the public interest." What would the Public Choice School say about equating "the government and the public interest?" If Hannesson wants to so blatantly contradict the findings of the Public Choicers, well and good. But at least he owes his audience an explanation of why he rejects their discoveries. This is not vouchsafed by him.[22]

Privatization (pp. 77–81) eloquently makes the case for considering ITQs as property rights, not "'privileges' revocable at any time without compensation." He thinks it is "ill-advised" that they cannot be the foundation for mortgages. He welcomes that "they have nevertheless been treated as property in marital dissolution cases." Hannesson likens failure to do so as "in many ways parallel to the difficulties in the former Soviet Union to establish private property rights to land." He mentions, quite correctly that this stance misallocates investment decisions toward the short run and away from the long run.

In our view, ITQs are not "real" private property. They are instead artificially concocted privileges devised by clever attorneys but which fail to reflect the natural relation between man and material. Politicians will find the temptation to hand out ITQs to crony friends irresistible. Why not have property rights in the things themselves, the fish, rather than merely in the rights to catch them. After all, we own our cars, our furniture, our houses, outright; we are not limited in these cases to a "right" to "catch" them. Second, why not apply these brilliant insights to the oceans themselves, as the very misleading title of his book would imply. And third, these concessions to the regulators are hard to reconcile with these statements supporting government interventionism (p. 81): ". . . property rights . . . are seldom if ever absolute, they function within constraints that vary from one kind of object to another and over time. . . . (P)roperty rights are embedded in society . . . and society can, similarly, restrict property rights. Residential housing is sometimes subject to rent control. The height of buildings to be erected on a given piece of land may be limited, particularly if it would spoil the view of somebody in the neighborhood."[23]

Also indicative of Hannesson's hostility to the free enterprise philosophy is his stance on how ITQs are to be doled out. On page 164, he expresses regret that "fishing rights such as ITQs have usually been given to boatowners only." In his view, they should have been given, also, "to ordinary crewmembers (who have no) investment in the industry." Thus he cossets the old leftist twaddle of a "worker's paradise." This blurring of the distinction between firm and laborer is certainly not compatible with the free capitalist system. Who is the owner? Who bears risk? Is it the former or the latter? To ask this is to answer it.

II. ZETLAND, *THE END OF ABUNDANCE: ECONOMIC SOLUTIONS TO WATER SCARCITY*

We shall subject the Zetland book to the same analysis as we employed for that by Hannesson: to what extent is Zetland's contribution compatible with what we have characterized as our libertarian free market approach, and when not, we shall criticize it.[24] As with Hannesson (2006) there are many positive elements in Zetland (2011). Let us list a few of them, before launching in to our critique. First and most important he brings to bear an explicitly economic analytic framework to address water issues, something rare and refreshing in this field. Replete with supply and demand curves and other aspects of the dismal science, Zetland ably criticizes both price ceilings and price floors as leading to shortages and surpluses, and this alone is an invaluable contribution.

What are some of the difficulties with this book from a free enterprise point of view? Let us now consider this statement of our author (p. 41–42):

> My suggestion for change, "some water for free, pay for more" (or Some for Free) is designed to cover costs, maintain equity, and prevent shortages for residential customers. . . . "Some for Free" works like this: First, every household (every meter) pays a service charge equal to the fixed cost of the water connection. Second, the number of people in the household determines how many units of cheap (or free) water the house receives. Third, the price of additional units is set high enough to reduce demand and prevent shortages, not cover costs. Higher prices will also produce revenue in excess of costs. . . . Fourth, excess revenue is rebated per capita to reduce the impact of higher service charges on individuals and restore the agency's accounts to breakeven. These rebates transfer money from people who use more water to people who use less water.

This, surely, cannot be a serious proposal, at least not one emanating from an economist with even the slightest adherence to free enterprise principles. Rather, it seems to stem from some sort of central planning mode that he made up as he went along.[25] If this is such a good idea why would it be employed for water but not other liquids such as beer, orange juice, gasoline, mercury? What would be the implication were this awkward[26] pricing scheme applied to cabbages, sealing wax, or rubber bands? Of course, when a new burger joint or ice cream parlor opens up, they sometimes give out samples as an advertising gambit. All well and good. But Zetland is advocating this Some for Free system on a permanent basis. It is his obligation to demonstrate why water is unique such that it calls for a convoluted pricing scheme which he fails to do. Zetland (p. 45) is exercised by the fact that the poor pay more for water:

> In Mexico City's shantytowns, for example, people without pipes get water from trucks. Truckers pay 50 pesos (about $4) to get 10,000 liters from city mains; then they sell 500 liters for 28 pesos (about $2), or 10 times the price.

That kind of thinking is that selfsame that has led to the widespread strife of the last century. The word "fair" sits uneasily in a book that supposedly offers an *economic* analysis of water scarcity. Zetland treads dangerously closely to a conflation between the normative and the positive, here. As far as the latter is concerned, not only do the poor pay more for water, this applies to all sorts of products. It is no secret, for example, that they are charged more for groceries. If it is any consolation to our author, however, profits tend to equalize for groceries (and many other goods) enjoyed by the wealthy and the indigent. Were this not so, there would be a tendency for grocers to move from low to high profit areas. No, the poor in Mexico do not need "decent" water management nor "Some for Free."

Rather what they are missing are the benefits of *laissez faire* capitalism which would tend to reduce costs in poor areas.[27] It does not seem likely that the poor paying 10 times the price of the rich emanates from the free enterprise system. Presumably, there is a congeries of restrictions on entry into this industry, or more truckers would come in to take advantage of this gigantic price differential.

Next, consider this statement (p. 23):

> Markets move water from those who have to those who want, using prices to balance supply and demand. Markets may not be fair in outcomes (rich people can still buy more than poor people), but they provide equal access. Market prices accurately reflect value and scarcity, but they can be high.

Why is it not "fair" that Bill Gates and Oprah Winfrey have more dollar votes than the rest of us, many, many more of them? Have they not contributed more value to our economy than virtually all other people? Have they not created far more wealth than the average person? Zetland's is a strange stance for an economist to take, on several grounds. First, it conflates the normative and the positive, the twain of which shall never (at least properly) meet. These are totally different universes of discourse, and his confusion of them is problematic. Second, if markets move water (and everything else under the sun) from those who in their own estimation have too much to those who have too little, and "accurately reflect value and scarcity," does this not indicate "fairness" at least in some sense of that word? Third, we are viewing Zetland through free enterprise eyeglasses, so to speak, and this sentiment simply does not pass muster.

His understanding of monopoly is problematic. He says (p. 23): ". . . monopolists do not necessarily suffer from their mistakes. A firm that makes a mistake faces lower profits and defecting customers. A monopolist just raises prices." If this is referring to a government monopoly, such as the U.S. Post Office, or the FDA, or the NHTSA, or the IRS, then he has a point, although he overstates it. While it is true that these alphabet agencies do not necessarily suffer, even the political system, inefficient and cumbersome as it is, can impose restraints on them. For example, the thalidomide disaster did impact the FDA.[28] Instead of making type I errors, approving bad medicines, they resorted to those of type II, refusing to allow the production of good ones. However, this does not at all apply to the private monopolies he is discussing. If they do not maximize profits, they necessarily suffer from lower revenues than would otherwise be available to them. Nor can such a private firm "just raise prices." If it does, it will be pricing above the profit maximizing level, assuming it had located there beforehand.[29] This analytic framework is thus erroneous even from the neoclassical point of view let alone from the correct Austrian economic perspective.[30]

Nor can we allow Zetland to get away with his (p. 38) phrase, "water wasters." His problem is that he seems to think there is some sort of objective criterion for the proper amount of water to use. If he were but to embrace the subjectivism of the Austrian school he might realize this is a will o' the wisp. Alex showers for 5 minutes, Bob for 10, and Carl for 30. Who is the water waster? David washes his car every day, Edward every month and Frank only once per year. Again we ask, who is "wasting water?" We can substitute for water any other liquid such as beer, wine, milk, or indeed any other good or service, and would still be bereft of any non-ambiguous answer to the question. *De gustibus non disputandum.*[31] Despite how it appears to the nanny-staters; if the water user is freely willing to pay a market determined price, it is, *ipso facto*, not wasted at least from his *ex-ante* point of view.

Of course, it cannot be denied, there is a sense in which "wasting water" can be coherent. For example, if due to government intervention farmers pay $5 per acre foot of water, and city folk must fork over $500 for this amount of that fluid, then it is not unreasonable to say that the agriculturalists are wasting water, in that were they allowed to sell some of it, they would not use it to grow cotton in the desert. But this is very far removed from Zetland's use of this term.[32]

It would appear that in his view, feminism, of all things, can help water markets. He states (p. 46): "In the early 1990s, the Indian government amended its constitution to require that one-third of the leaders and members of village councils be women. . . . Villages where women had power had

60% more drinking water facilities."[33] Enquiring minds want to know: what does this have to do with the economics of water? Shall we unleash women power to other industries, and expect the same beneficial results? And if so, why does this not occur naturally, in the market place, given that, presumably, greater profits will accrue to businesses that follow this lead. Are females champions of the free enterprise system? If not, a bit of reconciliation needs to be done, if he still wishes to retain any semblance of support for the marketplace. One wonders, also, that women can become empowered in a nation where village elders sometime employ group rape as a punishment for women who wish to marry unsuitable husbands (AFP, 2014A, 2014B; Culp-Ressler, 2014).

Zetland's (p. 47) penchant for central planning modalities is never ending: ". . . it's important to think about how often customers see their bills. It's hard to change behavior when water bills and usage statistics arrive quarterly or annually . . . bills with a happy face for below-average use or unhappy face for above-average use are especially effective. People don't like the unhappy face." This does not bespeak much reliance on the free enterprise system. Why oh why are bills with happy or unhappy faces not used for restaurant meals, for auto repair, for psychiatric services? Do we not need to economize on these goods and services too? Why is water special? The answer emanating from this side of the net is that water is so special because it is not allowed to be part of the free enterprise system. If it were, then all of these suggestions would appear as silly as they would be for more ordinary items. Nor would there be any special reason to "conserve" water, under a regime of economic freedom, any more than any other good. We do not worry about the incidence of bills for insurance or cable tv. There is no need for faces, happy or otherwise, on bills for shoes. We need not compare how much ice cream we are consuming compared to our neighbors.

Zetland's treatment of the issue of dirty water is a mixed bag. A positive element is his statement (p. 60) that "Many (water managers) want federal subsidies for municipal wastewater treatment. These subsidies are not economically sound." Yes, indeed. But he takes back his support of capitalism by objecting on the ground that "they are targeted to public agencies, not private companies that also serve the public." Federal subsidies to local governmental agencies are mere book-keeping arrangements as far as the free enterprise system is concerned. The government is the government is the government, at whatever level. However, his implication is that federal subsidies to "private companies that also serve the public" would be justified, and it is difficult to see why he gives a pass to this type of cronyism. On the positive side of the ledger he (p. 61) notes that "market prices reflect the cost of pollution but they also provide incentives." He sees "a market solution to this issue. Los Angeles can auction its sludge; whoever wants it buy it (or be paid to take it)." But why should "Los Angeles," by which we assume he means the city government, do any such thing? In the free enterprise system, municipalities would not so intimately enter into the market. That is called interventionism, crony capitalism, public-private partnerships or economic fascism in some circles.

However, Zetland relies, heavily, albeit implicitly, on the work of Coase (1960), and this is highly problematic. For Coase, who won the Nobel Prize in economics, there are two states of the world. The zero transactions cost model and the realistic one where transactions costs are very high, higher than any possible gains from transactions. In Coase's view in the former case it matters not by one whit whether the court holds the polluter or the victim responsible for this cost. Putting wealth effects to the side, if the costs of stopping the polluter are greater than its benefits (to the two very different groups added up) then no matter what the findings of the court, the pollution will continue, and this is the wealth maximizing solution. Ditto for the very opposite. If the benefits of cessation are greater, there will be an end to this activity, no matter what the court rules. And what should the judge do in the real world of very high transactions costs? Rule so as to minimize costs. But this places the court in the role of a central planner. Why judges would have a comparative advantage, vis a vis the free enterprise system based on private property rights where pollution is always and everywhere seen as a trespass, is never explained, whether by Coase (1960) or Zetland. According to the latter (p. 63): "The end of abundance means that contamination is more costly, clean water is more valuable, and polluters should pay the cost of cleaning up their mistakes." That is a value judgment which fails by mis-understanding that all values are subjective. He fails, as does Coase, to ex-plain that it is the valuation placed on "clean water" by its owner in the first place that demands the polluter to pay. If pollution were interpreted as the trespass it really is, we would deal with it in a similar manner. Should folks in cities be able to dump their untreated, or treated human waste into lakes, rivers, oceans? The answer emanating from the authors of the present book is that this depends upon the views of the owners of these bodies of water. If they agree, then, fine. If not, not. Of course, if these waste products filter into the aquatic property of others they ought to be responsible to the full extent of the law.[34]

Zetland's "Some for Free" policy requires that prices rise as the consumer increases his water usage. This is barking mad. And nowhere is such an assessment more clear than in his discussion of the liquid life-style. Why? First, it violates the economic presumption of one price.[35] That is, there is a tendency for otherwise homogenous goods to be bought and sold at the same price. If not, then there are profits to be made from arbitrage. No one charges anyone more when they purchase additional units of ice cream or orange juice. If a vendor embarked upon such a mad scheme, the consumer would simply seek more rational options, perhaps after purchasing the earlier units at the lower price. There is this inexorable affinity for a single price to be reflected in reality, and schemes of the sort put forth by Zetland cannot overcome it.

This is especially important when it comes to what he (p. 65) calls the liquid life-style: not regarding water needed "to stay alive, clean and fed. It's not about the water that businesses need to operate. It's about the optional water that we use to improve our surroundings or have fun." We are now talking about keeping lawns and golf courses green, filling swimming pools and Jacuzzis, etc. And why does he propose prices proportional to quantity demanded? He wants to discourage "excessive" use of H_2O. But this is done with every other good or service without exception in the absence of prices increasing for additional use on a mandated basis. No one has to pay more for his second Mercedes, and even more and more for his third and fourth. In fact, if he were to buy four at once he would most likely be able to negotiate a price reduction. The very idea is silly, even though for some critics, this luxury automobile is hardly necessary. Why should water be any different than the Mercedes? Zetland hints (p. 67) that water is different from other goods since none of the usual dynamics of normal commodities apply as such to many consumers, and many gas stations are needed to create competition and dynamic prices to balance supply and demand.

But this simply will not do. For it opens up the obvious question, why not simply replace fiat allocation structures with the free market here too? In that case, H_2O would be no more in danger of shortages and surpluses than any other liquid, let alone any other good or service. Nor need we accept his notion that efficient markets need numerous participants. Competition is not a matter of numbers of competitors, but rather of free entry. There are thousands of taxi cabs in major cities, but this is hardly a competitive industry, thanks to restrictions on entry. In contrast, there may be only one grocery store in a small town, but as long as others are legally permitted to offer this service, that is a competitive scenario.

Perhaps Zetland is led astray by his reliance on the perfectly competitive model of neoclassical economics. He appears to reject the application of his *Free for Some* proposal for gasoline on this basis, since there are many suppliers. Perhaps Zetland could be weaned away from his view that water is so unique were he to peruse the Austrian school analysis of competition (Hazlitt, 1946).

Zetland is on firmer ground then he objects to government requests that we (p. 75) ". . . shower with a friend, pee twice before flushing. . . ." These intrusive rules are akin to fishing and hunting seasons, artificial limitations regarding the efficiency of fishing boats, such as net strength, number of fishermen, size of boat, etc. These are all attempts to preserve stocks. Instead, let us have a market with accurate price signals and all these problems are

solved, as they are in most corners of our economy. He is on firmer ground
with this (p. 76–77):

> We'd consume less water when prices go up in the same way that we consume
> less gasoline when prices go up. We'd take shorter showers, install high effi-
> ciency appliances . . . The key is that nobody would need to tell us to use less
> water.

All well and truly said. No, brilliantly articulated. But Zetland does not go
far enough. Why not push for full free enterprise in water, and private property rights throughout? Also, his analysis of "politicians, bureaucrats and
regulators" evades the fact that public administrators are hopelessly disqual-
ified. It focuses, correctly, on the incentive problem of socialism. But it
misses the Hayekian (1945) analysis based on prices as bearers of information, and the even more important Misesian (1922) insight about the impossibility of rational planning without market prices.

Zetland takes a step away from the free market environmentalist perspective when he advocates (p. 84): ". . . a 5 cent deposit on each bottle would
spur people to pick them up and turn them in, as many people worldwide
now do with deposits on glass bottles." What is his motive for supporting this
type of government interventionism into the marketplace? Likely, it is his
claim that (p. 84): "Plastic consumption can create a negative externality that
pollutes the ocean, a common-pool good that has no owner or defender."[36]
What is the libertarian solution to this challenge? Why, of course, privatize
the ocean and all other bodies of water; convert them from common pool
goods subject to negative externalities. In this way, the supposed externality
can be internalized. The private owners of lakes and rivers, etc., presumably,
can be relied upon to deal with the issue of people leaving bottles around on
their property, whether plastic or glass. Do movie theater owners, or the
managers of sports stadiums charge a 5 cent deposit on popcorn boxes or
candy wrappers, or plastic cups? They do not. Instead, they spread garbage
cans around and hire cleaners. The ocean owners might borrow a leaf from
them. Or, they may impose large fines on those who trespass their plastic and
glass bottles on property not belonging to themselves. The point is, on the
market entrepreneurs will find ways to deal with such challenges. The last
thing the free enterprise system needs is a centrally planned scheme to deal
with bottles of the sort proposed by our author.

Finally, there is Zetland's (p. 88–89) defense of socialism: "Several years
ago, I believed that public water utilities were staffed by bureaucrats who
cared more about their offices and short working hours than their customers
or services. I reckoned that for-profit companies would deliver better water
and lower costs. But then I learned more about professional civil servants and
local public managers who were skilled at balancing different needs (service,

employment, environment, sustainability) in their communities. I read a few too many case studies of for-profit companies that cut corners on quality while raising prices in arbitrary ways. I've concluded that success and failure can happen at private or public firms, in developed or developing countries."

Yes, there may be an exceptional bureaucrat who is skilled and highly motivated. And, certainly, some entrepreneurs are incompetent. But the former are not residual income claimants. They cannot earn profits and expand their base of operation, automatically. All too often, success in this realm is punished with a budgetary reduction, while squeaky wheel failures see their finances raised. And the latter are eventually enmeshed in bankruptcy; forced to exit the industry. On a more basic level, Zetland's support of socialism fails to even mention the blistering attacks on this system by the likes of Mises and Hayek. Certainly, any free market credentials Zetland may have once possessed are almost totally vitiated by this embrace of his of communism.

III. GARDNER AND SIMMONS, "THE ECONOMIC EFFECTS OF USING PROPERTY TAXES IN LIEU OF DIRECT USER FEES TO PAY FOR WATER"

Introduction

Let us now cast our baleful eye on Gardner and Simmons (2012A) which is an edited collection of essays. This publication, too, explicitly covers the economics of water, and is ostensibly oriented in a free market direction. It is, too, but not entirely. We cannot comment on every contribution to this book; instead, we shall criticize those aspects of it that deviate the most from the free enterprise philosophy.

It is more than unusual to comment on a "mere" introduction, which is usually limited to summarizing the essays that appear in an edited volume such as this. But, this one contains substantive material, and since we cannot cover each and every contribution to this publication, the introduction can stand as a substitute for many of them.

Our authors start off on the wrong foot. They say (2012A, 2, emphasis added by present authors): "This book contains many examples of how this . . . [establishing secure and transferable private water rights] . . . is being accomplished, particularly in the formation of water markets and *market-like* exchanges of water rights." Notice the rat in the woodpile? Why "market-like" as opposed to plain old ordinary "market" rights? Whenever a true free enterpriser reads "market-like" instead of "market," the red lights on this control panel start to flicker. Nor is this any typographical error. All through the collection market-like institutions such as TURFs, ITQs, IBCs, TERs, WQTs, etc., are offered as the closest discussion we can have to full free enterprise. To the contrary, our claim is we can have it all! At the very least, we can discuss it, analyze it. This anthology, unhappily, ignores the full *laissez faire* vision in water resources.[37]

On page 10 the confusion between free markets and "market-like" institutions appears once again, indicating the prior instance was no oversight: ". . . this program falls short of a real market in water quality management. The chapter describes the basic characteristics of *market-like* program design and stresses the arguments for why *market-like* approaches should be preferred." (Emphasis added.)

Nor can these editors be relied upon to see through the so called "public goods" market failure critique of the interventionists. They state (pp. 9–10):

> . . . the public trust doctrine originated as a supposition of a public right of access to waters, including those under which the submerged lands are privately owned, for the purposes of navigation and fishing. Why public rights to these particular uses? Because they are instream uses where consumption[38] use of the water is mostly non-rival and where property rights are costly to define and protect—representative "public goods" where markets notoriously have been known to fail.

There is more wrong here from the free enterprise point of view than you can shake the proverbial stick at. First of all, that is not at all why the "public trust doctrine" came to apply to water. It came about because of the aqua-socialist ethos of our society. There is also a public right of access to health-care (socialized medicine), to housing (public housing), to wealth (the welfare system), to non-discrimination (affirmative action), to retirement funding (Social Security) to just about anything the socialist ethos of our society can be thought to justify. Why should water be any different, given all these other "progressive" policies? Secondly, markets fail only in the fever swamps of mainstream economists. There is a gigantic literature to the contrary,[39] which none of the contributors of this volume, let alone its editors, condescend to counteract. They content themselves with blithely and uncritically accepting the false notion of market failure. Following, we address several contributions to Gardner and Simons:

Scarborough, "Buying Water for the Environment"

Question: Does Scarborough even claim to be a supporter of free market water? If not, if he is a simple fascist,[40] the reader may wonder why a critique of his piece belongs in this section of the book devoted to criticizing ostensibly free market analyses of water issues. Let us see.

Scarborough (2012, p. 76) sets himself the task of providing "a comprehensive review of the role of markets in restoring instream flows." He will rely on "market data" on this phenomenon. He implies he is in support of the "institutional battle over market implementation." He does not explicitly embrace free enterprise in this regard, but the fact that his essay was included in a compilation dedicated to that end justifies us in asking whether or not, and if so how closely, he adheres to this goal.

According to Scarborough (2012, p. 77): "There are basically four ways to protect instream flows." He lists them as follows (pp. 77–78): "First . . . state restrictions or regulations, . . . second, the public trust doctrine of the Endangered Species Act (ESA) . . . third . . . allow appropriation of water for instream uses . . . (for) private parties or state agencies . . . fourth, the method of OWT."[41] Nowhere in this list, perhaps thought unworthy of inclusion if thought of at all, would be a fully private *for* profit concern, that would completely own these water resources. Suppose he were discussing the protection of any other resource: farm land, forests, mines, whatever. Would he limit himself to these four options? Not if he were guided by free enterprise principles. Then, he certainly would have included fee simple[42] ownership whether appropriation by private, for profit enterprises or *In-Toto*. In short, his thinking resembles fascism in its conflating government, labor, and capital sectors and bearing little or no resemblance to *laissez faire* markets.

Another difficulty with Scarborough's contribution is that he does not seem able to distinguish market from non-market activity. Under the heading of "Market Activity" he has this to say (p. 83): "In recent decades, market activity for instream flows has expanded markedly. Between 1987 and 2007, state, federal and private entities combined acquired more than 10 million acre feet (AF) of water . . . Between 1987 and 2007, federal agencies entered into 215 leases and 25 permanent transfers. . . ."

Notice anything untoward in this report? Yes, when government, whether at the federal, state, or city level engages in purchases or sales of anything, water rights certainly included, it cannot be considered a "market" activity. Why not? This is because there is a fundamental difference between statism and free enterprise. In the latter case, all parties engage in commercial activities with their own money or property and with their own free will. In the former situation, the government does so with money mulcted from the taxpayer under threat of violence. The state can no more engage in a "market" activity than can a criminal gang with its own ill-gotten gains.

Critical is the distinction between the case where the government seizes assets, e.g., through its tax or confiscation systems, and when it purchases property from willing sellers. This cannot be denied. But, is it a relevant difference, regarding markets and free enterprise? It is not, for capitalism consists of *voluntary* actions between consenting parties. When the baleful hand of the government enters the picture, in *any* of its activities, whether on the supply or the demand side, whether it engages in purchases or seizures, it is not part of the market, since there is an element of the involuntary in *all* of its actions. In his Table 4.2, Scarborough (2012, 85) adds federal, state and private transactions, and calls the sum, again, "market activity."[43] At least when apples and oranges are added, the sum is fruit. Here, the dollars add up, of course, but from a libertarian point of view, it is simply illicit to add up these numbers. But are we having a mere verbal dispute? This is of course always a possibility, but it seems difficult to accept this hypothesis when he can aver (p. 89): "In other states, market transactions are generally limited to specific state and federal entities."

Here is yet another attack on the marketplace by Scarborough (2012, p. 90): "Another problem facing the private provision of instream flows is that they are often viewed as a common property resource, in which exclusion of or contracting with all beneficiaries is prohibitively costly. As such, theory suggests that instream flows would be produced below the efficient level if they are only provided by the private sector." But the "private sector" does not view *anything* as a common property resource. In fact it is safe to say that if an entity views anything as a "common property resource" it *cannot* be the truly private sector. "Common property resource" and "private sector" are anathema to one another; these two concepts constitute a contradiction in terms (except of course to the fascist or crony capitalist). As for in-stream flows or anything else for that matter being "produced below the efficient level" this of course can occur under free enterprise. But, not in equilibrium! As the capitalist system is always tending in precisely that direction, it is difficult to see how this can be considered anything other than the last best chance to *avoid* something being "produced below the efficient level."[44]

After having criticized this article as insufficiently disposed toward economic freedom, we would not want to leave the impression that it is a totally fascist essay. No, the moderate free enterprise perspective from which not only this chapter, but pretty much the entire Scarborough book is written from, does indeed contain some support for *laissez faire*. For example (p. 91): "Well-defined, enforced and transferable rights are critical components of a viable and efficient water market . . . Uncertainty in the entitlement to water or the ability to protect those rights from harm diminishes the incentive to pursue market transfers and reduces the expected gains from trade." Well stated!

Gardner, "Auctions of Water Rights"

The thesis of this contribution is that prices are more efficient, efficacious and appropriate for water allocation than are governmental command and control modalities such as taxation. Ordinarily, this would be a welcome contribution to the free enterprise literature. However, in this case, the conclusion is not so clear. Why not? Gardner's (p. 226) opening salvo is as follows:

If a certain level of conservation is desirable . . . the effectiveness of these mandated rules must be compared to the conservation efforts that will be made voluntarily by the final users themselves as they respond to higher water prices in lieu of property taxes. The argument advanced here is that voluntary price-induced conservation will usually be more flexible, pervasive, durable, and hence effective than command-and-control government regulations. This is not to say that government should have no role to play in conservation—educating water consumers, for example, about economically feasible conservation practices and technologies may be very useful.

A minor difficulty: where is the evidence that the statists have a comparative advantage in "educating water consumers"? Is not education, too, an aspect of the economy which if left in private hands will "be more flexible, pervasive, durable, and hence effective than command-and-control government regulations."[45] This obeisance to government effectiveness from a supposedly free market author shocks the conscience of libertarians.

As to the main contention that prices are more effective than taxes, this is of course true. But more than just a little wind is taken out of the sails of this contention when we realize that the "prices" do not occur in the real free market place, where private entrepreneurs reap the benefits thereof. Rather, the amounts of money paid for in these prices instead enters into the coffers of the greedy government, and this is not given its due weight by Gardner. And, not only is the government the recipient of this largesse, something to be regretted on its own account in the libertarian community, but this entity is also in charge of setting these "prices" in the first place. Experience with statism in this regard is not encouraging, at least not in terms of efficient allocation. For example, consider the *anti*-peak load pricing engaged in by government regarding roads, bridges, tunnels, etc. Yes, typically, the all-knowing government, the institution relied upon by Gardner in his advocacy of government pricing schemes inaugurates *anti*-peak load pricing, the direct opposite of what is needed for curing excess demand, whether for traffic or water.

How does this work? The bureaucratic highway authority charges, for example, $10 to cross a bridge. But, if the motorist purchases a monthly or yearly ticket, the price falls, say, to $7 per trip. Yet who is likely to use this thoroughfare when in short supply: the 9am to 5pm regular employee during peak load times, or the housewife who makes a sporadic shopping trip into the central city a few times per month or even year? Obviously, the former. It will not pay the latter to purchase a multiple use ticket, since she uses the service so rarely. But the workingman who commutes into the city some 22 times per month is precisely the one to use the facility during rush hour. Thus, the government *lowers* the price to the rush hour commuter, raising the peaks and lowering the troughs, compared to the situation that would prevail from a more rational pricing scheme.[46]

Peak load pricing consists of charging more during periods of high demand. More for hotels near ski lodges in the winter than in the summer. Anti-peak load pricing is the very opposite: charging less during times of great demand. Were any private enterprise to do this, it would of course decrease profits and risk bankruptcy. This of course does not apply to the state apparatus. An example of this is selling monthly tickets for bridges or tunnels, at reduced prices per trip. But those who purchase these overwhelmingly use them during the rush hours, times of peak demand. Thus, we have a case here of anti-peak load pricing.[47] For more on this see Block (2009C).

Gardner says (p. 231):

> Of course, because water prices are generally administratively set, some agency would have to be responsible for gauging supply and demand and setting efficient prices. An objection might be raised that governments have only weak incentives to manage such a system of efficient water prices, even if they have the responsibility and capacity to do so. This problem could be reduced if the pricing schedule as a function of available water supply were promulgated publicly and in advance of any particular supply conditions.

Once again, time dependent variable pricing is easy to track. Everyone knows when demand will be high: the cooking and showering hours. No special notification system is necessary. Imagine the statist system promulgating anything publicly. More likely, freedom of information lawsuits will have to be launched against them to force them to turn over any information.[48] What is amazing in the interchange is Gardner's naïve faith in government to set prices in a rational manner. The Soviets could not accomplish this task. What makes his recommendation any different from an American system of Sovietized water? And, how does Gardner reconcile his confidence in aquatic central planning with this statement of his (p. 232):

> Given what economists know empirically about price elasticity of demand for water . . . it is perplexing that water prices are so often ignored in water planning. . . . Of course, this neglect of price in planning implicitly assumes that demand for water is perfectly price inelastic. . . . This assumption is surely wrong and surely leads to costly errors (popularly known as the 'planners curse') . . .

One last deviation from market principles is offered in this essay (p. 243): ". . . another rationale can be given . . . for a progressive water fee schedule— to induce conservation. As water users pay higher marginal prices for (purchasing) increasing blocks of water, they will undoubtedly be motived to be more economical in its use." This statement suggests that Gardner has ulterior motives in that it speaks not to price variation adjusting in response to natural variations over time in supply and demand, but as a tool to "induce" a desired behavior.

While arbitrage tends to guarantee that there is one price for any given good or service,[49] in a free market due to economies of scale, large users will tend to pay a lower price, not a higher one. This applies to fluids other than water, and, indeed, to pretty much all goods and services on the market. Is it the case that only water needs to be economized upon? Of course not. Why, then, make an exception for this one resource. This can only stem from thinking there is something unique about H_2O, and from an economic point of view, this is highly problematic, Gardner to the contrary notwithstanding.

Zheng, "The Economics of Dam Decomminssioning for Ecosytem Restoration"

What this essay is doing in a book ostensibly organized to shed light on applying free market principles to water resources is not easy to discern.[50] To the present authors, the decision as to whether to decommission a dam is akin to the one concerning whether a factory should be shut down. In the latter case, it is none of anyone else's business. It is the owner of the plant who would determine whether or not to keep it going, and the presumption is that he would choose based on profit maximization considerations.

Perhaps dams are from Venus and factories are from Mars, but based on Zheng, et al (2012) one would think that the two issues have nothing whatsoever in common. Certainly, the "p" word, "profit," never rears its ugly head in their analysis. Rather, central planning type thinking is the order of the day as far as they are concerned.. To wit (p. 251): ". . . dam removal does not always promote a win-win situation in which all interested parties benefit, but involves social, economic and ecological trade-offs that require careful decision analysis."

To be sure this is true *ex post*. There is never any guarantee that human action will eventuate in mutual benefit between contracting parties. One or both of them may always regret his previous decision. But *ex ante* the only reason people act is to improve their life or economic situation. Did they not think this would occur, they would never enter into a commercial agreement in the first place. Suppose that X closes down his factory. As economists we may deduce that he did so because he thought the benefits would outweigh the costs. There would be no need for considering the views of any other people. This would not be a win-win situation. Rather, it would be plain old "win" in the singular, for X. Yes, his employees might be disappointed that X is closing down his plant, but this property belongs to X, not them.[51] Assuming they have no long range labor contract to the contrary, this action of X violates not one of their rights.

And what is this "careful decision analysis" that Zheng mentions? This turns out to be a complicated process that is more akin to central planning than to anything that occurs in the free marketplace.[52] Zheng sees (p. 252) "a pressing need for comprehensive studies of these issues" one that involves itself with "diverse stakeholders." Au contraire, the operator of a factory or a private dam, need not undertake any "comprehensive study" unless he thinks its benefits outweigh its costs. Never is heard a discouraging word about the possibility that these environmental planners might make a mistake. Never contemplated is the idea that since those who undertake these "studies" cannot be made to pay for their errors; thus, there is no automatic feedback mechanism that functions so as to reduce mis-steps of the planners.[53]

As for "stakeholders," these worthies are defined as those with no private property rights to any of the resources involved. In other words, they are busybodies, mixing in with the making of decisions about which they have no rights at all. The present authors are "stakeholders" in the decision of people to brush their teeth or not. That is, we do not own the toothbrushes, nor the toothpaste and certainly not the teeth in question, and yet we have the temerity to try to order others concerning these habits of theirs? Zheng (p. 268) mentions that "Incorporating stakeholder values is critical in decision-making, especially for difficult (cases)." For shame—Yes, your authors mean "FOR SHAME" because in fact so called stakeholders have no stake. Since they have nothing invested, they can pick up and move at will. Take an employee of the factory for example, at most he has a stake in his skill set that enables him to hold his job; but as soon as a better offer comes along, there is nothing to hold him to that particular factory. Rights and responsibilities are opposite sides of the same coin. According to that old song, "you can't have one without the other." But if "stakeholders" have no responsibilities, how can they have rights?

IV. GOODHUE, ET AL, "THE SACRAMENTO–SAN JOAQUIN DELTA AND THE POLITICAL ECONOMY OF CALIFORNIA WATER ALLOCATION"

If Zheng (2012) was an implicit call for central planning, Goodhue, et al (2012) is an explicit example of it. They start off as if they had never heard of the impossibility of making interpersonal comparisons of utility (p. 281, emphasis added): "Large-scale water problems . . . are inherently difficult to solve . . . Because of the system's complexity . . . it is virtually inevitable that stakeholders' interests will conflict under any chosen policy path. These conflicts would be relatively manageable in a world in which (1) property rights were fully defined, (2) benchmarks were available and generally accepted as *bases for interpersonal welfare comparisons*, and (3) interpersonal compensation was feasible. In such a world, the logical approach would be to choose the policy that maximized aggregate welfare, thus ensuring economically efficient outcomes. The winners could then compensate the losers to guarantee that all stakeholders ended up better off, thus ensuring that all equity effects are incorporated into the outcome. In water allocation problems, typically, none of the conditions listed ... will be satisfied."

Therefore, central planning will come to the rescue, to overcome these difficulties, particularly the second listed one, the fact that "*interpersonal welfare comparisons*" are impossible. That is the thesis of this contribution. It is exceedingly difficult to see how such an initiative can be made compatible with the free enterprise system. One can only look with dismay at yet another attempt to square the circle by demonstrating interpersonal welfare comparisons.[54] The stakeholders, by definition, have no property rights in the dispute (and no stake). Why, then, try to placate them? Because they can make political trouble if not paid off?

According to these authors (p. 281–282): ". . . environmental and agricultural stakeholders often value objectives like 'ecosystem health' or the 'agricultural way of life.' It is difficult to assign a precise property right to these diffuse objectives." Precisely. So why not ignore them? Or, to be consistent, we should accede to the claim of the poor who "value" the transfer of funds from the rich to them. Should such calls for outright theft be respected? Hardly. And yet that is the implication of what is being advocated by these authors.

V. ANDERSON AND LEAL, *FREE MARKET ENVIRONMENTALISM*

We are concerned with but a single chapter of Anderson and Leal (1991), the one entitled "Homesteading the Oceans." Based on this title, as in the case of Hannesson (2006) with a similar title, one would be justified in expecting an overlap with the present book: that the authors would advocate, and defend, the notion of private property rights in the oceans themselves, not merely as pertains to some small aspect of these bodies of waters, such as fish. In the event, we are disappointed with yet another quasi fraudulent title.

These authors start off improperly insofar as full ocean ownership is concerned, with their Table 9.1 on the basis of which they wax eloquent about "U.S. Fish Stocks Being Overfished." What are we interested in here: the fish, or the entire ocean? It would appear the former, not the latter. Under the heading of "The Ocean Commons" (p. 109) we read:

> . . . with open access, not all costs will be taken into account. Another fish
> taken from the stock can reduce the reproductive capacity of the fishery and
> raise search and capture costs for other fishers (sic).[55] Because these added

costs are external to an individual fisher (sic) who considers only his costs and benefits, over time there will be too many fishers (sic) in the fishery. . . . This race to the best fishing grounds is often manifest in the form of overcapitalization in radar, sonar, faster boats, and larger nets. The result is lower profits for the too many fishers (sic) investing in too much capital to catch too few fish.

All well and good and well stated as a exegesis of the tragedy of the commons. But what does this have to do with ownership of the *ocean*? We can surely be excused for thinking these authors are talking about property rights in *fish*, not the entire body of water in which they swim around. We find not a word about owning the oceans themselves. It cannot be denied that their analysis of disappearing fish is right on the mark. But we were looking for something else entirely, and did not find even a hint of it.

Why this rabid sounding concern of ours with ocean privatization as distinct from fish preservation? After all, not every book, article or chapter has to be about what we are interested in. It is perfectly reasonable to discuss the fishing industry, our seeming critique of pursuing this to the contrary notwithstanding. We do so for several reasons. One, product differentiation. We want to determine whether the present book is unique or not. If not, we intend to give full credit to those if any who have preceded us in the venture. Two, academic fraud. Why engage in mislabeling? If an author wants to do good scholarly work on the fishing industry, as we concede many of these authors we have criticized have done, why characterize these efforts as ocean privatization, when they are clearly nothing of the sort?[56]

VI. DEACON, "CREATING MARINE ASSETS: PROPERTY RIGHTS IN OCEAN FISHERIES"

Deacon (2009) is written as an explicit support for individual transferrable quotes (ITQs) for fish. He properly recognizes his effort not as in behalf of a *complete* defense of private property rights in water. Rather, he maintains, it points in that direction. He states (p. 2): "This essay explores the potential for further gains by a more complete application of the property rights approach." And again, he describes his efforts as (p. 3) "more complete treatment of fishing rights as 'property.'" He is advocating, then, *more* of an application of private property rights. More than what? It would appear he means more than the present system of no property rights at all, namely, common or no ownership at all.

What are private property rights? They are the right to use, rent, sell, and preclude others from so doing, with regard to a given resource. In other words Deacon does not pose much of a challenge to himself. He has set the bar for his analysis at a pretty low level in terms of defending capitalist institutions. However, he is in danger of not even attaining this rather limited goal (p. 3): "If these [ITQ] rights can be placed under easement, now a common strategy on land, then a new avenue is opened up for conservation groups or *government* decision makers to use a market approach to achieve conservation objectives" (emphasis added, and also material in parentheses supplied by present authors). But, surely, *government* decision making is not a move *toward* private property rights. Instead, it is anathema to such rights; this constitutes a move in the diametric opposite direction.[57]

This applies, also, to Deacon's opposition to "bottom trawling"[58] (p. 3). For this is the aquatic equivalent to clear cutting forests (Anderson, 2007; Laband, 2001; O'Neill, 2009; Rockwell, 2007; Tomlinson, 2004). But the latter is certainly compatible with free enterprise in land ownership. Farmers typically "clear cut" wheat, corn and other such crops. Whether this should apply to trees is surely an entrepreneurial decision, in the free enterprise philosophy, not one that should be ruled out of court, holus bolus, by third parties. And the same applies to bottom trawling. Under a regime of economic freedom, if this practice maximizes profits, it will be pursued; if not, then not. But the decision will rest with the owners of the property in question, not with outside agitators such as Deacon. Also problematic is his (p. 11) statement to the effect that:

> . . . independent fishers have no incentive to share in the provision of information and other public goods or to coordinate their actions. They are notorious for concealing the locations of fish concentrations and it is not uncommon for fishers to jockey for an advantageous position on the fishing grounds. This can be beneficial for members of a fleet fishing independently, but is wasteful for the fleet as a whole.

In the first place, there is no such thing as a "public good."[59] Information certainly does not qualify, at least while it is not yet "out there."[60] Second, why is it economically inefficient for firms to "conceal" trade secrets from one another. Third, this viewpoint implies that horizontal integration is always to be welcomed. One need not oppose antitrust laws[61] to see the flaw in this viewpoint. In the market, there is an optimal amount of merger, and this need not necessarily include 100% of the industry as Deacon implies. If it did, the tendency for business amalgamation would be overwhelming.[62] States Deacon (p. 18):

> . . . fishery governance by harvester-based organizations represents a logical next step beyond ITQ regulation . . . these organizations [are] vehicles for coordination to overcome the free rider aspects of enforcing property rights, to capture the public good benefit of sharing information on fish stocks, and to eliminate wasteful races to catch the best fish. The Chignik case illustrates the last two of these benefits, and adds to these the gains from providing non-enforcement public goods such as shared equipment and a highly refined allocation of effort.

Co-ops are indeed compatible with free enterprise, but they are but one institutional arrangement to pass muster in this regard. They may well be an improvement over ITQs, but the next step, surely, from the free enterprise point of view, is whatever the market decides upon, and they need not necessarily be cooperatives. Unfortunately, the latter desiderata nowhere appears in this publication. Is it not passing curious that the cooperative movement boasts a rather small share of the overall market in other industries? Nor are good and sufficient reasons lacking for this state of affairs (Klein, 2007).

Deacon (p. 18) is a bit too enamored of "central management" as a business practice. If firms voluntarily merge to take advantage of the "transactions costs" he mentions, well and good. But, surely, there is an optimal amount of centralization and decentralization in the free enterprise system, and this emanates from the market process. Why is our author lending his support to one side (or the other) of what should come about naturally from the working out of competitive forces? He certainly offers no reason as to why there is too little centralization or too much decentralization in the market, whether for water or any other good or commodity. This seems, merely, a taste of his; there is no reason to suppose any market failure in this regard, his personal preferences to the contrary notwithstanding.

Regarding Deacon's support for "centrally managing," has he slipped into advocacy of common ownership, or no ownership, e.g., communism? Possibly, but not necessarily. It all depends upon whether this scheme emanates from a full private property rights system, or, which is more likely, from the semi, demi, quasi market *mimicking* institutional arrangement he seems to favor.

He is an enthusiastic supporter of "easements" (p. 19–20). He defines ownership as having control over a "bundle of sticks," and easement as "a transaction in which a landowner cedes some sticks from his or her bundle for a specified duration . . . in exchange for compensation." This is all well and good, but a robust system of private property rights, which a true free market environmentalist would favor, includes this arrangement as but one option. Why favor easements, then, when this is merely one of several choices open in a vigorous property rights system; why not go whole hog, and embrace the full capitalist system? There would be no necessity for marine easements in a full private property rights system. The invisible hand would tend to ensure any benefits accruing from easements. Why single out this one mode of operation? Is it because water is more interconnected than land? We are vouchsafed no answer to this query.

In Deacon's view (p. 22): "Trawl fishing is the only way to harvest certain commercially valuable flat fish, but it is nonselective and results in bycatch.[63] Fishers can control bycatch to a degree, by avoiding critical areas, by taking care when employing gear, and by using more selective trawl equipment, but no individual has an incentive to do so." True, all too true.

But the answer is a full-blooded and complete private property rights system in the oceans, not any of these compromise positions favored by him. Full ownership will give the property holders all the "incentive to do so" that anyone would want.

Instead, this man from PERC (Property and Environment Research Center) states (p. 24): "One key change would be to allow fishers (sic) to agree to limitations on the gear used and areas fished with active permits, making it unnecessary for a conservation group to purchase permits and lease them back with restrictions." Is this a way of "treating existing fishing rights more consistently as property rights?" Hardly. These "limitations," instead, are orthogonal to that goal. It is too bad that Deacon cannot see his way clear to embracing the system supported by the present authors. His compromise position (p. 28) "is to treat existing harvest rights more completely as property . . . and extend . . . the property rights approach." No, we do not need extensions or more completeness. We need full-bodied property rights in the water, as on the land. This position of his tends to inhibit innovation. Why should fishermen be condemned to use the technologies of the past? Private property rights, full blown, would encourage inventions to enable a sustainable catch with the expenditure of fewer resources. It is only where titles are insecure that technological improvements are untenable.

Deacon comes so close to embracing a *laissez faire* system when he mentions (p. 32) ". . . a hypothetical sole ownership regime where such rights are completely delineated. With open access, TNC (The Nature Conservancy) could pay a fisher (sic) to refrain from unwanted actions, but another harvester not so encumbered would be motivated to enter and outcompete the fisher under easement. Under sole ownership, where one agent holds rights to make coordinated decisions on all aspects of the resource's use, TNC could proceed the same way it does with conservation easements on land, by negotiating a single agreement covering many aspects of the resource's use." We are tempted to award Deacon the proverbial cigar for so insightfully likening the water and the land, and contemplating "sole ownership" which we interpret as complete private property rights. However, we refrain from doing so, since on the very same page he seems to take back his equation of water and land: "There are of course differences in the marine and terrestrial cases. Unlike land, the marine resource is shared, so its condition depends on how all users treat it and makes it important to negotiate agreements with all users." Ah, well, can't win them all.

NOTES

1. Liberalism: "b: a theory in economics emphasizing individual freedom from restraint and usually based on free competition, the self-regulating market, and the gold standard c: a political philosophy based on belief in progress, the essential goodness of the human race, and

the autonomy of the individual and standing for the protection of political and civil liberties"—Merriam Webster on-line 2013.

2. They are widely, but undeservedly, seen as libertarian supporters of free enterprise and private property rights.

3. Individual Transferrable Quotas

4. Chordata is a taxonomic phylum (a ranking between kingdom [as in the "animal kingdom"] and class [as in "mammals"]) consisting of animals with a notochord (a hollow structure such as a spinal cord). However, the subject matter addressed herein includes other aquatic animals outside of the Chordata phylum such as jelly fish, sponges, etc. plus members of the plant kingdom living in or underwater.

5. Indeed older technology in the form of clips attached to the creatures would provide the equivalent of brands.

6. A marker may stem from hybridization or other breeding process to establish recognizable subspecies.

7. For a defense of the industrial revolution, see Ashton and Hudson. 1998; Berg, 1992; Crafts, 1985; Deane, 1979; Floud and Johnson, 2003; Floud and McCloskey, 1994; Hartwell, 1967, 1970, 1972; Hayek, 1954; Levin, 1998; McKendrick,1983; Mises, [1949] 1998; Nardinelli, 1990; Rosenberg and Birdzell. 1987; Shaffer, 2012; Taylor, 1975. Hannesson (p.7), no supporter of free enterprise also says of "Western industrialized countries . . . based on private property" that "This arrangement also is, or has been, highly controversial. Socialism arose in protest against it and its perceived injustice. That perception is not without foundation." Wrong, wrong, wrong. Socialism arose, rather, out of economic illiteracy, greed, and moral disintegration, and was and is responsible for millions and millions of deaths Block, 2006C; Branfman, 2013; Conquest, 1986, 1990; Courtois, et. al. 1999; DiLorenzo, 2006; Rummel, 1992, 1994, 1997).

8. Despite its technical truth, Hannesson's assertion is not a critique of capitalism as he apparently supposes; rather, it illustrates a major short coming of democracy. "A democracy cannot exist as a permanent form of government. It can only exist until the majority discovers it can vote itself largess out of the public treasury." —Attributed to Alexander Tytler by (Peterson, 1951).

9. Hannesson (p. 12) also takes a gratuitous slap at markets in used body parts, which could save thousands of lives were they but legalized (see on this Anderson and Barnett, 1999; Barnett, Andy, 1999; Barnett, Saliba, & Walker, 2001; Beard, Jackson & Kaserman, 2007–2008; Block, Whitehead, Johnson, Davidson, White and Chandler. 1999–2000; Block, 1987, 1988A, 1988B; Carey, 2002; Cherry, 1999; Clay and Block, 2002; Garner and Block, 2008; Healy, 2006; Hippen, 2008; Kaserman, 2002; Kaserman & Barnett, 2002; Malek, 2001; Richards, 2001; Taylor, 2005, 2006, 2007; Wilkinson, 2003; Young, 2004). Presumably, it is licit for people to donate their own body parts (*not* those of their "offspring"), but if this entirely legal act is accompanied by a payment, it ceases to be acceptable. One wonders how an author who favors privatization, even of ITQs, can be so dismissive of commerce.

10. We all know what this means. If seven billion people "own" all the oceans, virtually none of them do. The real owners, in the sense of being able to determine their use, will be a few dozen bureaucrats at the United Nations, or some such organization. If we all "own" supposedly "public" parks, museums, roads, why cannot we not sell our share of them? And, since we may not legally do so, we cannot be said to really own these amenities. For the reader who does not believe this, we have some land to sell you in Wyoming. It is very beautiful (though it has recently experienced a massive forest fire). There are lots of geysers. Some say it is a super volcano. It is cheap, first offer will be accepted.

11. Branding with computer chips might be one way of distinguishing "mine" salmon from "thine."

12. Salmon would be one obvious exception to this general rule.

13. One motive for fish migration patterns might be to escape sharks. But this species, in the sea, is equivalent to wolves, or lions, on the land. None of them are allowed in cattle ranches or places where buffalo herds are privately raised. In like manner, the movement of these tigers of the ocean would be severely limited. They would have their own terrain, just as in the case of land predators. These species are much too valuable to be hunted to extinction, but under any

reasonable commercial institution, they would not be allowed to range widely either. The present authors would not want to be characterized as, gasp!, speciesists, so we first mention protecting fish from sharks. But humans, too, fall victim to these sea creatures with razor blade teeth. Fewer than a dozen human beings are killed by sharks each year (Oceana. Undated) but they sure do scare the bejesus out of us.

14. The movie "Medicine Man" with Sean Connery illustrates this point.

15. Such a completely uninteresting species is unlikely because all living creatures fit within a biological niche, i.e., other plant(s) or animal(s) depend on its members for survival. The herdsman is highly interested in the health of the forage needed to maintain his stock.

16. Environmental green on the outside; they favor the "green" agenda. But communist red on the inside; their goal is to control the decision-making of other people, as in the USSR, North Korea, Cuba, Communist China. Is Hannesson a member of this group? There is no "settled science" on this.

17. For example, a super bubonic plague germ that could not safely be kept from spreading, even in an airtight laboratory

18. The first premise of Hannesson's thought accurately describes men's relation to goods that are plentiful. For the prehistoric fisherman standing on the shore, his prey appears as if by magic faster than his capability to catch them. The second is that of the spoiled child who, having been provided food as much as he needed his entire life, feels unjustly exploited that he must now, gasp, work for his livelihood.

19. "A minority may be right, and the majority is always in the wrong." —Ibsen, 1882

20. Hannesson borrows this execrable idea from Moloney and Pearse, 1979.

21. See on this: Reuters, 2014; Grigg, 2014. North (2014) demonstrates just how extensive is this government leasing of land it does not properly own west of the Mississippi River. Even less well demonstrated is the government's claim over water resources.

22. For readings in this school of thought, see Buchanan and Tullock, 1962; Buchanan, 1975; Buchanan, Tollison and Tullock, 1980; Krueger, 1974; Rowley, Tollison and Tullock, 1988. For an Austro libertarian critique, see Block, 2000; 2005E; Block and DiLorenzo, 2000, 2001; DiLorenzo, 1984, 1987, 1988, 1990, 2002; DiLorenzo and Block, 2001; Mackenzie, Unpublished; Pasour, 1986; Rothbard, 1997B, 2011A; Stringham, 2005.

23. For a critique of the position that views may be owned, see Block, 2008.

24. One of our motivations for this is simple product differentiation. We wish to distinguish our book from others who have written on this subject. Another, of course, is to get that proverbial one millionth of an inch closer to the Truth with a capital T: to shed light on the economics and politics of water ownership and provision.

25. For a critique of central planning, whether of the five year plan or any other variety such as in the present case, see Mises, 1922.

26. For one thing it would be a bookkeeping nightmare; for not only must the quantity be monitored but the population of each house: continually, with frequent updates and intra-billing period revisions.

27. That is assuming criminals do not make off with these investments, and, if they would, a more robust competition amongst water trucks would ensue.

28. For the case in favor of abolishing this organization, see Becker, 2002; Goodman, 2011; Gottlieb, 2010; Henninger, 1990; Higgs, 1994; Hoppe, 1993A; Kaitlin, et. al., 1987; Kazman, 1990; Klein and Tabarrok, Undated; Peltzman, 1973, 1974; 1987A, 1987B, 2005; Sardi, 2007; Steinreich, 2005; Thornton, 2012.

29. The aphorism is "couldof, wouldof." If a raise in price could have increased revenues, the private profit maximizing firm would presumably already have done precisely that.

30. For the Austrian theory as it relates to monopoly, see Anderson, et. al., 2001; Armentano, 1999; Barnett, et. al., 2005, 2007; Block, 1977, 1982, 1994; Block and Barnett, 2009; Boudreaux and DiLorenzo, 1992; Costea, 2003; DiLorenzo, 1996; DiLorenzo and High, 1988; Henderson, 2013; High, 1984–1985; McChesney, 1991; McGee, 1958; Rothbard, 2004; Shugart, 1987; Smith, 1983; Tucker, 1998A, 1998B.

31. There is no accounting for taste. We say this in spite of Stigler and Becker, 1977. For a critique see Callahan, 2001.

32. On water pricing see: Anderson, 1983, 1998A, 1998B; Anderson and Hill, 1996; Anderson and Snyder, 1997; Block, 1992, 2001A, 2001B; Hannesson, 2004, 2006; Motichek, Block and Johnson, 2008; Reyburn, 1992; Rothbard, 1955, 1956, 1985, 2007; Tucker, 2008; Whitehead and Block, 2002; Whitehead, Gould and Block, 2004.

33. In case critics of ours think we are making this up out of whole cloth, attributing to Zetland words he didn't really write, check this out for yourselves.

34. States Anderson, 1989: "Fortunately, there is a simple, effective approach available—long appreciated but under used. An approach based solidly on ... private property rights. If you took a bag of garbage and dropped it on your neighbor's lawn, we all know what would happen. Your neighbor would call the police and you would soon find out that the disposal of your garbage is your responsibility, and that it must be done in a way that does not violate anyone else's property rights."

35. If fact in so far as it exists, a variation of price is exactly the opposite of Zetland's concept. Price decreases with increased usage due to an economy of scale that the businessman passes on to his customer.

36. Here, he comes so *close* to embracing the thesis of the present book, that owners of bodies of water would defend them against marauders, and banish the common-pool tragedy of the commons.

37. The apogee of support for semi, demi, quasi, partial, market-like institutions, instead of real, full, robust market ones, is perhaps reached in Shabman and Stephenson (2012) who wax eloquent about these compromises.

38. In fact most in-stream uses are non-consumptive. For example, a shipping company depends on adequate H_2O in the channel but neither diverts it nor uses it up.

39. For a critique of the market failure fallacy, see Anderson, 1998; Barnett, et. al, 2005; Block, 2002; Callahan, 2000; Cowen, 1988; DiLorenzo, 2011; Guillory, 2005; Higgs, 1995; Hoppe, 2003; MacKenzie, 2002; Rothbard, 1985; Simpson, 2005; Tucker, 1989; Westley, 2002; Woods, 2009A, 2009B.

40. "Fascist" refers to one who holds to the, unfortunately, popular economic system of common control by cliques (government, labor, capital) of factors of production and has nothing to do with the racism associated with Nazism. Technically, these terms should never be conflated. On the other hand, fascism does tend to demand a totalitarian regime, whether democratic or not. Only when the ruling gang or dictator is racist, as apparently is often the case, will this association occur. A euphemistic term bandied about by politicians "crony capitalism" is similar to and frequently identical with fascism.

41. OWT refers to the Oregon Water Trust (p. 75), "a private nonprofit organization dedicated to restoring and preserving freshwater ecosystems."

42. "Fee simple is the greatest possible estate in land, wherein the owner has the right to use it, exclusively possess it, commit waste upon it, dispose of it by deed or will, and take its fruits. It represents absolute ownership of land, and therefore the owner may do whatever he or she chooses with the land. If an owner of a fee simple dies intestate, the land will descend to the heirs.

43. Swaim (2014) calls "preposterous" this mixing of private and public institutions, and characterizing both, not just the former, as part of the free market. He states: "... the fact that public funds account for about 86% of for profit colleges' total income does make the colleges' claim that they are a 'free-market' alternative preposterous." Equally preposterous are Scarborough's numerous confusions between public and private.

44. In making this claim we of course reject the notion of external economies or positive externalities being a market failure. It would take us too far afield to defend this statement in the present context, but the interested reader may consult this literature: Barnett and Block, 2007, 2009; Block, 1983, 1990B, 1992, 1993, 2003B; Cordato, 1992; Hoppe, 2003; Lewin, 1982; Rothbard, 1982; Santoriello and Block, 1996; Terrell, 1999.

45. In addition, it is your authors' contention that information regarding scarcity is included within the price when free markets govern. Therefore, even the ignorant know to save water when the price goes up.

46. In support of this argument see Port Authority, 2014. On the other hand, in Denver, motorists pay more—much more—for peak hour usage (on the order of $.50 non-peak vs

$12.00 peak; prepaid and non-prepaid have similar variations). See on this US DOT FHA, 2014. A similar situation occurs in Seattle where tolls are based not only upon time of day, but also in terms of traffic congestion at any point in time: WSDOT, 2015. Does this mean that governments can be trusted to engage in rational pricing schemes? Yes and no. No, in the sense that it took them a long time to incorporate peak load pricing, and in some jurisdictions, such as New York City, this has still not occurred. Yes, in that even statist bureaucrats, some of them, some of the time, will borrow from free market practice.

47. This phenomenon can be viewed differently: By selling many trips all at once, the toll collector realizes an economy of scale and/or easier cheaper transponder technology which he may pass on to the consumer. Single users on the other hand require a human toll collector or a license plate reader plus an individually mailed bill. Furthermore, with the former they are paid in advance while with the latter their payment is on-time or delayed. Bulk selling does not necessarily preclude peak demand pricing, for example: prices at 2:00 am: single pass $2.00, bulk ticket $0.25/pass; at 5:30 pm: single pass $10.00, bulk ticket $7.00/pass. On the day of the Big Game: even higher on both counts, but with the ratios intact. The bottom line is that we do not object to bulk passes per-se. They may save lots of labor. The problem with currently prevalent practice is that it also engages in anti-peak load pricing, when, as we have seen, it need not do so merely in order to take advantage of these economies of scale.

48. Of course in saying this we must abstract from the government's role in creating pamphlets so as to "educat(e) water consumers, for example, about economically feasible conservation practices and technologies, may be very useful." Here, we must concede, the state does *such* an "excellent" job.

49. A gallon of water at 7:00 pm is not the same product as a gallon at 3:00 am. Sometimes, people store water on their premises to save money by taking this product during off-peak hours. That can be economical if the consumer finds it worthwhile. Of course, storage carries its own cost, so such arbitrage may never entirely close the price differential between peak and non-peak hours.

50. On the other hand, it is not the only chapter in Gardner and Simmons, 2012, to call forth such an evaluation.

51. With regard to the employees, while it may be difficult to visualize in prospect, even they will tend to be better off, because working for a new vibrant enterprise tends to be more lucrative than hanging on to a dying one.

52. See for example Zheng, p. 253, table 10.1; p. 260, table 10.4.

53. One of your authors is reminded of the case of the new water plant for Northglenn, CO. Our firm was hired to do a study of whether it would be cost effective to change the city from dependency on a neighboring town to an independent system. We came to the conclusion that it would not be economical to do so. That was not the answer that city fathers wanted to hear. They hired another firm to give them the "correct" answer. Then they hired us to design the new water plant. After this system was in place, the price of water service skyrocketed to the extent that it depressed housing costs for years following. But at least the bureaucrats had their own independent system.

54. For critiques, see Barnett, 2003; Gordon, 1993; Herbener, 1979; Rothbard, 1997A.

55. According to Mirriam-Webster on-line 2013 the word "fisher" is now accepted usage. We insert "sic" whenever it is used, however, in support of ordinary language as it was used before the requirements of politically correct feminism were imposed on the culture. For the importance of saving the language from cultural Marxism, see Block 2000A, 2000B, 2006D. We insist that "fisherman" or "fishermen" is the correct usage.

56. A similar pattern emerges when political scientists object to large amounts of money being spent on politics as "buying elections." Nothing of the sort occurs when rich people donate money to political campaigns. In very sharp contrast indeed, "buying elections" has nothing to do with mere advertising, etc. Rather, it concerns paying voters to cast their ballots in one direction or the other (given a secret ballot, it may be difficult to determine whether there was a successful purchase or not, but this is entirely a different matter).

57. That well known sign "No trespassing, private property—U.S. Government" is a joke!

58. Scouring the ocean floor, leaving nothing, nothing, untouched.

232   *Appendix*

59. Barnett and Block, 2007, 2009; Block, 1983, 2000, 2003C; Bibliography, undated; Cowen, 1988; De Jasay, 1989; Holcombe, 1997; Hoppe, 1989; Hummel, 1990; Osterfeld, 1989; Pasour, 1981; Rothbard, 1985, 1997A; Schmidtz, 1991; Sechrest, 2003, 2004A, 2004B, 2007; Tinsley, 1999.

60. That information is not scarce once well-known, underlies the libertarian case against property rights in intellectual property. See on this Kinsella, 2001.

61. For the case against antitrust legislation, see footnote 30.

62. Rothbard (2004) makes the case against the One Big Firm.

63. Catching unwanted types of fish or material not aimed at by the fisherman.

Bibliography

Abelard, Peter. 1120. *Sic et Non*, Ed. Appleton, John Hoblyn and Sayce, Archibald Henry. 1881. *Dr. Appleton: His Life and Literary Relics*; London.

Acton, John Emerich Edward Dalberg. 1881. Cannes, April 24, per *Letters of Lord Acton to Mary, Daughter of the Right Hon. W.E. Gladstone*, 1904, (London, 1913 version).

Adie, Douglas K. 1988. *Monopoly Mail: Privatizing the United States Postal Service*, New Brunswick, N.J.: Transaction.

Adie, Douglas K. 1990a. *The Mail Monopoly: Analyzing Canadian Postal Service, Vancouver*: The Fraser Institute.

Adie, Douglas K. 1990b. "Why Marginal Reform of the U.S. Postal Service Won't Succeed," pp. 73–92, in *Free the Mail: Ending the Postal Monopoly*, Peter J. Ferrara, ed., Washington, D.C.: The Cato Institute.

Admiralty and Maritime Law Guide. Undated. "Circuit Court Admiralty Cases, Salvage," http://www.admiraltylawguide.com/ccsalvage.html. Accessed on 4–15–2015.

AFP. 2014A. "Tribal elders in India order gang-rape of woman." January 23; http://www.dawn.com/news/1082165. Accessed on 4–28–2015.

AFP. 2014B. "Suspects in court over India gang-rape 'punishment'" January 24; http://www.dawn.com/news/1082385. Accessed on 4–28–2015.

Ahart, John and Stiles, Gerald. 1991. "The Military's Entry into Air Interdiction of Drug Trafficking from South America," *A Rand Note*, http://www.rand.org/content/dam/rand/pubs/notes/2007/N3275.pdf. Accessed 4–21–2015.

Ahlbrandt, Roger. 1973. "Efficiency in the Provision of Fire Services." Public Choice 16 (Fall): 1–15.

Albright, Logan. 2013. "Libertarianism in One Sentence." November 22; http://mises.ca/posts/blog/libertarianism-in-one-sentence/?utm_source=Ludwig+von+Mises+Institute+of+Canada+Daily+List&utm_campaign=6c4f4db8fe-RSS_EMAIL_CAMPAIGN&utm_medium=email&utm_term=0_6c2fea3584-6c4f4db8fe-209944333#comments. Accessed on 4–28–2015.

Alcock, James. Undated. "The Empire at Its Widest Extent by 1920," *Historical Atlas of the British Empire*, http://www.atlasofbritempire.com/uploads/1920_Widest_Extent.GIF. Accessed on 5–4–2015.

Alexander, Jeff. 2008. "Indians: 'Our water is not for sale'." *The Muskegon Chronicle*. April 28; http://www.mlive.com/environment/index.ssf/2008/04/indians_our_water_is_not_for_s.html. Accessed on 4–28–2015.

Allen, Robert C. 2009. *Farm to Factory: A Reinterpretation of the Soviet Industrial Revolution*. http://press.princeton.edu/titles/7611.html. Accessed on 4–28–2015.

Almadhagi, Ahmed Noman; "Yemen and the USA: A Super-Power and a Small-state Relationship, 1962–1994"; *Library of Modern Middle East Studies*; I. B. Tauris; 1996.

Alston, Wilton D. 2007. "What Would Happen If the Post Office Had Competition?" June 6 https://www.lewrockwell.com/2007/06/wilton-alston/the-postal-monopoly/. Accessed on 4-28-2015.

Alvarez, Lisette and Campbell J. Robertson. 2013. "Cost of Flood Insurance Rises, Along With Worries" October 12; http://www.nytimes.com/2013/10/13/us/cost-of-flood-insurance-rises-along-with-worries.html?_r=0. Accessed 4-29-2015.

Alvarez, Lizette. 2013. "In South Florida, a Polluted Bubble Ready to Burst," *New York Times*, September 8, http://www.nytimes.com/2013/09/09/us/lake-okeechobee-in-florida-a-polluted-bubble-ready-to-burst.html?_r=0. Accessed on 4-28-2015.

Amato, David S. 2013. "Economic Fascism and the Power Elite." March 5; https://mises.org/daily/6375/. Accessed on 4-28-2015.

Ancient Ireland: http://www.youtube.com/watch?v=su9OqvBbSD0. Accessed on 4-28-2015.

Anderson, Andrew. 1993. "Salvage and Recreational Vessels: Modern Concepts and Misconceptions"; http://www.safesea.com/salvage/law/anderson/anderson_background.html. Accessed on 4-28-2015.

Anderson, Martin. 1989. *The Christian Science Monitor*, 4 January, p. 19, reprinted in Block, Walter E., ed. *Economics and the Environment: A Reconciliation*, Vancouver: The Fraser Institute.

Anderson, Terry. 1983. *Water Crisis: Ending the Policy Drought*. Baltimore, MD: Johns Hopkins Press.

Anderson, Terry L. 1998A. "The Rising Tide of Water Markets." *Journal des Economistes et des Etudes Humaines* 8(4, December): 425–39.

Anderson, Terry. 1998B. "Environment: California, High and Dry" *Hoover Digest*, No. 3.

Anderson, Terry and P.J. Hill, 1979. "An American Experiment in Anarcho-Capitalism: The *Not* So Wild, Wild West," *Journal of Libertarian Studies*, 3: 9–29; http://mises.org/journals/jls/3_1/3_1_2.pdf. Accessed on 4-28-2015.

Anderson, Terry L. and Peter J. Hill, 2004, *The Not So Wild, Wild West*, Stanford, CA University Press.

Anderson, Terry L. and Peter J. Hill, Editors. 1995. *Wildlife in the Marketplace*. Lanham, MD: Rowman & Littlefield.

Anderson, Terry L. and Peter J. Hill, editors. 1996. *The Privatization Process: A Worldwide Perspective*, Lanham, MD: Rowman & Littlefield Publishers.

Anderson, Terry, and Leal, Donald R., 1991, *Free Market Environmentalism*, San Francisco: Pacific Institute.

Anderson, Terry L. and Pamela S. Snyder. 1997. "Water Markets: Priming the Invisible Pump"; Washington, D.C.: Cato Institute.

Anderson, William. 1998. "Market Failure?" October 8; https://mises.org/library/market-failure. Accessed on 4-28-2015.

Anderson, William. 2005. "Katrina and the Never-Ending Scandal of State Management," September, 13; https://archive.mises.org/library/katrina-and-never-ending-scandal-state-management. Accessed on 4-28-2015.

Anderson, William L., and Andy Barnett 1999. "Waiting for Transplants." *The Free Market*, *17*(4). https://bastiat.mises.org/library/waiting-transplants. Accessed on 4-28-2015.

Anderson, William and Scott A. Kjar. 2008. "Hurricane Katrina and the levees: taxation, calculation, and the matrix of capital." *The International Journal of Social Economics*. Vol. 35, No. 8, pp. 569–578.

Anderson, William L. 2007. "Fires of the Feds: How the Government Has Destroyed Forests." October 25; https://mises.org/daily/2764/Fires-of-the-Feds-How-the-Government-Has-Destroyed-Forests. Accessed on 4-28-2015.

Anderson, William, Walter E. Block, Thomas J. DiLorenzo, Ilana Mercer, Leon Snyman and Christopher Westley. 2001. "The Microsoft Corporation in Collision with Antitrust Law," *The Journal of Social, Political and Economic Studies*, Vol. 26, No. 1, Winter, pp. 287–302.

Aquinas, Thomas. *Summa Theologica*, 1st Part of Part II, "Treatise on Law," 2274, http://www.ccel.org/ccel/aquinas/summa.pdf. Accessed on 4-4-2015.

Arabian Peninsula and Vicinity, Undated. Library of the University of Texas, Maps, http://www.lib.utexas.edu/maps/middle_east_and_asia/arab_pennisula.gif. Accessed on 4–16–2015.

Artistotle. 350 C.C. Politics, Book II, Part V, Benjamin Jowett translation, http://classics.mit.edu/Aristotle/politics.2.two.html. Accessed on 4–27–2015

Arkansas Game and Fish Association. 2010. "Lake Overcup draw down meeting scheduled." *Arkansas Outdoors Newsletter*; http://www.agfc.com/Pages/newsDetails.aspx?show=50. Accessed on 4–28–2015.

Armentano, Dominick T. 1999. *Antitrust: The Case for Repeal*. Revised 2nd ed., Auburn AL: Mises Institute.

Arnold, N. Scott. 1994. *The Philosophy and Economics of Market Socialism: A Critical Study*; New York: Oxford University Press.

Augustine. 426. *The City of God.*

Ashton, T.S. and Pat Hudson. 1998. *The Industrial Revolution 1760–1830*. Oxford University Press.

Associated Press. 2003. "Could methane bubbles sink ships?", *Science on NBC News.com*, http://www.nbcnews.com/id/3226787/ns/technology_and_science-science/t/could-methane-bubbles-sink-ships/#.VS_3XulFCB9. Accessed on 4–16–2015.

AutomotiveTv. 2008. *YouTube*, "Rinspeed's First Underwater Car," http://www.youtube.com/watch?v=sJC7E06IBXI. Accessed on 4–17–2015.

Bailey, Ronald. 1995. *The true state of the planet*. The Free Press.

Bardham, P. and J. Roemer. 1992. "Market Socialism: A Case for Rejuvenation." *Journal of Economic Perspectives.* Vol. 6, No. 3, pp. 101–116.

Barnett, Andy. 1999. "Die Waiting." *Mises Daily*. https://mises.org/library/die-waiting. Accessed on 4–28–2015.

Barnett, William II. 1988. "The Market for Used Human Body Parts," *The Free Market*, https://mises.org/library/market-used-human-body-parts. Accessed on 4–28–2015.

Barnett, William II. 1989. "Subjective Cost Revisited," *Review of Austrian Economics*, Vol. 3, pp. 137–138; http://www.mises.org/journals/rae/pdf/rae3_1_9.pdf. Accessed on 4–28–2015.

Barnett, William II. 2003. "The Modern Theory of Consumer Behavior: Ordinal or Cardinal," *Quarterly Journal of Austrian Economics;* Vol. 6, No. 1, Spring, pp. 41- 63. http://www.mises.org/journals/qjae/pdf/qjae6_1_3.pdf. Accessed on 4–28–2015.

Barnett, William II and Walter E. Block. 2007. "Coase and Van Zandt on Lighthouses," *Public Finance Review*, Vol. 35, No. 6, November, pp. 710–733.

Barnett, William and Walter E. Block. 2009. "Coase and Bertrand on Lighthouses," *Public Choice*; 140(1–2):1–13, http://dx.doi.org/10.1007/s11127–008–9375-x. Accessed on 4–28–2015.

Barnett, William, Walter E. Block and Michael Saliba. 2005. "Perfect Competition: A Case of 'Market-Failure,'" *Corporate Ownership & Control*. Vol. 2, No. 4, summer, p. 70–75.

Barnett, William II, Walter E. Block and Michael Saliba. 2007. "Predatory pricing." *Corporate Ownership & Control*, Vol. 4, No. 4, Continued—3, Summer; pp. 401–406.

Barnett, William II, and Michael Saliba. 2004. "A Free Market for Kidneys: Options, Futures, Forward, and Spot." *Managerial Finance*. 30 (5): 38–56.

Barnett, William II., Michael Saliba, & Deborah Walker. 2001. "A Free Market in Kidneys: Efficient and Equitable." *The Independent Review*, *V*(3), 373–385; https://www.independent.org/pdf/tir/tir_05_3_barnett.pdf. Accessed on 4–28–2015.

Bauch, Herbert. 2007. *Montreal Gazette*, "Should we sell our water to the U.S.?" November 28, http://www.canada.com/montrealgazette/news/story.html?id=24ca3d1d-fb73–4233-90 3b-ccd07dc00827. Accessed on 5–4–2015.

Bauer, Peter. 1981. "The Population Explosion: Myths and Realities," in *Equality, the Third World, and Economic Delusion*. Cambridge, Mass.: Harvard University Press.

BBC. 2015B. "Somaliland profile," *BBC News*, January 19, http://www.bbc.com/news/world-africa-14115069. Accessed on 5–4–2015.

BBC. 2015E. "Yemen crisis: Who is fighting whom?" *BBC News*, March 26, http://www.bbc.com/news/world-middle-east-29319423. Accessed on 5–6–2015.

BBC. 2015A. "Yemen profile—Timeline," *BBC News*, April 1, http://www.bbc.com/news/world-middle-east-14704951. Accessed on 5–4–2015.

BBC. 2015C. "Puntland profile", *BBC News*, April 20, http://www.bbc.com/news/world-africa-14114727. Accessed on 5–4–2015.

BBC. 2015D. *BBC News*, "Somalia profile—Timeline," May 5, http://www.bbc.com/news/world-africa-14094632. Accessed on 5–4–2015.

Beard, T. R., J. D., Jackson, and D. L. Kaserman, 2007–2008. "The Failure of U.S. Organ Procurement Policy." *Regulation,* *30*(4); http://connection.ebscohost.com/c/articles/28339693/failure-u-s-organ-procurement-policy. Accessed on 4–28–2015.

Becker, Gary. 2002. "Get the FDA out of the way and drug prices will drop." *Business Week*. September 16; http://www.bloomberg.com/bw/stories/2002–09–15/get-the-fda-out-of-the-way-and-drug-prices-will-drop. Accessed on 4–28–2015.

Bell, Rogers, TELUS. 2013. "If the government let a giant foreign corporation buy up half of Canada's water, you would be outraged," *Toronto Star*, Advertisement http://torontostar.newspaperdirect.com/epaper/viewer.aspx. Accessed on 5–4–2015.

Belov, Fëdor: 1955. *The History of a Collective Farm*. Frederick A. Praeger, Inc. As excerpted in Riha, Thomas, ed. 1964. *Readings in Russian Civilization*. Volume III: *Soviet Russia, 1917–1963*. Ch. 42.

Benjamin, Daniel. 2012. "Bye, bye bison." April 1; http://perc.org/articles/bye-bye-bison. Accessed on 4–28–2015.

Bennett, James T. 1980. *Better Government at Half the Price*. London: Green Hill Publishers.

Bennett, James T. and Thomas DiLorenzo. 1982. "Public Employee Unions and the Privatization of Public Services," *Journal of Labor Research*. Fall.

Bennett, James T. and Thomas DiLorenzo. 1989. *Unfair Competition: The Profits of NonProfits*. New York: Hamilton Press.

Bennett, James T. and Manuel H. Johnson. 1980. "Tax Reduction Without Sacrifice: Private Sector Production of Public Services." *Public Finance Quarterly* 8, no. 4 (October): 363–396.

Benson, Bruce L. 1989. "Enforcement of Private Property Rights in Primitive Societies: Law without Government," *The Journal of Libertarian Studies*, Vol. IX, No. 1, Winter, pp. 1–26; http://mises.org/journals/jls/9_1/9_1_1.pdf. Accessed on 4–28–2015.

Benson, Bruce L. 1990. "Customary Law with Private Means of Resolving Disputes and Dispensing Justice: A Description of a Modern System of Law and Order without State Coercion." *The Journal of Libertarian Studies*, Vol. IX, No. 2," pp. 25–42; http://mises.org/journals/jls/9_2/9_2_2.pdf. Accessed on 4–28–2015.

Benson, Bruce. 2005. "The Mythology of Holdout as a Justification for Eminent Domain and Public Provision of Roads." *Independent Review*. Vol. 10, No. 2, Fall, pp. 165–194.

Berg, Maxine. 1992. *The Age of Manufactures 1700–1820* (2nd ed.) New York City: Routledge.

Berman, Harold J., and Dasser, Felix J. 1990. "The 'New' Law Merchant and the 'Old': Sources, Content and Legitimacy," in Thomas E. Carbonneau, ed., Lex Mercatoria and Arbitration: A Discussion of the Law Merchant, Dobbs Ferry, N.Y.: Transnational Juris Publications.

Berzon, Alexandra and Kris Maher. 2014. "West Virginia Chemical-Spill Site Avoided Broad Regulatory Scrutiny," *The Wall Street Journal*, January 13, http://online.wsj.com/news/articles/SB10001424052702303819704579317062273564766?mod=djem10point, Accessed on 5–4–2015.

Blair, Roger D., Paul B. Ginsberg, and Ronald J. Vogel. 1975. "Blue Cross-Blue Shield Administration Costs: A Study of Non-Profit Health Insurers." *Economic Inquiry* 13 (June): 237–251.

Block, Walter E. 2008 [1976]. *Defending the Undefendable*. Auburn, AL: The Mises Institute; http://mises.org/books/defending.pdf. Accessed on 4–28–2015.

Block, Walter. 1977. "Austrian Monopoly Theory—a Critique," *The Journal of Libertarian Studies*, Vol. I, No. 4, Fall, pp. 271–279; http://www.mises.org/journals/jls/1_4/1_4_1.pdf. Accessed on 4–28–2015.

Block, Walter. 1980. "On Robert Nozick's 'On Austrian Methodology'." *Inquiry*, Vol. 23, No. 4, Fall, pp. 397–444; http://www.walterblock.com/wp-content/uploads/publications/on_robert_nozick.pdf. Accessed on 4-28-2015.

Block, Walter. 1982. *Amending the Combines Investigation Act*, Vancouver: The Fraser Institute; First Part: https://www.scribd.com/doc/252440414/A-Response-to-the-Framework-Document-1–29;Second Part: https://www.scribd.com/doc/252440427/A-Response-to-the-Framework-Document-30–60. Both accessed on 4-28-2015.

Block, Walter. 1983. "Public Goods and Externalities: The Case of Roads," *The Journal of Libertarian Studies: An Interdisciplinary Review*, Vol. VII, No. 1, Spring, pp. 1–34; http://www.mises.org/journals/jls/7_1/7_1_1.pdf. Accessed on 4-28-2015.

Block, Walter E. 1987. "A Free Market in Kidneys?" *The Freeman Ideas on Liberty*, August, p. 308.

Block, Walter. 1988. "Comment on Leland Yeager on Subjectivism," *Review of Austrian Economics*, Vol. II, pp 199–208; http://www.mises.org/journals/rae/pdf/r2_12.pdf. Accessed on 4-28-2015.

Block, Walter. 1988A. "Caveat Emptor," *The Freeman Ideas on Liberty*, May, pp. 180–181, http://www.unz.org/Pub/Freeman-1988may-00180?View=Search. Accessed on 4-28-2015.

Block, Walter E. 1988B. "The Case for a Free Market in Body Parts," Rockwell, Llewellyn H. ed. 1988. *Essays in the Economics of Liberty: The Free Market Reader*, California: The Ludwig von Mises Institute, pp. 270–272.

Block, Walter. 1990A. "Earning Happiness Through Homesteading Unowned Land: a comment on 'Buying Misery with Federal Land' by Richard Stroup," *Journal of Social Political and Economic Studies*, Vol. 15, No. 2, Summer, pp. 237–253.

Block, Walter. 1990B. "Resource Misallocation, Externalities and Environmentalism in the U.S. and Canada," *Proceedings of the 24th Pacific Northwest Regional Economic Conference*, pp. 91–94.

Block, Walter. 1992. "Institutions, Property Rights and Externalities: The Case of Water Quality," *Agriculture and Water Quality: Proceedings of an Interdisciplinary Symposium*, Murray H. Miller, J. E. FitzGibbon, Glenn C. Fox, R.W. Gillham and H.R. Whiteley, eds., Guelph Centre for Soil and Water Conservation, University of Guelph Press, pp. 191–208.

Block, Walter. 1993. "Society, Stakeholders, and Externalities," *Fraser Forum*, February, pp. 18–19.

Block, Walter. 1994. "Total Repeal of Anti-trust Legislation: A Critique of Bork, Brozen and Posner," *Review of Austrian Economics*, Vol. 8, No. 1, pp. 35–70.

Block, Walter E. 1998. "Roads, Bridges, Sunlight and Private Property: Reply to Gordon Tullock," *Journal des Economistes et des Etudes Humaines*, Vol. 8, No. 2/3, June-September, pp. 315–326.

Block, Walter. 1999. "Austrian Theorizing, Recalling the Foundations: Reply to Caplan," *Quarterly Journal of Austrian Economics*, Vol. 2, No. 4, winter, pp. 21–39.

Block, Walter E. 1999A. "Review Essay of Bethell, Tom, *The Noblest Triumph: Property and Prosperity Through the Ages*, New York: St. Martin's Press, 1998," in *The Quarterly Journal of Austrian Economics*, Vol. 2, No. 3, Fall, pp. 65–84.

Block, Walter E. 1999B. "The Gold Standard: A Critique of Friedman, Mundell, Hayek, Greenspan," *Managerial Finance*, Vol. 25, No. 5, pp. 15–33.

Block, Walter. 2000A. "Word Watch," April 20; https://mises.org/library/word-watch. Accessed on 4-28-2015.

Block, Walter. 2000B. "Watch Your Language," February 21; https://mises.org/library/watch-your-language. Accessed on 4-28-2015.

Block, Walter. 2001A. "Drowning in Manitoba, Water Privatization in Walkerton, Ontario," August 4; http://www.lewrockwell.com/block/block4.html. Accessed on 6-8-2015.

Block, Walter. 2001B. "Four Firemen Perish," July 27; https://www.lewrockwell.com/2001/07/walter-e-block/four-firemen-die-in-socialist-fire/. Accessed on 4-28-2015.

Block, Walter E. 2002. "All Government is Excessive: A Rejoinder to 'In Defense of Excessive Government' by Dwight Lee," *Journal of Libertarian Studies*, Vol. 16, No. 3, pp. 35–82.

Block, Walter. 2002A. "Homesteading City Streets; An Exercise in Managerial Theory," *Planning and Markets*, Vol. 5, No. 1, pp. 18–23; September.

Block, Walter. 2002B. "On Reparations to Blacks for Slavery," *Human Rights Review*, Vol. 3, No. 4, July-September, pp. 53–73.

Block, Walter. 2003A. "Realism: Austrian vs. Neoclassical Economics, Reply to Caplan," *Quarterly Journal of Austrian Economics*, Vol. 6, No. 3, Fall, pp. 63–76.

Block, Walter. 2003B. "National Defense and the Theory of Externalities, Public Goods and Clubs." *The Myth of National Defense: Essays on the Theory and History of Security Production*, Hoppe, Hans-Hermann, ed., Auburn: Mises Institute, pp. 301–334.

Block, Walter E. 2003C. "Private property rights, economic freedom, and Professor Coase: A Critique of Friedman, McCloskey, Medema and Zorn," *Harvard Journal of Law and Public Policy*, Vol. 26, No. 3, Summer, pp. 923–951.

Block, Walter E. 2003D. "Libertarianism vs. Objectivism; A Response to Peter Schwartz," *Reason Papers*, Vol. 26, Summer, pp. 39–62.

Block, Walter E. 2004. "Me and hurricane Ivan." September 20; http://www.lewrockwell.com/block/block44.html. Accessed on 6–8–2015.

Block, Walter E. 2005A. "Then Katrina Came." September 3. http://www.lewrockwell.com/block/block51.html. Accessed on 6–8–2015.

Block, Walter E. 2005B. "The Answer to Katrina." September 11. http://www.lewrockwell.com/block/block53.html. Accessed on 6–8–2015.

Block, Walter E. 2005C. "Government and the Katrina Crisis." *The Free Market*. Vol. 26, No. 10, October.

Block, Walter E. 2005D. "Government and the Katrina Crisis." *The Free Market*. Vol. 26, No. 10, October.

Block, Walter. 2005E. "Government and Market: A Critique of Professor James Buchanan's *What Should Economists Do?*" *Corporate Ownership & Control*, Vol. 3, No. 1, Fall, pp. 81–87 .

Block, Walter E. 2006A. "Coase and *Kelo*: Ominous Parallels and Reply to Lott on Rothbard on Coase," *Whittier Law Review*, Vol. 27, No. 4, pp. 997–1022.

Block, Walter E. 2006B. "Katrina: Private Enterprise, the Dead Hand of the Past, and Weather Socialism; An Analysis in Economic Geography." *Ethics, Place and Environment: A Journal of Philosophy & Geography*; Vol. 9, No. 2, June, pp. 231–241; reprinted in "Post-Katrina: Risk Assessment, Economic Analysis and Social Implications"—edited by Harry Richardson, Peter Gordon and James Moore. Edward Elgar Publishing.

Block, Walter. 2006C. "Deaths by Government: Another Missing Chapter." November 27; http://www.lewrockwell.com/block/block66.html. Accessed on 6–8–2015.

Block, Walter E. 2006D. "Saving Language" December 21. http://www.lewrockwell.com/block/block69.html. Accessed on 6–8–2015.

Block, Walter. 2007A. "Reply to Caplan on Austrian Economic Methodology" *Corporate Ownership & Control*, Vol. 4, No. 2, November, pp. 312–317.

Block, Walter. 2007B. "Anarchism and Minarchism; No Rapprochement Possible: Reply to Tibor Machan," *Journal of Libertarian Studies*, Vol. 21, No. 1, Spring, pp. 91–99.

Block, Walter E. 2008. "Homesteading, ad coelum, owning views and forestalling." *The Social Sciences*. Vol. 3, No. 2, pp. 96–103.

Block, Walter. 2009A. "Rejoinder to Hoppe on Indifference" *Quarterly Journal of Austrian Economics;* Vol. 12, No. 1: 52–59.

Block, Walter E. 2009B. "Rejoinder to Machaj on Indifference," *New Perspectives on Political Economy*, Volume 5, Number 1, pp. 65–71.

Block, Walter E. 2009C. *The Privatization of Roads and Highways: Human and Economic Factors*; Auburn, AL: The Mises Institute.

Block, Walter E. 2010A. "Libertarianism is unique; it belongs neither to the right nor the left: a critique of the views of Long, Holcombe, and Baden on the left, Hoppe, Feser and Paul on the right." *Journal of Libertarian Studies;* Vol. 22: 127–70.

Block, Walter E. 2010B. "Milton Friedman on Intolerance: A Critique." *Libertarian Papers*; Vol. 2, No. 41.

Block, Walter E. 2011A. "How Not To Defend the Market: A critique of Easton, Miron, Bovard, Friedman and Boudreaux." *Journal of Libertarian Studies;* Vol. 22, pp. 581–592.

Block, Walter E. 2011B. Review essay of Ostrom, Elinor. 1990. *Governing the commons: The evolution of institutions for collective action.* Cambridge, UK and New York, NY: Cambridge University Press; in *Libertarian Papers*, Vol. 3, Art. 21.

Block, Walter E. 2011C. "Governmental inevitability: reply to Holcombe." *Journal of Libertarian Studies*, Vol. 22; pp. 667–688.

Block, Walter E. 2011D. "Terri Schiavo: A Libertarian Analysis" *Journal of Libertarian Studies*; Vol. 22, pp. 527–536.

Block, Walter E. 2013A. "Was Milton Friedman a socialist" *Management Education Science Technology Journal* (MEST Journal); Vol. 1, No. 1, pp. 11–26.

Block, Walter E. 2013B. *Defending the Undefendable II: Freedom in all realms;* Terra Libertas Publishing House; http://www.amazon.com/Defending-Undefendable-II-Freedom-Realms/dp/1908089377/ref=sr_1_1?ie=UTF8&qid=1379098357&sr=8–1&keywords=freedom+in+all+realms. Accessed on 5–28–2015.

Block, Walter and William Barnett II. 2008. "Continuums" *Journal Etica e Politica / Ethics & Politics*, Vol. 1, pp. 151–166, June.

Block, Walter and William Barnett II. 2009. "Monopsony Theory." *American Review of Political Economy* June/December, Vol. 7(1/2), pp. 67–109.

Block, Walter E. with William Barnett II. 2010. "Rejoinder to Hoppe on indifference, once again." *Reason Papers*, Vol. 32, pp. 141–154.

Block, Walter E. and William Barnett II. 2012–2013. "Milton Friedman and the financial crisis," *American Review of Political Economy,* Vol. 10, No. 1/2, June, 2012–June 2013; pp. 2–17.

Block, Walter E. and Matthew Block. 1996. "Roads, Bridges, Sunlight and Private Property Rights," *Journal Des Economistes Et Des Etudes Humaines*, Vol. VII, No. 2/3, June-September; http://www.walterblock.com/wp-content/uploads/publications/block-block_roads-bridges-sunlight-property-1996.pdf. Accessed on 5–28–2015.

Block, Walter and Matthew Block. 2000. "Toward a Universal Libertarian Theory of Gun (Weapon) Control," *Ethics, Place and Environment*, Vol. 3, No. 3, pp. 289–298.

Block, Walter and Thomas J. DiLorenzo. 2000. "Is Voluntary Government Possible? A Critique of Constitutional Economics," *Journal of Institutional and Theoretical Economics*, Vol. 156, No. 4, December, pp. 567–582.

Block, Walter and Thomas J. DiLorenzo. 2001. "The Calculus of Consent Revisited," *Public Finance and Management*, Vol. 1, No. 3.

Block, Walter E. and Michael R. Edelstein. 2012. "Popsicle sticks and homesteading land for nature preserves." *Romanian Economic and Business Review*. Vol. 7, No. 1, Spring, pp. 7–13; http://www.rebe.rau.ro/REBE%207%201.pdf. Accessed on 5–28–2015.

Block, Walter v. Richard Epstein. 2005. "Debate on Eminent Domain." *NYU Journal of Law & Liberty*, Vol. 1, No. 3, pp. 1144–1169.

Block, Walter E. and Michael Fleischer. 2010. "How Would An Anarchist Society Handle Child Abuse?" October 13; https://www.lewrockwell.com/2010/10/walter-e-block/how-would-child-abuse-be-handled-in-an-anarchist-society/. Accessed on 6–8–2015.

Block, Walter. Joseph Horton and Debbie Walker. 1998. "The Necessity of Free Trade," *Journal of Markets and Morality,* Vol. 1, No. 2, October, pp. 192–200.

Block, Walter E. and Llewellyn H. Rockwell, Jr. 2007. "Katrina and the Future of New Orleans," *Telos*, Vol. 139, Summer, pp. 170–185.

Block, Walter and Patrick Tinsley. 2008. "Should the Law Prohibit Paying Ransom to Kidnappers?" *American Review of Political Economy*; Vol. 6, no. 2, December, pp. 40–45.

Block, Walter E., Roy Whitehead, Clint Johnson, Mana Davidson, Alan White and Stacy Chandler. 1999–2000. "Human Organ Transplantation: Economic and Legal Issues," *Quinnipiac College School of Law Health Journal*, Vol. 3, pp. 87–110.

Block, Walter and Guillermo Yeatts. 1999–2000. "The Economics and Ethics of Land Reform: A Critique of the Pontifical Council for Justice and Peace's 'Toward a Better Distribution of Land: The Challenge of Agrarian Reform,'" *Journal of Natural Resources and Environmental Law*, Vol. 15, No. 1, pp. 37–69.

Blundell, John. 2003. "Human tissue option is not a macabre option." April 7; http://www.iea.org.uk/in-the-media/media-coverage/human-tissue-option-is-not-a-macabre-option. Accessed on 5–28–2015.

Bly, Thomas R. et al. 2010. Fisheries District 10, "Lake Conway Management Plan Evaluation 2003–2009," http://www.agfc.com/fishing/Documents/LakeConwayMgmtPlanEval2003–09.pdf. Accessed on 5–8–2015.

Boardman, Anthony, and Aidan R. Vining. 1989. "Ownership and Performance in Competitive Environments: A Comparison of the Performance of Private, Mixed, and State-Owned Enterprises." *Journal of Law and Economics* 32: 1–33.

Borcherding, Thomas, ed. 1977. *Budgets and Bureaucrats: The Sources of Government Growth*, Durham, N.C.: Duke University Press.

Borcherding, T.E., B.C. Burnaby, W.W. Pommerehne, and F. Schneider, 1982, "Comparing the efficiency of private and public production: the evidence from five countries," *Zeitschrift fur Nationalokonomie*, 89, 127–56.

Boudreaux, Don. 2008. "Optimal Population?" April 8; http://cafehayek.com/2008/04/optimal-populat.html. Accessed on 5–28–2015.

Boudreaux, Donald J., and Thomas J. DiLorenzo, 1992. "The Protectionist Roots of Antitrust," *Review of Austrian Economics*, Vol. 6, No. 2, pp. 81–96.

Bradford, William; *History of Plymouth Plantation—1630–1647*; written between 1630 and 1651 in 2 vols., Boston, The Massachusetts Historical Society, Houghton Mifflin Company, 1912; http://mayflowerhistory.com/primary-sources-and-books/. Accessed on 5–28–2015.

Bradley J., Robert. 1981. "Market Socialism: A Subjectivist Evaluation," *The Journal of Libertarian Studies*, Vol. V, No. 1, Winter, pp. 23–40.

Brandly, Mark. 2002. "A Primer on Trade." November, 4; https://mises.org/library/primer-trade. Accessed on 5–28–2015.

Branfman, Fred. 2013 "World's Most Evil and Lawless Institution? The Executive Branch of the U.S. Government." *Alternet*. June 26; http://www.alternet.org/investigations/executive-branch-evil-and-lawless?paging=off. Accessed on 5–28–2015.

Brewer, Charlie. 2010. "Lake Overcup draw down." July 28; http://www.crappie.com/crappie/showthread.php/142964-lake-overcup-draw-down. Accessed on 5–28–2015.

The British Museum. Undated. "The Yellow River," http://www.ancientchina.co.uk/staff/resources/background/bg14/bg14pdf.pdf. Accessed on 4–16–2015.

Brouhard, Rod. 2014. "Emergency Water Supplies; Tips for Surviving a Disaster Without Running Water," *about health*, March 7, http://firstaid.about.com/od/emergencypreparation/qt/07_water_supply.htm. Accessed on 5–4–2015.

Brown, Lester T. 1963. *Man, Land and Food*, W. W. Norton & Company.

Brown, Lester T. 1972. *World Without Borders*, W. W. Norton & Company.

Brown, Lester T. 1981. *Building a Sustainable Society*. W. W. Norton & Company.

Brown, Lester T. 2009. *Plan B 4.0: Mobilizing to Save Civilization*. W. W. Norton & Company.

Brown, Lester T. 2011. *World on the Edge: How to Prevent Environmental and Economic Collapse*. W. W. Norton & Company.

Brown, Lester T. 2012. *Full Planet, Empty Plates: The New Geopolitics of Food Scarcity*. W. W. Norton & Company.

Brown, Pamela J. 1987. "Free Thought and Free Trade: The Analogy Between Scientific and Entrepreneurial Discovery Process," *The Journal of Libertarian Studies*, Vol. 8, No. 2, Summer, pp. 289–292; http://www.mises.org/journals/jls/8_2/8_2_8.pdf. Accessed on 5–28–2015.

Buchanan, James M. 1969. *Cost and Choice: An Inquiry into Economic Theory*, Chicago: Markham.

Buchanan, James M. 1975. *The Limits of Liberty*, Chicago: University of Chicago Press.

Buchanan, James M. 1979. "The General Implications of Subjectivism in Economics," in *What Should Economists Do?*, Indianapolis: Liberty Press.

Buchanan, James M. and G. F. Thirlby. 1981. *L.S.E. Essays on Cost*, New York: New York University Press.

Buchanan, James M., Robert D. Tollison, and Gordon Tullock, eds. 1980. *Toward a Theory of the Rent-Seeking Society*, College Station: Texas A&M University.

Buchanan, James M., and Gordon Tullock. 1962. *The Calculus of Consent: Logical Foundations of Constitutional Democracy*, Ann Arbor: University of Michigan.

Bull, Brian. 2013. "Major Salt Mine Under Lake Erie Resumes Operations," *ideastream*, http://www.ideastream.org/news/feature/major-salt-mine-under-lake-erie-resumes-operations. Accessed on 4–17–2015.

Butler, Samuel. 1917. "Reconciliation," *The Notebooks of Samuel Butler*, Chapter XXII, "Gaining One's Point," New York.

Butler, Stuart M. 1985. *Privatizing Federal Spending*. New York: Universe Books.

Butler, Stuart M. 1986. "Privatizing Bulk Mail," *Management*, 6, No. 1, pp. 6–8, 10–11, 34–35.

Butos, William and Roger Koppl. 1997. "The varieties of subjectivism: Keynes, Hayek on expectations." *History of Political Economy*, 29 (2), pp. 327–59.

Bylund, Per. 2012. "Man and matter: how the former gains ownership of the latter." *Libertarian Papers*, Vol. 4, No. 1; http://libertarianpapers.org/articles/2012/lp-4–1–5.pdf. Accessed on 5–28–2015.

Caleuche. Undated. "River Facts," *Mississippi River Resource Page*, http://www.mississippiriverresource.com/River/RiverFacts.php. Accessed on 4–14–2015.

Callahan, Gene. 2001. "De Gustibus Non Est Disputandum." April 27; http://mises.org/daily/666. Accessed on 5–28–2015.

Callahan, Gene. 2003. "Choice and Preference," February 10; https://mises.org/library/choice-and-preference. Accessed on 5–28–2015.

Callahan, Gene. 2000. "Market Failure Again?" April 4; http://www.mises.org/story/407. https://mises.org/library/market-failure-again. Accessed on 6–8–2015.

Campbell, Bruce and Ed Finn. 2006. *Living with Uncle, Canada-US Relations in an Age of Empire*, Toronto.

Campbell, Kate. 2013. "Groundwater, Subsidence Draw Additional Attention" November 27; *Ag Alert*, California Farm Bureau Federation. www.cfbf.com. Accessed on 5–28–2015.

Caplan, Bryan. 2007. *The Myth of the Rational Voter: Why Democracies Choose Bad Policies*. Princeton, N.J.: Princeton University Press.

Carden, Art. 2008. "Beliefs, bias, and regime uncertainty after Hurricane Katrina." *International Journal of Social Economics*. Vol. 35, No. 7, pp. 531—545; http://www.emeraldinsight.com/journals.htm?issn=0306–8293&volume=35&issue=7&articleid=1729161&show=html. Accessed on 5–28–2015.

Carey, D. 2002. "Let the Market Save Lives." *Mises Daily*. February 21; https://mises.org/library/let-market-save-lives. Accessed on 5–28–2015.

Carroll, Bruce. 2014. "ISIS Captures Nuclear Material From Iraq," *Legal Insurrection*, July 10, http://legalinsurrection.com/2014/07/isis-captures-nuclear-material-from-iraq/. Accessed on 4–21–2015.

Casey, Doug. 2010. "Doug Casey on Anarchy." March 31; http://www.caseyresearch.com/cwc/doug-casey-anarchy. Accessed on 5–28–2015.

Casey, Gerard. 2012. *Libertarian Anarchy: Against the State*. Bloomsbury Academic; http://www.amazon.com/dp/1441144676/ref=as_li_tf_til?tag=lewrockwell&camp=14573&creative=327641&linkCode=as1&creativeASIN=1441144676&adid=157FYFSMK265EK398 X47&&ref-refURL=http%3A%2F%2Fwww.lewrockwell.com%2Flewrockwell-show%2F tag%2FGerard-Casey%2F. Accessed on 5–28–2015.

Casselman, Anne. Undated. "10 Biggest Oil Spills in History; No, the 1989 Exxon-Valdez spill doesn't make the list." http://www.popularmechanics.com/science/energy/coal-oil-gas/biggest-oil-spills-in-history#slide-1. Accessed on 5–28–2015.

Cefaratti, Todd. 2014. "ISIS Says they Have Nuclear Weapons to Wipe Out Israel," *Tea Party News Network*, June 23, http://www.tpnn.com/2014/06/23/isis-says-they-have-nuclear-weapons-to-wipe-out-israel/. Accessed on 4–21–2015.

Center for Conservation Biology. 2005. "The two Simon bets." Stanford University. March 16; http://www.stanford.edu/group/CCB/Pubs/Ecofablesdocs/thebet.htm. Accessed on 5–28–2015.

Cervantes Saavedra, Miguel de. 1895. *The Ingenious Gentleman Don Quixote of La Mancha*, Ch. LVIII, translation by Henry Edward Watts, London.

Chamberlin, William Henry. 1937. *Collectivism: A False Utopia*. New York, N.Y.: A.C. MacMillan.

Chambers, Mark. 2008. "The Hurricane Severity Index—A New Method of Classifying the Destructive Potential of Tropical Cyclones," *ImpactWeather*, http://doctorflood.rice.edu/SSPEED_2008/downloads/Day2/4A_Chambers.pdf. Accessed on 5–3–2015.

Chamlee-Wright, Emily. 2008. "Signaling effects of commercial and civil society in post-Katrina reconstruction." *The International Journal of Social Economics*. Vol. 35, No. 8, pp. 615–626.

Chamlee-Wright, Emily and Daniel Rothschild. 2007. "Disastrous Uncertainty: How Government Disaster Policy Undermines Community Rebound," Mercatus Center; http://mercatus.org/publication/disastrous-uncertainty-how-government-disaster-policy-undermines-community-rebound. Accessed on 5–28–2015.

Chapman, John L. 2008. "The Privatization of Public Services," February 21; http://mises.org/story/2866. Accessed on 5–28–2015.

Cherry, Mark J., ed. 1999. *Persons and Their Bodies: Rights, Responsibilities, and the Sale of Organs*. Kluwer Academic Publishers.

CIA. 2015. Central Intelligence Agency, *World Fact Book*, "Yemen" and "Somalia," May 1, https://www.cia.gov/library/publications/the-world-factbook/geos/ym.html, and https://www.cia.gov/library/publications/the-world-factbook/geos/so.html. Both accessed on 5–4–2015.

CITES. 1973 [amended 1979, 1983]. "Convention on International Trade in Endangered Species of Wild Fauna and Flora," http://www.cites.org/eng/disc/text.php, Accessed on 4–20–2015.

Clarkson, Kenneth W. 1972. "Some Implications of Property Rights in Hospital Management." *Journal of Law & Economics* 15, no. 2 (October): 363–384.

Clay, Megan and Walter E. Block. 2002. "A Free Market for Human Organs," *The Journal of Social, Political and Economic Studies*, Vol. 27, No. 2, Summer, pp. 227–236; http://www.jspes.org/summer2002_clay.html. Accessed on 5–28–2015.

CNN. 2014. *CNN Library* Hurricane Statistics Fast Facts," http://www.cnn.com/2013/05/31/world/americas/hurricane-statistics-fast-facts/index.html. Accessed on 4–29–2015.

Coase, Ronald H. 1960. "The Problem of Social Cost," *Journal of Law and Economics*, 3:1–44.

Coase, Ronald H. 1974. "The Market for Goods and the Market for Ideas," *American Economic Review*, 64:384–91

Colander, David C. 1998. *Microeconomics*, Boston: Irwin-McGraw-Hill.

Coleman, John; "Take Ownership of Your Actions by Taking Responsibility"; *Harvard Business Review*; 2012 http://blogs.hbr.org/2012/08/take-ownership-of-your-actions/. Last visited 4–13–2015.

Colorado Department of Natural Resources, Undated, "Prior Appropriation Law" http://water.state.co.us/surfacewater/swrights/pages/priorapprop.aspx. Accessed on 4–13–2015.

Colorado, University of. Undated. "The Juan de Fuca Microplate System," *Geological Sciences*, http://www.colorado.edu/geolsci/Resources/WUSTectonics/PacNW/juan_de_Fuca_general.html. Accessed on 4–28–2015.

Commoner, Barry. 1990. *Making Peace with the Planet*, New York Pantheon Books.

Conquest, Robert. 1986. *The Harvest of Sorrow*, N.Y.: Oxford University Press.

Conquest, Robert. 1990. *The Great Terror*, Edmonton, Alberta: Edmonton University Press.

Conrad, Joseph. 1906. *The Mirror of the Sea* , Ch. XXXI, New York, pp. 177–178. Also can be found in the Doubleday special edition of 1928, p. 106.

Cook, R. M., A. Sinclair & G. Stefánsson. 1997. "Potential collapse of North Sea cod stocks." *Nature*. 385: 521–522, doi:10.1038/385521a0.

Cordato, Roy E. 1989. "Subjective Value, Time Passage, and the Economics of Harmful Effects," *Hamline Law Review*, Vol. 12, No. 2, Spring, pp.229–244.

Cordato, Roy E. 1992. *Welfare Economics and Externalities in an Open-Ended Universe: A Modern Austrian Perspective*, Boston: Kluwer.

Cordato, Roy E. 2004. "Toward an Austrian theory of environmental economics." *The Quarterly Journal of Austrian Economics*, Vol. 7, No. 1, Spring: 3–16; http://mises.org/journals/qjae/pdf/qjae7_1_1.pdf. Accessed on 5–28–2015.

Correa, Enrique. 2013. "Fox 8 Explores Salt Mine Below Lake Erie," *Fox 8 Cleveland*, http://fox8.com/2013/01/31/fox-8-explores-salt-mine-below-lake-erie/. Accessed on 4–17–2015.

Costea, Diana. 2003. "A Critique of Mises's Theory of Monopoly Prices." *The Quarterly Journal of Austrian Economics*. Vol. 6, No. 3, Fall, pp. 47–62; http://www.mises.org/journals/qjae/pdf/qjae6_3_3.pdf. Accessed on 5–28–2015.

Courier staff. 2014. "Lake Chicot drawdown begins this summer." *Game and Fish notebook* (January 23). http://www.couriernews.com/view/full_story/24434899/article-Game-and-Fish-notebook--Jan--23--2014. Accessed on 5–28–2014.

Courtois, Stephane, Nicolas Werth, Jean-Louis Panne, Andrzej Paczkowski, Karel Bartosek and Jean Louis Margolin. 1999. *The Black Book of Communism: Crimes, Terror, Repression*, trans. from French by Jonathan Murphy and Mark Kramer, Cambridge, MA: Harvard University Press.

Cowen, Tyler, ed. 1988. *The Theory of Market Failure: A Critical Examination*, Fairfax, VA: George Mason University Press; http://www.amazon.com/Theory-Market-Failure-Critical-Examination/dp/0913969133/ref=sr_1_1?ie=UTF8&s=books&qid=1200191409&sr=1–1. Accessed on 5–28–2015.

Cowen, Tyler. 2006. "An Economist Visits New Orleans: Bienvenido, Nuevo Orleans" April 19; http://mercatus.org/media_clipping/economist-visits-new-orleans-bienvenido-nuevo-orleans. Accessed on 6–11–2015.

Crafts, N. F. R. 1985. *British Economic Growth During the Industrial Revolution*. Clarendon Press.

Crain, W. Mark and Asghar Zardkoohi. 1978. "A Test of the Property Rights Theory of the Firm: Water Utilities in the United States." *Journal of Law & Economics* 21, no. 2 (October): 395–408.

Culpepper, Dreda and Walter E. Block. 2008. "Price Gouging in the Katrina Aftermath." *International Journal of Social Economics*; Vol. 35, No. 7, pp. 512–520.

Culp-Ressler, Tara. 2014. "Village Elders In India Order Gang-Rape To Punish Woman For Dating A Muslim Man." January 23; http://thinkprogress.org/health/2014/01/23/3195931/indian-village-council-gang-rape/. Accessed on 5–28–2015.

D'Aliesio, Renata. 2012. "Plans to export water, though unpopular, keep springing up." August 23; *Globe and Mail*. http://www.theglobeandmail.com/news/national/plans-to-export-water-though-unpopular-keep-springing-up/article578415/. Accessed on 5–28–2015.

Dalrymple, Jim. 2014. *BuzzFeed News*, "ISIS Militants Seize Nuclear Materials In Iraq That Could Be Used For WMDs," July 9, http://www.buzzfeed.com/jimdalrympleii/isis-militants-seize-nuclear-materials-in-iraq-that-could-be#.is29Z1E6y. Accessed on 4–21–2015.

Dalsan. 2015. "Somalia: Galmudug Protests Mogadishu Meeting," *All Africa*, February 6, Mogadishu, http://allafrica.com/stories/201502060267.html. Accessed 5–6–2015.

D'Amico, Daniel J. 2008. "Who's to blame for all the heartache?: A response to anti-capitalistic mentalities after Katrina." *The International Journal of Social Economics*. Vol. 35, No. 8, pp. 590–602.

Davies, David G. 1971. "The Efficiency of Public Versus Private Firms: The Case of Australia's Two Airlines." *Journal of Law & Economics* 14, no. 1 (April): 149–165.

De Alessi, Louis. 1982. "On the nature and consequence of private and public enterprises." *Minnesota Law Review* 67, October, 179–286.

Daugherty, Robert L. and Joseph B. Franzini, 1977. *Fluid Mechanics with Engineering Applications*; McGraw-Hill Book Company, New York.

Davies, David G. 1977. "Property Rights and Economic Efficiency—The Australian Airlines Revisited." *Journal of Law & Economics* 20, no. 1 (April): 223–226.

De Jasay, Anthony. 1989. *Social Contract, Free Ride: A Study of the Public Goods Problem*. Oxford University Press.

de Wolf, Aschwin, ed. 2004. *Ordered Anarchy: Festschrift Essays in Honor of Anthony de Jasay*. Arlington, VA: Singularity Press.

Deacon, Robert T. 2009. "Creating Marine Assets: Property Rights in Ocean Fisheries." *PERC Policy Series* No. 43. Political Economy Research Center: Bozeman, Montana, http://www.perc.org/sites/default/files/ps43.pdf. Accessed on 5–11–2015.

Deane, Phyllis. 1979. *The First Industrial Revolution* CUP.

Dellemacchine Gennaio/Giugno. 2011. Nuovaciviltàemacchine; *Liberalismo e Anarcocapitalismo*; La Scuola Austriaca Di Economia; Nuovaciviltà; Dellemacchine Rai Eri; Anno XXIX n° 1–2; Gennaio-Giugno. 1–2.

Delta Crisis. Undated. "The Sacramento San Joaquin Delta Crisis," *Water 4 Fish, Targeting California's Water Management*, http://water4fish.org/delta-crisis/. Accessed on 5–4–2015.

Department of Defense. 2007. "Base Structure Report." http://www.defenselink.mil/pubs/BSR_2007_Baseline.pdf. Accessed on 5–28–2015.

Dewenter, Kathrin, and Paul H. Malatesta. 2000. "State-Owned and Privately-Owned Firms: An Empirical Analysis of Profitability, Leverage, and Labor Intensity." *American Economic Review*.

DiLorenzo, Thomas J. 1984. "The Domain of Rent-Seeking Behavior: Private or Public Choice?", *International Review of Law and Economics*, December.

DiLorenzo, Thomas J. 1987. "Competition and Political Entrepreneurship: Austrian Insights into Public Choice Theory," *Review of Austrian Economics*, Fall.

DiLorenzo, Thomas J. 1988. "Property Rights, Information Costs, and the Economics of Rent Seeking," *Journal of Institutional and Theoretical Economics*, Spring.

DiLorenzo, Thomas J. 1990. "The Subjectivist Roots of James Buchanan's Economics," *Review of Austrian Economics*, Spring; Vol. 4, pp. 180–195.

DiLorenzo, Thomas J. 1996. "The Myth of Natural Monopoly," *Review of Austrian Economics*, Vol. 9, No. 2, pp. 43–58; http://www.mises.org/journals/rae/pdf/rae9_2_3.pdf. Accessed on 5–28–2015.

DiLorenzo, Thomas J. 1998. "The Feds versus the Indians." *The Free Market*. January, Volume 16, Number 1; http://www.independent.org/newsroom/article.asp?id=108. Accessed on 6–5–2015.

DiLorenzo, Thomas J. 2002. "George Stigler and the Myth of Efficient Government," *Journal of Libertarian Studies*, Fall.

DiLorenzo, Thomas J. 2004. *How capitalism saved America: the untold history of our country, from the pilgrims to the present*. New York: Crown Forum.

DiLorenzo, Thomas. 2006. "Death by Government: The Missing Chapter." November 22; https://www.lewrockwell.com/2006/11/thomas-dilorenzo/death-by-government/ https://antioligarch.wordpress.com/2011/03/20/death-by-government-the-missing-chapter/ Accessed on 6–5–2015.

DiLorenzo, Thomas J. 2009. May 13. "Never-Ending Government Lies About Markets." http://mises.org/daily/3446. Accessed on 6–5–2015.

DiLorenzo, Thomas. 2010. "The Culture of Violence in the American West: Myth versus Reality." *The Independent Review*, v. 15, n. 2, Fall 2010, pp. 227–239; http://www.independent.org/publications/tir/article.asp?a=803; Accessed on 6–5–2015.

DiLorenzo, Thomas. 2011. "A Note on the Canard of 'Asymmetric Information' as a Source of Market Failure." *Quarterly Journal of Austrian Economics*, Vol. 14, No. 2, 249–255, Summer; http://mises.org/journals/qjae/pdf/qjae14_2_6.pdf. Accessed on 6–5–2015.

DiLorenzo, Tom and Walter E. Block. 2001. "Constitutional Economics and the Calculus of Consent," *The Journal of Libertarian Studies*, Vol. 15, No. 3, Summer, pp. 37–56; http://www.mises.org/journals/jls/15_3/15_3_2.pdf. Accessed on 6–5–2015.

DiLorenzo, Tom and Jack High. 1988. "Antitrust and Competition, Historically Considered," *Economic Inquiry*, Vol. 26, No. 1, pp. 423–435, July.

Dirmeyer. Jennifer. 2008. "The futile fight against (human) nature: A public choice analysis of the US Army Corps of Engineers—special focus on Hurricane Katrina." *The International Journal of Social Economics*. Vol. 35, No. 8, pp. 627–638.

Disney, Walt and Joe Grant, et al. 1940. "The Sorcerer's Apprentice," *Fantasia*, clip: https://www.youtube.com/watch?v=T8gOh0wEgLg. Accessed on 5–8–2015.

Doane, Charles. 2013. "SALVAGE LAW: Do You Get to Keep an Abandoned Boat?" July 15; http://www.sailfeed.com/2013/07/salvage-law-do-you-get-to-keep-an-abandoned-boat/. Accessed 6–5–2015.

Dr. Strangelove. 1964. *Dr. Strangelove or: How I Learned to Stop Worrying and Love the Bomb*, http://www.imdb.com/title/tt0057012/quotes and https://www.youtube.com/watch?v=N1KvgtEnABY. Accessed on 5–4–2015.

D'Souza, Juliet D., Bernardo Bortolotti, Marcella Fantini; and William L. Megginson. 2000. "Sources of Performance Improvements in Privatized Firms: A Clinical Study of the Global Telecommunications Industry." Working paper, Price College of Business, University of Oklahoma. http://papers.ssrn.com/sol3/papers.cfm?abstract_id=263219. Accessed 6–5–2015.

Dutton, Judy. 2011. "Liquid Gold: The Booming Market for Human Breast Milk," *Wired*, May 17, http://www.wired.com/2011/05/ff_milk/. Accessed on 5–4–2015.

Ebeling, Richard. 2009. "The First Thanksgiving and the Birth of Free Enterprise in America." November 23.

Eberstadt, Nicholas. 1988. *The Poverty of Communism*. Transaction Books.

Ehrlich, Paul and Anne Ehrlich. 1981. *Extinction: The Causes and Consequences of the Disappearance of Species*; New York: Random House.

Ehrlich, Paul. 1968. *The Population Bomb*, New York: Sierra Club–Ballantine.

Encyclopædia Britannica, Editors. 2014. "Gulf of Aden," http://www.britannica.com/EBchecked/topic/5650/Gulf-of-Aden. Accessed on 5–4–2015.

England, Randy. 2013. "The state: what can we replace it with?" March 31.

Environment Canada. 2013. "Prohibition of Bulk Water Removal" July 17; http://www.ec.gc.ca/eau-water/default.asp?lang=En&n=1356EC91–1. Accessed 6–5–2015.

Ephesus. 2015. "Arcadian Street (Harbor Street)", http://www.ephesus.us/ephesus/arcadianstreet.htm, and photograph, http://www.teleporttelescopes.com/Europe11/Europe2011_photos/11-Ephesus/DSC_5173.jpg. Both accessed on 4–14–2015.

Epstein, Richard A. 1980. *A Theory of Strict Liability: Toward a Reformulation of Tort Law*. San Francisco, Cato Institute.

Epstein, Richard A. 1985. *Takings: Private Property and the Power of Eminent Domain*, Harvard University Press, Cambridge, Massachusetts and London, England.

Epstein, Richard A. 2005. "Blind Justices: The scandal of *Kelo* v. New London." *Wall Street Journal*. June 3. http://www.mrformansplanet.com/index_files/EpsteinonKelo.htm Accessed 6–5–2015.

Exxon Valdez Oil Spill Trustee Council, Undated. "Oil Spill Facts," http://www.evostc.state.ak.us/index.cfm?FA=facts.home. Accessed on 4–16–2015.

Fallingwater. 1997. http://www.wright-house.com/frank-lloyd-wright/fallingwater.html. Accessed on 5–3–2015.

Faunt, Claudia C. 2009. "Groundwater Availability of the Central Valley Aquifer, California; United States Geological Survey." http://pubs.usgs.gov/pp/1766/PP_1766.pdf. Accessed on 6–8–2015.

FBI. Undated. The Federal Bureau of Investigation, "The USS Cole Bombing," *Famous Cases and Criminals*, http://www.fbi.gov/about-us/history/famous-cases/uss-cole. Accessed on 5–4–2015.

FEMA. 2002. Federal Emergency Management Administration; National Flood Insurance Program, Program Description; August 1; https://s3-us-gov-west-1.amazonaws.com/dam-production/uploads/20130726–1447–20490–2156/nfipdescrip_1_.pdf. Accessed on 5–3–2015.

Fenech, Amy S. 2003. Arkansas Game and Fish Commission Fisheries Division and Lake Conway Citizen Advisory Committee, "Lake Conway Management Plan," http://www.agfc.com/fishing/Documents/LakeConwayMgmtPlan.pdf. Accessed on 5–8–2015.

Feshbach, Murray and Alfred Friendly, Jr. 1992. *Ecocide in the USSR: Health and Nature Under Siege*, New York, Basic Books.

Fitzgerald, Randall. 1989. *When Government Goes Private: Successful Alternatives to Public Services*, New York: Universe Books.

Fletcher, Charles R. Esq. Undated. Shumaker, Loop & Kendrick, LLP; "Water Rights In Florida: Public Perception v. Legal Reality" http://waterinstitute.ufl.edu/symposium/downloads/presentations/fletcher.pdf. Accessed 6–5–2015.

Floud, Roderick and Paul Johnson, eds. 2003. *The Cambridge Economic History of Modern Britain, Vol. I, Industrialisation, 1700–1860.* Cambridge University Press.

Floud, Roderick and D. McCloskey, eds. 1994. *The Economic History of Britain Since 1700*, Vol. I, 1700–1860, 2nd ed. Cambridge, U.K.: Cambridge University Press.

Foldvary, Fred E. 2002. "Letters of Marque and Reprisal," *The Progress Report*, http://www.freerepublic.com/focus/f-news/1035395/posts. Accessed 6–5–2015.

Frech III, H.E. 1976. "The Property Rights Theory of the Firm: Empirical Results from a Natural Experiment." *Journal of Political Economy* 84, no. 1 (February): 143–152; http://www.econ.ucsb.edu/~frech/Publications%20&%20Papers/Frech_Property_Natural_Experiment.pdf. Accessed on 6–8–2015.

French, Doug. 2012. "Property Means Preservation." May 31; http://mises.org/daily/5960/. Accessed 6–5–2015

Friedman, David. 1972. *Laissez Faire in Population: the Least Bad Solution*, New York: Population Council.

Friedman, David. 1977. "A theory of the size and shape of nations." *Journal of Political Economy*, 85:59–77.

Friedman, Milton interviewed by Phil Donahue, 1979, http://www.youtube.com/watch?v=RWsx1X8PV_A. Accessed on 4–13–2015.

Friedman, Milton and Rose Friedman. 1997. "The Case for Free Trade." *Hoover Digest* No. 4. http://www.hoover.org/research/case-free-trade. Accessed on 6–8–2015.

Friedman, Milton and Walter E. Block. 2006. "Fanatical, Not Reasonable: A Short Correspondence Between Walter E. Block and Milton Friedman (on Friedrich Hayek's *Road to Serfdom*)." *Journal of Libertarian Studies*, Vol. 20, No. 3, Summer, pp. 61–80; http://www.mises.org/journals/jls/20_3/20_3_4.pdf. Accessed 6–6–2015.

Friedman, Milton. 1962. *Capitalism and Freedom*, Chicago: University of Chicago Press.

Gaia, Vince. 2012. "How the world's oceans could be running out of fish." September 21; http://www.bbc.com/future/story/20120920-are-we-running-out-of-fish. Accessed 6–6–2015.

Galles, Gary. 2010. "A Tale of Two Colonies." November 25; http://heavensmydestination.blogspot.com/2010/11/tale-of-two-colonies-gary-galles-mises.html. Accessed 6–6–2015.

Galloway, Devin and Francis S. Riley. 1999. "San Joaquin Valley, California, Largest human alteration of the Earth's surface," Menlo Park, California. USGS; http://pubs.usgs.gov/circ/circ1182/pdf/06SanJoaquinValley.pdf. Accessed 6–6–2015.

Gardner, Delworth. 2012. "The Economic Effects of Using Property Taxes in Lieu of Direct User Fees to Pay for Water." in Gardner, B. Delworth and Randy T. Simmons, eds. 2012, pp. 1–15. *Aquanomics: Water markets and the environment.* New Brunswick, NJ: Transactions Publishers.

Gardner, B. Delworth and Randy T. Simmons, eds. 2012. *Aquanomics: Water markets and the environment.* New Brunswick, NJ: Transactions Publishers.

Gardner, B. Delworth and Randy T. Simmons. 2012A. "Introduction." in Gardner, B. Delworth and Randy T. Simmons, eds. 2012, pp. 1–15. *Aquanomics: Water markets and the environment.* New Brunswick, NJ: Transactions Publishers.

Garner, Richard and Walter E. Block. 2008. "Harvesting organs on the final frontier: a critique of Star Trek." Issue 2; pp. 65–75. *Ethics and Critical Thinking Journal.* http://www.franklinpublishing.net/ethics.html. Accessed 6–6–2015.

Garone, Phillip; *The Fall and Rise of the Wetlands of California's Great Central Valley*; The University of California Press; Berkeley, CA; April 2011; page 92.

Garrison, Roger. 1985. "A Subjectivist Theory of a Capital Using Economy," in O'Driscoll, Gerald P. and Rizzo, Mario, *The Economics of Time and Ignorance*, Oxford: Basil Blackwell.

Gedab News. 2014. "Eritrea Watches The Houthi Advance In Yemen," October 15, http://awate.com/eritrea-watches-the-houthi-advance-in-yemen/. Accessed on 5–4–2015.

Geography Site. 2006. "Rock Flour," http://www.geography-site.co.uk/pages/physical/glaciers/flour.html, Accessed 4–16–2015.

Goodhue, Rachel E., Susan Stratton Sayre and Leo K. Simon. 2012. "The Sacramento-San Joaquin Delta and the Political Economy of California Water Allocation." in *Aquanomics: Water Markets, Bureaucracy, and the Environment*, edited by B. Delworth Gardner and Randy T. Simmons.

Goodman, John C. 2011. "How Many Melanoma Patients Did the FDA Kill?" March 30; http://healthworkscollective.com/johncgoodman/20968/how-many-melanoma-patients-did-fda-kill. Accessed 6–6–2015.

Goodwin, Stefan 2006. *Africa's Legacies of Urbanization: Unfolding Saga of a Continent*, Lexington Books, Lanham, http://www.amazon.co.uk/Africas-Legacies-Urbanization-Unfolding-Continent-ebook/dp/B00AE1M1PC#reader_B00AE1M1PC. Accessed on 5–4–2015.

Google Images. Undated. https://www.google.com/search?q=sea+steading&tbm=isch&tbo=u&source=univ&sa=X&ei=ZU6TU_XKB_SssASm2YDADA&ved=0CDsQsAQ&biw=1600&bih=731, accessed on 4–14–2015.

Gordon, David. 1993. "Toward a Deconstruction of Utility and Welfare Economics," *The Review of Austrian Economics*, Vol. 6, No. 2, pp. 99–112; http://www.mises.org/journals/rae/pdf/RAE6_2_4.pdf. Accessed 6–6–2015.

Gordon, David. 1996. "What Remains of Socialism?: Book review of Arnold, N. Scott. 1994. *The Philosophy and Economics of Market Socialism: A Critical Study.* New York: Oxford University Press." *Mises Review*, Vol. 2, No. 2; http://mises.org/misesreview_detail.aspx?control=136. Accessed 6–6–2015.

Gordon, David. 1999. "Book review of Ollman, Bertel." 1999. *Market Socialism: The Debate Among Socialists. The Mises Review*, Vol. 5, No. 2; https://mises.org/library/market-socialism-debate-among-socialists-bertell-ollman. Accessed on 6–8–2015.

Gore, Al. 1992. *Earth in the Balance: Ecology and the Human Spirit*, Boston: Houghton-Mifflin.

Gorte, Ross W., Carol Hardy Vincent, Laura A. Hanson and Marc R. Rosenblum. 2012. "Federal Land Ownership: Overview and Data." *Congressional Research Service* https://www.fas.org/sgp/crs/misc/R42346.pdf. Accessed 6–6–2015.

Goto, Miki. 1975. "Pollution Problems of The Seto Inland Sea," *Pesticide Chemistry–3: Third International Congress of Pesticide (Helsinki 1974)*, International Union of Pure and Applied Chemistry, London, pp. 155.

Gottlieb, Scott. 2010. "The FDA Is Evading the Law." *The Wall Street Journal.* December 23; http://www.wsj.com/articles/SB10001424052748704034804576025981869663212. Accessed 6–6–2015.

Grant, James. 2015. "The Forgotten Depression." May 7; https://mises.org/library/james-grant-forgotten-depression. Accessed 6–7–2015

Greenpeace. 2014. *Greenpeace USA*, "Mission Statement," http://www.greenpeace.org/usa/en/about/, http://www.greenpeace.org/usa/en/campaigns/oceans/Our-Vision/. Both accessed on 4–20–2015.

Gregory, Anthony. 2006. "The Trouble with Just Compensation" December 5. http://mises.org/story/2379. Accessed 6–6–2015.

Gregory, Anthony. 2011. "Abolish the Police." May 26; https://www.lewrockwell.com/2011/05/anthony-gregory/abolish-the-police/. Accessed 6–6–2015.

Grigg, William Norman. 2014. "Ranchers vs. Regulators, The Clark County Range War;" LewRockwell.com, April 18, https://www.lewrockwell.com/2014/04/william-norman-grigg/ranchers-vs-regulators/. Accessed on 5–11–2015.

Grossman, Gregory. 1985. "The Second Economy in the U.S.S.R." http://www.dtic.mil/dtic/tr/fulltext/u2/a269615.pdf. Accessed 6–6–2015.

Grotius, Hugo. 1625. *Law of War and Peace (De Jure Belli ac Pacis)*, 3 volumes; translated by A.C. Campbell, London, 1814.

Guardian. 2013. "Canada to claim North Pole as its own" http://www.theguardian.com/world/2013/dec/10/canada-north-pole-claim. Accessed on 4–14–2015.

Guillory, Gil. 2005. "What Are You Calling Failure?" May 5; http://www.mises.org/story/ 1806. Accessed 6–6–2015.

Guillory, Gil & Patrick Tinsley. 2009. "The Role of Subscription-Based Patrol and Restitution in the Future of Liberty," *Libertarian Papers* 1, 12; http://libertarianpapers.org/2009/12-the-role-of-subscription-based-patrol-and-restitution-in-the-future-of-liberty/. Accessed 6–6–2015.

Gunning, J. Patrick. 1990. *The New Subjectivist Revolution: An Elucidation and Extension of Ludwig von Mises's Contribution to Economic Theory*, Savage, MD: Rowan and Littlefield.

Hanscom, Gregg. 2014. "Flood pressure: Climate disasters drown FEMA's insurance plans," *Grist.org*, January 13, http://grist.org/cities/flood-pressure-how-climate-disasters-put-femas-flood-insurance-program-underwater/. Accessed on 5–3–2015.

Hanke, Steve H. 1987A. "Privatization." In J. Eatwell, M. Milgate and P. Newman, eds., *The New Palgrave: A Dictionary of Economics*, v. 3. London: The Macmillan Press, Ltd.: 976–77.

Hanke, Steve H., ed. 1987B. Prospects for Privatization. New York: Academy of Political Science.

Hanke, Steve H., ed., 1987C. *Privatization and Development*, San Francisco: Institute for Contemporary Studies.

Hannesson, Rögnvaldur. 2004. The Privatization of the Oceans, in D.R. Leal (Ed.): *Evolving Property Rights in Marine Fisheries*, Lanham, MD: Rowman and Littlefield, pp. 25–48.

Hannesson, Rognvaldur. 2006. *The privatization of the oceans*. Cambridge, MA: The MIT Press.

Hanson, Stephanie and Eben Kaplan. 2008. "Somalia's Transitional Government," Council of Foreign Relations, *Backgrounder*, May 12, http://www.cfr.org/somalia/somalias-transitional-government/p12475. Accessed on 5–4–2015.

Hardin, Garrett. 1968. "Tragedy of the Commons," *Science,* 162: 1243–1248. http://die-off.com/page95.htm. Accessed 6–6–2015.

Hartwell, Ronald M., ed. 1967. *The Causes of the Industrial Revolution*. London: Methuen.

Hartwell, Ronald M., ed. 1970. *The Industrial Revolution*. Oxford: Blackwell.

Hartwell, Ronald M., ed. 1972. "The Long Debate on Povery: Eight Essays on Industrialization and the 'Condition of England,'" London: Institute of Economic Affairs.

Hasegawa, Kyoko. 2015. "New Japan volcano island 'natural lab' for life;" *Yahoo News Canada*; May, 16; https://ca.news.yahoo.com/new-japan-volcano-island-natural-lab-for-life-033356821.html. Accessed on 5–18–2015.

Hasnas, John. 1995. "The myth of the rule of law." *Wisconsin Law Review* 199; http://faculty.msb.edu/hasnasj/GTWebSite/MythWeb.htm. Accessed 6–6–2015.

Hawkins, John. 2011. *Townhall.com*, "10 Of The Best Economics Quotes From Milton Friedman," http://townhall.com/columnists/johnhawkins/2011/11/29/10_of_the_best_economics _quotes_from_milton_friedman/page/full. Accessed on 4–16–2015.

Hayek, Friedrich A. 1945. "The Use of Knowledge in Society." *American Economic Review* 35 (4): 519–530.

Hayek, F.A., ed. 1954. *Capitalism and the Historians* (essays by T.S. Ashton, L.M. Hacker, W.H. Hutt, B. de Jouvenel), Chicago: The University of Chicago Press.

Hayek, Friedrich A. 1979. *The Counter-Revolution of Science*, 2nd ed. Indianapolis, IN: LibertyPress.

Hayek, Friedrich A. 1990. *The Intellectuals and Socialism*, Fairfax, VA: Institute for Humane Studies; reprinted from the *University of Chicago Law Review*, Vol. 16, No. 3, Spring 1949; http://mises.org/document/1019. Accessed 6–6–2015.

Hazlitt, Henry. 2008 [1946]. *Economics in One Lesson*. Auburn, AL: Mises Institute; http:// mises.org/books/economics_in_one_lesson_hazlitt.pdf. Accessed 6–6–2015.

Healy, Kieran. 2006. *Last Best Gifts: Altruism and the Market for Human Blood and Organs*. Chicago: University of Chicago Press.

Heinrich, David J. 2010. "Justice for All Without the State." *The Libertarian Standard*. May 6; http://www.libertarianstandard.com/articles/david-j-heinrich/justice-for-all-without-the-state/. Accessed 6–6–2015.

Henderson, David R. 2013. "The Robber Barons: Neither Robbers nor Barons." *Library of Economics and Liberty.* March 4; http://www.econlib.org/cgi-bin/printarticle2.pl?file=Columns/y2013/Hendersonbarons.html. Accessed 6–6–2015.

Henninger, Daniel. 1990. "Will the FDA Revert to Type?" *The Wall Street Journal,* December 12, A16. http://www.econlib.org/library/Enc1/DrugLag.html. Accessed 6–6–2015.

Herbener, Jeffrey M. 1979. "The Pareto Rule and Welfare Economics," *Review of Austrian Economics,* Vol. 10 Num. 1, pp. 79–106; http://www.mises.org/journals/rae/pdf/RAE10_1_4.pdf. Accessed 6–6–2015.

Heraclitus of Ephesus. [1921] per Plato, *Cratylus,* 402a; *Plato in Twelve Volumes,* Vol. 12 translated by Harold N. Fowler, Cambridge, MA; Harvard University Press; London, William Heinemann Ltd.

Higgs, Robert. 1994. "Banning a Risky Product Cannot Improve Any Consumer's Welfare (Properly Understood), with Applications to FDA Testing Requirements." *The Review of Austrian Economics,* Vol.7, No. 2, pp. 3–20; https://mises.org/library/banning-risky-product-cannot-improve-any-consumers-welfare-properly-understood-applications. Accessed on 6–8–2015.

Higgs, Robert. 1995. "The Myth of 'Failed' Policies." *The Free Market.* June. Vol. 13, No. 6. http://www.independent.org/newsroom/article.asp?id=123. Accessed 6–6–2015.

Higgs, Robert. 2009. "Why We Couldn't Abolish Slavery Then and Can't Abolish Government Now." August 20; http://www.independent.org/newsroom/article.asp?id=2589. Accessed 6–6–2015.

Higgs, Robert. 2012. "What is the point of my libertarian anarchism?" January 16. http://www.badquaker.com/archives/1315. Accessed 6–6–2015.

Higgs, Robert. 2013. "The State—Crown Jewel of Human Social Organization." http://blog.independent.org/2013/04/03/the-state-crown-jewel-of-human-social-organization/. Accessed 6–6–2015.

High, Jack. 1984–1985. "Bork's Paradox: Static vs Dynamic Efficiency in Antitrust Analysis," *Contemporary Policy Issues,* Vol. 3, pp. 21–34.

Hipke, Deana C. Undated. "The Great Peshtigo Fire of 1871" http://www.peshtigofire.info/. Accessed on 4–16–2015.

Hippen, Benjamin E. 2008. "Organ Sales and Moral Travails: Lessons from the Living Kidney Vendor Program in Iran." *Cato Policy Analysis,* 614; http://www.cato.org/pub_display.php?pub_id=9273. Accessed 6–6–2015.

Holcombe, Randall. 1997. "A Theory of the Theory of Public Goods," *Review of Austrian Economics,* Vol. 10, No. 1: 1–10; http://www.mises.org/journals/rae/pdf/RAE10_1_1.pdf. Accessed 6–6–2015.

Hood, Grace. 2014. "CSU Study Brings Science To Solve South Platte River Problems;" Community Radio for Northern Colorado; 9:51am, Tue., January 14; http://www.kunc.org/post/csu-study-brings-science-solve-south-platte-river-problems. Accessed 6–6–2015.

Hoppe, Hans-Hermann. 1989. "Fallacies of the Public Goods Theory and the Production of Security," *The Journal of Libertarian Studies,* Vol. IX, No. 1, Winter, pp. 27–46; http://www.mises.org/journals/jls/9_1/9_1_2.pdf. Accessed 6–6–2015.

Hoppe, Hans-Hermann. 1993A. "A Four-Step Heath-Care Solution," *The Mises Institute Monthly,* vol. 11, no. 4 (April), http://mises.org/freemarket_detail.aspx?control=279. Accessed 6–6–2015.

Hoppe, Hans-Hermann. 1993B. *The Economics and Ethics of Private Property: Studies in Political Economy and Philosophy,* Boston: Kluwer.

Hoppe, Hans-Hermann, ed. 2003. "National Defense and the Theory of Externalities, Public Goods and Clubs." *The Myth of National Defense: Essays on the Theory and History of Security Production,* Hoppe, Hans-Hermann, ed., Auburn: Mises Institute.

Hoppe, Hans-Hermann. 2004. "Property, Causality, and Liability," *Quarterly Journal of Austrian Economics* 7, no. 4, Winters. pp. 87–95; http://mises.org/journals/qjae/pdf/qjae7_4_6.pdf. Accessed 6–6–2015.

Hoppe, Hans Hermann. 2005. "A Note on Preference and Indifference in Economic Analysis." *The Quarterly Journal of Austrian Economics,* Vol. 8, No. 4, Winter, pp. 87–91; http://mises.org/journals/qjae/pdf/qjae8_4_6.pdf. Accessed 6–6–2015.

Hoppe, Hans-Hermann. 2006A. "Natural Elites, Intellectuals, and the State." July 21; http://mises.org/daily/2214; http://mises.org/etexts/intellectuals.asp. Accessed both on 6–6–2015.

Hoppe, Hans-Hermann. 2006B. "Uncertainty and Its Exigencies: The Critical Role of Insurance in the Free Market" March 7; https://mises.org/library/uncertainty-and-its-exigencies-critical-role-insurance-free-market. Accessed on 6–8–2015.

Hoppe, Hans-Hermann. 2008. "Reflections on the Origin and the Stability of the State." June 23; http://www.libertarian.co.uk/lapubs/polin/polin193.pdf. Accessed 6–6–2015.

Hoppe, Hans Hermann. 2009. "Further Notes on Preference and Indifference: Rejoinder to Block." *The Quarterly Journal of Austrian Economics*, 12, No. 1, pp. 60–64; http://mises.org/journals/qjae/pdf/qjae12_1_5.pdf. Accessed 6–6–2015.

Hoppe, Hans-Hermann. 2011A. "Of Private, Common, and Public Property and the Rationale for Total Privatization," *Libertarian Papers* 3, 1. http://libertarianpapers.org/2011/1-hoppe-private-common-and-public-property/. Accessed 6–6–2015.

Hoppe, Hans-Hermann. 2011B. "State or Private Law Society." April 10; https://mises.org/library/state-or-private-law-society. Accessed 6–6–2015.

Hoppe, Hans-Hermann and Walter E. Block. 2002. "Property and Exploitation," *International Journal of Value-Based Management*, Vol. 15, No. 3, pp. 225–236; http://www.mises.org/etexts/propertyexploitation.pdf; reprint: NUOVA Civilta delleCIVILTÀ. Accessed 6–6–2015.

Hudik, Marek. Unpublished. "A Note on the Nozick Problem." Available from authors of the present volume.

Huebert, Jacob. 2010. *Libertarianism Today*. Santa Barbara, CA: Praeger http://www.amazon.com/Libertarianism-Today-Jacob-H-Huebert/dp/0313377545/ref=sr_1_fkmr0_1?s=books&ie=UTF8&qid=1370719921&sr=1-1-fkmr0&keywords=libertarianism+today.+huerbert. Accessed 6–6–2015.

Hugo, Victor. 1877. *Histoire D'un Crime*, p. 554, Nelson Éditeurs, Paris.

Hülsmann, Jörg Guido. 1999. "Economic Science and Neoclassicism." *Quarterly Journal of Austrian Economics*, Vol. 2 Num. 4, pp. 1–20; http://www.mises.org/journals/qjae/pdf/qjae2_4_1.pdf. Accessed 6–6–2015.

Hummel, Jeffrey. 1990. "National Goods vs. Public Goods: Defense, Disarmament and Free Riders," *The Review of Austrian Economics*, Vol. IV, pp. 88–122; http://www.mises.org/journals/rae/pdf/rae4_1_4.pdf. Accessed 6–6–2015.

Hurricane Severity Index. 2008. https://ams.confex.com/ams/28Hurricanes/techprogram/paper_139371.htm. Accessed on 4–29–2015.

Ibsen, Henrik Johan. 1882. *Enemy of the people*.

IndieGoGo. 1–2014. "Designing the World's First Floating City," https://www.indiegogo.com/projects/designing-the-world-s-first-floating-city. Accessed on 4–14–2015.

Ingebritsen S.E. and Marti E. Ikehara. 1999. "USGS: 'Sacramento-San Joaquin Delta, the sinking heart of the state.'" Menlo Park, California; pp. 83–94; http://pubs.usgs.gov/circ/circ1182/pdf/11Delta.pdf. Accessed 5–4–2015.

Inquisitr. 2014. "Cliven Bundy's Cattle Returned, Armed Stand-Off Ends," http://www.inquisitr.com/1210430/cliven-bundys-cattle-returned-armed-stand-off-ends/, accessed on 4–14–2015.

International Maritime Organization. 1989. "International Convention on Salvage," http://www.imo.org/About/Conventions/ListOfConventions/Pages/International-Convention-on-Salvage.aspx. Accessed 6–6–2015.

International Seabed Authority. Undated. "Polymetallic Nodules," http://www.isa.org.jm/files/documents/EN/Brochures/ENG7.pdf. Accessed on 4–16–2015.

ITOPF (The international tanker owners pollution federation limited). 2013. "Oil Tanker Spill Statistics." http://www.itopf.com/information-services/data-and-statistics/statistics/. Accessed 6–6–2015.

IWM, 2014. "The Aden Emergency," Imperial War Museums, History, http://www.iwm.org.uk/history/the-aden-emergency. Accessed on 5–4–2015.

James, George. 1995. "Somalia's Overthrown Dictator, Mohammed Siad Barre, Is Dead," *The New York Times*, January 3, http://www.nytimes.com/1995/01/03/obituaries/somalia-s-overthrown-dictator-mohammed-siad-barre-is-dead.html. Accessed on 4–6–2015.

Jankovic, Ivan and Walter E. Block. Forthcoming. "Tragedy of the Partnership: A Critique of Elinor Ostrom." *American Journal of Economics and Sociology.*

Jevons, William Stanley. 1871 [1965]. *The Theory of Political Economy*, 3d ed. London, New York, Macmillan and Co.

Johansen, David. 2002. "Bulk water removals, water exports and the NAFTA." January 31; http://publications.gc.ca/Collection-R/LoPBdP/BP/prb0041-e.htm. Accessed 6–6–2015.

Johansen, David. 2010. "Bulk Water Removals: Canadian Legislation." July 7; http://www.parl.gc.ca/Content/LOP/researchpublications/prb0213-e.htm. Accessed 6–6–2015.

Johnsson, Richard C.B. 2004. "On Ricardo and Free Trade." January 12; https://mises.org/library/ricardo-and-free-trade. Accessed on 5–28–2015.

Jones, John Paul. 1778. Letter to Le Ray de Chaumont, November 16; per Abbot, Willis John; *The Naval History of the United States*; 1890; p. 82.

Kaitin, K. I., B. W. Richard, and Louis Lasagna. 1987. "Trends in Drug Development: The 1985–86 New Drug Approvals." *Journal of Clinical Pharmacology* 27, August, 542–48.

Lantis, David, et al. 1970. *California Land of Contrast*, 2nd Ed. Belmont, CA.

Kaserman, D. L. 2002. "Markets for Organs: Myths and Misconceptions." *Journal of Contemporary Health Law and Policy*, 18; http://scholarship.law.edu/cgi/viewcontent.cgi?article=1222&context=jchlp. Accessed on 6–8–2015.

Kaserman, D. L. and A. H. Barnett, 2002. *The U.S. Organ Procurement System: A Prescription for Reform (Evaluative Studies)*. Washington D.C.: AEI Press.

Kazman, Sam. 1990. "Deadly Overcaution: FDA's Drug Approval Process." *Journal of Regulation and Social Costs* 1, no. 1, September: 35–54.

KELO et al. v. CITY OF NEW LONDON et al. certiorari to the Supreme Court of Connecticut; No. 04–108. Argued February 22, 2005—Decided June 23, 2005. Kelo v. City of New London, Connecticut, 545 U.S. 469, 125 S. Ct. 2655, 2671 (2005).

Kentucky. 2011. "Brief History of the National Flood Insurance Program," Common Wealth of Kentucky, Department for Environmental Protection, Division of Water, http://water.ky.gov/floodplain/Pages/BriefHistory.aspx, Accessed on 5–3–2015.

King, Seth. 2010. "*Daily Anarchist* Interviews Walter E. Block," September 9. http://dailyanarchist.com/2010/09/06/daily-anarchist-interviews-walter-block/. Accessed on 6–10–2015.

Kinsella, N. Stephan. 2001. "Against Intellectual Property," *Journal of Libertarian Studies*, Vol. 15, No. 2, Winter, pp. 1–53; http://www.mises.org/journals/jls/15_2/15_2_1.pdf. Accessed 6–7–2015.

Kinsella, Stephan N. 2003. "A libertarian theory of contract: title transfer, binding promises, and inalienability" *Journal of Libertarian Studies*, Vol. 17, No. 2, Spring, pp. 11–37; http://www.mises.org/journals/jls/17_2/17_2_2.pdf. Accessed 6–7–2015.

Kinsella, N. Stephan. 2005. "A Libertarian Defense of 'Kelo' and Limited Federal Power." August 28. http://archive.lewrockwell.com/kinsella/kinsella17.html. Accessed 6–7–2015.

Kinsella, Stephan N. 2006. "How we come to own ourselves" September 7; http://www.mises.org/story/2291. Accessed 6–7–2015.

Kinsella, Stephan. 2007. "The Blockean Proviso." September 11; https://mises.org/blog/blockean-proviso. Accessed 6–7–2015.

Kinsella, Stephan. 2009A. "Down with the Lockean Proviso." March 13; http://www.stephankinsella.com/2009/08/down-with-the-lockean-proviso/. Accessed 6–7–2015.

Kinsella, Stephan. 2009B. "Milton Friedman on Intolerance, Liberty, Mises, Etc." November 9; http://www.stephankinsella.com/2009/11/milton-friedman-on-intolerance-liberty-mises-etc. Accessed 6–7–2015.

Kinsella, Stephan. 2009C. "The Irrelevance of the Impossibility of Anarcho-Libertarianism." August 20; http://www.stephankinsella.com/2009/08/20/the-irrelevance-of-the-impossibility-of-anarcho-libertarianism/. Accessed 6–7–2015.

Kinsella, Stephan. 2009D. "Van Dun on Freedom versus Property and Hostile Encirclement." August 3; http://www.stephankinsella.com/2009/08/van-dun-on-freedom-versus-property-and-hostile-encirclement/. Accessed 6–7–2015.

Kinsella, Stephen. 2009E. "The Libertarian Approach to Negligence, Tort, and Strict Liability: Wergeld and Partial Wergeld." September 1; http://www.stephankinsella.com/2009/09/the-libertarian-approach-to-negligence-tort-and-strict-liability-wergeld-and-partial-wergeld/. Accessed 6–7–2015.

Kinsella, Stephan. 2010. "Legislation and Law in a Free Society." February 25; http://mises.org/daily/4147. Accessed 6–7–2015.

Kirzner, Israel, ed. 1986. *Subjectivism, Intelligibility and Economic Understanding*, New York: New York University Press.

Klein, Daniel B. and Alexander Tabarrok. Undated. "Is the FDA Safe and Effective?" http://www.fdareview.org/. Accessed 6–7–2015.

Klein, Peter G. 2006. "Why Intellectuals Still Support Socialism." November 15; http://mises.org/daily/2318/Why-Intellectuals-Still-Support-Socialism. Accessed 6–7–2015.

Klein, Peter. 2007. "Vaguely Defined Property Rights." April 4; http://organizationsandmarkets.com/2007/04/04/vaguely-defined-property-rights/. Accessed 6–7–2015.

Klein, Peter G. 2014. "The Endangered Species Act and the Double Coincidence of Wants." September 12; https://mises.org/blog/endangered-species-act-and-double-coincidence-wants. Accessed on 6–8–2015.

Kreuter, Urs P. and Linda E. Platts. 1996. "Why the Ivory Ban is Failing." *Christian Science Monitor*. March 20; http://perc.org/articles/why-ivory-ban-failing. Accessed 6–7–2015.

Krouse, Peter. 2013. "Cargill stops mining salt under Lake Erie out of safety concerns," *Cleveland.com*, http://www.cleveland.com/business/index.ssf/2013/08/cargill_salt.html. Accessed on 4–17–2015.

Krueger, Ann O. 1974. "The Political Economy of the Rent-Seeking Society," *American Economic Review*. Vol. 64, No. 3, June, pp. 291–303.

Laband, David N. 2001. "The Political Commons." June 21; http://www.mises.org/daily/711. Accessed 6–7–2015.

LaGrone, Sam. 2014. "Chinese Submarine Headed to Gulf of Aden For Counter Piracy Operations," *USNI News* (US Navy Institute), September 30; http://news.usni.org/2014/09/30/chinese-submarine-headed-gulf-aden-counter-piracy-operations. Accessed on 5–4–2015.

Landsburg, Steven E. 2008. "What to Expect When You're Free Trading." *The NY Times*. January 16; http://www.nytimes.com/2008/01/16/opinion/16landsburg.html?_r=1&scp=1&sq=Steven+E.+Landsburg&oref=slogin. Accessed 6–7–2015.

Law of the Sea. Undated. *The United Nations Law of the Sea Treaty Information Center*, http://www.unlawoftheseatreaty.org/, http://www.un.org/Depts/los/convention_agreements/texts/unclos/closindx.htm. Both accessed on 4–20–2015.

Leal, Donald. 1997. "How Fishing Communities Protect Their Future: We Don't Need Government to Regulate Fishing." *The Freeman*; February 1; http://www.fee.org/the_freeman/detail/how-fishing-communities-protect-their-future/#ixzz2oGK9mJzQ; http://www.fee.org/the_freeman/detail/how-fishing-communities-protect-their-future/#axzz2n09Gm9Zu. Both accessed 6–7–2015.

Leal, Donald R. 2000. "Let's Homestead the Oceans," *PERC Reports*, September; http://perc.org/articles/homesteading-oceans. Accessed 6–7–2015

Leclerc, René. 2012. "Understanding the Sacramento River Valley Before Levees and Dams"; California Extreme Precipitation Symposium; June 26. http://cepsym.org/Sympro2012/leclerc_prnfmt.pdf. Accessed 6–7–2015.

Leeson, Peter T. 2007. "An-*arrgh*-chy: The Law and Economics of Pirate Organization," *Journal of Political Economy*, Vol. 115, No. 6, pp. 1049–1094.

Leeson, Peter T. 2009. "Want to Prevent Piracy? Privatize the Ocean," *National Review*, April 13; http://www.nationalreview.com/corner/180288/want-prevent-piracy-privatize-ocean-peter-t-leeson. Accessed on 6–8–2015.

Leeson, Peter T. 2011. *The Invisible Hook: The Hidden Economics of Pirates*. Princeton University Press.

Levin, Michael. 1998. "Scrooge defended." December 14; http://mises.org/daily/110. Accessed 6–7–2015.

Lewin, Peter. 1982. "Pollution Externalities: Social Cost and Strict Liability." *Cato Journal*, vol. 2, no. 1, Spring, pp. 205–229.

Lind, Michael. 2012. "Thank you, Milton Friedman: How conservatives' economic hero helped make the case for big government." August 7; http://www.salon.com/2012/08/07/thank_you_milton_friedman/. Accessed 6–7–2015.

Lindsay, Cotton M. 1976. "A Theory of Government Enterprise." *Journal of Political Economy* 84 (October): 1061–1077.

Lipka, Lawrence J. 1970. "Abandoned Property at Sea: Who Owns the Salvage 'Finds'?" *William & Mary Law Review*, Vol. 12, No. 1, http://scholarship.law.wm.edu/cgi/viewcontent.cgi?article=2713&context=wmlr. Accessed 6–7–2015.

Locke, John. 1764. *The Two Treatises of Civil Government*; ed, Thomas Hollis, London; Book 2, Of Civil-Government. http://oll.libertyfund.org?option=com_staicxt&staticfile=show.php%Ftitle=222. Accessed 6–7–2015.

Locke, John. 1948. *An Essay Concerning the True Origin, Extent and End of Civil Government*, in E. Barker, ed., *Social Contract*, New York: Oxford University Press, pp. 17–19.

Lombardo, Gary A. and Robert F. Mulligan. 2003 "Resource allocation: a Hayekian paradigm for maritime conglomerates." *Quarterly Journal of Austrian Economics*. Vol. 6, No. 1 (SPRING): 3–21; https://mises.org/journals/qjae/pdf/qjae6_1_1.pdf. Accessed 6–7–2015.

Long, Roderick. 2004. "Libertarian Anarchism: Responses to Ten Objections." https://mises.org/library/libertarian-anarchism-responses-ten-objections. Accessed 6–7–2015.

Long, Roderick. 2007. "Easy rider." September 11; http://aaeblog.com/2007/09/11/easy-rider/. Accessed 6–7–2015.

Lora, Manuel. 2006. "What Happened to Katrina Aid? " March 3; http://www.mises.org/story/2064. Accessed 6–7–2015.

Lora, Manuel. 2007. "If You Love Nature, Desocialize It." May 10; http://mises.org/daily/2539. Accessed 6–7–2015.

Lovley, Erika. 2009. "Ron Paul's plan to fend off pirates," Politico, April 15, http://www.politico.com/news/stories/0409/21245.html. Accessed on 4–21–2015.

Maceina, Mike; Slipke, Jeff; and Grizzle, John. 1999. "Electric Fences for Fish?," *Highlights of Agricultural Research*, Vol 46, No. 4, Winter; Auburn University http://www.aaes.auburn.edu/comm/pubs/highlightsonline/winter99/electricfence.html. Accessed on 4–27–2015.

Machaj, Mateusz. 2007A. "A Praxeological Case for Homogeneity and Indifference," *New Perspectives on Political Economy*. Vol. 3, No. 2, pp. 231–238; http://pcpe.libinst.cz/nppe/3_2/nppe3_2_5.pdf. Accessed 6–7–2015.

Machaj, Mateusz. 2007B. "Market Socialism and the Property Problem: Different Perspective of the Socialist Calculation Debate." *Quarterly Journal of Austrian Economics* 10:257–280 http://mises.org/journals/qjae/pdf/qjae10_4_1.pdf. Accessed 6–7–2015.

Machan, Tibor R. 2010. "Milton Friedman and the Human Good," June 7; http://mises.org/daily/4451/Milton-Friedman-and-the-Human-Good. Accessed 6–7–2015.

Machan, Tibor. Undated. "Self-Ownership & the Lockean Proviso." http://88.167.97.19/albums/files/TMTisFree/Documents/Economy/Mises/journals/scholar/Machan9.pdf. Accessed 6–7–2015.

Mackenzie, Doug W. Unpublished. "Politics and Knowledge: Expectations Formation in Democracy" Working Paper, presented at the Southern Economics Conference, 2005.

MacKenzie, Doug W. 2002. "The Market Failure Myth." August 26; https://mises.org/library/market-failure-myth. Accessed 6–7–2015.

Madwin, Gayle. Undated. localwiki, Yuba-Sutter, District 10, https://localwiki.org/yuba-sutter/District_10, Accessed on 5–3–2015.

Malakoff Diggins State Historic Park. Undated. "The Sawyer Decision," http://malakoffdigginsstatepark.org/?page_id=568. Accessed on 5–3–2015.

Malakunas, Karl. 2015. "World should fear China's actions in South China Sea: Philippine leader," *Yahoo News*, http://news.yahoo.com/philippines-warning-over-chinas-actions-south-china-sea-092122697.html. accessed on 4–14–2015.

Malcolm, Norman. 1958. *Ludwig Wittgenstein: A Memoir*, Oxford: Oxford University Press.

Malek, Ninos P. 2001. "Sell Your Kidney, Make a Profit." *Mises Daily*. April 20, http://mises.org/daily/660. Accessed 6–10–2015.

Malek, Ninos P. 2012. "To Protect and Conserve." April 2; http://mises.org/daily/5983/. Accessed 6–7–2015.

Maltsev, Yuri. 1996. "Murray N. Rothbard as a critic of socialism." *Journal of Libertarian Studies*.12:1 (Spring): 99–119; http://mises.org/journals/jls/12_1/12_1_5.pdf. Accessed 6–7–2015.

Marcus, B. K. 2009. "The Enterprise of Customary Law." June 29; http://bkmarcus.com/2007/06/. Accessed 6–7–2015.

Maritime Security. 2013. "Turkey Closes Bosphorus To Tankers During Storm," Asia, http://maritimesecurity.asia/free-2/maritime-security-asia/turkey-closes-bosphorus-to-tankers-during-storm/. Accessed on 4–16–2015.

Maybury, Richard J. 1999. "The Great Thanksgiving Hoax." November 20; http://mises.org/daily/336. Accessed 6–7–2015.

McChesney, Fred. 1991. "Antitrust and Regulation: Chicago's Contradictory Views," *Cato Journal*, Vol. 10, No. 3, Winter, pp. 775–778.

McClendon, Russell. 2010. "10 of the most endangered whales on Earth." June 23; http://www.mnn.com/earth-matters/animals/stories/10-of-the-most-endangered-whales-on-earth. Accessed 6–7–2015.

McConkey, Michael. 2013. "Anarchy, Sovereignty, and the State of Exception: Schmitt's Challenge." *The Independent Review*, v. 17, n. 3, Winter, pp. 415–428. https://www.independent.org/pdf/tir/tir_17_03_05_mcconkey.pdf. Accessed on 6–8–2015.

McDonnell, Lawrence. 1962. *Rivers of California*, Pacific Gas and Electric Company, San Francisco.

McGee, John S. 1958. "Predatory Price Cutting: The Standard Oil (New Jersey) Case," *The Journal of Law and Economics*, October, pp. 137–169.

McGee, Robert W. 2008. "An economic and ethical analysis of the Katrina disaster." *International Journal of Social Economics.* Vol. 35, No. 7, pp. 546–567; http://www.emeraldinsight.com/journals.htm?issn=0306–8293&volume=35&issue=7&articleid=1729162&show=html. Accessed 6–7–2015.

McGee, Robert W. and Walter E. Block. 1994. "Pollution Trading Permits as a Form of Market Socialism and the Search for a Real Market Solution to Environmental Pollution," *Fordham University Law and Environmental Journal*, Vol. VI, No. 1, Fall, pp. 51–77.

McKendrick, Neil, et al. 1983. *The Birth of a Consumer Society...Eighteenth-Century England.* Bloomington, IN: Indiana University Press.

McKenzie, Richard B. 2015. "My California Water Is an Undiluted Bargain; I pay $.002—two-tenths of a cent—per gallon. Hike the price and raise my incentive to conserve." May 5; http://www.wsj.com/articles/my-california-water-is-an-undiluted-bargain-1430781715. Accessed 6–5–2015.

McTigue, Maurice. 2004. *Making Government Accountable: Reform Lessons from New Zealand*; Mercatus Center/George Mason University; http://www.amazon.com/Making-Government-Accountable-Lessons-Zealand/dp/B0010JTPDI. Accessed 6–7–2015.

Megginson William and Jeffry Netter. 2001. "From State to Market: A Survey of Empirical Studies on Privatization," *Journal of Economic Literature* 39, no. 2, June.

Menger, Carl. 1950[1871]. *Principles of Economics.* Editors and translators, James Dingwall and Bert F. Hoselitz, Glencoe, IL: Free Press; http://www.mises.org/etexts/menger/principles.asp. Accessed 6–7–2015.

Messynessychic. 2013. "Marville2," http://www.messynessychic.com/2013/10/11/lost-paris-documenting-the-disappearance-of-a-medieval-city/marville2/. Accessed on 4–14–2015.

Mises, Ludwig von [1922] 1981. *Socialism: An Economic and Sociological Analysis.* Translated by J. Kahane. Indianapolis: Liberty Fund; http://mises.org/books/socialism/contents.aspx. Accessed 6–7–2015.

Mises, Ludwig von. [1949] 1998. *Human Action,* Scholars' Edition. Auburn: Mises Institute, http://www.mises.org/humanaction/pdf/HumanActionScholars.pdf. Accessed 6–7–2015.

Mises, Ludwig von. [1944] 1969. *Bureaucracy,* New Rochelle, N.Y.: Arlington House; http://www.mises.org/document/875/Bureaucracy. Accessed 6–7–2015.

Missouri Pacific Historical Society. 2015. "MoPac's First 125 Years," http://mopac.org/index.php/corporate-history/73-missouri-pacific-railroad. Accessed on 5–8–2015.

Moloney, David and Peter Pearse. 1979. "Quantitative Rights as an Instrument for Regulating Commercial Fisheries." *Journal of the Fisheries Research Board of Canada*. Vol. 36, No. 7, July, pp. 859–866; http://www.nrcresearchpress.com/toc/jfrbc/36/7; doi: 10.1139/f79–124. Accessed 6–7–2015.

Molyneux, Stefan versus Michael Badnarik. 2009. "How much government is necessary?" July 5; https://www.youtube.com/watch?v=6_k93op7_Pc. Accessed on 6–8–2015.

Molyneux, Stefan. 2008. "The Stateless Society: An Examination of Alternatives." https://www.lewrockwell.com/2005/10/stefan-molyneux/the-stateless-society-an-examination-of-alternatives/. Accessed 6–7–2015

Monsen, J. R., and K.D. Walters. 1983. *Nationalized Companies*. New York: McGraw-Hill.

Montana. 2012. "Water Rights in Montana." Montana Department of Natural Resources and Conservation, et al; http://leg.mt.gov/content/publications/environmental/2012-water-rights-handbook.pdf. Accessed on 4–29–2015.

Moore, Stephen. 1987. "Privatizing the U.S. Postal Service," in Stephen Moore and Stuart Butler, eds., *Privatization,* Washington: Heritage Foundation.

Moore, Stephen and Stuart Butler, eds., 1987. *Privatization*, Washington: Heritage Foundation.

Moore, Thomas G. 1990. "The Federal Postal Monopoly: History, Rationale, and Future," pp. 61–72, *Free The Mail: Ending the Postal Monopoly* ed. Peter J. Ferrara. Washington, D.C.: CATO Institute.

Mosby, Joe. 2014. "Anglers find success at Overcup." *Log Cabin Democrat*. April 12; http://thecabin.net/news/2014–04–12/anglers-find-success-overcup#.U4d11E9OWM8. Accessed 6–7–2015.

Motichek, Amy, Walter E. Block and Jay Johnson. 2008. "Forget Ocean Front Property, We Want Ocean Real Estate!" *Ethics, Place, and Environment*; Vol. 11, Issue 2, June, pp. 147–155.

Mulligan, Robert F. and Gary A. Lombardo. 2008. "Entrepreneurial Planning in a Regulated Environment: the U.S. Federal Maritime Commission and the Maritime Industry." *Quarterly Journal of Austrian Economics*. 11:106–118; https://mises.org/journals/qjae/pdf/qjae11_2_3.pdf. Accessed 6–7–2015.

Murphy, Robert P. 2004. "Can Trade Bring Poverty?" December 24. https://mises.org/library/can-trade-bring-poverty. Accessed 6–7–2015.

Murphy, Robert P. 2005A. "But Wouldn't Warlords Take Over?" July 7; http://mises.org/story/1855. Accessed 6–7–2015.

Murphy, Robert P. 2005B. "How the Market Might Have Handled Katrina," November 17. http://www.mises.org/story/1968. *Accessed* 6–7–2015.

Murphy, Robert P. 2007. *The Politically Incorrect Guide to Capitalism*. Regnery.

Murphy, Robert P. 2010. "Overrating Government Service." March 15; http://mises.org/daily/4131?utm_source=Ludwig+von+Mises+Institute+of+Canada+Daily+List& utm_campaign=e4794b19d8-RSS_EMAIL_CAMPAIGN&utm_medium=email& utm_term=0_6c2fea3584-e4794b19d8-274221537. Accessed 6–7–2015.

Murphy, Robert P. 2013A. "Where Are the Rothbardian Defense Agencies?" December 14; https://mises.ca/posts/blog/where-are-the-rothbardian-defense-agencies/. Accessed 6–7–2015.

Murphy, Robert P. 2013B. "Drug Gangs and Private Law." December 17; http://mises.ca/posts/blog/drug-gangs-and-private-law/. Accessed 6–7–2015.

Murrell, Peter. 1983. "Did the Theory of Market Socialism Answer the Challenge of Ludwig von Mises? A Reinterpretation of the Socialist Controversy," *History of Political Economy*, Spring 15(1), pp. 92–105.

Myers, Ransom A., Jeffrey A. Hutchings, and Nicholas J. Barrowman. 1997. "Why do fish stocks collapse? The example of cod in Atlantic Canada"; *Ecological Applications*, 7: 91–106. http://dx.doi.org/10.1890/1051–0761(1997)007[0091:WDFSCT]2.0.CO;2; http://www.esajournals.org/doi/abs/10.1890/1051–0761(1997)007%5B0091:WDFSCT%5D2.0.CO%3B2. Both accessed 6–7–2015.

Nardinelli, Clark. 1990. *Child Labor and the Industrial Revolution*. Bloomington: Indiana University Press.

National Flood Insurance Program. 2012. http://www.fema.gov/national-flood-insurance-program; http://www.floodsmart.gov/floodsmart/pages/about/nfip_overview.jsp. Both accessed 6–7–2015.

Nedzel, Nadia and Walter E. Block. 2007. "Eminent Domain: A Legal and Economic Analysis," *Government Law and Policy Journal;* Vol. 9, No. 1, Spring, pp. 70–73; reprinted as: Nedzel, Nadia and Walter E. Block. 2007. "The Demise of Eminent Domain," *One On One: A Publication of the General Practice Section of the New York State Bar Association*, Vol. 28, No. 2, Winter, pp. 49–53.

Nedzel, Nadia and Walter E. Block. 2008. "Eminent Domain: A Legal and Economic Critique." *University of Maryland Law Journal of Race, Religion, Gender, and Class*; Vol. 7, No. 1, pp. 140–171; http://www.walterblock.com/publications/. Accessed on 6–8–2015.

Nelson, Peter Lothian. 2015B. "The Libertarian Way to Provide a Park-like Experience." *Liberty.me, Liberal Ed*. 8-25. https://peterlothiannelson.liberty.me/the-libertarian-way-to-provide-a-park-like-experience/. Accessed on 8-29-2015.

Nelson, Peter Lothian. 2015A. "To Homestead a Nature Preserve." *Liberty.me, Liberal Ed*. July 14. https://peterlothiannelson.liberty.me/to-homestead-a-nature-preserve/. Accessed on 8-29-2015.

Nimoy, Leonard and Harve Bennett, 1986. "The Voyage Home;" *Star Trek IV*. http://www.amazon.com/Star-Trek-IV-Two-Disc-Collectors/dp/B000083C49. Accessed on 4–14–2015.

NOAA. Undated. "What is a dead zone?" National Oceanic and Atmospheric Administration, National Ocean Service, http://oceanservice.noaa.gov/facts/deadzone.html. Accessed on 4–16–2015.

NOAA. 2011. National Oceanic and Atmospheric Administration, National Weather Service Weather Forecast Office—New Orleans/Baton Rouge: http://www.srh.noaa.gov/lix/?n=ms_flood_history. Accessed on 4–29–2015.

North, Gary. 1976. "Educational Vouchers: The Double Tax," *The Freeman*, Vol. 26, No. 5; http://www.thefreemanonline.org/columns/friedman-and-north-on-vouchers/. Accessed 6–7–2015.

North, Gary. 2011. "Just Say No to School Vouchers . . . Again." June 30; http://www.garynorth.com/public/8202.cfm. Accessed 6–7–2015.

North, Gary. 2012. "Detours on the Road to Freedom: Where Milton Friedman Went Wrong." http://www.garynorth.com/public/9862.cfm. Accessed 6–7–2015.

North, Gary. 2014. "What Is at Stake in the BLM vs. Bundy Showdown." April 17, https://www.lewrockwell.com/2014/04/gary-north/use-youtube-instead-of-violence/. Accessed 6–7–2015.

North, Gary and Milton Friedman. 1993. "Friedman and North on Vouchers." July 1; http://www.fee.org/the_freeman/detail/friedman-and-north-on-vouchers/#axzz2nGM6q4us. Accessed 6–7–2015.

Northwestern Hawaiian Islands Multi-Agency Education Project. Undated. "French Frigate Shoals," http://www.hawaiianatolls.org/about/ffs.php. Accessed 4–28–2015.

Nove, Alec. 1993. *An economic history of the U.S.S.R.*, 3rd edition; Penguin http://books.google.com/books/about/An_Economic_History_of_the_U_S_S_R.html?id=vyX6 PH0NYScC. Accessed 6–7–2015.

Nozick, Robert. 1974. *Anarchy, State, and Utopia*. New York: Basic Books.

Nozick, Robert. 1977. "On Austrian Methodology," *Synthese*, Vol. 36, 1977, pp. 353–392; reprinted in *Socratic puzzles*. Harvard University Press, 1997.

Nutter, G. Warren. 1957. "Some observations on Soviet industrial growth." National Bureau of Economic Research, Issues 55–59; http://books.google.com/books/about/Some_observations_on_Soviet_industrial_g.html?id=oLoSAQAAMAAJ. Accessed 6–7–2015.

Oceana. Undated. Shark Attack Statistics, http://usa.oceana.org/shark-attack-statistics. Accessed on 5–11–2015.

O'Neill, Ben. 2009. "The Victorian Bushfires." February 25; https://mises.org/daily/3343/The-Victorian-Bushfires. Accessed 6–7–2015.

O'Neill, Ben. 2010. "Choice and Indifference: A Critique of the Strict Preference Approach." *Quarterly Journal of Austrian Economics,* Vol. 13, No.1, pp. 71–98, Spring; http://mises.org/journals/qjae/pdf/qjae13_1_4.pdf. Accessed 6–7–2015.

Ollman, Bertel, ed. 1998. *Market Socialism: The Debate Among Socialists.* Routledge.

Olson, Charles B. 1979. "Law in Anarchy." *Libertarian Forum.* Vol. XII, No. 6, November-December, p. 4.

Osterfeld, David. 1986. *Freedom, Society and the State: An Investigation into the Possibility of Society without Government.* San Francisco, CA: Cobden Press; http://mises.org/books/osterfeld_freedom.pdf. Accessed 6–7–2015.

Osterfeld, David. 1989. "Anarchism and the Public Goods Issue: Law, Courts and the Police," *The Journal of Libertarian Studies,* Vol. 9, No. 1, Winter, pp. 47–68; http://www.mises.org/journals/jls/9_1/9_1_3.pdf. Accessed 6–7–2015.

Ostrom, Elinor. 1990. *Governing the Commons,* Cambridge Press.

Pasadena. 1949. SCOCAL, City of Pasadena v. City of Alhambra, 33 Cal.2d 908 http://scocal.stanford.edu/opinion/city-pasadena-v-city-alhambra-25978. Accessed on 5–4–2015.

Pasour, Jr., E. C., 1981, "The Free Rider as a Basis for Government Intervention," *The Journal of Libertarian Studies,* Vol. V, No. 4, Fall, pp. 453–464; http://www.mises.org/journals/jls/5_4/5_4_6.pdf. Accessed 6–7–2015.

Pasour, E. C., Jr. 1986. "Rent Seeking: Some Conceptual Problems and Implications." *Review of Austrian Economics* 1: 123–43; http://mises.org/journals/rae/pdf/RAE1_1_8.pdf. Accessed 6–7–2015.

Paul, Ellen Frankel. 1987. *Property Rights and Eminent Domain.* Livingston, New Jersey: Transaction Publishers.

"Paul, Ron." Undated. "'Ron Paul' On the Inner Contradictions of Limited Government." http://www.youtube.com/watch?v=7o4kiWpqoeg&feature=PlayList&p=9645F6A68683F679&playnext=1&playnext_from=PL&index=4. Accessed 6–7–2015.

Pejovich, Svetozar. 1979. *Life in the Soviet Union: A Report Card on Socialism.* Fisher Institute. http://books.google.com/books/about/Life_in_the_Soviet_Union.html?id=_ZSZAAAAIAAJ. Accessed 6–7–2015.

Peltzman, Sam. 1973. "An Evaluation of Consumer Protection Legislation: The 1962 Drug Amendments." *The Journal of Political Economy.* Vol. 81, No. 5, Sept-Oct, pp. 1049–1091.

Peltzman, Sam. 1974. *Regulation of Pharmaceutical Innovation: The 1962 Amendments.* Washington, D.C.: American Enterprise Institute for Public Policy Research.

Peltzman, Sam. 1987a. "Regulation and Health: The Case of Mandatory Prescriptions and an Extension." *Managerial and Decision Economics* 8(1): 41–6.

Peltzman, Sam. 1987b. "The Health Effects of Mandatory Prescriptions." *Journal of Law and Economics* 30(2): 207–38.

Peltzman, Sam. 2005. Regulation and the Natural Progress of Opulence. Washington: AEI-Brookings Joint Center on Regulatory Studies, pp. 15–6.

Peterson, Elmer. 1951. "This is the Hard Core of Freedom," *Daily Oklahoman,* December 9, p. 12A.

Peterson, J.E. 2009. "The Arabian Peninsula in Modern Times: A Historiographical Survey of Recent Publications," http://www.jepeterson.net/sitebuildercontent/sitebuilderfiles/peterson_arabian_peninsula_historiography.pdf. Accessed on 5–4–2015.

Pezzaglia, Phil. 2011. "Floods of 1972," *River News-Herald and Isleton Journal, Exploring Rio Vista's Past,* February 16, http://rivernewsherald.org/history_2–16–2011.html. Accessed on 5–3–2015.

Photobucket. Undated. http://s199.photobucket.com/user/Doc_Olds/media/Olds%20Car%20Stuff/Hummer/Vacation%2007/Forum%20Stuff/normal_aerial8.jpg.html. Accessed on 4–28–2015.

Pitney, Jr., John J. and Levin, John-Clark. 2014. *Private Anti-Piracy Navies: How Warships for Hire are Changing Maritime Security,* Lexington Books, Lanham MD.

Plato. 1914. [Alexander Kerr] *The Republic of Plato,* Book VIII, Chicago.

Plato. 360. *Timaeus,* 48e-52d, Benjamin Jowett translation, http://classics.mit.edu/Plato/timaeus.html. Accessed on 4–28–2015.

Plaut, Martin. 2013. "Ethiopia and Kenya help dismember Somalia," *New Statesman*, September 3, http://www.newstatesman.com/africa/2013/09/ethiopia-and-kenya-help-dismember-somalia. Accessed on 5–6–2015.

Polynational. 2014. "Saudi-Yemeni War," *The Polynational War Memorial*, March 8, http://www.war-memorial.net/Saudi-Yemeni-War-3.298. Accessed on 5–4–2015.

Poole, Robert. 1976. *Cutting Back City Hall*, New York: Reason Press.

Popeo, Daniel. 1988. "Privatizing the Judiciary." August 1; http://www.fee.org/the_freeman/detail/privatizing-the-judiciary/. Accessed on 6–7–2015.

Port Authority of New York & New Jersey. 2014. "Bridges and Tunnels," December 7, https://www.panynj.gov/bridges-tunnels/tolls.html. Accessed on 5–20–2015.

Priest, George. 1975. "The History of the Postal Monopoly in the United States," *Journal of Law and Economics*, Vol. 18, No. 33, pp. 33–80.

Proudhon, Pierre-Joseph. 1966 [1840]. *What Is Property?* New York: Howard Fertig. Quoted from Stewart Edwards (ed.) 1969. *Selected Writings of Pierre-Joseph Proudhon*. New York: Anchor Books.

Proudhon, Pierre-Joseph. 1851. *Idée Générale de la Révolution au XIXᵉ Siécle*, Paris.

Pufendorf, Samuel. 1673. *Natural law and the law of nations (De officio hominis et civis prout ipsi praescribuntur lege naturali)*.

Puffert, Douglas J. 2000. "The Standardization of Track Gauge on North American Railways, 1830–1890," *The Journal of Economic History*, December, vol. 60, no. 4, https://campus.fsu.edu/bbcswebdav/users/jcalhoun/Economic_Standards/Puffert%20-%20The%20Standardization%20of%20Track%20Gauge.pdf. Accessed 5–8, 2015.

Racanelli, P. J., 1986, United States v. State Water Resources Control Bd., 182 Cal. App. 3d 82 [227 Cal. Rptr. 161]: http://law.justia.com/cases/california/calapp3d/182/82.html. Accessed on 4–13–2015.

Rand, Ayn. 1957. *Atlas Shrugged*, New York: Random House.

Rand Corp. 2013. "Asymmetric Warfare," *Rand Corporation*, October 7, http://www.rand.org/topics/asymmetric-warfare.html. Accessed on 5–6–2015.

Raskin, Max, Scott A. Kjar, Robert Rahm. 2008. "What is seen and unseen on the Gulf Coast." *The International Journal of Social Economics*. Vol. 35, No.7, pp. 490–500.

Raunek. 2012. "How to Handle a Ship in Congested (High-Traffic) Waters?" *Marine Insight*, http://www.marineinsight.com/marine/marine-news/headline/how-to-handle-a-ship-in-congested-high-traffic-waters/. Accessed on 4–16–2015.

RBC Radio. 2014. "Somalia: Puntland cuts its ties with Federal Government following announcement of Central State," *RBC Raxanreeb*, August 1, http://www.raxanreeb.com/2014/08/somalia-puntland-cuts-its-ties-with-federal-government-following-announcement-of-central-state/. Accessed on 5–6–2015.

Regan, Shawn. 2014. "A peaceable solution for the range war over grazing rights." *Wall Street Journal*, p. A15, April 23; http://perc.org/articles/peaceable-solution-range-war-over-grazing-rights. Accessed on 6–7–2015.

Regis, Ed. 2004. "The Doomslayer: The environment is going to hell, and human life is doomed to only get worse, right? Wrong. Conventional wisdom, meet Julian Simon, the Doomslayer." *Wired*. http://www.wired.com/wired/archive/5.02/ffsimon_pr.html. Accessed on 6–7–2015.

Reichert, William O. 1980. "Natural Right in the Political Philosophy of Pierre-Joseph Proudhon." *The Journal of Libertarian* Studies Vol. IV, No 1 (Winter), pp. 77–91; http://mises.org/journals/jls/4_1/4_1_5.pdf. Accessed on 6–7–2015.

Reno, William. 2011. *Warfare in Independent Africa, New Approaches to African History*; Cambridge.

Reyburn, Mary. 1992. "California's Water Shortage is Government's Fault," *The Free Market*, Vol. 10, No. 3, March, pp. 4–5.

Ricardo, David. 1821 [1912]. *The Principles of Political Economy and Taxation*, 3rd ed., London: J. M. Dent.

Rice, Leonard and Michael White. 1991. *Engineering Aspects of Water Law*; Krieger Pub Co; April; http://www.amazon.com/Engineering-Aspects-Water-Leonard-Rice/dp/089464548X. Accessed on 6–7–2015.

Richards, Janet Radcliffe. 2001. "Organs for sale." *Indian Journal of Medical Ethics*. Vol. 9, No. 2, April-June; http://ijme.in/index.php/ijme/article/view/1279/2850. Accessed on 6–8–2015.

Riley, Brian; Miller, Terry. 2014. "Congress Should Get Smart and Cut Tariffs to Boost Trade Freedom," *The Heritage Foundation*, http://www.heritage.org/research/reports/2013/10/congress-should-get-smart-and-cut-tariffs-to-boost-trade-freedom. Accessed 5–4–2015.

Rizzo, Mario J. 1979. "Uncertainty, Subjectivity, and the Economic Analysis of Law," in Mario J. Rizzo (ed.), *Time, Uncertainty, and Disequilibrium*, Lexington, MA: Lexington Books, pp. 71–90.

Rizzo, Mario J. 1980A. "The Mirage of Efficiency," *Hofstra Law Review*, Vol. 8, pp. 641–658.

Rizzo, Mario. 1980B. "Law Amid Flux: The Economics of Negligence and Strict Liability in Torts," *Journal of Legal Studies*, 9(2): 292–318.

Robbins, Lionel. 1928. "The Optimum Theory of Population" in *London Essays in Economics: in Honour of Edwin Cannan*, eds. T. Gregory and H. Dalton.

Robbins, Lionel. 1966. "Lecture two: population and returns." *The Theory of Economic Development in the History of Economic Thought*. pp. 22–33; London: Macmillan, St Martin's; http://library.mises.org/books/Lionel%20Robbins/The%20Theory%20of%20Economic%20Development.pdf. Accessed on 6–7–2015.

Rockwell Jr., Llewellyn H. 1998. "Vouchers: Enemy of Religion," 1 September. https://mises.org/library/vouchers-enemy-religion. Accessed on 6–7–2015.

Rockwell Jr., Llewellyn H. 2000A. "Education and the Election." https://www.lewrockwell.com/1970/01/lew-rockwell/school-vouchers-rip/. Accessed on 6–7–2015.

Rockwell Jr., Llewellyn H. 2000B. "Why Not Feel Sorry for BP?" May 5; https://www.lewrockwell.com/2010/05/lew-rockwell/why-not-feel-sorry-for-bp/. Accessed on 6–7–2015.

Rockwell Jr.. Llewellyn H. 2002. "Vouchers: Another Name for Welfare." July 2. https://www.lewrockwell.com/2002/07/lew-rockwell/vouchers-are-welfare-2/. Accessed on 6–7–2015.

Rockwell, Jr., Llewellyn H. 2007. "Land Socialism: Playing With Fire." October 24; https://mises.org/daily/2761. Accessed on 6–7–2015.

Rockwell, Jr., Llewellyn H. 2014A. *Against the State: An Anarcho-Capitalist Manifesto*. Rockwell Communications LLC.

Rockwell, Jr., Llewellyn H. 2014B. "What Libertarianism Is, and Isn't." March 31; http://www.lewrockwell.com/2014/03/lew-rockwell/what-libertarianism-is-and-isnt/. Accessed on 6–7–2015.

Rockwell, Jr., Llewellyn H. and Walter E. Block. 2010. "The Economics and Ethics of Hurricane Katrina." *American Journal of Economics and Sociology*. Vol. 69, No. 4, October, pp. 1294–1320.

Rocky Mountain Buffalo Association. 2015. http://www.buffaloranchers.com/. Accessed on 5–11–2015.

Roemer, John and Pranab Bardhan. 1992. "Market Socialism: A Case for Rejuvenation." *Journal of Economic Perspectives*. Summer.

Roland, Denise. 2012. "World fish stocks declining faster than feared." September 28; http://www.ft.com/intl/cms/s/2/73d14032–088e-11e2-b37e-00144feabdc0.html#axzz2oGV52IvF. Accessed on 6–7–2015.

Rome, Gregory and Walter E. Block. 2006. "Schoolhouse Socialism." *Journal of Instructional Psychology*, Vol. 33, No. 1, pp. 83–88; https://www.questia.com/library/journal/1G1-144014466/schoolhouse-socialism. Accessed on 6–9–2015.

Roos, Maurice. 2007. "A Half Century of Watching California Floods," California Department of Water Resources, *DWR News* Summer, http://www.water.ca.gov/climatechange/docs/Roos-flooding.pdf. Accessed on 5–3–2015.

Rosenberg, Nathan and L.E. Birdzell. 1987. *How the West Grew Rich: The Economic Transformation of the Industrial World*, New York, N.Y.: Basic Books.

Rothbard, Murray N. 1955. "The Ownership and Control of Water." *Ideas on Liberty*, No. 3. New York: Foundation for Economic Education, November, pp. 82-87 (written anonymously).

Rothbard, Murray N. 1956. "Concerning Water." *Freeman*, March, pp. 61–64.

Rothbard, Murray N. 1961. "A Fable for Our Times By One of the Unreconstructed." https://www.lewrockwell.com/2014/09/murray-n-rothbard/a-fable-for-our-time/. Accessed on 6–7–2015.

Rothbard, Murray N. (2004 [1962]). *Man, Economy and State*, Auburn AL: Ludwig von Mises Institute, Scholar's Edition; http://www.mises.org/rothbard/mes.asp. Accessed on 6–7–2015.

Rothbard, Murray N. 1963. "War, Peace, and the State." The Standard , April, pp. 2–5; 15–16; http://mises.org/rothbard/warpeace.asp; Accessed on 6–7–2015.

Rothbard, Murray N. 1965. "The Anatomy of the State." *Rampart Journal*, Summer, pp. 1–24. Reprinted in Tibor R. Machan (ed.), *The Libertarian Alternative*. Chicago: Nelson-Hall Co., 1974, pp. 69–93; http://mises.org/easaran/chap3.asp. Accessed on 6–7–2015.

Rothbard, Murray N. 2006 [1970]. "Anarcho-Communism." *The Libertarian Forum*, Vol. II, No. 1, January 1, p. 4; http://mises.org/library/death-wish-anarcho-communists. Accessed on 4–13–2015; originally appeared as "The Death Wish of the Anarcho-Communists," *The Libertarian Forum*, January 1, 1970.

Rothbard, Murray N. 1971. "Milton Friedman Unraveled." *Individualist*, February, pp. 3-7; https://mises.org/sites/default/files/16_4_3.pdf. Accessed on 6–9–2015.

Rothbard, Murray N. 1973. *For a New Liberty,* Macmillan, New York; http://www.mises.org/rothbard/newliberty.asp; http://mises.org/rothbard/newlibertywhole.asp. Accessed both on 6–7–2015.

Rothbard, Murray N. 1974. "Justice and Property Rights: The Failure of Utilitarianism." *Egalitarianism As a Revolt Against Nature and Other Essays*. Washington, D.C.: Libertarian Review Press; https://mises.org/daily/4047/. Accessed on 6–7–2015.

Rothbard, Murray N. 1975. "Society Without a State." *The Libertarian Forum*, volume 7.1, January.

Rothbard, Murray N. 1977. "Do you hate the state?" *The Libertarian Forum*, Vol. 10, No. 7, July; http://www.lewrockwell.com/2014/04/murray-n-rothbard/do-you-pass-the-rothbard-test/. Accessed on 6–9–2015.

Rothbard, Murray N. 1979. "Comment: The Myth of Efficiency," in Mario J. Rizzo (ed.), *Time, Uncertainty, and Disequilibrium*, Lexington, MA: Lexington Books: pp. 91–96.

Rothbard, Murray N. 1982. "Law, Property Rights, and Air Pollution," *Cato Journal*, Vol. 2, No. 1, Spring; reprinted in *Economics and the Environment: A Reconciliation*, Walter E. Block , ed., Vancouver: The Fraser Institute, 1990; http://www.mises.org/rothbard/lawproperty.pdf. Accessed on 6–7–2015.

Rothbard, Murray N. 1985. "Bankruns and Water Shortages." *The Free Market*. Auburn, AL: The Ludwig von Mises Institute, September, pp. 3–4.

Rothbard, Murray N. 1985A. "Airport Congestion: A Case of Market Failure?" *The Free Market*. Auburn, AL: The Ludwig von Mises Institute, January, https://mises.org/library/airport-congestion-%E2%80%94-case-market-failure. Accessed on 6–7–2015.

Rothbard, Murray N. 1989A. "Why Not Feel Sorry for Exxon?" *Liberty Magazine*. July. https://mises.org/library/why-not-feel-sorry-exxon. Accessed on 6–7–2015

Rothbard, Murray N. 1989B. "World War I as Fulfillment: Power and the Intellectuals." *The Journal of Libertarian Studies*, Vol. 9, No. 1, Winter, pp. 81–125. Reprinted in *The Costs of War*, by J. V. Denson (ed.). New Brunswick, NJ: Transaction Publishers, 1998, pp. 203–254. Also appears in 2nd Edition, 1999.

Rothbard, Murray N. 1994. "Vouchers: What Went Wrong?" *The Free Market*. Auburn, AL: The Ludwig von Mises Institute, January, pp. 1, 8.

Rothbard, Murray N. 1995. *Making Economic Sense*. Auburn, AL: Mises Institute; http://mises.org/econsense/econsense.asp. Accessed on 6–7–2015.

Rothbard, Murray N. 1997A. "Toward a Reconstruction of Utility and Welfare Economics." *The Logic of Action One: Method, Money, and the Austrian School*. Glos, UK: Edward Elgar Publishing Ltd., pp. 211–254.

Rothbard, Murray. 1997B. "Buchanan and Tullock's 'The Calculus of Consent," *The Logic of Action II*, UK: Edward Elgar Publishing Limited, pp. 269–274.

Rothbard, Murray N. 1997C. "The single tax: economic and moral implications" and "A reply to Georgist criticisms," *Logic of Action One: Applications and Criticisms from the Austrian School*. London: Elgar, pp. 294–310.

Rothbard, Murray N. 1998 [1982]. *The Ethics of Liberty*, New York: New York University Press.

Rothbard, Murray N. 2006. "What Really Happened at Plymouth." November 23; http://mises.org/daily/2395/. Accessed on 6–7–2015.

Rothbard, Murray N. 2007. "Who Owns Water?" *Mises Daily*, June 15; http://mises.org/daily/2553. Accessed on 6–7–2015.

Rothbard, Murray N. 2011A. "Buchanan and Tullock's 'The Calculus of Consent," Chapter 5; *Economic Controversies*. Auburn, AL: Mises Institute.

Rothbard, Murray N. 2011B. "Malthus and the Assault on Population." August 2; http://mises.org/daily/5501/. Accessed on 6–7–2015.

Rotman, Michael. 2014. "Cuyahoga River Fire"; *Cleveland Historical*; January 1, http://clevelandhistorical.org/items/show/63#.VT7U0OlFCB8. Accessed on 4–27–2015.

Rowley, Charles Kershaw, Robert D. Tollison, Gordon Tullock. 1988. *The Political Economy of Rent-Seeking*. Springer.

Rozeff, Michael S. 2005. "Original Appropriation and Its Critics." September 1. https://www.lewrockwell.com/2005/09/michael-s-rozeff/original-appropriation-and-its-critics/. Accessed on 6–7–2015.

Rubin, Jeff. 2010. "Water: Canada's most valuable resource." *Globe and Mail*." November 4; http://www.theglobeandmail.com/report-on-business/rob-commentary/water-canadas-most-valuable-resource/article1391659/. Accessed on 6–7–2015.

Rummel, R. J. 1992. *Democide: Nazi Genocide and Mass Murder*. Rutgers, New Jersey: Transaction Publisher.

Rummel, R. J. 1994. *Death By Government*, New Brunswick, NJ: Transaction.

Rummel, R. J. 1997. *Statistics on Democide*. Center on National Security and Law, University of Virginia.

Russo, Mitch. 2010. "Fact Sheet—Sacramento River Flood Control Project—Weirs and Flood Relief Structures"; California, State of; Department of Water Resources; Division of Flood Control http://www.water.ca.gov/newsroom/docs/WeirsReliefStructures.pdf. Accessed on 5–3–2015.

Reuters. 2014. "After Nevada Ranch Stand-Off, Emboldened Militias Ask: Where Next?" *Newsweek*, April 17, http://www.newsweek.com/after-nevada-ranch-stand-emboldened-militias-ask-where-next-246691. Accessed on 5–11–2015.

Ruwart, Mary. 1993. *Healing our world: The Other Piece of the Puzzle*. SunStar Press; revised edition.

SAFCA. 2008. "Sacramento Area Flood History," Sacramento Area Flood Control Agency, http://www.safca.org/history.html. Accessed on 5–4–2015.

Sailor, Steve. 2013; "The Simon-Ehrlich Bet (and the nonbet)," http://isteve.blogspot.ca/2013/09/the-simon-ehrlich-bet-and-nonbet.html. Accessed on 04–27–2015.

Sakoff, A. 1962. The private sector in Soviet agriculture. *Mthly. Bull. Agr. Econ.* 11:9.

Salisbury, David F. 2003. "What Does a Voucher Buy? A Closer Look at the Cost of Private Schools." *Cato Institute Policy Analysis*, No. 486, August 28.

Salonia, LCdr Mark J. 1990. "The U.S. Navy's Future in Drug Interdiction," Global Security, http://www.globalsecurity.org/military/library/report/1990/SMJ.htm, Accessed on 4–21–2015.

Sandle, Tim. 2013. "Humpback whales could be dropped as an endangered species." December, 22; http://www.digitaljournal.com/news/environment/humpback-whales-could-be-dropped-as-an-endangered-species/article/364474; http://www.digitaljournal.com/news/environment/humpback-whales-could-be-dropped-as-an-endangered-species/article/364474#ixzz2oGRMfllO. Accessed both on 6–7–2015.

Santoriello, Andrea and Walter E. Block. 1996. "Externalities and the Environment," *The Freeman*, November, Vol. 46, No. 11, pp. 755–756, http://www.thefreemanonline.org/featured/externalities-and-the-environment/; reprinted in *El Diario*, (Bolivia), July 1997. Accessed on 6–7–2015.

Sardi, Bill. 2007. "The FDA has blood on its hands." May 16; https://www.lewrockwell.com/2007/05/bill-sardi/the-fda-has-blood-on-its-hands/. Accessed on 6–7–2015.

Savas, E. S. 1987. *Privatization*. Chatham, N.J.: Chatham House Publishers.

Savas, E.S. 1979. "Refuse Collection: A Critical Review of the Evidence." *Journal of Urban Analysis*. Vol. 6, pp. 1–13.

Savas, E.S. 1982. *How to Shrink Government: Privatizing the Public Sector*. Chatham House Publishers: Chatham, N.J.

Savas, E. S. 2000. *Privatization and Public—Private Partnerships*. Chatham, N.J.: Chatham House Publishers.

Scahill, Jeremy. 2013. "Their Intention and Our Intention Is the Same Somalia, 1993–2004"; *Dirty Wars: The World Is a Battlefield*; Section 10. Nation Books; New York.

Scarborough, Brandon. 2012. "Buying Water for the Environment." In Gardner, B. Delworth and Randy T. Simmons, eds. 2012, pp. 75–105. *Aquanomics: Water Markets and the Environment*. New Brunswick, NJ: Transactions Publishers.

Scarpeleggia, David. 2012. "A missed opportunity to protect Canada's water sovereignty." October 11; http://www.ipolitics.ca/2012/10/11/a-missed-opportunity-to-protect-canadas-water-sovereignty. Accessed on 6–7–2015.

Schmidtz, David. 1991. *The Limits of Government: An Essay on the Public Goods Argument*, Boulder Co: Westview Press.

Schoenbach, Victor J. 2000. Studying populations—basic demography; http://www.epidemiolog.net/epid168/lectures/Demography.pdf, page 2. Accessed on 6–7–2015.

Schumpeter, Joseph A. 1942. *Capitalism, Socialism and Democracy*, New York: Harper.

Scott, James C. 2009. *The Art of Not Being Governed: An Anarchist History of Upland Southeast Asia*, Yale University Press, New Haven & London.

The Seasteading Institute. Undated. http://www.seasteading.org/?intro=close, Accessed on 4–14–2015.

Sechrest, Larry. 2003. "Privateering and National Defense: Naval Warfare for Private Profit," pp. 239–74, *The Myth of National Defense: Essays on the Theory and History of Security Production*, edited by Hans-Hermann Hoppe, Ludwig von Mises Institute, Auburn, Alabama.

Sechrest, Larry. 2004A. "Public Goods and Private Solutions in Maritime History." *The Quarterly Journal of Austrian Economics*. Vol. 7, No. 2. Summer, 3–27; http://www.mises.org/journals/qjae/pdf/qjae7_2_1.pdf. Accessed on 6–7–2015.

Sechrest, Larry. 2004B. "Private Provision of Public Goods: Theoretical Issues and Some Examples from Maritime History," *ICFAI Journal of Public Finance*, August, Vol. II, No. 3, 45- 73; http://88.167.97.19/albums/files/TMTisFree/Documents/Economy/Mises/journals/scholar/Sechrest7.pdf. Accessed on 6–9–2015.

Sechrest, Larry. 2007. "Privately Funded and Built U.S. Warships in the Quasi-War of 1797–1801," *The Independent Review*, Summer, Vol. 12, No. 1: 101–113.

Seldon, Arthur. 1968. *The Price of Blood*. London: Institute of Economic Affairs; Hobart Papers; http://files.libertyfund.org/files/1456/Seldon_0820.07.pdf. Accessed on 6–7–2015.

SFWMD. 2015. South Florida Water Management District, "Restoring Lake Okeechobee," May 14; http://my.sfwmd.gov/portal/page/portal/xweb%20protecting%20and%20restoring/lake%20okeechobee. Accessed on 5–14–15.

Shabman, Leonard and Kurt Stephenson. 2012. "Market-like Water Quality Trading: Why it Matters and How to Make it Happen." in Gardner, B. Delworth and Randy T. Simmons, eds. 2012. *Acquanomics: Water Markets and the Environment*. Transaction Publishers. http://www.amazon.com/Aquanomics-Environment-B-Delworth-Gardner/dp/1412845785/ref=sr_1_1?s=books&ie=UTF8&qid=1393465796&sr=1–1&keywords=gardner%2C+delworth. Accessed on 6–7–2015

Schick, Rabbi Moses, per Leon Wieseltier. 2015. *Jewish Review of Books*, "The Argumentative Jew," Winter.

Shaffer, Butler. 2004. "The Case for Ebenezer." December 13; https://mises.org/library/case-ebenezer. Accessed on 6–7–2015.

Shaffer, Butler. 2012. *The Wizards of Ozymandias: Reflections on the Decline and Fall.* Auburn, AL: The Mises Institute; http://library.mises.org/books/Butler%20Shaffer/ The%20Wizards%20of%20Ozymandias_Vol_2.pdf. Accessed on 6–7–2015.

Sharp, Gwen. 2010. "Comparing Oil Spills." July 9; http://thesocietypages.org/socimages/ 2010/07/09/comparing-oil-spills/. Accessed on 6–7–2015.

Shugart II, William F. 1987. "Don't Revise the Clayton Act, Scrap It!," 6 *Cato Journal*, 925.

Simmons, Randy, and Kreuter, Urs P. 1989. "Herd Mentality: Banning Ivory Sales is No Way to Save the Elephant," *Policy Review*, Fall, pp. 46–49; http://agrilifecdn.tamu.edu/kreuter/ files/2013/01/Simmons-Kreuter-1989_3.pdf. Accessed on 6–7–2015.

Simon, Julian. 1981. *The Ultimate Resource*, Princeton: Princeton University Press.

Simon, Julian, 1990. "The Unreported Revolution in Population in Population Economics." *The Public Interest.* Fall: 89–100.

Simon, Julian. 1996. *The Ultimate Resource II.* Princeton U. Press.

Simpson, Brian. 2005. *Markets Don't Fail.* New York, N.Y.: Lexington Books.

Smith, Adam. [1776] 1979. *An Inquiry into the Nature and Causes of the Wealth of Nations*, Indianapolis, IN: Liberty Fund.

Smith, E. Michael. 2012. "California Extreme Super Flood"; http://chiefio.wordpress.com/ 2012/11/29/california-extreme-super-flood/. Accessed on 6–7–2015.

Smith, Hedrik. 1976. *The Russians.* Quadrangle.

Smith, Jr., Fred L. 1983. "Why not Abolish Antitrust?," *Regulation*, Jan-Feb, 23; http://cei.org/ op-eds-and-articles/why-not-abolish-antitrust. Accessed on 6–7–2015.

Smith, Robert J. 1981. "Resolving the Tragedy of the Commons by Creating Private Property Rights in Wildlife," *Cato Journal* 1 (Fall): 439–468; http://www.cato.org/sites/cato.org/ files/serials/files/cato-journal/1981/11/cj1n2–7.pdf; http://cei.org/studies-other-studies/re-solving-tragedy-commons-creating-private-property-rights-wildlife. Accessed on 6–7–2015.

Sorokanich, Robert 2014. "A Tantalizingly Brief Glimpse Inside Fabien Cousteau's Underwater Lab," *Gizmodo*, http://gizmodo.com/a-tantalizingly-brief-glimpse-inside-fabien-cousteaus-u-1600786309. Accessed on 4–17–2015.

Southgate, Henry. 1862. *Many Thoughts of Many Minds, Being a Treasury of Reference*; Griffin, Bohn, and Company; London.

Sowell, Thomas. 1983. *The Economics and Politics of Race: An International Perspective.* New York: Morrow.

Sowell, Thomas. 2000. *Jewish World Review*, "Wake up, parents!," http:// www.jewishworldreview.com/cols/sowell081800.asp. Accessed on 4–29–2015.

Speiser, Frank. 2005. "Imminent Eminent Domain: Paying Tribute in Collectivist Society." June 28; http://www.strike-the-root.com/51/speiser/speiser1.html. Accessed on 6–7–2015.

Spiro, Andreas. 2012. "What Do Ron Paul, Northwest Biotherapeutics, And Novartis Have In Common?" September 12; http://seekingalpha.com/article/856731-what-do-ron-paul-north-west-biotherapeutics-and-novartis-have-in-common. Accessed on 6–7–2015.

Spooner, Lysander. 1966 [1870]. *No Treason: The Constitution of No Authority and A Letter to Thomas F. Bayard*, Larkspur, Colorado: Rampart College; http://jim.com/treason.htm. Accessed on 6–7–2015.

Steinreich, Dale. 2005. "Playing God at the FDA." May 2; http://mises.org/daily/1805. Accessed on 6–7–2015.

Stigler, George J. and Gary S. Becker. 1977. "De Gustibus Non Est Disputandum," *American Economic Review*, 67: 76–90; http://www.jstor.org/stable/1807222. Accessed on 6–7–2015.

Stringham, Edward, ed. 2005. *Anarchy, State, and Public Choice.* Cheltanham, UK: Edward Elgar.

Stringham, Edward, ed. 2007. *Anarchy and the Law: The Political Economy of Choice*, Somerset, NJ: Transaction Publishers; http://www.amazon.com/Anarchy-Law-Political-Economy-Choice/dp/1412805791. Accessed on 6–7–2015.

Stringham, Edward. 2008. "Economic Value and Cost Are Subjective." *The Handbook of Austrian Economics*, Peter Boettke (editor), Cheltenham, UK: Edward Elgar Publishing.

Stringham, Edward P and Nicholas A. Snow. 2008. "The broken trailer fallacy: Seeing the unseen effects of government policies in post-Katrina New Orleans." *International Journal of Social Economics.* Vol. 35, No. 7, pp. 480–489; http://www.emeraldinsight.com/journals.htm?issn=0306–8293&volume=35&issue=7&articleid=1729156&show=html.   Accessed on 6–7–2015.

Suez. 2008. "Canal History," Suez Canal Authority, http://www.suezcanal.gov.eg/sc.aspx?show=8. Accessed on 5–4–2015.

Sullivan, Louis Henri. 1902. "Education," *Brickbuilder*, vol. 11, #6, p. 115.

The Sutter Butte Flood Control Agency. 2010. "Flood Aware/Flood Prepare," *The Appeal Democrat*, http://www.sutterbutteflood.org/downloads/2010updates/flood_aware_prepare.pdf. Accessed on 5–3–2015.

Suzuki, David and David McKibben. 2004. *The David Suzuki Reader: A Lifetime of Ideas from a Leading Activist and Thinker*. Greystone Books.

Suzuki, David and Ian Hanington. 2012. *Everything Under the Sun: Toward a Brighter Future on a Small Blue Planet*. Greystone Books.

Suzuki, David, Amanda McConnell and Adrienne Mason. 2007. *The Sacred Balance: Rediscovering Our Place in Nature*. Greystone Books.

Swaim, Barton. 2014. "The College Money Vortex." *Wall Street Journal*. March 14, p. A11. http://online.wsj.com/news/articles/SB10001424052702304250204579431002568739162. Accessed on 6–7–2015.

Tacitus. 98. *De vita et moribus Iulii Agricolae*, posted on the Latin Library by John W. Thomas, http://www.thelatinlibrary.com/tacitus/tac.agri.shtml. Accessed on 4–28–2015.

Tahoe, Lake. 2011. "Crowds flock to Lake Tahoe beaches," *Lake Tahoe News*, http://www.laketahoenews.net/2011/07/crowds-flock-to-lake-tahoe-beaches/.   Accessed   on 4–28–2015.

Tannehill, Morris and Linda Tannehill. [1970] 1984. *The Market for Liberty*, New York: Laissez Faire Books.

Tannehill Morris and Linda. 2001. "Arbitration of Disputes." July 1; http://mises.org/daily/5404. Accessed on 6–7–2015.

Taylor, Arthur J. 1975. *The Standards of Living in Great Britain*. Methuen.

Taylor, James Stacey. 2005. *Stakes and Kidneys Why Markets in Human Body Parts are Morally Imperative*. Ashgate Publishing.

Taylor, James Stacey. 2006. "Why the 'Black Market' Arguments Against Legalizing Organ Sales Fail." *Res Publica* 12 (2).

Taylor, James Stacey. 2007. "A 'Queen of Hearts' Trial of Organ Markets: Why Scheper-Hughes's Objections to Markets in Human Organs Fail." *Journal of Medical Ethics* 33 (4): 201–204.

Telecommunications Industry. Undated. "Working paper," Price College of Business, University of Oklahoma.

Terrell, Timothy D. 1999. "Property Rights and Externality: The Ethics of the Austrian School." *Journal of Markets and Morality*. Vol. 2, No. 2, Fall; http://www.marketsandmorality.com/index.php/mandm/article/view/626. Accessed on 6–9–2015.

The New York Times, Various dates. "Ali Abdullah Saleh," http://topics.nytimes.com/top/reference/timestopics/people/s/ali_abdullah_saleh/index.html. Accessed on 5–4–2015.

The Thoreau Institute. 1998. "Inside the Bureau of Land Management," *Different Drummer*, http://www.ti.org/blmintro.html#RTFToC1, Accessed on 4–14–2015

Thierer, Adam. 1992. *Judgement Day: The Case for Alternative Dispute Resolution*. Adam Smith Institute; http://www.adamsmith.org/wp-content/uploads/judgement-day.pdf. Accessed on 6–9–2015.

Thomas, Ellen. Undated. "Clathrates: little known components of the global carbon cycle," Wesleyan.edu, *Notes on paleoceanography (and various lectures)*, http://ethomas.web.wesleyan.edu/ees123/clathrate.htm. Accessed on 4–16–2015.

Thompson, Dixon. 2013. "Water for Sale? A look at the Complex Issue of Bulk Water Export," *Policy Horizons Canada*, October 28, http://www.horizons.gc.ca/eng/content/feature-article-%E2%80%93-water-sale-look-complex-issue-bulk-water-export.   Accessed   on 5–4–2015.

Thoreau, Henry David. 1854. *Walden or, Life in the Woods*; Internet Bookmobile, Library of America version; p.139; http://www.eldritchpress.org/walden5.pdf.   Accessed   on 4–17–2015.

Thoreau, Henry David. 1900. "The Fisher's Boy"; Stedman, Edmund Clarence; *An American Anthology, 1787–1900*; #301; Boston.

Thornton, Mark. 1999. "The Government's Great Flood." September, Volume 17, Number 9; https://bastiat.mises.org/library/governments-great-flood-0. Accessed on 6–7–2015.

Thornton, Mark. 2012. "Drugs: The Good, the Bad, and the Ugly." October 3; https://mises.org/library/drugs-good-bad-and-ugly. Accessed on 6–9–2015.

Times-Picayune. 2011. "1965: Hurricane Betsy smashes ashore near New Orleans," December 8,http://www.nola.com/175years/index.ssf/2011/12/1965_hurricane_betsy_smashes_a.html. Accessed on 5–3–2015.

Tinsley, Patrick. 1998–1999. "Private Police, A Note." *Journal of Libertarian Studies*, Vol. 14, No. 1, Winter, pp. 95–100; http://www.mises.org/journals/jls/14_1/14_1_5.pdf. Accessed on 6–7–2015.

Tomlinson, Charles. 2004. "The Myth of the Tree Shortage." September 24; http://mises.org/daily/1625/. Accessed on 6–7–2015.

Tucker, Jeffrey. 1989. "Book Review: The Theory Of Market Failure Edited by Tyler Cowen" *The Freeman: Ideas on Liberty,* Vol. 39 No. 7 July; http://www.thefreemanonline.org/columns/book-review-the-theory-of-market-failure-edited-by-tyler-cowen/. Accessed on 6–7–2015

Tucker, Jeffrey. 1998A. "Controversy: Are Antitrust Laws Immoral?" *Journal of Markets & Morality.* Vol. 1, No. 1, March, pp. 75–82; http://www.marketsandmorality.com/index.php/mandm/article/view/664. Accessed on 6–9–2015.

Tucker, Jeffrey. 1998B. "Controversy: Are Antitrust Laws Immoral? A Response to Kenneth G. Elzinga." *Journal of Markets & Morality.* Vol. 1, No. 1, March, pp. 90–94; http://www.marketsandmorality.com/index.php/mandm/article/view/666. Accessed on 6–9–2015.

Tucker, Jeffrey. 2008. "Rain, Rain, Go Away" February 26; https://mises.org/library/rain-rain-go-away. Accessed on 6–7–2015.

Tullock, Gordon. 1996. "Comment on 'Roads, Bridges, Sunlight and Private Property,'" by Walter E. Block and Matthew Block," *Journal des Economistes et des Etudes Humaines*, Vol. 7, No. 4, December, pp. 589–592.

Twain, Mark. 1883. *Life on the Mississippi,* Boston.

Twain, Mark. 1901. "Osteopathy," *Mark Twain's Speeches,* New York.

United Nations. Undated. "Oceans," http://www.un.org/en/sustainablefuture/oceans.asp. Accessed on 4–14–2015.

United Nations. 1982. "United Nations Convention on the Law of the Sea." http://www.un.org/Depts/los/convention_agreements/convention_overview_convention.htm; http://www.un.org/Depts/los/convention_agreements/texts/unclos/unclos_e.pdf. Accessed both on 6–7–2015.

US BOR, U.S. Department of the Interior, Bureau of Reclamation. 1987. *Design of Small Dams*; Third Edition.

US Corps of Engineers. 1992. *Reconnaissance Report, Yolo Bypass, California*; March.

US Corps of Engineers. 1999. *Sacramento and San Joaquin River Basins, California, Post-Flood Assessment for 1983, 1986, 1995, and 1997,* Chapter 2, March.

U.S. Fish and Wildlife Service. 2013. "CITES & Elephants: What is the 'global ban' on ivory trade?" November; http://www.fws.gov/le/pdf/CITES-and-Elephant-Conservation.pdf. Accessed on 6–7–2015.

US DOT FHA. 2014. "II. What Is Congestion Pricing?" Federal Highway Administration, July 31, http://ops.fhwa.dot.gov/publications/congestionpricing/sec2.htm. Accessed on 5–20–2015.

U.S. Submarine Structures, LLC. Undated. http://www.ussubstructures.com/h2o.html. Accessed on 4–17–2015.

Utt, Ronald D. 2005. *The Heritage Foundation*, "The Bridge to Nowhere: A National Embarrassment," http://www.heritage.org/research/reports/2005/10/the-bridge-to-nowhere-a-national-embarrassment. Accessed 4–29–2015.

Vance, Laurence M. 1996. "Friedman's Mistake." *The Free Market.* Vol. 14, No. 11. November; https://mises.org/library/friedmans-mistake. Accessed on 6–7–2015.

Vance, Laurence M. 2005. "The Curse of the Withholding Tax" April 21; http://mises.org/daily/1797. Accessed on 6–7–2015.

Vance, Laurence M. 2010. "Same Empire, Different Emperor." February 11; http://www.informationclearinghouse.info/article24648.htm. Accessed on 6–7–2015.

Vance, Laurence M. 2012. "My Antiwar Odyssey." August 22; http://www.lewrockwell.com/2012/08/laurence-m-vance/my-antiwar-odyssey/. Accessed on 5–18–2015.

Vining, Aidan R., and Anthony E. Boardman. 1992. "Ownership versus Competition: Efficiency in Public Enterprise." *Public Choice* 73: 205–39.

Voltaire. 2010. "The Prude Woman," http://fr.wikisource.org/wiki/La_B%C3%A9gueule. Accessed on 4–29–2015.

Vuk, Vedran. 2006A. "Journalism and Underwater Basket Weaving" June 21. https://www.lewrockwell.com/2006/06/vedran-vuk/journalism-and-underwater-basketweaving/. Accessed on 6–7–2015.

Vuk, Vedran. 2006B. "Socialist Man in the Big Easy." September 25; https://mises.org/library/socialist-man-big-easy. Accessed on 6–7–2015.

Vuk, Vedran. 2008. "Taking advantage of disaster: misrepresentation of housing shortage for political gain." *The International Journal of Social Economics*. Vol. 35, No. 8, pp. 603–614.

Walker, Douglas M. and John D. Jackson. 2008. "Market-based 'disaster relief': Katrina and the casino industry." *The International Journal of Social Economics*. Vol. 35, No.7, pp. 521–530.

Walras, Leon. 1874. Principe d'une theorie mathematique de l'echange. *Memoire lu a l'Academie des sciences morales et politiques* (Seances des 16 et 23 about 1873) Paris, Guillaumin.

Wapshott, Nicholas. 2012. "A Lovefest Between Milton Friedman and J.M. Keynes." July 30; http://www.thedailybeast.com/articles/2012/07/30/nicholas-wapshott-a-lovefest-between-milton-friedman-and-j-m-keynes.html. Accessed on 6–7–2015.

Ward, Alex. 2012. "Won't sell up? Enjoy living in the middle of a motorway! Road is built around a house after elderly Chinese couple refuse to move." November 22; http://www.dailymail.co.uk/news/article-2236746/Road-built-building-couple-refuse-China.html. Accessed on 6–7–2015.

Watner, Carl. 1982 "The Proprietary Theory of Justice in the Libertarian Tradition." *Journal of Libertarian Studies*. Vol. 6, No. 3–4, Summer/Fall, pp. 289–316; http://mises.org/journals/jls/6_3/6_3_6.pdf. Accessed on 6–7–2015.

Watson. Paul Joseph. 2014. "Harry Reid Calls Cliven Bundy Supporters 'Domestic Terrorists,'" *Infowars.com*, April 17, http://www.infowars.com/harry-reid-calls-cliven-bundy-supporters-domestic-terrorists/. Accessed on 5–11–2015.

Washington, Booker T. 1901. *Up from Slavery*, Chapter XI, as published in *The Outlook*, vol. 67, p. 121, Jan. 12.

Wenzel, Robert. 2012. "How Milton Friedman Helped Make the Case for Big Government." August 9; http://www.economicpolicyjournal.com/2012/08/how-milton-friedman-helped-make-case.html. Accessed on 6–7–2015.

Wenzel, Robert. 2013. "Robert Ringer's Strawman Anarchist." February 2; https://www.lewrockwell.com/2013/02/robert-wenzel/robert-ringers-strawmananarchist/. Accessed on 6–7–2015.

Westley, Christopher. 2002. "The Myth of Market Failure" June 14; http://www.mises.org/story/982. Accessed on 6–7–2015.

Westley, Christopher, Robert P. Murphy and William L. Anderson. 2008. "Institutions, incentives, and disaster relief: The case of the Federal Emergency Management Agency following Hurricane Katrina." *International Journal of Social Economics*. Vol. 35, No. 7, pp. 501–511; http://www.researchgate.net/publication/23648944_Institutions_incentives_and_disaster_relief_The_case_of_the_Federal_Emergency_Management_Agency_following_Hurricane_Katrina. Accessed on 6–9–2015.

What is CITES? http://www.cites.org/eng/disc/what.php; http://www.cites.org/. Accessed on 6–7–2015.

White, Lawrence H., 1978, "Privatization of municipally-provided services," *The Journal of Libertarian Studies*, Vol. 2, No. 2, Summer, pp. 187–197.

Whitehead, Roy and Walter E. Block. 2002. "Environmental Takings of Private Water Rights: the Case for Full Water Privatization," *Environmental Law Reporter*, October, pp. 11162–11176.

Whitehead, Roy, Catherine Gould and Walter E. Block. 2004. "The value of private water rights: from a legal and economic perspective," *Albany Law Environmental Outlook Journal*. Vol. 9, No. 2, pp. 315–343; http://heinonline.org/HOL/LandingPage?handle=hein. journals/alev9&div=15&id=&page=. Accessed on 6–9–2015.

Wilcke, Richard R. 1999. "An appropriate ethical model for business, and a critique of Milton Friedman," https://www.independent.org/pdf/tir/tir_09_2_2_wilcke.pdf. Accessed on 5–28–2015.

Wilder, Mark A. 2000. "Application of Salvage Law and the Law of Finds to Sunken Shipwreck Discoveries." *Defense Counsel Journal*, January; http://www.rms-republic.com/reference/Volume67No1Article6.pdf. Accessed on 6–7–2015.

Williams, Walter E. 1999. "Population control nonsense." *Jewish World Review*; Feb. 24; http://www.jewishworldreview.com/cols/williams022499.asp. Accessed on 6–7–2015.

Wittman, Donald. 2000. "The Wealth and Size of Nations." *Journal of Conflict Resolution*. Vol. 44, No. 6, pp. 868–884.

Wood, J. Stuart. 2008. "The finance of Katrina." *The International Journal of Social Economics*. Vol. 35, No. 8, pp. 579–589.

Woods, Thomas E. Jr. 2009A. "Krugman Failure, Not Market Failure" June 19; https://www.lewrockwell.com/2009/06/thomas-woods/krugman-failure-not-market-failure/. Accessed on 6–7–2015.

Woods, Thomas E. Jr. 2009B. "Response to the 'Market Failure' Drones" June 10; http://mises.org/story/3503. Accessed on 6–7–2015.

World Bank. 1979. "Yemen Arab Republic—Development of a traditional economy. A World Bank country study." Washington, D.C. http://documents.worldbank.org/curated/en/1979/01/828138/yemen-arab-republic-development-traditional-economy. Accessed 5–4–2015.

Worldatlas.com. Undated. http://www.worldatlas.com/aatlas/infopage/gulfofaden.htm, Accessed 5–4–2015.

World Wildlife Fund. 2013. "Whales." http://worldwildlife.org/species/whale. Accessed on 6–7–2015.

Worstal, Tim. 2013. "But Why Did Julian Simon Win The Paul Ehrlich Bet?" *Forbes*. January 13; http://www.forbes.com/sites/timworstall/2013/01/13/but-why-did-julian-simon-win-the-paul-ehrlich-bet/. Accessed on 6–7–2015.

WSDOT. 2015. "Toll Rates," Washington State Department of Transportation, http://www.wsdot.wa.gov/Tolling/TollRates.htm. Accessed on 5–20–2015.

Yablonski, Brian. 2007. "Bisonomics." *PERC Report*. Volume 25, No.3, Fall; http://perc.org/articles/bisonomics. Accessed on 6–7–2015.

Yates, Steven. 2002a. "Vouchers and Government Control." July 6; http://www.rense.com/general26/gvvt.htm. Accessed on 6–7–2015.

Yates, Steven. 2002b. "Refuting the voucherites." July 13; http://www.schoolandstate.org/Knowledge/Vouchers/MainVoucherPage.htm. Accessed on 6–7–2015.

YemenWeb.com. 2011. "Yemen—The Arabian Dream Where Wonders Never Cease—Ancient Yemen," http://www.yemenweb.com/History.htm. Accessed 5–4–2015.

Young, Adam. 2002. "Arbitration on Trial." July 17; https://mises.org/daily/1002/Arbitration-on-Trial. Accessed on 6–7–2015.

Young, Adam. 2004. "Organ Donations: Socialism or Laissez-Faire?" *Mises Daily*. January 07; http://mises.org/daily/1414. Accessed on 6–7–2015.

Young, Andrew T. 2008. "Replacing incomplete markets with a complete mess: Katrina and the NFIP." *The International Journal of Social Economics*. Vol. 35, No. 8, pp. 561–568.

Young, Andrew and Walter E. Block. 1999. "Enterprising Education: Doing Away with the Public School System," *International Journal of Value Based Management*, Vol.12, No. 3, pp. 195–207.

Yunker, James A. 1995. "Post-Lange Market Socialism: An Evaluation of Profit-Oriented Proposals." *Journal of Economic Issues*, September. http://www.wiu.edu/users/miecon/wiu/yunker/postlang.htm. Accessed on 6–7–2015.

Zetland, David. 2011. *The End of Abundance: Economic Solutions to Water Scarcity*. Mission Viejo, CA: Aguanomics Press.

Zheng, Pearl Q., Benjamin F. Hobbs and Joseph F. Koonce. 2012. "The Economics of Dam Decomminssioning for Ecosystem Restoration: Making Informed Decisions to Remove Aging U.S. Dams." in Gardner, B. Delworth and Randy T. Simmons, eds. 2012, pp. 1–15; *Aquanomics: Water Markets and the Environment*. New Brunswick, NJ: Transactions Publishers.

Zizka, Paul. 2015. "Frozen bubbles in Canadian lakes—in pictures," *The Guardian*, http://www.theguardian.com/world/gallery/2015/feb/02/frozen-bubbles-in-canadian-lakes-in-pictures. Accessed on 4–16–2015.

Index

Abelard, Peter, 21, 29n22, 233
Acton, John, 201, 233
ad coelum, 47n17, 62, 93n22, 98, 112n10, 173, 174, 238
Adams, John Quincy, 168n90
Adie, Douglas, 19n4, 165n42, 233
Aden: City, 250; Gulf of, x, 157, 159, 161, 162, 168n83, 245, 252
Admiralty, 49, 50, 51, 52, 53n4, 233
affirmative action, 216
agrarian reform, 239
agriculture, 23, 50, 167n64, 237, 261
Ahart, John, 125, 233
Ahlbrandt, Roger, 19n4, 165n42, 233
Alaska, 12n5, 84, 104n10
Albright, Logan, 53n7, 233
Alcock, James, 168n86, 233
Alexander, Jeff, 155, 233
Alexander the Great, 12n3
Allen, Robert C., 28n8, 111n1, 233
Allen, Woody, 286
alluvial fan, 94n36
Almadhagi, Ahmed Noman, 168n86, 234
Al-Qaeda, 124
Al-Shabab, 169n104
Alston, Wilton D., 19n4, 165n42, 234
Alvarez, Lisette, 131, 134, 234
Amato, David S., 46n5, 234
American Arbitration Association, 22
American Indians, 155
American Stock Exchange, 22

anarchism, anarcho-capitalism, xiii, 2, 15, 169n95, 198, 234, 238, 239, 241, 243, 249, 251, 253, 254, 256, 257, 259, 260, 262, 263, 266
Anderson, Andrew, 51, 53n6, 234
Anderson, David, 154
Anderson, Martin, 230n34, 234
Anderson, Terry, 18n2–19n4, 28n3, 46n10, 80, 111n1, 120n3–120n4, 165n42, 198n1, 202, 223, 225, 230n32, 234
Anderson, William L., 92n4, 228n9, 229n30, 230n39, 234, 266
Andrus Island, 165n32
anglers, 66, 255
Antarctica, 3
antitrust, 225, 232n61, 234, 235, 240, 244, 249, 254, 263, 265
The Appeal Democrat, 264
aquanomics, 246, 247, 262
aquasocialism, 7, 14n27, 148
aquifer, 1, 6–8, 11, 14n34–14n35, 35n7, 60, 105, 106, 107–110, 110, 111, 112n2–112n8, 113n14, 113n18, 149, 149–150, 150, 151–152, 153, 166n56, 182, 182–183, 202, 245
Aquinas, Thomas, 2, 12n4, 234
Arab, 159, 267
Arabian Peninsula, 66, 159, 235, 257
Arboga, California, 165n32
Aristotle, 2, 235
Arizona, 40

Arkansas, 87, 193, 199n5, 200n16, 235, 245, 285
Arkansas Game and Fish Association, 200n16, 235, 245
Armentano, Dominick T., 229n30, 235
Arnold, N. Scott, 13n21, 235, 247
artesian, 11, 14n34, 106–109, 112n3, 112n5
Ashton, Thomas Southcliffe, 228n7, 235, 248
Associated Press, 64, 235
Atlantic Ocean, 61, 176
Atlas Shrugged, 47n18, 258
atmospheric, 14n36, 60, 256
Augustine, St., 2, 12n3, 235
Austrian economics, xiii, 63, 198, 235, 237, 238, 240, 243, 244, 247, 249, 250, 253, 255, 257, 262, 263, 286

Badnarik, Michael, 28n3, 46n10, 255
Bailey, Ronald, 13n22, 235
Bakersfield, California, ix, 150, 166n56
Baltistan, 53n1
Bardhan, Pranab, 13n21, 259
Barnett, Andy H., 228n9, 234, 235
Barnett, William, 13n21, 45, 63, 72n24, 72n28, 93n13, 198n1, 229n30, 230n39, 230n44, 231n54, 232n59, 235
barnyardization, 6
Barre, Mohamed Siad, 159, 250
Barrowman, Nicholas J., 255
Bartosek, Karel, 243
Baton Rouge, Louisiana, 256
Bauch, Herbert, 154, 235
Bauer, Peter, 13n13, 235
Beard, Thomas Randolph, 228n9, 236
Becker, Gary S., 229n28, 229n31, 236, 263
Beijing, China, 42–43
Bell, Rogers, 236
Belov, Fëdor, 28n8, 111n1, 236
Benjamin, Daniel, 111n1, 120n4, 236
Bennett, Harve, 256
Bennett, James T., 19n4, 165n42, 236
Benson, Bruce L., 18n2–19n3, 28n3, 46n10, 62, 94n30, 198n1, 236
Berg, Maxine, 228n7, 236
Bering Sea, 119
Berman, Harold J., 28n4, 198n1, 236
Berzon, Alexandra, 147, 236

Bethell, Tom, 237
Better Business Bureau, 22
Birdzell, L.E., 228n7, 259
Blair, Roger D., 19n4, 236
Block, Matthew, 46n8, 47n17, 47n21, 94n30, 104n5, 239, 265
Blockean Proviso, 73, 73n37
Blundell, John, 168n81, 240
Bly, Thomas R., 199n5, 240
Boardman, Anthony E., 19n4, 165n42, 240, 266
Bohai Sea, 94n36
Borcherding, Thomas, 19n4, 165n42, 240
Bortolotti, Bernardo, 19n4, 245
Bosphorus, 72n18, 254
Boston, Massachusetts, 117, 240, 242, 247, 249, 265
Boudreaux, Don, 13n13, 229n30, 238, 240
Boxer Rebellion, 94n36
Bradford, William, 28n9, 37, 240
Bradley J., Robert, 13n21, 240
Brandly, Mark, 167n75, 240
Branfman, Fred, 228n7, 240
Brannon Island, 165n32
Brewer, Charlie, 200n16, 240
Britain (Great Britain, Also see England), 94n36, 125, 126, 159, 160, 168n90, 169n103, 243, 246, 264
Brouhard, Rod, 148, 240
Brown, Lester T., 13n13, 240
Brown, Pamela J., 167n75, 240
Bruce, Lenny., 286
Buchanan, James, 72n24, 229n22, 238, 240–241, 244, 261
Buena Vista Lake, 166n56
bulk mail, 241
Bull, Brian, 101, 241
Bundy, Cliven, 40, 206, 250, 256, 266
Bunkerville, Nevada, 40
Butler, Samuel, 171, 241
Butler, Stuart M., 19n4, 165n42, 241, 255
Butos, William, 72n24, 241
Bylund, Per, 12n9, 46n7, 241

Cache la Poudre River, 94n24
California, ix, 139–140, 141, 142, 144, 147, 149, 150, 151, 152, 153, 166n58, 167n62, 167n64, 176, 179, 202, 222, 234, 237, 244, 245, 246, 247, 251, 252,

254, 258, 259, 261, 263, 265, 286
California Farm Bureau, 166n53, 241
Callahan, Gene, 229n31, 230n39, 241
Cambridge, Massachusetts, 235, 243, 245, 248, 249
Cambridge, UK, 239, 246, 257, 258
Camp Lemonnier, 160
Campbell, Bruce, 154, 241
Campbell, Kate, 149, 241
Canada, 42, 154–156, 167n71–167n73, 167n77, 168n85, 236, 237, 241, 245, 247, 255, 261, 262
Canadian Postal Service, 233
capitalism, 7, 13n21, 26, 89, 201–203, 209, 211, 217, 228n8, 230n40, 244, 246, 248, 255, 262
Caplan, Bryan, 145, 237, 238, 241
Carbonneau, Thomas E., 236
Carden, Art, 92n4, 241
Carey, Douglas, 228n9, 241
Cargill, 101, 252
Caribbean, 123, 127
Carquinez Strait, 150, 151, 165n29, 166n56
Carroll, Bruce, 124, 241
Cascade Mountains, 13n19
Casey, Doug, 18n2–19n3, 46n10, 120n3, 241
Casey, Gerard, 28n3, 46n10, 241
Casselman, Anne, 7, 241
Cato Institute, 233, 234, 245, 249, 252, 254, 255, 261, 263
Cefaratti, Todd, 124, 241
Central Intelligence Agency,. *See* CIA
Central Park, 148
Central Valley of California, 140, 144, 147, 149–151, 153, 166n56, 167n62, 245, 246
Cervantes, Miguel, 149, 242
Chamberlin, William Henry, 46n3, 242
Chambers, Mark, 142, 242
Chamlee-Wright, Emily, 92n4, 242
Chandler, Stacy, 228n9, 239
Chapman, John L., 19n4, 165n42, 242
Cherry, Mark J., 228n9, 242
Charleston, West Virginia, 147
China, 21–22, 24, 42, 94n30, 94n36, 127, 158, 229n16, 253
chordata, 202, 228n4

CIA (Central Intelligence Agency), 160, 168n86, 168n91, 169n100, 242
Cicero, 12n3
CITES (Convention on International Trade of Endangered Species of Wild Fauna and Flora), 115–116, 116, 120n1, 242, 265, 266
City of God, 2, 12n3, 235
City of Pasadena v. City of Alhambra, 150, 257
civil government, 253
civil society, 242
Clarkson, Kenneth W., 19n4, 242
Clay, Megan, 228n9, 242
Clemens, Samuel,. *See* Twain, Mark
Cleveland, Ohio, 101
Coase, Ronald, 72n27–72n28, 184, 212–235, 238, 242
Coast Range, 150, 165n29
Colander, David C., 13n22, 242
Coleman, John, 31, 242
collectivism, 46n3, 242
Colorado Department of Natural Resources,, 35n7, 242
Colorado, 35n7, 135, 164n11, 286
Colusa Basin, 165n27
Commoner, Barry, 13n13, 242
commons, tragedy of, 7, 8, 13n12, 14n26, 18, 19n7, 21, 22, 23, 35, 39, 56, 62, 76, 109, 111n1, 115–116, 150, 153, 163, 169n107, 181, 224, 230n36, 248, 263
communism: Black Book of, 243; Party, 13n21
competition, 24, 25, 26, 149, 159, 213, 227n1, 229n27, 234, 235, 236, 244, 266
competitive advantage, 17, 98
Conquest, Robert, 228n7, 242
Conrad, Joseph, 49, 242
conservation, 112n2, 166n53, 219, 220, 224, 227, 231n48, 237
Conservation Fund, 40
continuum, 44, 45, 94n35, 113n15, 172, 239
Convention on International Trade of Endangered Species of Wild Fauna and Flora,. *See* CITES
Cook, R. M., 7, 242
Cordato, Roy E., 14n26, 72n24, 230n44, 242–243

Correa, Enrique, 101, 243
Costea, Diana, 229n30, 243
Cosumnes River, 165n32
Courier News, 200n16, 243
Courtois, Stephane, 228n7, 243
Cowen, Tyler, 92n4, 230n39, 232n59, 243, 265
Crafts, N. F. R., 228n7, 243
Crain, W. Mark, 19n4, 243
crony capitalism, 46n5, 164n15, 211, 230n40
Cuba, 22, 160, 229n16
Culpepper, Dreda, 92n4, 243
Culp-Ressler, Tara, 210, 243
culture of violence, 244
Cuyahoga River fire, 261

dam, 77, 81, 89, 141, 143, 144–145, 146, 165n31, 167n64, 221, 252, 265, 268
D'Aliesio, Renata, 167n72, 243
Dalrymple, Jim, 124, 243
Dalsan Radio (Mogadishu), 168n91, 243
D'Amico, Daniel J., 92n4, 243
Dasser, Felix J., 28n4, 198n1, 236
Daugherty, Robert L., 71n14, 243
Davidson, Mana, 228n9, 239
Davies, David G., 19n4, 165n42, 243
Deacon, Robert, 202, 224–227, 244
De Alessi, Louis, 19n4, 165n42, 243
Deane, Phyllis, 228n7, 244
Defending the Undefendable, 200n27, 236, 239, 285
De Jasay, Anthony, 232n59, 243
de Jouvenel, B., 248
Delamere, Henry, 141
Delta Crisis, 152, 244
Delta-Mendota Canal, 151
democracy, 228n8, 241, 253, 262
Denmark, 47n13
Department of Defense, 47n15, 244
Department of Water Resources (California), 259, 261
Dewenter, Kathrin, 19n4, 165n42, 244
de Wolf, Aschwin, 198n1, 243
DiLorenzo, Thomas J., 18n2, 19n3, 19n4, 28n3, 46n4, 46n10, 72n24, 111n1, 120n4, 198n1, 228n7, 229n22, 229n30, 230n39, 234, 236, 239, 240, 244
Dirmeyer, Jennifer, 92n4, 244

disaster relief, 77, 89, 142, 266
Disney, Walt, 199n12, 244
Djibouti, Republic of, 160
dollar vote, 27, 145, 166n43, 209
Doane, Charles, 53n6, 245
Donahue, Phil, 31, 246
double coincidence of wants, 117, 252
drawdown cone, 11, 14n35, 107, 112n7, 150, 151, 243
Dr. Strangelove, 44, 245
drug approval, 251
D'Souza, Juliet D., 19n4, 245
Dubai, 72n32
Dutton, Judy, 168n82, 245

Earth, 3, 3–4, 5, 7, 12n3, 13n13, 13n18, 21, 22, 39, 49, 53, 53n8, 55, 58, 61–62, 63, 68, 71n9–71n10, 71n14, 97, 102, 112n9–112n11, 120, 149, 155, 163n4, 167n77, 173, 192, 195, 199n10, 206, 246, 247, 254
East India Company, 128
Eastwood, Clint, 149
Easy Rider, 253
Eatwell, J., 248
Ebeling, Richard, 46n4, 245
Eberstadt, Nicholas, 28n8, 111n1, 245
Ecclesiastes, 154, 167n69
ecology, 171, 247
economic history, 246, 256, 258
economics, xiii, 5, 12n5, 15, 28n19, 63, 82–83, 93n11, 103, 171, 198, 206, 210, 212, 213, 215, 221, 227n1, 229n24, 234, 285–286, 286
Economics in One Lesson, 248, 285
Edelstein, Michael R., 46n7, 73n37, 239
Edinburgh, Scotland, 24
educational vouchers, 256
efficiency, 17, 127, 128, 194, 213–214, 233, 240, 243, 249, 259, 260
Ehrlich, Anne, 13n13, 13n22, 245, 261, 267
Ehrlich, Paul, 13n13, 13n22, 245, 261, 267
Elk River, 147, 148
emergent vegetation, 14n30, 35n5, 181
eminent domain, 77, 89, 90, 93n5, 94n30, 236, 239, 245, 256, 257, 263
Encyclopædia Britannica, 245

endangered species, 7, 115, 116, 217, 252, 261
England, 46n10, 51, 117, 159, 174, 202, 245, 248, 254
England, Randy, 46n10, 245
enterprise, 127, 129, 139, 144–145, 147–148, 148, 162, 163n6, 165n23, 166n50, 201, 204, 207, 208, 209, 210, 211–212
environment, 1, 7, 24, 27, 34, 40, 56, 167n72, 201, 202, 223, 234, 237
Environment Canada, 245
Ephesus, Turkey, 29n21, 157, 245
Epstein, Richard, 46n7, 46n8, 71n6, 93n5, 94n30, 164n19, 239, 245
Eritrea, x, 246
estuary, 133, 151–152, 163n1, 192
ethics, 16, 21, 38, 238, 239, 246, 249, 255, 259, 261, 264
Ethiopia, 120n7, 160, 235, 258
Everglades, 131, 132, 134, 136, 137, 138
exceedance, 92, 95n39
externalities, 214, 230n44, 237, 238, 242, 249, 252, 261
Exxon Valdez Oil Spill Trustee Council, 71n17, 245

Fallingwater, 144, 165n39, 245
Fannie Mae, 17, 111
Fantini, Marcella, 19n4, 245
fascism, 211, 217, 230n40, 234
Faunt, Claudia C., 150, 151, 245
FBI (Federal Bureau of Investigation), 168n90, 245
Feather River, 140, 141, 165n25, 165n32
Federal Bureau of Investigation, See FBI
Federal land ownership, 247, 255
Federal Maritime Commission, 255
FEMA (Federal Emergency Management Agency), 165n38, 245, 248, 256
Fenech, Amy S., 199n5, 245
Feshbach, Murray, 28n8, 111n1, 245
Finland, 47n12
Finn, Ed, 241
fish stocks, 7, 83, 204, 205, 223, 225, 255, 259
Fitzgerald, Randall, 19n4, 165n42, 245
FitzGibbon, J. E., 237
Fleischer, Michael, 239

Fletcher, Charles R., 135, 246
flood insurance, 138, 139, 141, 141–142
floodplain, 79, 81, 91, 139, 142, 144, 147, 251
Florida, xi, 131, 132, 133, 135, 142, 164n8, 176, 179, 234, 246, 262
Floud, Roderick, 228n7, 246
Foldvary, Fred E., 129n6, 246
Frech III, H.E., 19n4, 165n42, 246
Freedom Industries, 147, 148, 166n48
French, Doug, 111n1, 120n3, 246
French Frigate Sholes, 5, 256
Friedman, David, 13n13, 246
Friedman, Milton, 13n20, 13n21, 28n13, 31, 92n2, 93n12, 93n16, 164n15, 237, 238, 239, 246, 251, 253, 256, 260, 265, 266, 267
Friendly, Jr., Alfred, 28n8, 111n1, 245
future of liberty, 248

Gaia, Vince, 7, 246
Galles, Gary, 46n4, 246
Galloway, Devin, 151, 166n52, 167n62, 246
Gardner, B. Delworth, 202, 215, 216, 218, 219, 220, 220–221, 231n50, 246, 247, 262, 268
Garner, Richard, 228n9, 246
Garone, Phillip, 140, 246
Garrison, Roger, 72n24, 246
Gates, Bill, 209
gauging supply, 220
GDP (Gross Domestic Product), 8, 22, 28n5
Gedab News, 159, 246
General Land Office (now part of the BLM), 46n9
Genesis, Book of, 16, 108, 112n11
The Geography Site, 93n19, 247
Gillham, R.W., 237
Ginsberg, Paul B., 19n4, 236
Global Positioning System,. *See* GPS
gold, 112n11, 140, 177, 179, 180, 185, 188, 190, 227n1, 237
Goodhue, Rachel E., 202, 222, 247
Goodman, John C., 229n28, 247
Goodnight, Charles, 72n32
Goodwin, Stefan, 168n91, 247
Google Images, 28n10, 247

Gorbachev, Mikhail, 168n78
Gordon, David, 13n21, 231n54, 247
Gordon, Peter, 238
Gore, Al, 13n13, 247
Gorte, Ross W., 28n6, 247
Goto, Miki., 71n17, 247
Gottlieb, Scott, 229n28, 247
Gould, Catherine, 230n32, 267
government, 10, 12n5, 12n6, 15, 16–18,
    18n2, 22, 24, 25, 27, 28n3, 28n6,
    28n19, 40, 55, 60, 70, 73n37, 76, 78,
    82, 92n2, 97, 100, 101, 105, 111, 115,
    118, 119, 124, 125, 126, 127, 128, 129,
    129n5, 129n7, 129n11, 139, 143, 144,
    146, 147, 148, 149, 152, 153, 154, 155,
    156, 157, 159, 160, 161, 163n6,
    165n42, 166n50, 168n82, 169n95, 182,
    184, 192, 202, 204, 206, 206–207, 207,
    210, 211, 213, 214, 217, 218–219, 220,
    224, 228n8, 229n21, 230n40, 230n46,
    231n48, 231n57
GPS (Global Positioning System), 56, 65,
    65–66, 71n2, 71n4, 73n35
Grant, James, 247
Grant, Joe, 244
Great Britain,. *See* Britain.
Greenland (Denmark), 47n13
Greenpeace, 72n29, 115, 118, 119, 120,
    247
Greenspan, Allan, 237
Gregory, Anthony, 18n2, 19n3, 28n3,
    46n10, 94n30, 247
Grigg, William Norman, 229n21, 247
Grizzle, John, 253
Gross Domestic Product, See GDP
Grossman, Gregory, 28n8, 111n1, 247
Grotius, Hugo, 12n9, 46n7, 72n29, 247
groundwater, 11, 14n33, 60, 106, 107,
    108–109, 111, 149, 150, 151, 153,
    167n63, 241, 245
The Guardian, 42, 247, 268
Guillory, Gil, 18n2–19n3, 28n3, 46n10,
    198n1, 230n39, 248
Gulf Coast (of the Gulf of Mexico), 147,
    258
Gulf of Farallones, ix, 151, 152
Gulf of Mexico, viii, 41, 188, 192, 195
Gunning, J. Patrick, 72n24, 248

Hanington, Ian, 13n13, 264
Hanke, Steve, 19n4, 165n42, 248
Hannesson, Rögnvaldur, 201, 202–203,
    204–206, 207, 208, 223, 228n8–228n9,
    229n16, 229n18, 229n20, 230n32, 248
Hanscom, Gregg, 143, 248
Hanseatic League, 51
Hardin, Garrett, 248
Hanson, Laura, 247
Hanson, Laura A., 247
Hanson, Stephanie, 168n91, 248
Hartwell, Ronald M., 248
Hasegawa, Kyoko, 248
Hasnas, John, 248
Hawkins, John, 248
Hardy Vincent, Carol, 247
Hassan, Sheikh Mohamud, 169n104
Hawaii, 5, 256
Hayek, Friedrich A., 72n24, 129n11, 172,
    214, 215, 228n7, 237, 241, 246, 248,
    286
Hazlitt, Henry, 17, 145, 213, 248, 285
Healy, Kieran, 168n81, 228n9, 248
Heaton, Tony,– 40
Heinrich, David J., 18n2–19n3, 28n3,
    46n10, 248
Henderson, David R., 229n30, 249
Henninger, Daniel, 229n28, 249
Herbener, Jeffrey M., 231n54, 249
Heraclitus of Ephesus, 157, 249
herd mentality, 263
Higgs, Robert, 18n2–19n3, 28n3, 46n10,
    198n1, 229n28, 230n39, 249
High, Jack, 229n30, 244, 249
Hill, Peter J., 18n2, 19n4, 28n3, 46n10, 80,
    111n1, 120n3–120n4, 165n42, 198n1,
    230n32, 234
Hipke, Deana C., 72n25, 249
Hippen, Benjamin E., 228n9, 249
Hobbs, Benjamin F., 268
Holcombe, Randall, 232n59, 238, 239, 249
Hood, Grace, 113n17, 249
Hoover Dike, 131, 133–134, 136, 137, 138,
    139
Hoppe, Hans-Hermann, 12n9, 18n2, 19n3,
    28n3, 46n7, 46n10, 93n13, 94n29,
    129n11, 164n19, 165n36, 198n1,
    229n28, 230n39, 230n44, 232n59, 238,
    239, 249–250, 262

Horn of Africa, 160
Horton, Joseph, 167n75, 239
Houthi, 246
Hudik, Marek, 93n13, 250
Huebert, Jacob, 18n2–19n3, 28n3, 46n10, 53n7, 62, 250
Hudson, Pat, 228n7, 235
Hugo, Victor, 37, 250
Hülsmann, Jörg Guido, 93n13, 250
Human Action, 254
human life, 133, 258
human tissue, 240
Humboldt River, 71n16
Hummel, Jeffrey, 232n59, 250
humpback whales, 261
hurricane, 22, 24, 132, 142, 144, 163n2, 242
Hurricane Betsy, 142, 265
Hurricane Carla, 142
Hurricane Ivan, 238
Hurricane Katrina, 77, 142, 164n8, 234, 238, 239, 241, 242, 243, 244, 253, 254, 255, 259, 263, 266, 267
Hurricane Severity Index, 142, 163n2, 242, 250
Hutchings, Jeffrey A., 255
Hutt, W. H., 248
hydraulic conductivity, 107, 112n5
hydraulic grade line, 14n34, 109, 112n3
hydraulic mining, 140

Ibsen, Henrik Johan, 167n74, 229n19, 250
Idaho, 67
Idrsids, 159
Ikehara, Marti E., 250
Illinois, 193
Imperial War Meµseums,. *See* IWM.
Indian Ocean, 159, 187
IndieGoGo, 28n10, 250
indifference, 82, 238, 239, 249, 250, 253, 257
Individual Transferable Quotas,. *See* ITQs
industrial revolution, 202, 203, 228n7, 233, 235, 243, 244, 248
Ingebritsen S.E., 167n64, 250
injustice, 137, 139, 164n18, 228n7
Inland Sea,. *See* Seto
An Inquiry into the Nature and Causes of the Wealth of Nations, See *The Wealth*

of Nations
Inquisitir, 250
insurance, 44, 50, 68, 81, 88, 138, 139, 141, 142, 143, 144, 147, 165n36, 192, 211, 234, 245, 248, 250, 251, 256
International-Convention-on-Salvage,. *See* salvage.
International Maritime Organization, 250
International Seabed Authority, 72n20, 250
The International Tanker Owners Pollution Federation Limited,. *See* ITOPF
intolerance, 238, 251
in toto,. *See* ownership concepts for water bodies
Iona, 29n21
Ionia,. *See* Iona
Iowa, 50, 193
Iran, 24, 249
ISIL, ISIS (Islamic State of Iraq and the Levant), 124, 241, 243
Italian, 132, 159, 169n103
ITOPF (The International Tanker Owners Pollution Federation Limited), 7, 250
ITQs (Individual Transferable Quotas), 5, 6, 71n5, 83, 93n16, 202, 204, 205, 207, 215, 224, 225, 226, 228n9
ivory, 177, 252, 263, 265
IWM (Imperial War Meuseums), 168n86, 250

Jackson, John D., 236, 266
Jackson Plan, 141
James, George, 168n91, 250
Jankovic, Ivan, 14n26, 111n1, 251
Japan, 21, 22, 47n14, 117, 121n10, 158, 168n85, 248
Jevons, William Stanley, 28n7, 251
Johansen, David, 155, 167n72, 251
Johnson, Clint, 228n9, 239
Johnson, George Clayton, 28n14
Johnson, Jay, 230n32, 255
Johnson, Manuel H., 19n4, 165n42, 236
Johnson, Paul, 228n7, 246
Johnsson, Richard C.B., 167n75, 251
Jones, John Paul, 115, 118, 251
JSOC (Joint Special Operations Command), 160
Juan de Fuca Plate, 13n19, 242

justice, 12n3, 118, 164n18, 165n24, 236, 239, 245, 248, 260, 266

Kaitin, K. I., 251
Kaplan, Eben, 248
Kaserman, D. L., 228n9, 236, 251
Kazman, Sam, 229n28, 251
Kelo, Susette, et al. v. City of New London, Connecticut, et al., 94n30, 238, 245, 251
Kentucky, 88, 142, 251
Kenya, 160, 258
Kern "Lake," ix, 166n56
Keynes, John Maynard, 172, 241, 266
King, Seth, 18n2, 19n3, 28n3, 46n10, 198n1, 251
Kinsella, Stephan, 12n9, 13n21, 18n2, 19n3, 28n3, 39, 46n7, 46n10, 51, 52, 53n6, 71n6, 73n37, 94n30, 164n19, 198n1, 232n60, 251, 252
Kipling, Rudyard, 120n6
Kirzner, Israel, 72n24, 252
Kjar, Scott A., 92n4, 234, 258
Klein, Daniel B., 229n28, 252
Klein, Peter G., 116, 129n11, 226, 252
Knights Landing, California, ix, 140
Koonce, Joseph F., 268
Korea, 3, 21, 22, 47n14, 229n16
Kreuter, Urs P., 111n1, 120n3, 252, 263
Krouse, Peter, 101, 252
Krueger, Ann O., 229n22, 252

Laband, David N., 225, 252
LaGrone, Sam, 158, 252
laissez faire, 26, 89, 201, 203, 209, 215, 217, 218, 227, 246, 267
Lake Conway, 183, 189, 199n5, 240, 245
Lake Erie, 11, 101, 241, 243, 252
Lake Michigan, 155
Lake Okeechobee, 131, 132, 133, 134, 137, 139, 234, 262
Lake Overcup, 235, 240, 255
Lake Pontchartrain, 187, 188, 189, 192, 194, 196
Lake Tahoe, 7, 264
land reform, 239
Landsburg, Steven, 167n75, 252
Lantis, David, 251
Lasagna, Louis, 251

law, 2, 6, 7, 8, 12n3, 12n4, 12n6, 15, 17, 35n7, 40, 44, 45, 47n20, 49, 50, 51, 52, 53n4, 53n6, 57, 58, 63, 70, 71n14, 73n37, 83, 84, 89, 91, 93n5, 93n8, 113n16, 117, 134, 135, 136, 143, 173, 174, 178, 182, 204, 212, 225, 233, 234, 236, 238, 239, 240, 242, 243, 244, 245, 247, 248, 250, 251, 252, 253, 254, 255, 256, 257, 258, 259, 260, 261, 263, 265, 267
Law of Salvage,. *See* salvage
Law of the Sea, 8, 49, 51, 53n6, 58, 117, 204, 252, 265
Laws of Oleron, 51
Leal, Donald, 14n26, 202, 223, 234, 248, 252
lebensraum, 124
Leclerc, René, 140, 252
Lee, Dwight, 237
Leeson, Peter T., 129n1, 168n85, 252
Leo XIII, Pope, 75
letter of mark and reprisal, 126
levees, 79, 81, 94n36, 131, 133, 141, 142, 143, 144, 145, 146, 167n64, 234, 252
Levin, John-Clark, 257
Levin, Michael, 228n7, 252
Lewin, Peter, 164n19, 230n44, 252
liability, 9, 56, 57, 68, 85, 88, 92, 136, 138, 145, 164n19, 245, 249, 251, 252, 259
libertarian, xiii, xiv, 10, 16, 28n17, 29n22, 33, 39, 40, 43, 44, 45, 47n12, 47n16, 50, 52, 53n7, 62, 63, 64, 67, 68, 69, 73n37, 80, 81, 83, 88, 89, 90, 94n29, 94n30, 102, 103, 113n15, 113n16, 124, 125, 126, 128, 129n2, 139, 143, 144, 148, 152, 162, 164n19, 165n36, 178, 185, 197, 198, 201, 208, 214, 217, 219, 228n2, 229n22, 232n60, 233, 234, 236, 237, 238, 239, 240, 241, 244, 246, 248, 249, 250, 251, 253, 254, 257, 258, 259, 260, 265, 266, 285, 286
liberty, 6, 24, 149, 237, 239, 240, 248, 249, 251, 253, 254, 260, 261, 262, 263, 264, 265, 285
limited government, 50, 251, 257
Lind, Michael, 13n21, 253
Linda, California, 165n32
Lindsay, Cotton M., 19n4, 165n42, 253
Lipka, Lawrence J., 53n6, 253

Locke, John, 2, 8, 12n9, 38, 39, 46n7, 49, 253
Lockean proviso, 39, 73n37, 251, 253
Loess Plateau, 94n36
Lombardo, Gary A., 50, 253, 255
London, 125, 233, 236, 242, 245, 247, 248, 249, 251, 253, 258, 259, 261, 262, 263
Long Range Navigation,. *See* LORAN
Long, Roderick, 18n2, 19n3, 28n3, 46n10, 73n37, 198n1, 238, 253
Lora, Manuel, 92n4, 111n1, 120n3, 253
LORAN (Long Range Navigation), 56, 65, 66, 71n3
Louisiana, 142, 164n8, 186, 193, 194
Lovley, Erika, 129n6, 253
Lower 9th Ward (New Orleans), 166n46

Maceina, Mike, 14n25, 253
Machan, Tibor, 13n21, 39, 238, 253, 260
Machaj, Mateusz, 13n21, 93n13, 238, 253
Mackenzie, Doug W., 229n22, 230n39, 253
Madison, James, 126
Madwin, Gayle, 141, 253
Maher, Kris, 236
Malakoff Diggins State Historic Park, 140
Malakunas, Karl, 42, 253
Malatesta, Paul H., 19n4, 165n42, 244
Malcolm, Norman, 46n1, 253
Malek, Ninos P., 111n1, 120n4, 228n9, 253, 254
Malthus, Thomas, 13n13, 13n22, 261
Maltsev, Yuri, 46n3, 254
management, 40, 67, 76, 138, 139, 163n6, 207, 209, 216, 226, 234, 239, 240, 241, 242, 244, 245, 262
manganese nodules, 62, 64, 69, 72n20
Manhattan, NY, 24, 112n10
Marcus, B. K., 28n4, 62, 198n1, 254
Margolin, Jean Louis, 243
marine assets, 202, 224, 244
Marine Insight, 258
maritime industry, 255
Maritime Security, 72n18, 254, 257
market failure, 82, 216, 226, 230n39, 230n44, 235, 241, 243, 244, 253, 260, 265, 266, 267
market socialism, 13n21, 235, 240, 247, 253, 255, 257, 259, 267

markets, 5, 17, 119, 168n81, 171, 201, 202, 204, 209, 210, 213, 215, 216, 217, 228n9, 230n45, 234, 237, 239, 244, 246, 247, 251, 262, 263, 264, 265, 267, 268
Mars, 53, 60, 104n10, 146, 167n75, 221
Marx, Karl, 168n78
Marysville, California, 140, 141, 286
Mason, Adrienne, 264
Massachusetts, 24, 240, 245
Maybury, Richard J., 46n4, 254
McChesney, Fred, 13n21, 229n30, 254
McClendon, Russell, 7, 254
McCloskey, Donald, 228n7, 238, 246
McConkey, Michael, 18n2, 19n3, 28n3, 46n10, 254
McConnell, Amanda, 13n13, 264
McDonnell, Lawrence, 166n56, 254
McGee, John S., 229n30, 254
McGee, Robert, 13n20, 13n21, 92n4, 93n15, 254
McKendrick, Neil, 228n7, 254
McKenzie, Richard B., 254
McKibben, David, 13n13, 264
McTigue, Maurice, 93n17, 254
Mediterranean Sea, 123, 158
Megginson, William L., 19n4, 165n42, 245, 254
Menger, Carl, xiii, 28n7, 117, 254
Mercatus Center, 242, 254
Mercer, Ilana, 234
Messynessychic.com, 29n21, 254
methane clathrate, 62, 64, 72n21
Mexico: City, 209; United States of, 209
Miami, Florida, 132
Microsoft, 234
migration, 6, 62, 86, 205, 228n13
Milgate, M., 248
Miller, Murray H., 237
Miller, Terry, 259
minarchism, 238
Minnesota, 186, 193, 194, 243
Mises Institute, Ludwig von, 233, 235, 236, 237, 238, 248, 249, 254, 255, 260, 261, 262, 263, 285
Mises, Ludwig von, xiii, 46n3, 72n24, 82, 86, 94n28, 120, 215, 228n7, 229n25, 248

Mississippi River, viii, 5, 41, 59, 77, 87, 88, 105, 140, 142, 147, 177, 183, 186, 187, 191, 192, 193, 194, 195, 196, 197, 229n21, 241, 265

Missouri: River, viii; state, 88, 193

Missouri Pacific Historical Society, 199n4, 254

Mogadishu, Somalia, 160, 161, 169n104, 243

Moloney, David, 229n20, 255

Molyneux, Stefan, 18n2, 19n3, 28n3, 46n10, 198n1, 255

monopoly, 25, 28n16, 28n19, 78, 149, 210, 229n30, 233, 234, 236, 243, 244, 255, 258

monopsony, 239

Monsen, J. R., 19n4, 255

Montana, 67, 135, 244, 255

Montana Department of Natural Resources and Conservation, 255

Moon, 53, 58, 60, 104n10, 146, 167n76

Moore, James, 238

Moore, Stephen, 19n4, 165n42, 255

Moore, Thomas G., 19n4, 165n42, 255

Mosby, Joe, 200n16, 255

Mother Lode, 140

Motichek, Amy, 230n32, 255

Mount Trumbull Wilderness, 40

Mt. Hood, 13n19

Mt. Rainier, 13n19

Mulligan, Robert F., 50, 253, 255

Murphy, Robert P., 13n22, 18n2, 19n3, 28n3, 46n10, 92n4, 167n75, 198n1, 255, 266

Murrell, Peter, 13n21, 255

Myers, Ransom A, 7, 255

NAFTA (North American Free Trade Agreement), 155, 251

Nardinelli, Clark, 228n7, 255

national defense, 238, 249, 262

National Flood Insurance Program,. *See* NFIP

National Ocean Service, 256

National Oceanic and Atmospheric Administration,. *See* NOAA

National Weather Service, 256

natural law, 2, 258

natural monopoly, 28n19, 244

Nature Conservancy, 227

navy, 124, 125, 126, 127, 128, 158, 162, 168n90, 252, 261

Nazism, 230n40

Nebraska, 125

Nedzel, Nadia, 46n8, 94n30, 256

negligence, 148, 251, 259

Netter, Jeffry, 19n4, 165n42, 254

Nevada, 3, 40, 71n16, 206, 261

New Democratic Party (Canada), 155

New England Aquarium, 117

New London, See *Kelo, Susette*

New Orleans, Louisiana (Big Easy), 112n5, 112n10, 140, 142, 144, 147, 166n46, 177, 188, 189, 239, 243, 256, 263, 265, 285, 286

New York, NY, 24, 230n46

Newfoundland, Canada, 202

Newman, P., 248

NFIP (National Flood Insurance Program), 139, 141, 142, 143, 245, 251, 256

Nimoy, Leonard, 7, 256

Ninth Circuit Federal Court, 174

NOAA (National Oceanographic and Atmospheric Administration), 71n17, 140, 256

North, Gary, 13n20, 13n21, 93n16, 229n21, 256

North American Plate, 13n19, 68

North Carolina, 117

North Korea, 3, 22, 229n16

Northwestern Hawaiian Islands Multi-Agency Education Project, 256

Norway, 47n13

Nove, Alec, 28n8, 111n1, 256

Nozick, Robert, 63, 93n13, 237, 250, 256

Nutter, G. Warren, 28n8, 111n1, 256

objectivism, 238

ocean, 4, 6, 8, 9, 21, 42, 49, 50, 52, 55, 57, 59, 65, 68, 70, 83, 93n18, 97, 98, 100, 115, 118, 119, 121n10, 124, 151, 176, 182, 191

Oceana, 228n13, 256

O'Driscoll, Gerald P., 246

Ogaden region, x, 160

Ohio, 101, 142, 147

oil drilling rigs, 7

oil spills, 5, 7, 55, 241, 263

Oliverhurst, California, 165n32
Ollman, Bertel, 13n21, 247, 257
Olson, Charles B., 198n1, 257
O'Neill, Ben, 93n13, 225, 256–257
Ontario, 155, 237
Oregon Water Trust, 230n41
organ procurement and sales, 168n82, 236,
   239, 242, 246, 248, 249, 251, 259, 264,
   267
Oroville Dam, ix, 165n31
Osterfeld, David, 46n5, 232n59, 257
Ostrom, Elinor, 14n26, 19n7, 111n1, 239,
   251, 257
Ottawa, 42–43
Ottoman Empire, 159
ownership concepts for water bodies: in
   toto, 9, 31, 32, 33, 34, 91, 171, 172,
   176, 180, 181, 182, 183, 185, 186, 187,
   189, 191, 192, 193, 194, 196, 197, 198;
   prior appropriation, 31, 33, 34, 35n7,
   79, 80, 84, 86, 135, 136, 164n13, 171,
   172, 176, 180, 181, 182, 183, 184, 185,
   186, 187, 189, 190, 191, 194, 198, 242;
   riparian, 9, 10, 14n30, 31, 33, 34, 35,
   35n5, 36n10, 78, 79, 83, 91, 98, 99,
   135, 136, 175, 178, 180, 181, 185, 186,
   191, 193, 195

Pacific Ocean, 21, 150, 151, 166n56
Paczkowski, Andrzej, 243
Pakistan, 50, 53n1
Panne, Jean-Louis, 243
Pareto, Vilfredo, 249
Pasadena, City of v. City of Alhambra,
   150, 257
Pasour, Jr., E. C., 229n22, 232n59, 257
Paul, Ellen Frankel, 12n9, 46n7, 94n30,
   257
Paul, Ron, 3, 129n6, 253, 257, 263, 285,
   286
peace, 4, 10, 21, 40, 42, 58, 72n29, 99,
   103, 115, 119, 120, 131, 158, 178, 206,
   239, 242, 247, 258, 260
Pearse, Peter, 229n20, 255
Pejovich, Svetozar, 28n8, 111n1, 257
Peltzman, Sam, 229n28, 257
Pennsylvania, 165n39
permeability, 11, 107, 112n5
Persian Gulf, 158

Peterson, Elmer, 228n8, 257
Peterson, J. E., 168n86, 257
Pezzaglia, Phil, 165n32, 257
Philippines, 21, 253
Photobucket, 257
phreatic water surface, 14n36, 109, 112n9,
   127
piracy, 55, 71n7, 123, 124, 127, 128,
   129n1
pirate, 12n3, 44, 123–124, 125, 127, 128,
   129, 129n3, 159, 161, 162, 252, 253
Pitney, Jr., John J., 129n10, 257
planning, 168n78, 183, 208, 211, 214, 220,
   221, 222, 223, 229n25, 255
Plato, 14n31, 85, 123, 249, 257
Platts, Linda E., 111n1, 120n3, 252
Plaut, Martin, 168n91, 258
Plymouth Plantation, 24, 28n9, 37, 240,
   261
political economy, 172, 198, 222, 239, 241,
   244, 246, 247, 249, 251, 252, 253, 255,
   257, 258, 261, 263
pollution, 7, 9, 13n20, 55, 60, 63, 64,
   72n19, 78, 99, 103, 107, 131, 134, 137,
   164n16, 211, 212, 247, 250, 254–252,
   260
pollution trading permits, 254
Polynational War Memorial, 258
Pontifical Council, 239
Poole, Robert, 19n4, 165n42, 258
Popeo, Daniel, 28n4, 198n1, 258
population, 3, 7, 13n10, 52, 58, 66, 103,
   112n2, 119, 120, 131, 132, 133, 134,
   152, 155, 158, 160, 161, 229n26, 235,
   240, 245, 246, 259, 261, 262, 263, 267
Port Authority of New York and New
   Jersey, 258
poverty, 23, 37, 245, 255
praxeology, 253
precipitation, 4, 60, 71n12, 132, 140,
   164n8, 252
preference, 82, 166n43, 177, 206, 226,
   241, 249, 250, 257
Pribilof Canyon, 119
Priest, George, 19n4, 165n42, 258
prior appropriation,. *See* ownership
   concepts for water bodies
privateer, 126, 161, 162, 169n102, 262

privatization, 1, 4, 6, 7, 8, 16, 22, 25, 49,
　52, 78, 83, 115, 138, 148, 157, 165n42,
　168n78, 168n80, 172, 198, 201, 204,
　207, 224, 228n9, 234, 237, 238, 242,
　248, 250, 254, 255, 262, 266–267
property rights, 1, 2, 4, 6, 7, 8, 11n1, 16,
　18, 21, 33, 37, 38, 42, 43, 44, 46n5,
　47n11, 51, 52, 56, 57, 60, 65, 66, 67,
　68, 76, 77, 79, 89, 91, 97, 99, 100, 111,
　132, 135, 139, 147, 153, 164n12, 175,
　177, 178, 196, 199n10, 202, 204, 207,
　218, 224, 226, 231n57, 239, 246, 250,
　251, 263
property taxes, 43, 215, 219, 246
Prosser, William, 174
Proudhon, Pierre Joseph, 1, 11n1, 46n5,
　139, 258
public choice, 12n5, 169n101, 203, 207,
　233, 244, 263, 266
public goods, 216, 225, 237, 238, 243, 249,
　250, 257, 262
public sector, 17, 165n42, 262
public services, 236, 242
Pufendorf, Samuel, 12n9, 46n7, 258
Puffert, Douglas J., 199n4, 258
Puntland, Somalia, 161, 236, 258

Qanyare, Mohamed Afrah, 160
quantitative rights, 255

Racanelli, P. J., 34, 79, 258
Rahm, Robert, 92n4, 258
Rand, Ayn, xiii, 43, 47n18, 258, 285
Rand Corp., 161, 258
Raskin, Max, 92n4, 258
rational voter, 241
RBC Radio, 168n91, 258
Reclamation District 10, 141
Red Dragon, 129n10
Red Sea, 158
Redding, California, 150
refuse collection, 262
Regan, Shawn, 40, 258
Regis, Ed., 13n22, 258
Reichert, William O., 46n5, 258
Reno, William, 168n91, 258
rent seeking, 12n5, 169n101, 257
Rerum Novarum, 75
restitution, 248

Reverie, Tennessee, 87
Reuters, 229n21, 261
Reyburn, Mary, 229n31, 258
Ricardo, David, 167n75, 251, 258
Rice, Leonard, 36n10, 258
Richard, B.W., 251
Richards, Janet Radcliffe, 228n9, 259
Richardson, Harry, 238
rift zone, 200n21
Riley, Brian, 167n73, 259
Riley, Francis S., 151, 166n52, 167n62,
　246
Rime of the Ancient Mariner, 167n70
Riparian,. *See* ownership concepts for
　water bodies
River Don, 59
Rizzo, Mario, 72n24, 164n19, 246, 259,
　260
robber barons, 97, 249
Robbins, California, ix
Robbins, Lionel, 13n13, 259
Robertson, Campbell J., 134, 234
Rockwell, Llewellyn H., Jr., xiii, 7, 13n20,
　53n7, 92n4, 93n16, 165n37, 225, 237,
　239, 259
Rocky Mountain Buffalo Association, 259
Roemer, J., 13n21, 235, 259
Roland, Denise, 7, 259
Rome, Gregory, 13n20, 93n16, 259
Roos, Maurice, 165n32, 259
Rosenberg, Nathan, 228n7, 259
Rosenblum, Marc R., 247
Rothbard, Murray N., xiii, 6, 7, 12n9,
　13n13, 14n26, 15, 18n2–19n3, 28n3,
　35n4, 39, 40, 46n5, 46n7, 46n10, 49,
　50, 53n7, 58, 62, 63, 71n8, 72n19,
　72n24, 73n37, 79, 82, 89, 93n16, 100,
　103, 104n2, 127, 129n11, 136, 164n16,
　164n19, 173, 175, 175–176, 177, 178,
　180, 183, 185, 186, 187, 190, 196, 198,
　199n14, 200n23, 229n30, 255,
　260–261, 285, 286
Rotman, Michael, 7, 261
Rowley, Charles Kershaw, 229n22, 261
Rozeff, Michael S., 12n9, 46n7, 261
Rubin, Jeff, 155, 167n72, 261
Rule of Law, 248
Rummel, R. J., 228n7, 261

Russia (also *see* U.S.S.R.), 59, 168n78, 236, 263
Russo, Mitch, 141, 261
Ruwart, Mary, 261

Sacramento: City of, ix, 140, 141, 165n40, 166n46; County, 165n32; River, ix, 10, 47n13, 87, 139, 140, 141, 151, 160, 165n26, 165n27, 165n32, 166n56, 203, 252, 261, 265; Valley, 140, 141, 141–142, 165n27, 167n62–167n63
Sacramento Area Flood Control Agency (SAFCA), 261
Sacramento-San Joaquin Delta, 165n32, 166n58, 202, 222, 244, 247, 250
Sailor, Steve, 13n22, 261
Sakoff, A., 28n8, 111n1, 261
Saleh, Ali Abdallah, 159, 264
Saliba, Michael, 228n9, 235
Salisbury, David F., 13n20, 93n16, 261
Salonia, Mark J., 125, 261
salvage, 49, 50, 51, 52, 53n3, 53n6, 233, 234, 250, 253
Salvage Law, 51, 245, 267
San Francisco: City of, ix, 150, 151, 286; Bay, ix, 140, 150, 152, 165n29, 166n56, 167n64
San Joaquin: River, ix, 151, 165n32, 166n56, 167n60, 167n61, 265; Valley, 142, 149, 151, 165n27, 166n56, 167n62, 167n65, 246
San Luis Canal Co., 166n53
San Luis Reservoir, ix
San Pablo Bay, ix, 140, 165n29, 166n56
Sandle, Tim, 7, 261
Santoriello, Andrea, 230n44, 261
Sardi, Bill, 158, 229n28, 262
Savas, E. S., 19n4, 165n42, 262
Sawyer Decision (*Woodruff vs. North Bloomfield Gravel Mining Company*), 140, 253
Scahill, Jeremy, 160, 169n99, 262
Scandinavia, 123
Scarborough, Brandon, 216, 218, 230n43, 262
Scarpeleggia, David, 167n73, 262
Schiavo, Terri, 239
Schick, Rabbi Moses, 171, 262
Schmidtz, David, 232n59, 262

Schoenbach, Victor J., 13n11, 262
Schumpeter, Joseph, 15, 262
Schwartz, Peter, 238
Scott, Arnold N., 235, 247
Scott, Gottlieb, 247
Scott, James C., 198n1, 262
Scott, Rick, 131
Scotland, 24
Seasteading Institute, 28n10, 53, 262
Sechrest, Larry, 50, 232n59, 262
Seldon, Arthur, 168n81, 262
Seto Inland Sea, 247
Sevier River, 71n16
Shabman, Leonard, 230n37, 262
Shaffer, Butler, 18n2, 28n3, 46n10, 228n7, 262–263
Shandong Peninsula, 94n36
Sharp, Gwen, 7, 263
Shasta Dam, 10, 77, 141, 142, 165n31
Shugart II, William F., 229n30, 263
Siberia, 104n10
Simmons, Randy T., 111n1, 120n3, 202, 215, 216, 231n50, 246, 247, 262, 263, 268
Simon, Julian, 13n13, 13n22, 111n1, 120n4, 241, 258, 261, 263, 267
Simon, Leo K., 247
Simpson, Brian, 230n39, 263
Sinclair, A., 242
Singapore, 72n18
slave, slavery, 11n1, 16, 31, 125, 238, 249, 266
Slipke, Jeff, 253
Smith, Adam, 26, 28n7, 103n1, 167n75, 168n78, 263, 264
Smith, Jr., Fred L., 229n30, 263
Smith, E. Michael, 263
Smith, Hedrik, 28n8, 111n1, 263
Smith, Robert J., 14n26, 19n7, 263
Snow, Nicholas A., 92n4, 263
Snyman, Leon, 234
Snyder, Pamala S., 230n32, 234
Social Security, 216
socialism, 7–8, 13n21, 14n27, 18, 67, 72n29, 75, 115, 118, 120n3, 135, 148, 149, 201, 214, 214–215, 216, 228n7, 235, 237, 238, 239, 240, 247, 248, 252, 253, 254, 255, 257, 259, 262, 266, 267
socialized medicine, 216

Solomon (King), 154
Somalia, Federal Republic of, 127, 158, 159, 160, 161, 162, 168n85, 168n91, 169n94–169n95, 169n97, 169n99, 169n103, 169n104, 236, 242, 243, 248, 250, 258, 262
Somaliland: province of Somalia, x, 161, 169n103, 235; British, x, 159, 169n103; Italian, x, 159, 169n103
Sorokanich, Robert, 104n8, 263
South China Sea, 22, 253
South Florida, xi, 131, 132, 133, 139, 234
South Florida Water Management District, 262
South Platte River, 249
Southeast Asia, 158, 262
Southgate, Henry, 12n2, 263
sovereignty, 254, 262
Soviet Union,. *See* U.S.S.R.
Sowell, Thomas, 13n13, 164n10, 263
species extinction, 5, 13n12, 55, 56, 66, 111n1, 115, 116, 204, 205, 228n13, 245
Speiser, Frank, 94n30, 263
Spiro, Andreas, 263
Spooner, Lysander, xiv, 18n2, 19n3, 28n3, 46n10, 79, 263
St. Augustine,. *See* Augustine, St.
St. Lucie River, 131, 132, 133
Standard Oil, 254
stateless society, 255
Stefánsson, G., 242
Steinreich, Dale, 229n28, 263
Stigler, George J., 229n31, 244, 263
Stiles, Gerald, 233
Stratton Sayre, Susan, 247
strict liability, 245, 251, 252, 259
Stringham, Edward, 18n2, 19n3, 28n3, 46n10, 72n24, 92n4, 198n1, 229n22, 263
subduct, 13n19, 68, 192
subjective value, 242
subjectivism, 63, 72n24, 210, 237, 240, 241, 252
subsidence, 11, 106, 107, 110, 112n6, 150, 151, 153, 166n58, 167n64, 241
Suez Canal, 168n87, 264
Suisun Bay, 140, 165n29
Sullivan, Louis Henri, 55, 264
Summa Theologica, 12n4, 234

Sutter (California): County 13n32: Basin, ix, 140, 141, 165n27; Bypass, 141
Sutter Butte Flood Control Agency, 141, 264
Suzuki, David, 13n13, 264
Swaim, Barton, 230n43, 264
Sweden, 47n13

Tabarrok, Alexander, 229n28, 252
TAC (Total Allowable Catch), 5, 6
Tacitus, 131, 264
Tamiami Trail (Highway 41), xi, 134
Tannehill, Morris and Linda, 18n2–28n4, 46n10, 198n1, 264
Taylor, Arthur J., 228n7, 264
Taylor, James Stacey, 228n9, 264
taxonomic phylum, 228n4
technological units, 190, 193, 197
Telecommunications Industry, 264
Tennessee, 87, 88, 193
Tennessee Valley Authority (TVA), 10, 77, 90
TERs (Tradeable Emissions Rights), 13n20
Terrell, Timothy D., 230n44, 264
Territorial Use Rights in Fisheries (TURFs), 5, 6, 205, 215
thalweg, 84, 93n20
Thierer, Adam, 264
Thirlby, G. F., 72n24, 240
Thomas, Ellen, 72n21, 264
Thompson, Dixon, 154, 264
Thoreau, Henry David, 1, 97, 118, 264–265
Thoreau Institute, 46n9, 264
Thornburg v. Port of Portland, 174
Thornton, Mark, 92n4, 229n28, 265
The Times-Picayune, 142, 265
Tinsley, Patrick, 18n2–19n3, 28n3, 46n10, 129n2, 198n1, 232n59, 239, 248, 265
Tollison, Robert D., 229n22, 241, 261
Tomlinson, Charles, 225, 265
Total Allowable Catch,. *See* TAC
Tracy, California, 167n59, 167n60
trade freedom score, 167n73
Tradeable Emissions Rights,. *See* TERs
tragedy of the commons, 8, 19n7, 23, 109, 263
Tripoli, Libya, 123

trireme, 123, 124
Tucker, Jeffrey, 229n30, 230n32, 230n39, 265
Tullock, Gordon, 94n29, 229n22, 237, 241, 261, 265
Turner, John, 155
Twain, Mark, 105, 147, 265
Two Treatises of Government, 253
typhoon, 22, 158, 187, 192

uncertainty, 45, 218, 241, 250
Union of Soviet Socialisn Republics,. *See* U.S.S.R.
United Islamic Courts, x, 161
United Nations, 13n10, 28n5, 49, 50, 53n2, 72n29, 117–118, 160, 169n97, 204, 228n10, 252, 265
United Nations Convention on the Law of the Sea (UNCLOS), 117, 204, 252, 265
United States, 35n7, 80, 125, 129n8, 133, 155, 158, 160, 163n2, 233, 245, 251, 258, 286
University of Colorado, 13n19, 242, 286
U.S. Army Corps of Engineers, 133, 134, 141, 145, 244, 265
U.S. Bureau of Land Management, 40, 41, 46n9, 206, 256, 264
U.S. Department of Defense, 47n15, 244
U.S. Department of the Interior, 46n9, 265
U.S. Fish and Wildlife Service, 265
US Federal Highway Administration, 230n46, 265
U.S. Food and Drug Administration, 17, 210, 236, 247, 249, 251, 252, 262, 263
U.S. Geological Survey (USGS), 166n53, 245, 246, 250
U.S. Post Office, 18, 76, 111, 210, 233, 234, 255, 258
U.S. Submarine Structures, 104n8, 265
U.S.S.R. (Union of Soviet Socialisn Republics), 3, 7, 22, 23, 50, 111n1, 229n16, 245, 247, 256
Utah, 71n10, 71n16
Utt, Ronald D., 164n21, 265

Vaiont Dam, Italy, 132
Vance, Laurence M., 13n20, 13n21, 47n15, 93n16, 168n90, 265, 266
Venus, 221

Vietnam, 21, 125
Vikings, 123
Vining, Aidan R., 19n4, 165n42, 240, 266
Virginia, 24, 168n90
Vogel, Ronald J., 19n4, 236
Voltaire, François-Marie Arouet, 165n24, 266
vouchers, 13n20, 93n16, 100, 256, 259, 260, 267
Voyage Home, Star Trek, 256
Vuk, Vedran., 92n4, 266

Walden, 97, 118, 264
Walker, Deborah, 167n75, 228n9, 235, 239
Walker, Douglas M., 92n4, 266
Wall Street Journal, 236, 247, 249, 264
Walras, Leon., 28n7, 266
Walters, K.D., 19n4, 255
Wapshott, Nicholas, 13n21, 266
War of 1812, 125
war on terror, 160
Ward, Alex, 94n30, 266
warships, 127, 128, 257, 262
Washington, Booker T., 31, 266
Washington, DC, 44, 47n15, 146, 251
Washington State Department of Transportation,. *See* WSDOT.
water allocation, 35n7, 218, 222
water cycle, 4, 9, 36n8, 57, 58, 59, 70, 93n10, 111, 176
water quality, 134, 216, 237, 262
Water Resources (California): Control Board, 258; Department of, 259, 261
water rights, xiv, 14n30, 34, 35n7, 41, 47n11, 75, 79, 91, 108, 135, 136, 138, 215, 217, 218, 246, 255, 267
water shortage, 111, 157, 200n22, 208, 213, 258, 260
Watner, Carl, 12n9, 46n7, 266
Watson, Paul Joseph, 206, 266
The Wealth of Nations (An Inquiry into the Nature and Causes of the Wealth of Nations), 263
Wenzel, Robert, 13n21, 18n2, 19n3, 28n3, 46n10, 266
Werth, Nicolas, 243
West Virginia, 147
West Virginia American Water, 147
wetland, 103, 112n10, 140, 165n28, 246

Westley, Christopher, 92n4, 230n39, 234, 266
White, Alan, 228n9, 239
White, Lawrence H.,, 19n4, 165n42, 266
White, Michael, 258
Whitehead, Roy, 71n6, 228n9, 230n32, 239, 267
Whiteley, H.R., 237
Wilcke, Richard R., 13n21, 267
Wilder, Mark A., 53n6, 267
Williams, Walter E., 13n13, 267
Wilton, Alston, 234
Wilton, California, 165n32
Winfrey, Oprah, 209
Wisconsin, 72n25, 193, 286
Wisconsin Law Review, 248
withholding tax, 266
Wittman, Donald, 13n13, 267
Wood, J. Stuart, 92n4, 267
Woodruff vs. North Bloomfield Gravel Mining Company See: Sawyer Decision
Woods, Thomas E. Jr., 230n39, 267
Worldatlas.com, 267
World Bank, 168n86, 267
world population prospects, 13n10
World War II, 159
World Wildlife Fund, 7, 267

Worstal, Tim, 13n22, 267
WSDOT (Washington State Department of Transportation), 230n46, 267

Yablonski, Brian, 267
Yahya, Hamid ed-Din al-Mutawakkil, 159
Yates, Steven, 13n20, 93n16, 267
Yeatts, Guillermo, 46n7, 239
Yellow River, 94n36, 240
Yemen, Republic of, 158–159, 160, 161, 162, 168n86, 168n90, 234, 235–236, 242, 246, 258, 267
YemenWeb.com, 267
Yolo Bypass, 141, 265
Young, Adam, 13n20, 28n4, 92n4, 93n16, 198n1, 228n9, 267
Yuba (California): City, ix, 140, 141, 165n32; County, 165n32; River, ix, 165n32
Yunker, James A., 13n21, 267

Zardkoohi, Asghar, 19n4, 243
Zetland, David, 202, 208, 209, 210, 211–215, 230n33, 230n35, 268
Zhemchug Canyon, Bering Sea, 119
Zheng, Pearl Q, 221–222, 231n52, 268
Zizka, Paul, 72n21, 268

About the Authors

Walter E. Block is Harold E. Wirth Endowed Chair and Professor of Economics, College of Business, Loyola University New Orleans, and senior fellow at the Mises Institute. He earned his PhD in economics at Columbia University in 1972. He has taught at Rutgers, SUNY Stony Brook, Baruch CUNY, Holy Cross and the University of Central Arkansas. He lectures widely on college campuses, delivers seminars around the world and appears regularly on television and radio shows. He is the Schlarbaum Laureate, Mises Institute, 2011; and has won the Loyola University Research Award and the Mises Institute's Rothbard Medal of Freedom, 2005; theDux Academicusaward, Loyola University, 2007.

Prof. Block counts among his friends Ron Paul and Murray Rothbard. He was converted to libertarianism by Ayn Rand. Block is old enough to have once met Ludwig von Mises, and shaken his hand. Block has never washed that hand since. So, if you shake his hand (it's pretty dirty, but what the heck) you channel Mises.

Block is a leading Austrian School economist and an international leader of the freedom movement. His earliest work *Defending the Undefendable* (first edition Fleet 1976, latest edition Mises 2008, translated in 12 languages) is now, more than 30 years later, still regarded as a classic of libertarianism. This collection of essays, which argues in behalf of societal villains as economic scapegoats based on the principles of nonaggression, forces its reader to think and to rethink his initial knee-jerk emotional responses, and to gain a new and far sounder appreciation of economic theory and of the virtues and operations of the free market economy. Block's writing was inspired by Henry Hazlitt, the author of the most widely read economics text *Economics in One Lesson*. Block's latest book is *Yes to Ron Paul and Liberty*.

Block has been a fixture in the libertarian movement for some four decades. He actually met F.A. Hayek, and was friends with, and mentored by, Murray Rothbard. His contributions to academic libertarianism and to Austrian economics have been prodigious. Block's writings continue to challenge the conventional wisdom (or ignorance) of how economics works and will retain its freshness for decades to come. His public speaking style has been described as a combination of that of Woody Allen, Lenny Bruce and Murray Rothbard

Dr. Block has written almost 500 articles for peer-reviewed refereed journals, 21 books, and literally thousands of op eds for magazines and newspapers. Block appears widely on radio and television. He is a contributor to such scholarly journals as *The Review of Austrian Economics*, *Journal of Libertarian Studies*, *The Journal of Labor Economics*, and the *Quarterly Journal of Austrian Economics*. He is currently Harold E. Wirth Eminent Scholar Endowed Chair and Professor of Economics, College of Business Administration, at Loyola University New Orleans.

Peter Lothian Nelson is a professional engineer in the state of Colorado and previously in Wyoming. His engineering specialty includes water resources, hydrology, open channel design, storm drainage, underground pipelines, and other water related issues. Mr. Nelson was president of PL Nelson Engineering from 2007 until 2014 and frequently served as an expert witness.

He has a masters degrees in divinity and engineering from Nashotah House and the University of Colorado, respectively. He has had the pleasure of meeting and discussing policy and economics with Ron Paul during his first presidential run and with Murray Rothbard and Leonard Reed during visits to Denver. He has taken courses from Michael Ramsey, Archbishop of Canterbury. Nelson presents and teaches at engineering and church conventions.

Mr. Nelson currently lives in Estes Park and Denver. He is married (Jeanne) with two children: Patrick and Rebecca. He comes originally from Northern California including Marysville, Oakland, Alameda, San Francisco, and Sonoma. He has also lived in Wisconsin, New Jersey, and Washington, DC. His outside interests include philosophy, history, theology, economics, and genealogy. Members of Peter's family have been in the area currently within the United States dating back to 1624.

www.ingramcontent.com/pod-product-compliance
Lightning Source LLC
Chambersburg PA
CBHW021810270326
41932CB00007B/127